Emotional Abuse

5 Books in 1:

Codependency + Narcissism + Narcissistic abuse + Emotional and narcissistic partner abuse + Borderline personality disorder

Dr. Keith Sam

Table of Contents

Codependency

Introduction 11

Chapter 1 What is Codependency? 14

Chapter 2 Symptoms of Codependency 18

Chapter 3 Crossing De-Nile to Recovery 22

Chapter 4 So, Are You Codependent? 30

Chapter 5 Getting Started in Recovery 32

Chapter 6 What Made You Codependent? 36

Chapter 7 Healing Your Wounds — Freeing Your Self 41

Chapter 8 Welcome to the Real You 47

Chapter 9 Building Self-Esteem and Self-Love 56

Chapter 10 Finding Pleasure 60

Chapter 11 Letting Go and Non-attachment 74

Chapter 12 Speaking Up 81

Chapter 13 Relating to Your Family, Friends, and Lovers 90

Chapter 14 Making Relationships Work 101

Chapter 15 Following Your Bliss 109

Chapter 16 The People-Pleaser 117

Chapter 17 Being Assertive 122

Chapter 18 The essential dictionary to understanding narcissistic abuse 126

Conclusion 143

Narcissism

Introduction 149
Chapter 1 What is Narcissism? 152
Chapter 2 Scoring Narcissistic Traits 156
Chapter 3 Healthy and Extreme Narcissism.. 169
Chapter 4 Real Narcissistic People... 181
Chapter 5 Techniques to Handle Narcissists 193
Chapter 6 What Happens Next... 206
Chapter 7 Assessing the Situation Objectively.. 214
Chapter 8 Reverse Discourse and Narrative Therapy/ NLP Reframing
....225
Chapter 9 Alternative Healing Methods Explained............................239
Chapter 10 Your Brain in love, sex and the Narcissist 248
Chapter 11 Effects Of Narcissistic Abuse... 261
Conclusion 269

Narcissistic abuse

Introduction 275

Chapter 1 What is the Narcissistic abuse? 287

Chapter 2 Identifying Your Inner Strengths 294

Chapter 3 Self Control & Self-Responsibility 299

Chapter 4 Reprogramming the self-talk 310

Chapter 5 Redefining your Inner Circle 320

Chapter 6 Rebuilding Self-Trust 325

Chapter 7 Speaking your Trust 337

Chapter 8 Taking New Risks 344

Chapter 9 Let go of the fight to win and the your need for Justice 356

Chapter 10 Release the immediate pain and feelings of loss 364

Chapter 11 Release and heal the connection to the Narcissist 377

Chapter 12 Speaking your truth to the family and community 382

Chapter 13 Speaking your truth to the family and community 395

Chapter 14 Relationships With A Narcissist 402

Conclusion 412

Emotional and narcissistic partner abuse

Introduction 417
Chapter 1 What Is Narcissistic Abuse? 419
Chapter 2 What Causes Narcissism? 432
Chapter 3 Who is The Narcissist? 444
Chapter 4 Narcissistic Personality Disorder 461
Chapter 5 Narcissistic Manipulation Tactics 476
Chapter 6 Learning The Language Of Narcissist: Who Abusers Use Anything And Everything Against Their Victims 489
Chapter 7 The Essential Dictionary To Understanding Narcissistic Abuse 502
Chapter 8 Dating Emotional Predators 514
Chapter 9 The Narcissistic Translator 527
Chapter 10 Have A Love Affair With Yourself? 532
Conclusion 535

Borderline personality disorder

Introduction 541
Chapter 1 The World of the Borderline Disorder 545
Chapter 2 The Borderline Society 560
Chapter 3 Communicating with the Borderline 569
Chapter 4 Taking Back Control of Your Life 582
Chapter 5 BPD and Successful Treatment 604
Chapter 6 What Is Your BPD Type 607
Chapter 7 Addressing and Changing Negative Behaviors and Patterns of BPD 615
Chapter 8 Reconstructing Your World and Building a New You 630
Chapter 9 Maintain success on a personal level 644
Chapter 10 Using mindfulness to manage emotions 658
Chapter 11 The Narcissist's Target 671
Conclusion 681

CODEPENDENCY

STOP CONTROLLING OTHERS AND BOOST YOUR SELF-ESTEEM. HOW TO SPOT AND SURVIVE THE HIDDEN GASLIGHT EFFECT, SAVE RELATIONSHIPS AFFECTED BY ADDICTION, ABUSE, TRAUMA OR TOXIC SHAMING

Introduction

Before you can put codependency completely behind you, you have to love, respect and come to terms with the real you. For so long, you have been trapped in a cycle of caring for others, putting them first, and denying your own true self. Now, take the time to get to know you and find the courage to love yourself for who you are.

Step One: Discover Who You Are As an Individual

People in codependent relationships commonly define themselves in terms of their relationships. They might be a caring wife, a good daughter, a loving mother or a faithful friend. All these roles can be important to you, but for now, think of who you are as a person apart from these roles.

Get out your journal again and make a list of the things you like. Write down the things that make you happy and the things that make you sad. Mention activities and events you enjoy.

Then, write down the things that make you different from other people. Avoid judging yourself as you think of these things. Also, keep to those things that are unique to you as a person rather than you as a member of a relationship.

Step Two: Accept Who You Are Not

Perhaps you have buried the real you to protect yourself or to take care of your partner's needs. You do things you do not like to do, just as everyone must at some time in their life. The difference in a codependent relationship is that you lose sight of your distaste for the role, the activity or the conversations. You become the role, despite the fact that it causes you to put aside what benefits you.

So, spend some time thinking about things, people, thoughts, behaviors and emotions that you do not identify with or want to include in your life. You have probably already realized that you do not like your partner's addictions. Yet there is more to who you are than that one issue.

Write down those things you disagree with or do not enjoy in your daily life. Write down activities or events you would not want to participate in. Write down the names of people you do not want to be part of your life.

Step Three: Realize Your Limitations

Take the concept of what you are not a step further and think about what your limitations are, both in the codependent relationship and in other parts of your life. For instance, you do not have the power to end your partner's addiction. You cannot get inside your partner's mind and figure out what will change his behavior. You are not physically strong enough to withstand constant physical abuse without injury or pain. In short, you are not superhuman.

Aside from these limitations, shared by all humans, you have other more personal limitations. Is there a limit to your capacity to help your partner? Is there a limit to your patience? Write down some examples of things you cannot do that others can. Realize that you can become stronger, but you will always have limitations. Everyone does.

Step Four: Look for Your Strengths

Now, look for your strengths. Your first reaction as someone who struggles with codependency issues might be your caretaking ability. Set that aside for now and think about your other positive qualities. Think about the things you are good at now and those you excelled in during your childhood. Consider the positive values you adhere to and that make you different from other people. Make a list of the great things that make you who you are.

Step Five: Explore Your Needs for Personal Growth

As you contemplate your weaknesses and limitations, it is common to feel bad about yourself and judge yourself harshly. Understand and remember that criticizing yourself has no value and is a total waste of time. Instead, take your personal weaknesses as indications of issues where you can improve. Write down some things you want to do, skills you want to develop and qualities you want to magnify in yourself. Then, start taking steps to make those self-improvements.

Step Six: Express Your Self Respect

Once you have a solid sense of who you are and what you want out of life, express those thoughts, needs and wants assertively and often. The more you show your respect for you, the more your self-esteem improves. You are a good person regardless of what anyone, including your partner, might say or do. Allow yourself to feel good about who you are, and don't let fear stop you from telling the world.

Chapter 1 What is Codependency?

Being in a codependent relationship is much like taking a ride on a never-ending rollercoaster of emotion. It doesn't matter on which side of the codependency coin you are, whether you are a pleaser, a fixer, an addict, or a caregiver; one relies on the other for a complete sense of who they are.

The first step on the road to recovery from a codependent relationship is to understand what it means. Codependency, like several psychological concepts, can be highly confusing, but in simple terms is nothing but relationship addiction. It is a behavioral and psychological condition, where one individual is excessively reliant on another for their identity, self-worth and validation.

Some experts are of the view that it is an obsessive preoccupation with other people's problems in a bid to meet one's own neglected emotional needs; while others suggest codependency is an unhealthy pattern of excessive dependence on other people and their approval to find your identity. A third opinion is that codependency is a relationship condition where the real issue stems from an individual's lack of relationship with himself or herself.

A widely prevalent codependent definition suggests growing up being dependent on someone who in turn is dependent on an element that is non-dependable. It could be drugs, alcohol, overeating, or an excessive indulgence in sex – anything compulsive and overdone.

With all these differing and confusing definitions, it is no wonder codependency is so hard to understand. If you have read this far you might be thinking about how you ended up in a codependent relationship. Below I have listed the main ways codependency manifests.

Learnt Behavior

Observing older members in the family often teaches codependency. Children in homes where both partners share an unhealthy, destructive or abusive relationship are more prone to be a part of codependent relationships themselves. They observe, learn and invariably internalise the behaviour to display similar behaviour patterns in their future relationships as they move into adulthood.

Repressing an Issue Within A Relationship

Dysfunctional families breed codependency by their inability to acknowledge the existence of a problem. Underlying issues such as shame, anger, pain and jealously are often brushed under the carpet without being resolved. The issues can stem from addiction (alcohol, drugs, sex or gambling), abuse (mental, physical and sexual), or chronic mental or physical illness. Rather than talking about these issues or tackling them head on, there is a tendency to repress the core problem.

Addiction

The term codependent was initially used as synonym for enabler. Enablers 'helped' addicts with their highly compulsive tendencies by taking control of the situation and assuming personal responsibility for the addict; often by rationalising their behaviour, protecting them by making excuses, and covering up for their actions. Within a codependent relationship where one partner is an addict, there is tendency to deny the consequences of the addict's dysfunctional behavioural patterns, and although done with the very best of intention, does nothing but prolong the situation.

Codependency was a term first coined by Alcoholics Anonymous, and primarily centred on the problem of compulsive alcohol addiction, where the family and well meaning friends of the addict unwittingly encouraged and supported their addiction by enabling their dysfunctional behaviour.

Abuse

In an abusive relationship, the suffering family member stifles his emotions and disregards his own requirements to turn into some sort of 'survivor'. They get habituated to denying or ignoring tricky emotions. They don't communicate, detach themselves from the underlying issue and avoid confrontation, often shutting out others outside of the relationship. They begin to become an extension of the abuser, denouncing all thoughts and feelings of their own and begin to base their sense of self-worth on what the abuser thinks of them. This lack of feelings and mistrust invariably leads to impaired psychological and identity development.

Mental Health/Physical Disability (the caring role)

In relationships where one person suffers from a mental health condition, or physical disability, another assumes the caring role. This can create a situation where the carer, takes control of everything on behalf of the other person, to the extent of preventing the person with the condition or disability from reaching their true potential. The carer will take over everything, often quite simple tasks that the other person could quite easily do for himself or herself. This will all be done in the name of caring, but in reality this is just another example of a codependent relationship, and similar to an abusive relationship, the other person learns to keep quiet and to accept what they are told without question.

Although the strategies you will find in the following chapters can be used with whatever codependent relationship you may find yourself in; for the purposes of this book, we will be primarily focusing on intimate relationships between two people.

Chapter 2 Symptoms of Codependency

Your mind and body operate as a "smart system" that is capable of evaluating for your needs and determining what you will need to do in order to meet those needs. You have built a library of activities and events that you use to help you meet your needs and your "smart system" evaluates and chooses what it believes to be the best option(s) in order to deal with whatever is happening at the moment.

Because no other person can live your life for you, it follows that if you are unhappy or uncertain or uneasy, then you are the only person on this planet who can do anything about it. No one else can do that for you. And, that is why it is important that you take full and complete responsibility for your life.

The rules that govern how your life plays out are:

1. Everything you do or have is the result of the choices you make.

2. You will always experience what you create (through your choices).

3. You can do anything you want, any time you want, anywhere you want, as long as you're willing to pay the price... without whining or blaming.

Our initial suggestions concerning making change is to address the topics of gratitude and responsibility:

1. by developing an "attitude of gratitude" you will find it much, much easier to overcome those

beliefs that hold you back – we call them limiting beliefs. For those who feel they have little or nothing to be grateful for, we will show you how to assess and evaluate for the good things in your life.

2. by taking responsibility for every action you undertake – regardless of the hand you were dealt in life – you will not get lost in the "blame game" that defines victimhood.

WHAT? BE RESPONSIBLE FOR MY ACTIONS EVEN WHEN THERE IS SOMEONE ELSE TO BLAME?

Absolutely. Blaming is a depressing and useless exercise that fixes nothing and is not a pretty thing to watch. However, if you do only those things that are in your own Best Interest you won't suffer from guilt, anxiety, inferiority, or even drinking, drugging or excessive eating in an attempt to "deal" with your problems. By taking responsibility for your own thoughts and actions you can learn to feel better about yourself. And, when that happens your Codependent behaviours will no longer be your "default" setting.

And that's a major win.

The point at which responsibility for self comes into your life is the point where you get to pick your own direction and discover what and who you want to be – and Dynamic Discovery will show you how to do just that.

Relationships

Relationships are a huge part of human life. We have relationships with people, places and things. Some are good (happy), some are bad (unhappy). The quality of your relationships is governed by your behaviours, meaning how you act. And how you act is based upon your values and beliefs, which may be at odds with those around you and would explain why you sometimes engage in conflict or are out of step with the rest of society.

Codependent relationships are typically derived from emotional and behavioural conditions that are often not satisfying and are sometimes unhealthy, one-sided, emotionally crippling, and abusive. This type of behavior is also known as "relationship addiction".

Now, this is not to say that so-called normal intimate relationships are all springtime and flowers, because they're not. Every intimate relationship has its ups and downs but that is not the issue here: Codependent persons are addicted to helping others and need to be needed. And, sometimes this need is so powerful that the other person becomes locked into being needy. Enabling is the word for this behavior.

This type of relationship may not be in your long-term Best Interest because it does not meet the definition whereby Best Interest is defined as not being deliberately hurtful or harmful to yourself or anyone else.

Our process for self-evaluation will allow you to determine for yourself what to do in order to meet your "real" needs. Because no other person can live your life for you, it follows that you are the one person on this planet who can make the changes required so that you can get what you really, really, really want – happiness, or peace, or contentment, or calm. And, no one else can do that for you.

Please remember this: The human being is the only creature on earth that is not a prisoner of its programming but the master of it, and therefore no human needs to live with unhappiness, guilt, resentment, etc., for one more day because we have all been gifted with the ability to effect change.

Let that sink in…

You have been gifted with the ability to effect change. Change how you think and feel and change your life.

Chapter 3 Crossing De-Nile to Recovery

Often times all the above leads to dysfunction in marriages, this becomes the cause and effect of troubled parenthood and dysfunction in Family, on a whole. The troublesome marriages end up in a divorce or separation, for which the children bears the fruits.

Parenthood as a Co-dependency Parameter

Co-dependent Parents

Co-dependency of Fear in Parenthood is one of the most general occurrences of co-dependency in parenthood.

1. Over consciousness: one of the effective stabilizing of a parent's co-dependency is through their acts from over-consciousness. As they are perpetually worried about their kids, they establish a argument that is paranoid, whenever the kid raises a topic.

2. Holding authority over all personal decisions: is one category of parents, who tend to believe that they have the right to exert authority over all of their child's decisions, regardless of their importance.

3. Over-bonding Parenthood: some parents try to bond too much to their kids by becoming

the creepy or interfering element in their personal space, peace and calms that the kid grows up to be paranoid of everything in their life. For example, a kid hates anyone touching their stuff in a shared hotel room. This owes to the fact that her mom had a nosy habit of going through her personal belongings by utilizing the excuse of cleaning her room. One day in her hostel, the friends, unaware of this fact, try to surprise her by cleaning the room. She reacts vehemently to their surprise. This is one of the impacts of over-bonding parents who create an image of creepiness or endless interference on their account, toward the kids.

4. Having No respect for the Kids: another category of poorly co-dependent parenthood is reflected through having no respect for the kids. This arises from a constant judgement of the kid being irresponsible, incompetent, unable and worthless, from the parent. Hence, the parent consistently makes remarks that emphasizes their lack of respect, honor and positivity towards the kid. This recurrent disapproval from the parent can mold the kid into a terribly depressed, clueless, dishonest and useless person with perpetual failures.

5. Comparing the kids with others: this is one of the worst aspects of poor parenthood, where the parents keep on comparing their kid's and expectation against the peer group of neighbor's,

brother's, sister's, relative's kids grades, achievements and scores.

6. Biased relationship with kids: sometimes parents end up treating kids separately within the family. Exemplifying, in a family of kids- 1 boy and 1 girl, mother's undue affection towards the son, can instill a sense of abandonment for the girl child while a father's attachment towards the daughter can result in the son in the family feeling detached from the dad.

7. Control-freaks: yes, this category of co-dependent parents also exist. Parents who exert and execute their desires upon the dreams and ambitions of the kids figure into this category of control-freaks. They specify hard and fast rules that control the academic and personal life of their kids, without any relations, breaks or rewards for the same.

8. Recurrent punishments: another aspect of co-dependent parenthood is where the parents involve the kids in recurrent and regular punishments for their deeds. Control-freaks type of parents establishes hard rules, for which they make strict punishments, regardless of the deed. This instils a sense of fear, hatred and discontent towards the parents.

9. Unsatisfied attitude: this arises from the perpetual comparisons and discontent from the parents towards their kids. Gradually the child

ends up disbelieving in his or her abilities, skills, talents and dreams owing to the feeling of not making the parents ever happy. Lack of appreciation for good deeds, mature decisions and responsibilities bring about a constant depression and despair in the kid.

10. Perfectionists: some parents become too inflexible that they deny any fun or frolic to their kids. Their ideals of perfection remain the limits, restrictions and discontent for the kids. This inflexibility not only damages the parent-child relationship, but also brings about mentally unsatisfied kids.

Co-dependent Kids

Co-dependent kids are the kind of children who believe that their parents should be responsible for each of their deeds. Hence, they consult and counsel with their parents to achieve anything or take any a decision. This is due to their psychological belief of lacking confidence in the self about taking any decision by themselves. Co-dependent kids fear of the day that their parents will not be there, to guide them. Some of the main cause and effects of co-dependent behavior towards parents are:

1) Worried Attitude: the first and foremost cause and effect of a co-dependent child is his worried attitude. The worried behavior is consistent regarding taking any a decision, doing anything or even forming an opinion about something.

2)   Perpetually Clueless: almost all co-dependent kids share this attitude as they feel clueless when they lack guidance from their parents. They do not know of an independent route or path unless guided by their parents beforehand.

3)   Empathies with parents too much: co-dependent kids empathies with their parents too much that their experiences are all lived by through their parent's shoes. Empathy involves relaxing one's own desires that the subject ends up feeling more than obliged to the parents.

4)   Call parents for everything: a co-dependent child ends up seeking his parents counsel under all circumstances, regardless of its importance. There is no independent identity, plan or resolutions and hence the child lacks any motive of the own, to achieve anything.

5)   Worried about crowd or loneliness: another primary defining aspect of a co-dependent child is his or her worry about facing the crowd or being lonely, in the absence of parents. Co-dependent kids cannot are highly introverted sans their parents support.

6)   Love Addict: another important category of co-dependent children are the love-addicts, Casanovas or playboys. This kind of children become addicted to hunting for love due to the detachment they feel with their parents. Co-dependent children who miss their parents love, care and affection believes in being content through a relationship or constant dosage of intimacy shared with a person.

7) Having parent's dream as own dream and none of the own: often, the kids who are overly co-dependent, end up believing in their own existence as something that is heavily obliged to making their parent's dreams come true.

8) Self-sabotage: when a child ends up believing that parent's dreams, fantasies and desires are above their own, they end up sabotaging their own commitments, desires, fancies and whims to pave way for the parents dreams and ambitions coming true.

9) No self-respect: a co-dependent kid has very low self-confidence, self-esteem and self-respect that he does not believe in his own potential of realizing his dreams, as there are none. Gradually such a kid turns into a terrible automaton without no individual aim, personal success or ambition.

Family as a Co-dependency Parameter

Co-dependent parenthood and co-dependent parent-child relationship in the longer run can induce a dysfunction in the entire family. Certain times the co-dependency manhandled in a marriage are a cause of dysfunction in the family. A co-dependence scenario of troubling parenthood gives rise to co-dependent kids who pave way for a dysfunction in the family, on a full scale.

Some of the harmful effects of dysfunction in a family due to co-dependence is through

1) Lack of emotional contentment is one of the basic effects of a dysfunctional family as the kids and the parents

both feel that the family is draining much of their positivity into it, rather than making themselves feel positive or content.

2)   Lack of Communication instils a huge gap in the family members as in the due course of time, each family member resorts to avoiding the company of the rest for one's own peace.

3)   Divorce: this is one of the direct effects of poorly handled marital co-dependencies. When co-dependency becomes irresolvable, parents can end up in suggesting divorce or separation, which can directly affect the physical, mental and emotional psyche of the kid.

4)   De-valuing the suggestion of the family members: with the growing discomfort, individual members of the family ends up valuing the suggestions and remarks of other family members on a lesser and increasingly lesser honor.

5)   Lack of Love: another important effect upon a family owing to inter-dependent co-dependent parameters is the experience of immense lack of love. This instils a feeling of needing to search for love outside the family, even becoming a love addict in the process.

6)   Lack of Self-respect: another quite important aspect of co-dependency in a family is the lack of self-respect among individuals as well as lack of respect for each other. This induces a feeling of constantly minimizing the value of one's family as well as dismissing the same with

worthlessness. This also instils in the family, a sense of lack of aims, ambitions and achievements.

7) Lack of Freedom individually, due to controlling, hard and punishing authoritarian patriarchy by the co-dependent parents/ kids;

Chapter 4 So, Are You Codependent?

Addiction to Food in Co-dependency

Food enablers are the co-dependent factors of increasing or adding to one's obesity or overeating disorders. Co-dependent partners that can add to one's eating disorders can be the parent, the kids, the partners or the friends. Due to the aforementioned harmful effects of co-dependency, some of the emotional imbalances of anxiety, restless, hypersensitivity, depression and stress can add to venting out the same through over-eating.

Spouses of the food-a-holics will try to please their partners by cooking exotic delicacies that render the subject and the partner to become obese on their own. Even though the co-dependent tries to limit the food intake of the partner and put down rules of healthy food diets, the love and other factors of co-dependent makes them the food enablers that lead to the obesity of both, in the due time. One's lack of communication and other misunderstanding inclusive of the intimacy issues can pull the reasons for venting out the aspects of anxiety through eating. Co-dependents should instead show the delight of delicacy through healthy diet.

Another theory of psychology dictates that co-dependency itself arises from a family dysfunction of overeating or obesity. When someone in a family has the habit of overeating, the children and other family members are also invited to the sumptuous dining, every time the food addict has a rush or pang, hence inducing the same overeating disorder in the rest of the family. This also teaches the family that overeating is a pleasant vent out or resolution for one's anxieties depression and stress.

Workaholics as part of co-dependency Parameter

Do you feel that the undue business tours and official appointments of our partner is leaving you lonely, unsatisfied, compromised and confined without any bliss in your relationship? Then your co-dependency is largely dependent on your partner's workaholic nature.

Workaholism is one of the biggest cause and effects of maintaining stability in a family, A workaholic patriarchal or simply, the head in a family enables the rest of the family to feel incomplete and discontent with the time spent with the workaholic. This induces a dissatisfactory co-dependence on account of the subject. They tend to adjust, compromise and fake affection to mask the absence and dissatisfaction with the concerned workaholic. Gradually, the rest of the family grown into a dysfunction of perspective that work is the only duty one should regard and respect. This instils a sense of detachment with morals, humanity, warmth and family values as each individual member of the family grows to regard their work of utmost importance.

Exemplifying, a highly workaholic businessperson father or mother can instill in their kids a sense of loneliness, detachment and ideology that is centered on the belief of delivering just productivity, money and profit as the morals of their life. The kid learns to regard his work more than his own family, and hence run to work even at his girl's deathbed.

Chapter 5 Getting Started in Recovery

While no two relationships are exactly the same, neither are codependent relationships. There is a great deal of diversity and variables within relationships, and at any given time, codependency can exist or not exist. This is why experts in the field of psychology have trouble identifying what exactly a codependent relationship is. What we do know is that people with certain personality types are prone to this type of relationship and that these habits are often learned early on, usually in childhood.

While it is possible for anybody to have healthy relationships, those who grew up with parents in healthy, well-adjusted relationships tend to have a leg up against those who were raised in a household constantly engrossed in emotional turmoil and disagreement. The idea of nature versus nurture says that the personality traits of a person are variable both by the genes of the person, but also the environment they grew up in. It would be hard to ignore the fact that a child would be affected by their environment, but also by genes from their parents.

While it may seem obvious that a child from a broken home would grow up and mimic the same habits, we must also consider the role that codependency between parent and child has on future relationships. Studies show that children who are coddled by their parents and who rely on the parents for everyday tasks will be attracted to a mate who will do the same for them.

If a parent consistently takes care of a child's every need, especially when doing things the child could easily do for themselves, they lack the confidence it takes to make it out on their own. This could be anything from cooking, cleaning, doing laundry, or even having the parents deal with conflicts between friends and classmates. When a parent plays too big of a role in their child's life, they actually teach them that they don't need to try, because someone will always be there to take care of them when times get tough. Unfortunately, as these children get older and begin looking for spouses, they look for someone they can depend on. While finding a mate you can rely on is a good trait, depending on them to do the things they can do themselves is selfish, and perpetuates the codependent relationship they had with the parent.

Another offshoot of this is with very strict parenting. Having a laundry list of rules to follow during childhood teaches discipline, but there is a fine line between learning life skills and becoming a prime candidate for a codependent relationship. Often times, if the rules are not followed, the parent can become angry or disappointed, and the child learns that they are doing well by the mood of the parents. The child can feel happy when they please their parents, and all self-worth is established through these means. The child's sole source of emotional well-being comes from the parents, and not from their own self-esteem. What they learn is that doing things right or wrong, in a very black and white way, is the basis of a good relationship. As they enter find spouses, they will carry out the same relationship. They become dependent on making their spouse happy, and if they don't their self-esteem diminishes. What perpetuates it even further is if their spouse depends on them to do simple tasks for them, making the relationship highly one-sided.

Certain personality traits are often seen in codependent relationships, and if you tend to relate to these traits, it may be time to take a closer look at your relationships. While it is not your destiny to be codependent, you may be more susceptible if you are a people pleaser. This type of person avoids conflict and will do whatever is necessary to avoid it. In childhood, these kids are often the teacher's favorite, never getting in trouble, as defying the rules would cause conflict and make their parents unhappy, the stem of their self-worth.

Further down the line, this person may fall victim to an emotionally of physically abusive relationship, as the burden of sticking up for themselves and ending a relationship would impose on their abuser. They would rather stay in the relationship than going through the conflict of ending it. Their self-esteem is so dependent on the wants and needs of their abuser, that leaving would cause inner turmoil as well, which is why so many people end up staying in these types of relationships.

People who are prone to depression or anxiety are also good candidates for codependency. Although the scientific community has not officially recognized codependency disorder as an official diagnosis, links are clear between mental disorders like anxiety and depression and codependency. This is likely because all three problems are usually caused by issues with self-esteem. When self-worth is defined by how you are perceived by others, it becomes difficult to cope with someone being unhappy with you. To remedy this, people often enter into codependent relationships in order to make them happy, or defying this lowers self-esteem, leading to anxiety and depression. Either way, it can be a very tough habit to break.

Codependency is also perpetual between generations. The environment you were raised in often dictates how you will raise your own children. The habits and parenting skills you were exposed to early on stick with you, and unless a valiant effort is made to teach your children a different way of life, you will likely end up parenting your kids the same way your parents raised you. In the case of a dysfunctional, codependent upbringing, this leaves little hope that your child will have a different life.

The good news is, once the habits you have developed can be recognized as dysfunctional or co-dependent, it becomes much easier to change those habits. You cannot stop what you don't recognize as a problem. Therefore, just by reading this book and recognizing that you may have some codependent habits, you can change that in yourself so that future generations will benefit from strong, healthy relationships with friends and loved ones.

Chapter 6 What Made You Codependent?

By now, you may recognize that you are in a codependent relationship. You may rely heavily on one friendship in particular, or pay extra attention to your spouse. It is natural to gravitate toward certain people, so don't overanalyze every relationship you are in. Still, it important to take stock of your relationships and begin to recognize if you are being used, or if you are using someone else. There are two sides to this equation, and it is important to establish healthy boundaries with friends and loved ones.

How do you know if you are being used? This one should be pretty simple to spot, but not always. Take inventory of your friends. Is there someone who consistently calls you for help with things? Looking after their kids? Getting yard work done? While you may be happy to help, is that person reciprocating the favors? If that person comes to rely on you to babysit, but never helps with your kids, or simply expects it from you, it may be time to set some boundaries. While that person may not be able to reciprocate in an appropriate manner, they should at least be grateful, and be cognizant of your time and energy.

In a spousal relationship, this may be harder to spot. In any relationship, roles are established early on. An over-eager spouse may want to take care of their loved ones every need, offering to cook, clean, wait on them hand and foot. While this may seem like a way to show affection, it can quickly turn into a codependent relationship. Unless the partner can reciprocate in some way, it may seem like the relationship is very one-sided. Over time, the over-eager spouse will become tired and a bit resentful that their partner is taking advantage of their good nature. However, by this time, they may feel like their self-esteem is reliant on how their spouse feels about them, likely a habit they developed earlier in life.

Being used can have many definitions. Someone may rely on you financially, or for help getting places if their car is broken. Your intentions are likely good, and just doing favors for someone doesn't mean you are codependent. You may be, however, if you start going out of your way, putting your own life on hold, to help someone else, especially when it is out of guilt. This is the ultimate definition of being used. Often times, if you are reliable and always there for someone, the moment you are not may make you feel guilty. This guilt could stem from your own feelings of inadequacy, or from the person you constantly help to make you feel guilty. Either way, the relationship has escalated to an unhealthy level, and it is time to set some boundaries. Yes, boundaries are discussed a lot, we will get to how to manage these relationships later on in the book.

This may be particularly difficult to pinpoint if a relationship has been this way most of your life. Of course, we are talking about a long-standing relationship between an adult child and their parents. It is important to stay in touch and take care of the people who raised you, but that relationship can get out of control as well. For example, let's say you suspect you may be in a codependent relationship with your own mother. In this case, your parents are divorced, and your mom lives on her own. She is constantly calling you to help mow the lawn and do daily tasks for her. You begin to forgo your own responsibilities to be at her beckoned call. One day, you decide to take a day trip with your own kids. Mom calls first thing in the morning and asks for help with something at her house. You explain that you are going out, but your mother makes you feel guilty, saying things like, " I only raised you", or "If it doesn't get done now, it will never get done", anything to make you feel guilty for having your own life. This type of relationship develops over time and is usually the result of codependency starting from early childhood. Your mother may not have had successful relationships in her past, specifically with her parents, and is bringing that to the relationship with you.

We often see this sort of relationship between mothers and their daughters in law. TV shows and movies have been dedicated to these relationships, in which the mother believes that nobody can take good care of her son, and anybody who tries is doomed to disappoint her. The mother is dependent on her son needing her for her own self-worth. Once she realizes that her son is grown and does not depend on her, she may lash out at his significant other, or the son, making both parties feel guilty for not spending more time.

How do you know if you are the user? Again, take stock of the relationships you are currently in. Is there one friend you always rely on to bail you out? Do you ever pay back the favor, or are you accustomed to them helping you? Another big one, do you feel upset when that person cannot help and do you give them an attitude, or act ungrateful when they can't step away?

In your personal relationship, do you expect your significant other to be with you all of the time? If they want to spend time with friends do you get jealous or upset? Do you make them feel guilty when they hang out with other people? These things may be difficult to face, and if they are, it is a good indicator that you are in a codependent relationship. If this sounds like you, it may mean that your self-esteem has been dictated by relationships like this in the past. It doesn't mean that this cannot be changed.

Perhaps one of the most difficult codependency relationships to deal with is one with addiction involved. If you are involved with someone with a drug addiction, gambling habit or something similar, it is likely that this person was not this way when you entered the relationship. Had you met them on the street in their current state, these facts would have been a major red flag for you to step away. Unfortunately, that person you are in love with was once a different person, and was not on drugs, or spending every night at gambling at the casino.

It is hard to come to terms with letting this relationship go because you see what was, and what potential is there in this person. Instead, you let the dysfunction continue, hoping that eventually, the person you knew and loved will come to their senses. This is exactly what happens with parents of drug addicts as well. Their sweet son or daughter is in there somewhere, and they are very susceptible to being manipulated by that person. That person will become dependent on their willingness to help, while their loved one becomes guilted into continuing to help them. Unfortunately, this just enables bad habits and the likelihood that they will snap out of it on their own is slim to none. If you make it easy for a drug user to continue abusing drugs, they don't have a good reason to stop.

Chapter 7 Healing Your Wounds — Freeing Your Self

In the last section, I examined the chart with circles and you should utilize this to assist you with deciding on whether you are being bona fide in your life or not, Remember, the inward circle speaks to your True Self. Nonetheless, your actual self is perpetually changing relying on the manner in which that you carry on with your life. In spite of the fact that the center you doesn't change, your mentalities change with time. The following circle is simply the depreciated and this is the place you at present are. You don't feel like you have that much worth and you sense that you don't have much decision in your life, however that is the place you are incorrect. On the off chance that you utilize the third circle and assess circumstances, you can gain from them and proceed onward from codependency so you turn out as the Ideal individual you might want to be.

The word perfect is abstract. One individual needs a certain something and another gets bliss from different things. To assist you with seeing what you get euphoria from, I might want you to plunk down and record the things you are appreciative for every day on the grounds that these will assist you with evaluating your situation from an increasingly positive point of view. Peruse your rundown of appreciation every prior day you endeavor to make yourself feel positive about what your identity is. At that point, take a gander at any circumstance that is giving you issues and work out the various situations which can prompt you turning into the perfect individual. How about we demonstrate to you a model,

You have a great deal of housework to do today. You feel overpowered. You additionally realize that there won't be sufficient cash to take care of the tabs this month.

This is your actual circumstance right now in time. What would you be able to do to transform it?

1) Get the housework done rapidly so you possess more energy for yourself.

2) Decide to set yourself an objective and keep it to the extent the housework is concerned.

3) Do the occupations that you realize will be taken note.

4) Look at your actual monetary circumstance so you are not stressed over something that truly isn't that awful.

5) Work out ways that you can spare a little to assist you with paying your bills.

6) Think about others much more terrible off who don't have a rooftop over their heads.

7) Think that you are so fortunate to have a home.

You have to work out your very own solutions to your own issues throughout everyday life, except you have to come to choices that help you to be not so much mutually dependent but rather more free. For instance, Nicole was in the very same circumstance as portrayed previously. She generally considered herself to be immaterial. Her first need was her better half who was a medication fiend. Everything went on his propensity. She had no cash left. What she didn't see was that it was conceivable to take care of the tabs just by removing something different of her spending. She was an awesome cook and figured out how to make heavenly dinners on a strict spending plan and set away enough cash so the bills could be paid without her better half realizing that she had held back. She really began to appreciate the cooking procedure and increased a great deal of fulfillment from the autonomy it gave her just as having the option to impart this to her better half. To the extent the housework was concerned, she gave herself a set time inside which to do the housework so she had time left over for herself. That was an irregularity. How she did this was to reveal to herself that what wasn't done by a set time would be left to one more day. She set objectives for critical things and did these, however really shocked herself at accomplishing more than she arranged.

Consistently you get difficulties. Consistently you get an opportunity to handle life in a superior manner that gives you more and there's nothing amiss with setting aside that effort for you. You have to develop your fellowships. You have to locate that perfect self that lies in the outside circle and when you do, you start to feel more grounded and progressively positive about yourself. While you are mutually dependent, you will in general put your very own needs on the back rack and that is never going to add to satisfaction. You will wind up detesting what you feel compelled to do with your life however it's just your codependence that powers you. On the off chance that you develop your very own confidence by permitting yourself a tad of delight – paying little heed to the conditions you are in – you can really give your adored one more since satisfaction checks. Glad individuals give more. Take a gander at the kinships you have with glad individuals and what you find is that you don't fear their visits. You don't feel awful about their inspiration. When you are upbeat, individuals will feel like that about you too.

No one but you can help yourself in this circumstance. Obviously, there are guides who are master in this field, yet this book is about YOU and what YOU can do individually to assist you with regaining the accompanying:

• Pride in yourself

• Happiness in your heart

• Gratitude for your life

• Love for yourself

What you may not understand is that codependency wrecks lives and it's not simply your life that is being destroyed. It is harmful and changes your general perspective on life and your connections and breeds so much lament, despondency and sharpness. By figuring out how to cherish yourself, you proceed onward and can carry on with a more joyful life and subsequently offer more to your loved ones than you ever could while you clutch the need to please others. Venture off the indirect that is wrecking your life and start to see past it.

I need you to return to part two and take a gander at the activity there where you need to choose the little things that you need to do in your life. These can be miniscule advances. They don't need to be colossal things. Possibly you deny yourself of things since you believe you don't merit them. Its rubbish, however it's what you accept. Right now is an ideal opportunity to break free from that servitude. Quit doing it to yourself and ensure that consistently, you do at any rate one thing that is your decision. It could be something as straightforward as:

• Treating myself to a peach

• Washing my hair and utilizing a conditioner

• Dressing in my pleasant garments

• Picking up the telephone and conversing with a dear companion

• Buying myself a lot of blossoms

• Eating a lot of grapes

• Trying out another eye cosmetic

• Practicing yoga

• Dancing before a stay in shape move video

You get one took shots at this life and it doesn't need to be drudgery. Quit causing yourself to do things that you despise any longer and allow yourself twenty minutes per day to accomplish something that you need to do. You need to rediscover the perfect you and you will never do that while you are mutually dependent. Your life doesn't rotate around the life of another person. It might interlace with the life of another person, however every individual is an island and that island takes into account fun here and there, just as obligation.

On the off chance that that is the manner by which you see yourself presently, it's an ideal opportunity to change your perspective. Obviously, you feel that you have to help your friends and family, yet the thing that matters is that a mutually dependent individual is eager to endure conduct that is in opposition to their prosperity. That is unfortunate, however it doesn't win you any pats on the back with the individual you make that penance for. Leave it speechless by figuring out how to cherish yourself.

Chapter 8 Welcome to the Real You

Be on guard for passing into our old practices. Codependency is dynamic; reusing can be as well. We can stall out, waste our time, at that point find we've gotten ourselves all the more profoundly settled in the refuse.

Regardless of whether our reusing knowledge keeps going six minutes or a half year, our natural response is normally one of refusal, disgrace, and self-disregard. That is not the exit plan.

That is the route in more profoundly.

We escape, or through, a reusing procedure by rehearsing acknowledgment, self-sympathy, and self-care. These demeanors and practices may not come as easily as disavowal, disgrace, and disregard. We've gone through years rehearsing disavowal, disgrace, and disregard. In any case, we can figure out how to rehearse more beneficial options, notwithstanding when it feels clumsy. A few proposals for doing that pursue.

Rehearsing Healthier Alternatives

The initial move toward traversing a reusing circumstance is distinguishing when we're in it. Here are some notice signs.
1

Feelings Shut Down. We may go numb and start solidifying or overlooking emotions.

We come back to the mentality that emotions are pointless, wrong, unjustified, or insignificant. We may reveal to ourselves very similar things about needs and needs.

Impulsive Behaviors Return. We may start habitually eating, caretaking, controlling, working, remaining caught up with, burning through cash, taking part in sexual practices, or whatever else we urgently do to abstain from inclination.

Unfortunate casualty Self-Image Returns. We may begin feeling, thinking, talking, and acting like an injured individual once more. We may start concentrating on others, or resort to accusing and scapegoating. A decent piece of information that I'm "in it" is the point at which I hear myself whimpering about how somebody is getting along either to me, or how terrible something is. My voice starts to grind on my nerves.

Self-esteem Drops. Our degree of confidence may drop. We may stall out in self-loathing or disgrace. We may turn out to be excessively disparaging of ourselves as well as other people.

Hairsplitting and sentiments of not being sufficient may return.

Self-Neglect Starts. Disregarding the little and huge demonstrations of self-care that are an ordinary piece of our recuperation routine may show we're near a reusing circumstance. Surrendering our day by day schedule is another sign.

The Crazies Return. All the old muck can return. This incorporates: return of tension and dread; feeling detached from individuals and our Higher Power; issues dozing (to an extreme or excessively little); personality hustling; feeling overpowered by perplexity (or just overpowered); trouble thinking plainly; feeling irate and angry; feeling regretful in light of the fact that we feel that way; feeling urgent, discouraged, denied, undeserving, and disliked. We may get into the "overs": overtired, exhausted, overcommitted, overextended, excessively delicate; or the "unders": came up short on, overlooked, underspent, starved, and sickly.

A proceeding with physical condition can be a notice sign that something is bothering at our psyches and feelings. We may start pulling back from and maintaining a strategic distance from individuals. An arrival to affliction or the "perseverance mode" is another notice sign. This would incorporate continuing the conviction that we can't appreciate life or have a ton of fun today, this week, or this month; life is something to be "traversed," and perhaps one week from now or one year from now we can be cheerful.

The Behaviors Return Too. When we're into a reusing circumstance, any or all the adapting practices may return.

Caught! Feeling caught, accepting we have no decisions, is an exceptionally speculate frame of mind.

Not That Again. It's conceivable to advance to the threat zone during reusing.

Side effects here incorporate incessant physical ailment, synthetic reliance, ceaseless despondency, or potential dreams about suicide.

After we've recognized an arrival to our old ways, the following stage is basic. We state,

"Uh oh! I'm doing it once more." This is called acknowledgment and trustworthiness. It's useful to come back to ideas like weakness and unmanageability as of now. In case we're working a Twelve Step program, this is a decent time to work Step One. This is classified "give up." Now comes the possibly troublesome part. We let ourselves know, it's alright, I did it once more. This is designated "self-sympathy."

Myths

Accepting any of the accompanying legends about reusing may make recuperation more troublesome than should be expected.

• I ought to be further along than I am.

• If I've been recouping for various years, I shouldn't have issues with this any longer.

• If I was working a decent program, I wouldn't do this.

• If I'm an expert in the recuperation, psychological wellness, or general helping field, I shouldn't have this issue.

• If my recuperation was genuine, I wouldn't do this.

• People wouldn't regard me on the off chance that they realized I thought, felt, or did this.

• Once changed, a conduct is gone until the end of time.

• I couldn't in any way, shape or form be doing this once more. I know better.

- Oh, no! I'm starting over from the beginning.

These are fantasies. On the off chance that we trust them, we have to attempt to change what we accept. It's alright to have issues. It's alright to reuse. Individuals who work great projects and have great recuperations reuse, regardless of whether they're experts. It's alright to do "it" once more, notwithstanding when we know better. We haven't gone right starting over from the beginning. Who knows? We may gain from it this time.

On the off chance that we demand accusing or feeling embarrassed, we can give ourselves a constrained time to do that. Five to fifteen minutes ought to be sufficient.

Dealing with Ourselves

After we've acknowledged ourselves and given ourselves an embrace, we pose ourselves two inquiries.

- "What do I have to do to deal with myself?"
- "What am I expected to learn?"

Regularly, oneself consideration ideas we have to practice are essential:

- acknowledgment,
- give up,
- reasonable assessment of what we can control,
- separation,
- expelling the person in question,
- managing emotions,

- paying attention to what we need and need,
- defining limits,
- settling on decisions and assuming liability for them,
- defining objectives,
- getting fair,
- giving up, and
- giving ourselves immense portions of affection and sustaining.

Intentionally concentrating on our recuperation program, conversing with sound individuals, employing ourselves with contemplations and positive musings, unwinding, and doing fun exercises help as well.

We have to recover our equalization.

Dealing with ourselves at work may require some unique contemplations than thinking about ourselves at home. Certain practices might be suitable at home yet could bring about loss of our activity. We might not have any desire to tell the manager how distraught we are at him. Self-care is self-obligation.

Codependency is a pointless cycle. Mutually dependent emotions lead to self-disregard, self-disregard prompts more mutually dependent sentiments and practices, prompting progressively self-disregard, and around we go. Recuperation is an all the more empowering cycle. Self-care prompts better sentiments, more beneficial emotions lead to progressively self-care, and around that track we travel.

I don't know unequivocally what you have to do to deal with yourself. In any case, I realize you can make sense of it.

Something else I don't know is the thing that exercise you're learning. It's everything I can do to get familiar with my own. I can't reveal to you how to understand the specific encounters throughout your life, yet I can disclose to you this: among you and your Higher Power, you will make sense of that as well.

Try not to stress. In the event that you don't comprehend, or in the event that you aren't prepared to become familiar with your exercise today, that is alright. Exercises don't leave. They continue introducing themselves until we learn them. What's more, we'll do that when we're prepared and all is good and well.

Tips

In spite of the fact that I don't have a recipe for self-care and learning life's exercises, I've gathered a few hints that may help during reusing.

• If it feels insane, it likely is. Regularly when we keep running into an insane framework, our first response is still to think about what's up with us. We can confide in certain individuals, yet we can't confide in everybody. We can confide in ourselves.

• If we're ensuring ourselves, something might undermine us. Possibly a trigger is helping us to remember the past times or an old message is attacking us. Here and there, somebody in our present is undermining us, and we're attempting to imagine they're most certainly not. In case we're ensuring ourselves, it gets who or what is frightening us, and what we're shielding ourselves from.

• When one strategy for critical thinking falls flat, attempt another. Once in a while, we stall out.

We experience an issue, choose to explain it a specific way, come up short, at that point more than once, once in a while for a considerable length of time, attempt to take care of that issue similarly, despite the fact that that way doesn't work. Regroup and take a stab at something different.

• Self-will doesn't work any preferred during recuperation over it did previously. Giving up works. In some cases in reusing, we're experiencing the way toward denying an issue that is crawling into our mindfulness. We're attempting to stay away from it or defeat it by applying more prominent measures of self-will. At the point when self-will comes up short, attempt give up.

• Feelings of blame, pity, and commitment are to the mutually dependent as the primary beverage is to the heavy drinker. Watch out for what occurs straightaway.

• Feeling pitiful and baffled since we can't control a person or thing isn't equivalent to controlling.

• Trying to recover our misfortunes for the most part doesn't work. "On the off chance that I think back and gaze at my misfortunes excessively long, they gain on me," says one man. "I've figured out how to take them and run."

• We can't at the same time set a limit and deal with the other individual's feelings.

• Today isn't yesterday. Things change.

• We don't need to accomplish more today than we can sensibly do. In case we're worn out, rest. In the event that we have to play, play. The work will complete.

Chapter 9 Building Self-Esteem and Self-Love

People usually consider themselves as caring people. They express the care through actions. There is, however, a little known and darker side to this act of caring for other people and which is neither talked about enough nor well fathomed.

One behavior associated with codependency is caretaking – which is not ideal – and should be replaced by caregiving. Codependency causes you to have unhealthy relationships, and caretaking is one of those qualities that should not be exercised.

Differences between Caregiving and Caretaking

There are vital differences between caregiving and caretaking. In a healthy relationship, the happier and healthier you both are, the more you do caregiving rather than caretaking. Caretaking is a dysfunctional behavior that can still be changed. It should be lessened, or better yet, eliminated if possible. Your objective is to do as much caregiving and as less caretaking as you can – in order to experience more contentment, peace and happiness in your relationships.

Caregiving

When someone needs care and assistance, whether caused by a chemical dependency, chronic medical state, or being cured from any illness, the one who provides the nurturing is called the caregiver. The caregiver is possibly a friend, family member, or health professional. This person gives support and comfort to another when necessary. The assistance is provided with kindness and compassion, emerging from a place filled with love and without any expectations of receiving something as payment. Caregivers can rely on and acknowledge the patient's position on his or her chosen path and will not meddle nor try to change it.

Caretaking

A caretaker also extends a helping hand when needed. He can be a friend, family member, or professional. This person gives what he or she thinks as comfort and support, and usually waits for something in return -- he "gives to get". A caretaker may attempt to modify the outcome and not allow the patient's path take its natural course. Through a caretaker's eyes, what he or she does is out of love; however, there is possibly a subconscious or underlying motive of fear.

Here are other ways on how you can distinguish caregiving from caretaking:

Caretaking

- Worry
- Crosses boundaries
- Think they understand what's best for other people
- Immediately rush into action when a problem comes up
- Consider self-care as a selfish act, and therefore avoids it
- Usually attracts needy people

- Focuses on the problem
- Uses "you" a lot

Caregiving

- Solve problems and take action
- Respects boundaries
- Only know what's good for themselves
- Wait to be asked for help before taking action
- Practice self-care to take care of others
- Usually attracts healthy people
- Focuses on the solution
- Uses "I" more

You cross the line between caregiving and caretaking when your personal energy is channeled to others who are perfectly able of taking care of themselves. This is usually triggered by caring too much, or the choice of doing more than you should as caring, when in fact, it is already caretaking.

What makes caretaking so hard to detect by the untrained eye to spot is about the actions of the person being camouflaged under the idea of caring. More often than not, the person who's also a caretaker is unaware of what they are doing simply because it feels a lot like love and intimacy although it's actually not.

Of course, you always want to have a smooth flowing relationship. No one wants to be with someone who's unhappy all the time. You care and provide all the attention that you can shower to your partner. But how do you know if it's no longer "caring", but instead being "codependent"?

Problems start to arise when helping starts to feel hurting; you feel fear, and this is where your relationship is based on. Clearly, this isn't good, as this ends up not being healthy for everyone involved. Simply put, caretaking starts from insecurity. It's a codependency hallmark wherein you are in a need to be in control. Caregiving, on the other hand, is an illustration of love and kindness.

For a caretaker, it can be quite a revelation to realize that it's better to be liked and appreciated for who you are, instead of being liked and appreciated just because you gave someone what he or she needed at that time. Being with someone doesn't have to come with reasons or conditions.

Chapter 10 Finding Pleasure

Identifying a codependent relationship is tricky. It is often disguised in any individual's willingness to adapt to other people's needs.

People in general consciously or unconsciously assign all the people in their lives a role to assume. They then deal with these people based on what they think these people want from them. In essence, it's like presenting a puppet show of your life. You may not realize it, but you are orchestrating the whole show based on what you conceptualize in your head.

There are people who are somewhat oblivious of the "roles" they assume, some seem to be detached, and others run along the lines of being codependent. In order to put an end to or overcome a codependent relationship, you need to recognize a person who "suffers" from codependency.

You will find in the succeeding paragraphs some of the most common codependent "roles." Do not be surprised if you recognized yourself in more than one. In addition, you will find some strategies on how you can change the script so nobody becomes the codependent party.

   1. Martyr

For martyrs, suffering is virtuous. They are happy when they were able to put the needs of their loved ones ahead of their own. They are the ones who would be the first one to take on an extra project and always the last person to leave the office. They would pick up the tab voluntarily even if they are broke.

Recognize the signs? It might have been the concept that your parents and your religious belief has instilled in you.

The Issue: You might not have realized it yet, but when sacrifice is your norm when it comes to relationships with loved ones, friends, and colleagues, you tend to neglect your own needs to be loved and cared for. While these are the things that you are hoping to get by giving more than you can give, chances are your efforts can backfire. When you don't get what you want from the relationship, you'll begin to resent these very same people to whom you've extended your help.

How to Overcome: Begin to care for yourself

It is important that you understand the difference between self-care and selfishness. You have to realize that you are not being selfish if you opt to leave the office on time or if you want to go out with friends once in a while. Also, it isn't rude if you ask to split the bill if you can't afford to shoulder everything. You have to begin to care for yourself because no one else will. Ernest Hemingway, an American author and journalist, once said, "My health is the main capital I have and I want to administer it intelligently." If we don't have our health, we have nothing left to give. It's similar to the idea of how to respond to an emergency in a plane crash: put on your oxygen mask first before helping others or else you are no help to either of you.

2. Savior

A savior takes pride in being the one to solve all conflicts. He is the one who's always there to lend money when a friend needs it, even if he is equally broke.

The Issue: There is no denying that everyone does need help sometimes and it is not bad to help. However, if you feel it is your personal mission to be the one to give comfort to others, even to the point of creating discomfort on your part, it is not healthy. You are telling the people you've helped that they are hopeless without you. You teach them to become overly dependent on you. As a result, you've created a relational dynamic that will continuously suck energy, time and resources out of you. People can learn to take advantage of this. They can even manipulate you to get what they want. When people get used to you being their savior, they quickly react when you don't perform that role in their life.

How to Overcome: Empower

It is always a good thing to help; it's a win-win situation because you feel good when you are able to be of help. However, you have to examine your real purpose for helping other people. It is also important to analyze if it is also doing them good. Being there for them is one thing but preventing them from being self-reliant is another. There are people whom you have helped once who come in for another and then another until they are totally dependent on you that they do nothing to improve their own situation. It's not rude to occasionally say "no." When you save people from their problems, you may actually be robbing them of a lesson that they need to learn for themselves. If you feel that helping other people is the only time that you are needed and loved, then you are not in a healthy relationship at all.

3. Adviser

Are you an adviser? You probably have an ability to look into someone else's problems and offer solutions and advice. The adviser is not too good a listener, though.

The Issue: People come to you because you give good advice. You feel happy because they constantly come to you to hear what you have to say. You assume that they lack self-esteem to even solve their own problems. In reality, though, advisers are the ones who are really insecure and they feel needed when people come to them. They are the ones who lack self-esteem. They want to feel in charge and in control and the only way they can do that is to tell someone what they have to do.

How to Overcome: Set boundaries

If someone comes to you and pours their heart out, try to listen to them for a change. Just by listening, you are able to help your friend or your loved one. You don't have to tell them what to do. Let them make the decision themselves. Let them see for themselves the perfect solution to their problems. You can give them your two cents' worth but only after you have listened to them, and do not tell them what to do. Give them options and then let them decide. Do not tell them outright that they have to do this or that. Respect their own judgment; be a friend and just listen. Ultimately, people need to come to their own conclusions about their problems.

4. People Pleaser

The people pleaser is the one who always volunteers to organize something for the community. They are the ones who volunteer to fix everything. They bask in the glory of being "appreciated" for their hard work in initiating gatherings, parties, and fund drives.

The Issue: It is not really a problem if you are the go-to person when it comes to social gatherings, but it becomes a problem when you begin to feel that doing so becomes a chore yet you cannot say "no" because you don't want them to stop liking you. People-pleasing is passive manipulation. You do things for other people because you can get something from them.

How to Overcome: Learn to Say No

It is not your loss if you say "no." The next time the office needs a volunteer, think twice before stepping up to do the task. Analyze if people are indeed going to dislike you if you didn't volunteer. Are you up for another task? Don't you have other important things to do at home? Learn to say "no" not because you don't want to do it but because there are other more important things that you need to do. There is always a time for everything. Besides, the world won't fall apart if you say "no." You can be replaced. People are capable of finding other people to help.

5. The Person who Says "Yes" All the Time

Have you ever been in a situation when you had to say "yes" when you really wanted to say "no?" Did you resent your action? A person who says "yes" all the time is one who keeps his discomfort to himself.

You can't tell your friends what you really feel for fear of offending them. You can tell your partner that you are upset because you didn't want to start a fight.

The Issue: A healthy relationship is one in which both parties or a group of friends are in total honesty with each other. If you avoid conflicts so you just say "yes" when you meant to say "no," there is a disconnect somewhere in the honesty department there.

In the office, there is something that you are uncomfortable with but you are too afraid to tell your boss for fear that you might lose your job. With your partner, you are afraid to trigger an argument because you fear that they might leave you. So, you hide the feelings inside. When this happens, you might end up resenting them and eventually ruin your relationships.

How to Overcome: Be Honest

If you don't speak up, you will not resolve anything. Your partner might not be aware that there is a problem already until it blows up in your faces. It takes courage to tell the truth but it is liberating. You can tell the truth without hurting someone else's feelings. Talking about a problem doesn't always equate to creating conflicts; this is just the healthier way of bringing up unresolved issues to find solutions.

Did you identify yourself in any of these? You were able to hurdle the first step to making changes in your life: awareness of the "problem." Acceptance that there is a problem is critical in making improvements.

Reclaiming Yourself from Codependency

People become codependent longer than they should because they are scared of being alone or feel accountable for their partner's happiness. They may say their desire to break free – but end up staying instead. Others may go away but end up committing the similar self-damaging mistakes once they get in a new relationship. The adrenaline rush felt when they experience passionate feelings toward someone can be captivating. For a lot of people, the rationale behind extreme emotional reliance on a partner is codependency – a tendency to put other's needs before their own.

No matter how hopeless it may appear, codependent people can still break free from their emotional struggles. Regardless of how low they may have felt during their worst moments, they can still recover from this condition.

Raising Your Self-Esteem

Self-esteem is an assessment of someone's worth, or how an individual judge himself. It's also defined as a person's competency in coping with life's basic challenges, and deserving of happiness. Self-esteem one of codependency's main symptoms, and it has to be addressed as soon as possible.

Codependents often have sensitive self-esteem combined with the fear of abandonment or rejection. The "esteem" they have is based on how others see them and perceive their character. They live by solving problems of other people, and this boosts their morale in a distorted way. If something goes awry, they take the blame and bear the guilt. They fill up their schedule to focus on one person – they have this feeling of being needed, and this feeling overcomes everything else.

Codependents usually come from dysfunctional, troubled, or repressed families. They deny it, though, hence the failure of solving their personal issues brought by them being codependents.

They take the blame for almost everything yet also blames others for everything. They reject compliments but are saddened when they don't get complimented. They are scared of being rejected yet reject themselves. They don't think they will be loved or liked, so they tend to show others they are lovable enough to be accepted by other people.

How should you reclaim your self-esteem?

- Challenge any self-defeating thoughts or beliefs about self-worth. You don't have to confirm anything to anyone about yourself.

- See yourself in a loving relationship that fulfills your desires and meets your needs. If your present relationship is damaging, look at ways on how you self-sabotage and observe your own behaviors.

- Tell yourself everyday that it's healthy to receive help from others, and it's an indication of strength rather than weakness. Friendships, counseling, and other online resources can be ultimately helpful to guide you in looking for a happy relationship.

- Become aware of any negative judgments you have about yourself. Don't be harsh; you have to be kind and compassionate on yourself.

- Don't be afraid of rejection; go ahead and get involved in intimate and loving relationships. Concede and let go of your shield, and allow others in your life.

Have you considered that you're just hooked on the pain brought by love? If yes, then remind yourself that you risk your chances of having happy and healthy relationships where your needs can be fulfilled. Are you afraid of being alone? Are you scared of taking a risk? By doing so, you prevent yourself from seeking the happiness and love you deserve.

Focus on your healing and your personal growth – by doing so, you'll begin to transform your life and attract others who are in the same emotional level as you.

Overcoming Guilt and Resentment

Sometimes, guilt is good. Guilt can make people empathize, take the right course of action and to make themselves better individuals. After guilt, forgiveness of oneself should always follow as it's an essential key to life and relationships. For many, however, self-acceptance still remains hard to get hold of due to unhealthy guilt, and this guilt can stay with a person for years, decades, or even for a lifetime.

Guilt is a possible persistent source of pain. You keep on reminding yourself to condemn yourself and to be guilty, and it ends up destroying you and meddling with your goals. Guilt brings anger and resentment, not only to yourself but to people around you.

Why should negative feelings such as guilt, resentment and anger be avoided? One, they absorb your energy. Two, they bring illness and depression. Three, they prevent you from having happiness, success and fulfilled relationships. They hinder you from moving on and stop you from moving forward.

Codependents usually have guilt within them. It's common for them to accept the blame and feel responsible for another's wrongdoings because of their lack of self-esteem. Guilt, however, should be differentiated with shame; shame is when you feel inadequate and inferior, and tends to underestimate yourself and your relationships.

How do you overcome these feelings of shame, guilt and resentment? Ask these questions to yourself, and follow the steps.

- Take responsibility if you've been rationalizing your actions. Tell yourself, "Yes, I did it." Look back and remember what happened. Think about how you felt, and think about other people involved in the process. Consider what were your needs during those times, and if they were met. If those needs weren't met, then why weren't they?

What were your motives in doing so? Was there any catalyst for such behavior? Is this catalyst connected to a person or an event in your past? You can write them all down, with a dialogue that includes your feelings.

- While growing up, how were your feelings and mistakes handled? Were you judged for them? Punished? Forgiven? Were people hard on you because of those mistakes? Were you somehow made to feel ashamed?

- How do you judge yourself? Are they really based on your personal faith and principles, or are they based on someone else's approval? Do you still need someone else's support before you go for something that you like? Don't aim to live up on another person's expectations – there are instances on which you'll never get their approval, and in doing so, you might end up sacrificing your own happiness and wants.

- Are your current actions matched with your true values? If not, think of your thoughts, emotions and beliefs that made you do your actions. What may have led you to abandon your values? In violating your values, you end up hurting yourself, which is more painful than hurting someone else.

- How did these conflicts affect you and other people? Take note of those people that you've hurt, and remember that you've hurt yourself as well. Reflect on how you can make amends and ask forgiveness from these people – how can you make things better? Can you still do something to ease the pain?

- If someone did you wrong, you'd possibly forgive them easily. Why then would you treat yourself differently? Do you think it benefits you to punish yourself continually?

- There's nothing wrong with making mistakes as long as you learn from them. Remorse is acceptable – even healthy – and it leads to creating corrective action. You'll learn how to act differently. Write yourself a letter filled with appreciation, understanding and forgiveness. Repeat these words to yourself: I forgive myself. I'm innocent. I love myself.

- Surround yourself with people who won't judge you for your past. Share to them what you did. Avoid secrecy to avoid further prolonging guilt and shame.

What is a healthy and humble attitude? You believe you're at fault but you still forgive yourself. Others were wrong, yet you forgive them. You regret the things that happened in the past yet you understand it was just a part of being human, and you ended up learning from your mistakes and you gain experience.

Yes, that is a healthy attitude.

Separating Responsibilities

Another vital task that codependents have to understand is how to separate responsibilities for themselves and for others. They react on other people's concerns. As these problems become more intense, codependents' reactions are more intense as well. They tend to be more involved in the process, hence keeping them in a chaotic state, as well as the people around them. Their energies are focused on other people and their problems which makes them less attentive to their own lives.

In rescuing, codependents aim to take care of people who can perfectly live their own lives. They dwell on problems they don't have control over, and can be upset when things go wrong. What they don't know is that rescuing these people from their responsibilities doesn't help them grow but instead makes them evade the outcome of their actions more. Love makes codependents undertake in manipulative behavior. Their intentions are to help, and they end up being people who force things to happen using too much effort and energy.

Codependents fail to realize that other people don't need controlling, and these people would usually have no interest in obtaining the outcome the Codependent is aiming for. Codependents must understand as well that people will simply do what they wish to do regardless if they're wrong or right, or if they're hurting themselves.

Codependents who do another person's task doesn't help the person be better by rescuing them -- they instead actually teach them to be more dependent, and will lead to them taking advantage of the Codependent. In return, the codependent becomes resentful, overburdened, and ultimately vengeful and upset simply because they do things they don't wish to do.

Chapter 11 Letting Go and Non-attachment

As people grow up, they learn to become more independent. Life events such as college, marriage, and having a family are trademark examples of a person becoming independent. However, codependent people struggle to reach the average person's independence. This can be problematic for a number of reasons because independence has major benefits. One benefit is independence can boost a person's confidence. When a person is learning to become more independent, this means that they are learning to rely on themselves. This leads to the person needing to become more sure and self-reliant in their decision making. This, in turn, leads to the person building their confidence.

Another reason why confidence is important is that it can lead to a person to become less reliant on other people. The most obvious explanation for why this is true is when a person becomes more independent, they do not need to rely on other people as much as they used to be. As a result, the person is able to learn that it is okay to be on their own and they are also more likely to appreciate another person's help when it does happen, especially when help is needed.

Independence is also a way to alleviate a person's stress levels. Once a person no longer needs to constantly rely on other people, they are less likely to be dissatisfied or stressed out when they are making plans. They only need to rely on themselves.

One other way independence can be beneficial is because of self-value is improved. When a person becomes more independent, they are able to trust their instincts and themselves in general. Trusting one's self shows that they value themselves and their ability to make decisions. People also tend to feel accomplished when they work through something on their own.

For the people who struggle with independence, there are ways to improve reliance on one's self. It can be uncomfortable and overwhelming to take the necessary steps to independence, but the end result is worth the hard times in the beginning.

The first way to improve someone's independence is to take the time to learn more about one's self. People can feel unsure of who they are. This is especially true for codependent people because their identity is usually attached to whoever they have become dependent on. A person might find that they tend to say yes or no to things that they do not necessarily want to do because they are so focused on appeasing other people.

A great way to learn more about one's self is to start journaling. The main benefits of doing this are that the person will begin to understand how they are feeling, why they make certain behavioral decisions, and why they act in certain ways. This will lead to independence because the person will begin feeling more confident in knowing who they are and understanding how their thought patterns work. Reflecting on how one feels and thinks about certain situations also lead to a new level of trust the person has in themselves and their instincts. The person will also likely learn more about what they want out of life that meets their own needs rather than someone else's needs. The end result of understanding one's self is the person will also be able to reason which areas of their life should take on more independence and when the independence should begin setting in.

Another way to become more independent is to stop asking other people for permission. While there are instances where a second opinion is welcome, it is important that people learn to think for themselves and not relying on other people to do the decision making. Once a person learns to stop asking other people for permission, then they can gain independence. This is because when a person stops relying on other people to make plans, they are, in turn, learning to trust that their own mind and emotions can make the best decision for a given situation.

If a person is too dependent on getting other people's opinions or permission, then they have become overly dependent on the other person's ideas. This will not help a person gain independence; it actually hurts their chances of reaching independence. When people ask for someone else's opinion or permission, they probably already have the same idea in their own head. Their goal is to gain the approval of the other person. This means that the next time a person is looking to ask for someone's permission or approval, they should look at their own answer first and go along with their instincts. When a person is able to be more aware of their instincts then their thoughts and emotions seem more reliable as well. There becomes no need to ask for permission, which means their independence is strengthened.

The next way to become more independent is if the codependent person learns how to be more assertive with other people. When a person becomes confident that someone will agree with them or not tell them "no," then they might start to become dependent on that individual. Codependent people are notorious for being agreeable with other people in order to avoid being abandoned or rejected. Once the codependent person is able to stop themselves from always giving in to what other people want, a newfound independence will take its place.

One's ability to learn how to be more assertive will actually allow them to know when to tell a person "no" and when it makes sense for them to say "yes." In turn, the codependent person can see when it is important for them to put themselves first.

Learning how to puts one's own needs before other people, when necessary, can lead to not only independence but self-value as well. Codependent people can become so dependent on helping other people and putting their needs ahead of one's own needs. This can lead to the codependent forgetting about themselves and what they actually want to be doing.

It is important to be assertive in relationships and with other matters of life. For example, if a codependent person finds that a fellow employee is asking them to take care of work that is not the codependent person's responsibility, this may be because the fellow employee knows the codependent person says "yes" often. This can lead to unnecessary stress for the codependent person.

The codependent person should start saying "no" more often so that they can focus more on their own needs. They should also remember that the people who truly care for the codependent person will accept when they say "no" and want the codependent person to take the time to look after themselves.

Setting aside time for alone time and alone dates can also lead to independence. The codependent can go about doing this by thinking about doing certain things that they normally do with others. It could be responsibilities such as grocery shopping or running errands, but the alone dates could also be going to a coffee shop and catching up on some reading over a cup of coffee or going to a movie.

The act of fitting in some alone time not only allows the person to increase their independence and feeling comfortable with one's own company, but alone dates can improve a person's confidence and self-esteem.

When codependent people set aside time once a month to take advantage of alone dates, then they can build up their sense of self-worth. This also means that the codependent person no longer needs to wait for other people to be available to do something; they only need to depend on themselves to be ready.

Alone dates can also be viewed as a form of self-love because the codependent person is showing themselves that they are comfortable being alone and themselves in general. The act of being alone is actually great when to let go of the negative and shameful thoughts that often arise when a codependent person finds themselves alone.

One final way to build a codependent person's independence is to provide emotional support for one's self rather than seeking support from someone else. It is not only true for codependent people but others as well, to seek help from other people when one is feeling down or overwhelmed. The mind believes that other people can provide them with the comfort and advice that will lift their spirits. There is nothing wrong or abnormal about turning to other people for support. However, when a person becomes too dependent on receiving support from other people rather than turning to one's self for support, then this will only fuel their codependent tendencies.

It is extremely important to learn how to gain support from one's self because once a person is capable of getting emotional support from themselves then they will learn how to take control of their emotions and the course of their life. A person's ability to comfort themselves rather than relying on other people to do so is actually how a person can achieve emotional support from one's self.

The emotional support a person gains from themselves can prove to them that they are not only capable of physically taking control of their life, but mentally they can as well. This is especially rewarding for codependent people because their mind is the largest obstacle standing in their way of trusting in their self.

Once a person takes the necessary steps towards gaining independence, then they too can reap the benefits that independence can bring them. It will take time and effort to work through the mental barriers preventing codependent people from maintaining independence. Yet, it is important to push through the discomfort and fear in order to trust in one's self.

Chapter 12 Speaking Up

Welcome to the second phase of the codependency recovery action plan. Self-esteem essentially means what you think of yourself. It's about how you treat, respect, and love yourself. Codependents gain a sense of self-esteem based on the opinions of other people. This is why codependents lack self-esteem and self-confidence because, in order to love and respect yourself fully, you need to feel confident that you accept yourself exactly as you are. Some people are motivated to keep improving themselves through their lives. They accept themselves for who they are without putting pressure on themselves to change. Codependents are obsessed with gaining the appreciation and approval of others. They use people-pleasing habits so that they can see in themselves what others see. Due to their avoidance behaviors and patterns, their self-confidence is lowered as well because they learn that through avoidance comes failure. With failure comes trying harder, but through a codependents effort in trying harder, it can be interpreted as controlling and manipulating their way through life. This is an unhealthy cycle that only contradicts growth and repeats history.

People with low self-esteem feel defeated or abandoned when they have a set-back or suffer a major disappointment in their lives. They believe they failed because they weren't good enough, which leads to doubt and mistrust. When someone has a healthy level of self-esteem, they don't let bad things define what they feel about themselves. They can tell the difference between making mistakes and being a reflection of their mistakes. Someone who displays a high level of self-esteem can see their mistakes and learn from them. They can quickly reflect on their decisions and what got them to make that mistake, then learn from it and push forward. Codependents who don't have high self-esteem see errors as a failure, which discourages them and they don't learn; instead, they avoid. Avoidance lowers self-esteem and self-improvement efforts. Individuals with high self-esteem genuinely know and value themselves.

Signs of someone with high self-esteem are:

- Trusting themselves.

- Loving themselves.

- Believing that things will work out with effort in situations they can control.

- Rewarding themselves after progression or they have completed a goal.

- Showing compassion for others.

- Taking responsibility for their actions.

- Positive and optimistic.

- Feeling competent and confident about their individuality.

- Knowing they are unique and comfortable in their skin.

- Holding firm boundaries to maintain their self-esteem and self-worth.

If you are codependent, you may ask other people their opinion of something that only you can answer about yourself. You might beat yourself up and disregard compliments if others direct them toward you. Codependents lack self-esteem, which means they often doubt themselves and their ability to grow. They don't feel worthy enough to try new things, and they lack boundary control. Having low self-esteem can affect all aspects of one's life, which can lead to a downward spiral of continuous negative habits. However, you can learn and develop self-esteem over time and with effort, you can transform it into self-worth and confidence.

One of the first steps to achieving this goal in building self-esteem is to detach yourself from codependency. If you are codependent, you first need to realise that you cannot solve everyone's problems. If you are involved with a codependent, then creating healthy boundaries and learning the signs can help you evaluate your deterring strategies.

Disengage with Love and Kindness

When you hear the word detach, you might think of it as disappearing, pushing away, or withdrawing. Staying away from codependency doesn't mean you need to do any of these; it means to let go of the characteristics of codependency. These include letting go of control, anxiety and excessive worries, blame, or feeling ashamed and guilty for everything. Think of detachment from codependency as distancing yourself from what makes you prone to codependent traits but still keeping your real sense of self. To do this, give yourself some boundaries. Every time you catch yourself trying to control people or situations, stop and think about how you can do things differently. Every time you obsess and avoid things, fight against these enforced thoughts and don't avoid or obsess. While all this seems easier said than done, it will take mindfulness and practice to get it right. Some examples of the disengaging processes are:

Emotionally

- Only do things according to what you can control; the rest isn't worth stressing about.

- Avoid making snap decisions regarding important life events. For example, instead of making a spontaneous decision, think about it for a few hours.

- Instead of controlling everything, give the control to someone else and ignore the itch to jump in.

- Allow others to make choices for themselves.

- The only problems that you can control are your own, give advice but don't take other's issues into your own hands.

- Question your expectations of yourself. Are they unrealistic and far-fetched?

Physically

- Walk away to breathe after a disagreement or rising conflict.

- Choose against visiting a toxic person in your life.

- Do not get yourself into compromising situations.

Codependency takes years of brain wiring and restructure, as habits form and take residence in your memories, promoting unstable patterns throughout your life. Detaching yourself from codependency will take courage, effort, and resilience. Remember to congratulate yourself after every accomplishment; this will help your brain reconnect the neurons that your past and experiences have damaged. While you work on viewing codependency as a toxic friend that is not a part of you, building self-esteem and confidence can help in ridding yourself of codependent habits for good.

Building Self-Esteem

It's not just codependency that can stem from a traumatic childhood; low self-esteem also resembles trauma. Any form of neglect or lack of attention while in the early development years can trigger low self-esteem. Starting at an early age, we learn from behaviors, methods, and parental guidance. Sometimes, families can be dysfunctional, which alters the young mind to view the world as a scarier place than it is, which makes no room for imperfections. From having a low view and reflection of oneself, people can miss out on opportunities they don't feel confident enough to accomplish. This results in feeling powerless to change things as they also don't feel confident enough to handle such a significant change. Here are some things you can do to boost your self-esteem.

Challenge the Inner Critic

Most of the time, low self-esteem is believing in your negative thoughts. These negative thoughts are the voice behind the cruel inner critic who defeats you for everything you do and makes you doubt yourself in your quest for success. Despite what your internal critic says to you, you must think about everything you have overcome. Think about your achievements, the problems you have solved (even if they weren't yours) the positive relationships you have created, and quiet the bully by reminding yourself that you have strengths too. When your brain says, 'you can't do that,' challenge it by saying 'I will try.'

Take Care of Yourself

Taking care of your physical wellbeing can also promote mental and spiritual wellbeing. Part of taking care of your physical self is paying close attention to your hygiene and your appearance. When you look good, you feel good. However, do not go overboard in needing to have every blemish covered up; instead, be okay with the things that make you stand out. Make sure your clothes are clean and smell nice. Eat healthy food that boosts your immunity and overall mood. Take care of the stress that seems to weigh you down. Keep an exercise schedule and continue to increase serotonin levels through healthy workouts. Do things you enjoy or that you are good at.

If you don't know what you are good at doing, make a list of all your strengths and achievements. Within that list, you will see the hidden talents you might have that you didn't know about. For example, your list could look like this:

- Got A's in Maths and English.
- Won a sporting award at school.
- Got promoted at my job.
- Helped a friend move to a new house.
- Painted a masterpiece.
-

Within the list of achievements, you can see that you are good at Maths and English, you excelled at painting, and you were helpful towards your companions. When you choose what to do next, try painting another picture, creating a blog, or building a business plan. Are you more creative, or are you more of a critical thinker? Can you revise your finances or help a friend budget? Do things you exceed at and your self-esteem will increase because you feel good about these things.

Try New Things

Trying new things can be a scary experience for some people because they are afraid of failure. Most codependents help others work on new things and observe on the sidelines because that's how they define their self-esteem. However, instead of watching someone do something new, join in with them. Have you ever gone on a road trip just for fun with no destination? Have you ever walked up to a stranger and started a conversation? Think of something you're good at, but also something you fear, and dip your toes in. When you accomplish something new, your self-esteem will rise, especially when you reward yourself after every attempt, even if you fail.

Avoid Toxicity

As much as a codependent likes to avoid things, they don't avoid toxicity. To reverse this behavior, pay attention to the underlying problems that you have avoided. Replace natural avoidance patterns with avoiding toxic people and toxic habits instead. This method is a great technique to boost self-esteem and confidence levels. Another way you can avoid toxic people is to create solid boundaries and learn to put your foot down. Codependent personalities are prone to having people take advantage of them, so if a codependent can learn to identify toxicity and walk away, it can help in breaking the abusive cycle. As much as people can be toxic, situations can also be toxic. A toxic situation can be where you don't feel safe, someone is bullying you, or there is always a crisis happening. In these circumstances, the best thing to do is practice your mindfulness strategies, then plan your escape route. Once you get yourself out of the dramatic situation, you can work on some relaxation methods like deep breathing, taking a bath, and talking to a close friend. When your mind is fresh and bright, start by avoiding the toxic triggers that lead you into the situation, to begin with. Other aspects that can gain self-love, self-esteem, and confidence are learning how to respect yourself and acknowledge your self-worth.

Acknowledging Self-Worth

Self-esteem and self-worth are very similar in the fact that they both reflect how we feel about ourselves. However, self-worth is knowing that you have the power and control to make all of what you think (or don't think) about yourself happen. For example, if you lack self-esteem, it means that you don't feel competent enough to see yourself as a unique and reliable individual. If you lack self-worth, it means that even if you had the drive to accomplish all your goals and dreams, you don't feel like you deserve to have them. Self-esteem can be defined and increased by what you do and how you carry yourself and your behaviours. Whereas, self-worth is determined by what you believe can be done and accomplished by what you feel you deserve. In short, self-worth is more about who you are not defined by what you do.

Much of building self-worth is by developing your self-esteem; however, to acknowledge your self-worth is to believe that you deserve respect and validation. Self-worth is the fundamental point of self-acceptance. So, gaining some insight into developing more self-worth, recognise when those thoughts of comparison creep through. When your mind says 'you will never be a superstar' challenge it with, 'I already am.' You don't have to believe this thought straight away; defeat your inner critic one idea at a time. Another way to build self-worth is knowing when to have compassion for yourself and when to push yourself forward. When we do too much of one thing, we are striving for perfection. When we do too little, we become complacent or lazy. A balance between the two is having compassion when you fail and being your own best friend when you aren't at your best. Also, by pushing yourself forward past your fears and failure can change the tone in how you feel about yourself, which is what boosting self-worth is all about.

Chapter 13 Relating to Your Family, Friends, and Lovers

Roles

The definitions for codependence can become so broad and convoluted that it seems like almost everybody could be considered codependent in some way shape or form. It gets so diluted that it would be impossible to not fall into one of those categories. Instead look at codependent relationships as a specific type of dysfunction in that someone helps another (read enables) to underachieve, be irresponsible, lack maturity, be addicted, procrastinate, or encourage or hide mental health issues, etc.

Within the dysfunctional family unit we will see the emergence of roles as a way for children to cope with the chaos and drama.

Human beings are funny creatures.

Because we are social animals we will always try to impose a social structure to make sense of our world.

It falls into very predictable patterns.

Keep in mind that the following characteristics may appear in children and adults that are not codependent.

That's not the assumption to make here, otherwise everyone could be considered codependent.

Rather, look at it like this: When someone is exhibiting codependent tendencies the roles we will discuss below will help us identify this person's place in a codependent relationship.

The roles can be based off of their personalities, birth order, or a combination of factors.

We will discuss the following to gain a better understanding of each one and later we will delve into how to treat them in the healing section.

Keep in mind that these roles can change over time and individuals can also hold more than one role simultaneously.

The Addict

Substance abuse is very common in children from dysfunctional homes including alcohol and drug abuse.

The addict in this role lives in a chaotic state and the way they primarily deal with their life is by escaping.

The physical and psychological dependency becomes so ingrained that they identify and make substance abuse a priority in their lives.

They will lie, cheat, and steal to maintain their addiction.

Within the family unit we see the addict take center stage as everything seems to revolve around them.

It does several things, it gives the family something else to focus on rather than their own internal, individual suffering as well as allowing the other dysfunctional roles to flourish.

The Responsible Child or Hero

This is the child that is older than he or she seems.

They take on a parental role at a very early age.

He or she is very responsible and may look great on the outside.

Usually they are great students, athletes, the prom queen.

This is the child parents look to, to say they are doing a fine job in raising their kids.

The family hero can grow up to be controlling and judgmental.

The judgment can extend to others but they are actually judging themselves just as harshly.

This person may have a lot of material success where you see high incomes, the perfect house etc. They are very competitive and driven.

Unfortunately, this stems from insecurity.

This person, the hero, because of his or her rigid and controlling nature and seeming success that you see on the outside will have a very difficult time admitting that there's even a problem.

Now this isn't to say that all high achievers are codependent.

All I am saying is that if there is dysfunction in a family, then this is one of the role that can appear.

Don't confuse this with somebody that becomes a high achiever because they are driven and they want to find success.

Not every driven and successful person is considered codependent.

The Scapegoat

The next role is the child that acts as the scapegoat for all things.

This is the child that gets in trouble for everything.

Trouble seems to find them even if they are not looking.

What is happening is the child is acting out the anger and frustration that the family is ignoring.

This child provides distraction from the real issues.

He or she gets in trouble at school, that is how they get attention.

The only attention they know is the negative type.

This is the child who grows into the teenager who becomes addicted to drugs, becomes pregnant, or gets the girlfriend pregnant.

The scapegoat is usually the most sensitive and that is why there is so much tremendous hurt inside of them.

They cannot put a name on the dysfunction, they just know there is something wrong in the family.

The scapegoats end of growing up to be very cynical and distrustful with a lot of hatred and can be very self-destructive.

It's safe to say there is probably a lot of overlap with the addict.

This person on the other hand is the one that, because their problems are right there on the surface, may seek help first.

They can be the first one to admit that there is a problem and they are not covering anything up.

Everything is right there in the open.

The Mascot

The Mascot

This child is essentially taking responsibility for the emotional well-being of the family.

The class clown.

The funny one.

They want to divert the family's attention from all of the hurt and the anger and the emotional hardships.

A lot of times, this is the person that distracts the attention from the addict.

This person is valued for their kind heart, their ability to stop everything and listen to their friend when they have a problem. Incredibly generous.

Their self-identity is centered on helping others so much so that they do not meet their own needs.

This is the person that cannot receive love, only give it.

It is like they do not take on friendships.

Rather, they become the therapist for their friend.

The mascots tend to get into abusive relationships because they are there to save that person.

You will see them become social workers, therapists, nurses.

In other words, help oriented occupations.

Ruled by guilt and very low self-worth they work hard to never get in arguments with people.

They run their lives by being very agreeable and not wanting to be the bad guy.

This is your quintessential people pleaser.

It is very difficult to overcome this.

It takes a lot of therapy and a lot of self-love for them to come out of this and to understand that it's not their fault, and they are not responsible for everything that goes wrong in other people's lives.

They fit the classic role of the codependent person that is so one-sided and not balanced that they give everything they have and get nothing in return.

The Lost Child

This role tries to disappear.

This is the person that gets lost in fantasy books, plays a lot of video games, watches a lot of movies and TV.

This happens because they do not want to deal with what is going on at home.

They withdraw from from the chaos and deny that there is a problem at all.

So much so that they don't even bother getting angry.

They just withdraw emotionally.

They suffer very low self-esteem and are unable to feel as they get older.

This is the person that does not want to get into a relationship and they have intimacy issues.

These people end up becoming socially isolated.

That is the only way they know how to remain safe and avoid being hurt.

You will see a lot of artists and writers who express themselves through their medium rather than become people that deal with their problems.

At the same time they can hide behind characters or the roles they play.

Again, keep in mind, just because these roles exist does not mean that everyone that is a high achiever is a controller that just because you like to write, doesn't mean you are a lost child.

This is simply a way of identifying roles in a dysfunctional family.

To show that dysfunction is present.

This shows the different roles, if the family is seeking treatment and looking to classify the roles.

They can be tailored to each one as we move into recovery.

Normal Childhood

What if my childhood was normal?

The question comes up a lot, I get it.

You may not have been raised with an alcoholic or an abusive parent.

However, codependency is passed down from generation to generation.

So even if you live in a home where they didn't do these things perhaps your parents experienced it and they are going to end up modeling that behavior to you.

Example: your dad is not an abusive individual towards you, but perhaps he is a workaholic and is never around.

He is a good dad overall and he is trying but he learned this behavior.

He has learned avoidance as a coping mechanism from his family growing up which can lead to issues down the road for his children.

Or maybe, mom was raised in a home where there was a lot of verbal abuse and she is determined to raise her children in an environment that does not support that.

But perhaps that comes off with a repression of feelings.

I am not saying that this is necessarily something terrible but at the same time it is a learned behavior that she cannot control if she is not aware.

The behavior of repressing feelings is now passed on, maybe not the verbal abuse though.

The fact of the matter is we are all human beings, we all have issues, we all do things that are not perfect.

That's what makes us who we are.

There is no such thing as a perfect family.

So a perfect childhood is not possible.

Nobody is perfect.

You would need not just one but two perfect people working together in perfect unison, all the time in order to prevent bad habits and bad imprinting from mom and dad.

It's okay.

The point is we have to understand and recognize it when we do, then the healing can begin.

Discussing Characteristics of Codependency with Jim

"Whoa, this stuff really hits home for me. I mean I can see all of those roles playing out in my family."

"Like what?" I asked.

"Well, my sister got hooked on Vicodin in high school and it seemed like there was always drama with her and we were always doing everything we could to keep her out of trouble and get her into rehab or something."

"How is she doing now?"

"She ended up going to this rehab place in Arizona but from what I hear she's struggling."

"Sorry to hear that."

"Yeah, it sucks for her kids too and I'm seeing the pattern in them as well."

"How so?"

"Well, her oldest is going into seventh grade and seems to be the one taking care of the two younger ones. She gets them off to school and she gets herself ready. My sister is always bragging about her and what a great kid she is. It's true too, she's a great kid. I feel like I'm talking to an adult when we talk. Poor kid's had to grow up too fast though."

"So, the daughter has taken on a care taking role in the family it looks like."

"Yup, that's what I see there too." He said.

"How do you see yourself in what we talked about?"

"You mean what role did I play?"

"Exactly."

"I guess I was the responsible one. I think because I was the oldest. That's why I feel so much for my niece. It's hard watching what she's going through because the pressure she puts on herself is crazy."

"And you can relate, right?"

"Yup, I can. Also, I remember my little brother was always joking around. Heck, he's still like that, he can't seem to be serious about anything. I always wondered why he was like that, now it makes sense."

"It's funny how predictable the roles we adopt are." I said.

"But I don't want to change who I am, I mean I want to keep my personality the way it is you know, I'm not looking to change my outlooks and all that."

"Look at it this way, you aren't looking to change your personality, that's what makes you unique. See it more as you are looking to become your authentic self, one that is true to who you are. Does that make sense?"

He paused lost in thought. "Yeah, that does make sense. A lot of sense actually."

Chapter 14 Making Relationships Work

Often codependency continues to perpetuate due to different reasons. As a codependent person, you must make an effort to understand the reasons that sustain codependency so that you can look for ways to overcome those. You are your own enemy and which is why you struggle to overcome codependency. Sabotaging yourself becomes a constant thing assuming that you don't deserve a good life. Of course, you might have made some mistakes in your past, who doesn't? But not forgiving yourself for past mistakes is not the right decision. You start denying your own strengths and thoughts. There are different ways of self-sabotage, including codependency, aggression, an abusive relationship, denial, and more.

Even after realizing codependency, you will not be able to overcome it because of self-sabotage which can make you feel unworthy which triggers codependency even deeper. To treat codependency, you must believe that you are worthy. You should think of the way a person with self-love would handle the situation that you are in. A person with self-love will not select unhealthy options that might hurt their mind and body.

If you can't love yourself yet, try to fake it for some time and so you will gradually make it true. Self-sabotaging is closing the actual view, which is why you are struggling to see the reality, so when you fake it, you will be able to clear the path slowly, but firmly. If you consider factors like anger, denial, and shame, they perpetuate codependency pretty easily. Hence, you must educate yourself about the factors so you can overcome them.

Anger and denial regarding codependency and your partner

Codependency should not be denied because it is dangerous. If you are denying it, it means you are not ready to accept and change, hence it will continue to remain. Instead of facing the problems in your life, you try harder to save others from facing their problems. The same behavior repeats itself when you deny the fact that you are codependent. Basically, there are different types of denial that you will learn below. Once you understand the types, you can take necessary measures.

Denial Your Partner's Behavior

Denying your partner's behavior is one of the common denials, but you can overcome it. You deny that your partner is addicted and his or her addiction causes a lot of problems in your life. Yet, you are not ready to accept it, which is why codependency perpetuates in your life. This kind of denial is common because codependents have been facing similar situations from their childhood. They might have grown up with parents who are addicts, so it looks normal to them.

The addicts and dependents have gotten used to been taken care of, so they are not ready to take responsibility. And codependents are okay with that because they like to take care of others.

If you deny your partner's behaviors, you must understand that you are walking towards a dangerous destination. You must acknowledge the reality and work accordingly because a relationship can ruin your life if you don't handle it wisely. You must accept the fact that you are not responsible for their behaviors. If they are addicted or relying on you for almost everything, it means you have created the path for it. You should not let anyone hurt you just because you are codependent. Also, if you deny your partner's behaviors, it doesn't mean that you don't care about them. Of course, you are bothered, but you just don't see the seriousness, or you somehow build up reasons to justify the act. This is the typical behavior of someone who loves their partner, but the love codependents show is extra. They don't make an effort to correct the mistakes; they just ignore them. However ignorance will make things worse.

Denial of Codependency

When you are confronted about codependency, you will deny it, and that's the very first step. You can clearly see that you are codependent, but you are not ready to accept it because you think it's a situation that has made you a codependent. You try to blame the situation and people so that you don't have to discuss codependency. Most codependents don't want to discuss it because they think it will worsen the pain, but it will not. This is one of the reasons why you deny that you are codependent.

Another reason is you are not someone who seeks help from others so if you accept that you are a codependent you'd have to get help from others to treat it. This kind of mentality leads you towards a destructive path. You don't like the fact that someone is taking care of you and being responsible for your behaviors because, for a long time, you've been doing it for others. You don't want others to make you happy as it triggers self-examination at a point. When you are codependent, you can easily avoid self-examination, which is why you turned down help from others.

Denying your true nature, which is codependency, will help you to stay away from professional help and admitting your codependent nature. On the other hand, some codependents don't seek professional help, but they try to treat themselves all alone. They believe that they can figure out the problem by talking to close friends and reading reliable books and articles. But sometimes, this can be dangerous depending on the level of codependency that you have. You may be ashamed to seek help, so you try not to get in touch with professionals. But remember, it is not a wise move.

Denial of Feelings

This is another type of denial which deals with a codependent's feelings. You are not ready to discuss how you feel, and ultimately, you end up denying your feelings. Normally, codependents can easily understand what other people feel and worry about. Plus, codependents spend a lot of time helping others to feel better. But they deny their own feelings which create resentment in their hearts. Codependency gives rise to obsession. When you are obsessed, you get distracted from what's important. Similarly, when you are obsessed with your partner, it will be hard to focus on your feelings because you are worried about your partner's feelings more than yours. If you think about your own feelings and how you have been doing, you will have no solid answers because you have denied your feelings.

Even if you understand your physical pain, you will not understand emotional pain because you are blinded by codependency. Also, growing up, you have not had an environment that lets you share your emotions and feelings. You may have always been the one to listen, not the one to speak. Moreover, you don't understand the reason why you should share your feelings when nobody is there to comfort or listen. Hence you keep denying your feelings from childhood. Actually, feelings serve a purpose even if they are not positive feelings. Through feelings, you understand what you need and don't. If you want to interact with people, you must have the ability to share your feelings. How do feelings help you become better at interacting while overcoming codependency?

- If you are angry, you will be reacting to make changes.

- If you are sad, you will empathize and value human connections.

- If you fear, you will keep dangers at bay even if they are emotional dangers.

- If you are guilty, you will have values that you respect.

- If you feel ashamed, you will not harm others.

- If you feel lonely, you will strengthen your connection with others.

Likewise, every negative feeling serves a purpose. When you deny your own feelings, you won't be able to move forward in life. You will bottle up your feelings for years, and it will always be there in your subconscious mind. When you accumulate pain, you will not be able to overcome it. Instead, constant denial might be your answer. What will happen when you continue to deny your feelings? You will end up depressed, and depression isn't as easy as you think!

Maybe you don't, but most codependents treat resentment as a shield to hide anger. Of course, your past or childhood would have been unpleasant and difficult. Maybe you couldn't express what you feel because nobody bothered to listen but that doesn't mean it will repeat in the future unless you want it to repeat. If you stop denying your feelings, you will be able to lead a healthy and happy life. It is important to talk to your partner and explain how you feel because unlike other healthy relationships, your partner will not understand your feelings. Not because he or she doesn't understand others, but because you have been hiding your feelings from them.

Unresolved feelings will repeat itself. If you overcome denial and anger, you will be able to overcome codependency too. But if you don't, it will perpetuate. And you must learn about the snowball effect to understand sustaining codependency.

The Snowball Effect

This is a concept discussed in psychology to understand something that is not only related to codependency but also many other things in life. We all have dealt with the snowball effect in life. Many times in life, you would have dealt with situations that you thought wouldn't blow up this big, but before you know it, the situation becomes a huge mess. This is metaphorical to a snowball that rolls down the hill and forms something huge. Just like that, the negative feelings and thoughts about yourself can snowball into something huge, and before you know it, there would have been a huge mess. You will not be able to cope with yourself when the snowball gets smashed and creates a huge mess! Certain thoughts make the whole process of opening up to your partner difficult, and some of them are:

- You tend to jump into conclusions without focusing on the evidence.

- You tend to generalize even if you see a single negative thing to support certain activity.

- You often catastrophize because you only think about the worst possible outcome.

- You easily filter the positive things into negative.

- You set strict rules regarding the unrealistic expectation of yours and others.

These negative feelings will increase your anxiety and enhance your negative mindset. When your mind is filtered through these feelings, it can be complicated to see things in the right way. You will not make an effort to change or to motivate yourself to overcome codependency because your mind is filtered that way. If negative emotions and behaviors snowball down the hill, you will not be able to stop it successfully. Hence, you must stop it when it started. Well, stopping the snowball where it started might impossible, but it is not. If you follow a few essential points, you will be able to do it.

- The critical point is to break the chain. Start by challenging a few thoughts and looking at them objectively.

- Write your feelings down or talk to a close friend about it. Also, when talking to them about your feelings if they have something to say, let them because listening is also essential.

- Don't skip your day-to-day activities because when you have a routine, you will be able to distract negative thinking for some time.

- Do engage in mindful activities, exercises, and yoga.

These tips might look simple, but they are not as easy as they sound because consistency and patience are two essential things when you are trying to overcome codependency. If you try to move out of this vicious cycle in one go, you are likely to get hurt. Instead, baby steps will help you overcome codependency without creating a mess. Don't let your mind snowball in the process of healing, so even the process of healing should be done step by step.

Not to forget that a professional can help you out of this vicious circle simply because he or she has the skills and required education. Hence, don't step back if you need professional help.

Chapter 15 Following Your Bliss

If you've been in an abusive relationship before, you know the feeling—constantly worrying that the other shoe will drop. Things might be completely fine within that moment, but you cannot help but feel that things are about to fail somehow. You know that, no matter how good things may be in the moment, that it will not always be that good, and because of that, you cannot help but feel uneasy. This is because, whether you know it consciously or not, you recognize the cycle abuse follows. It goes from a state of idealization to devaluation before finally reaching the discard stage, at which point, the narcissist attempts to hoover you up and start the cycle all over again.

This cycle can be incredibly difficult to break, especially since the narcissist keeps you interested in him and hoping things could get back to the way they were through revisiting the idealization stage, even though it frequently is fleeting and gives way to devaluation quickly. Through each of these stages, the behaviors change, but the one thing that remains consistent is the victim's fear of things escalating and of further abuse.

Idealize

The first step in the cycle is idealization. When you are idealized, you are made to feel as though you are important and desired by the narcissist. You are likely showered with attention and made to believe that you are deeply loved. The narcissist puts you on a pedestal with kind words, making you feel valued, and you eat it up. Especially if you have been starved for this sort of love or affection for any meaningful amount of time by the narcissist during the devalue and discard stages, the idealization stage is like a breath of fresh air after diving a little too deep for your skills and comfort. Just as the lack of oxygen burning your lungs and clouding your mind gets to the point of unbearable, you breach the surface and cannot get enough fresh air, the lack of love in your relationship follows the same pattern. When you are finally met with the love you have been craving, you feel as though you cannot get enough of it and you want more.

This keeps you hooked to the narcissist, and he understands your fixation on the affection. He then uses it as a weaponized to further idealize you. This is referred to as love bombing. Love bombing is the act of showering a person with praise, kind words, gifts, and other tokens of love or appreciation with the hopes of making the other person hooked on the narcissist. While it sounds as though it would be pleasant, and many people would love to literally be bombed with love, the narcissist weaponizes the love, using it to manipulate his victim, and that is what makes it so insidious. He knows that what he is doing is using the victim's feelings to keep her bound to him, and he does it anyway because it suits him.

For example, imagine that you are in a relationship with a narcissist. You love him with all your heart, but you are also frequently the victim of screaming, being blamed, gaslighting, and isolation from friends and family. The narcissist, after a particularly bad argument, has chosen to shift back to the idealization stage in the cycle. He can sense that you want to leave the relationship, and because of that, he decides to tell you how much he loves and values you. He may leave little notes of affection on your desk before work, or send you flowers or delivery of your favorite food for lunch. He may take you on fancy dates and ask you to go out to dinner with him in hopes of rekindling the love for him that you have been withdrawing from as you have debated leaving. Suddenly, you once again feel like you are the center of his universe, and while you still feel as though you fear you will go back to the way things were when the narcissist abused you last, you are also hopeful that this stage will last forever this time.

Devalue

Unfortunately, no matter how much you may want to cling to the idealization stage, you quickly find the relationship returning to old ways. The narcissist begins to use old tactics again. He stops being so interested in you and likely has begun demeaning you again. His manipulation is ramping up again, and he likely leaves you feeling hurt and confused most of the time. Things are not necessarily bad yet, but the tensions are rising once more.

At this stage, narcissists feel as though they have wasted enough time and energy lavishing their targets with love and affection. Narcissists love shortcuts and the paths of least resistance, and they will take the easiest path to what they want. He feels as though he has sufficiently hooked his target again when he begins the devalue stage. This means he can start to act out the abuse again with what he hopes is little consequence. He begins to belittle his target again, knowing that it will knock her off of the pedestal he placed her atop, and knowing that the result will be the target scrambling to please the narcissist to climb back up. The devaluation stage typically ends with a big blowout of sorts—perhaps the narcissist hurts the victim, or cheats on the victim, or does something else major that is the result of culminating tensions that have steadily been increasing like the pressure within a volcano that is ready to explode at any moment.

Returning to the example begun in the Idealize stage, you may have noticed that your partner has been making snide comments more frequently than he had been. You knew that you felt hurt and upset by the narcissist's choice in words, but when you confronted him, he told you that you were overreacting and that you should let it go and move on. Confused and uncomfortable, you let it go, but you can tell that tensions have gotten worse. Eventually, he hits you and threatens you with serious harm if you were to ever leave him, marking the escalation and explosion of the devaluation stage. You have been clearly made aware that you do not matter to the narcissist through his words and actions and are now left reeling and attempting to deal with the consequences.

Discard

The discard stage occurs when the narcissist wants to make it clear that you have lost any usefulness you once had. Through abandoning his victim, he makes it clear that the only purpose his victim served was to serve him, and him alone. When he decides that you are no longer serving him to his contentment or that he has found a new toy to pursue instead, he abandons you altogether to get his narcissistic supply fix elsewhere.

At this stage, despite abandoning you, he also gets the satisfaction of knowing that he has hurt you deeper than anyone else ever could simply by leaving you behind and refusing to speak or acknowledge you in any way, shape, or form. You may know that you are better off free of him, but you feel hurt and miss him all the same because you have always loved him despite the abuse he has inflicted.

Repeat

This cycle, once it has been played through, repeats again. The narcissist, when he feels as though you have suffered enough, or he feels as though you may be getting ready to move on from him, will magically reappear, telling you how important you are to him and how leaving you was his biggest mistake. This is called hoovering you back in. Like the hoover vacuum from which the technique draws its name, he attempts to suck you in with sweet words and promises he will never fulfill. He does not care about lying to you because as far as he is concerned, all that matters is his own feelings.

Escaping the Cycle

When you are finally ready to leave the cycle of abuse, you have finally acknowledged that things are not likely to ever change. You finally recognize that in order to better yourself, you have to escape. This is, unfortunately, the most dangerous time for abuse victims, as their abusers rarely are willing to let their victims leave willingly. The narcissist almost definitely will put up a fight to keep you around, but what is important is to recognize that the only way to end the abuse for good is to drop the narcissist for good. Your life will be far happier and healthier if you do.

Leave when it is safe

The first step toward escaping the cycle is escaping the relationship. You need to create a plan to leave and follow through with it. Remember, you must leave when it is safe for you to do so. This is oftentimes when the abuser is at work or attending some other sort of hobby or prior obligation that typically keeps him busy for a regular amount of time away from home. With the abuser preoccupied, you are free to begin moving out. You may be able to request a police escort if you feel unsafe with the idea of leaving while the narcissist is gone, particularly if you fear that he may become irrationally angry and abusive when he realizes you are leaving.

Avoid explaining or downplaying abuse

Once you have escaped, the next step is to make sure you do not say anything or think anything that may devalue what you have been through. Do not minimize the abuse the narcissist put you through—the more specific and honest you are with yourself, the more likely you are to remain firm in your convictions and leave the narcissist for good. However, if you were to try to explain away the abuse, you would likely be more willing to put up with attempts to talk or work out your relationship.

Recognize the cycle—and do not fall for the hoover

By recognizing the cycle of abuse, you regain some of your power. You recognize that the happy periods are little more than oscillations within a cycle, and that cycle will return to violence and abuse again in the future. You know that the abuse will come again, and when you devalue and depersonalize it to that point, you are far more likely to stay away. Just as you would have no qualms avoiding a dog that you knew bit unprovoked, remembering the abuse the narcissist has inflicted can help you stay strong and keep your distance.

Acknowledge your power

No matter what the narcissist may want you to believe, you have power. You have the power to make your own decisions. You have the power to control your own actions and manage your own emotions. You have the power to decide to disengage from the narcissist permanently, and not allow the narcissist to dictate how everything should go. When you acknowledge that you are capable of living by yourself and that you are powerful enough to take care of yourself and your loved ones, you are far more likely to resist the narcissist's hoover attempts.

Reach out to others in moments of weakness

The last step, when breaking the cycle of abuse is to remember to reach out to others. If not some sort of group of friends or family, try seeking out support online or from other people you think or know have been through your situation. Reach out to these people during moments of weakness, when you may be missing the narcissist or wishing things would be different. The plus side to finding people who have been through your situation before you is that they can not only guide and offer advice, they can also show you what your future holds. If you see other people living life happily, you can see that happiness is out there, so long as you put in the effort to attain it.

Chapter 16 The People-Pleaser

On the surface, People-Pleasers just want everyone to be happy. However, People-Pleasers don't believe they're worthy of love unless others love them. To get that love, a People-Pleaser will do everything they can to make people like them. While an independent, empowered person believes they are inherently worthy of love, a People-Pleaser feels that they must earn it by being a social chameleon and changing into whoever the person they're with would like best. With their significant other, a People-Pleaser will put on a happy mask and work very hard to always be what they believe their partner wants, be it "The Breadwinner," "The Domestic Goddess," or "The Pillar of Strength." They'll say "yes" to everything and always defer to their partner's desires because they believe that will make them lovable.

The consequences of being a People-Pleaser are quick and painful. A People-Pleaser is immediately at risk for becoming a doormat to their partner, and if their partner is abusive in any way, the People-Pleaser's life will be miserable. Always prioritizing their partner's needs instead of their own can cause a lot of pain for the People-Pleaser. They won't be able to talk about it with their partner, because a People-Pleaser hates discussing negative emotions, believing it will make their partner stop loving them.

Even if their significant other isn't abusive, it will be hard for them to respect a People-Pleaser, because they'll start to see the People-Pleaser as spineless. They'll get frustrated when the codependent won't be able to make a decision without them, or talk about anything that might be controversial or reveal a difference of opinion. Basically, the partner of a People-Pleaser may get bored with the relationship.

Read on for some signs that you might be a People-Pleaser in your relationship:

• You always go to great lengths to meet your partner's every desire, including canceling plans with other people to do what your partner wants, neglecting work and other hobbies, doing something sexual that makes you uncomfortable, and so on.

• You never say "no," but you feel guilty when you even consider saying no to your partner.

• You're always anxious and apologizing just in case you might have done or said something your partner didn't like.

• You don't feel good about yourself unless your partner is happy with you and giving you compliments, affection, etc.

• You avoid confrontation and have developed systems for skirting around hard topics like finances, politics, and so on.

• When you feel sad, upset, or any other emotion that you feel your partner won't want to see, you shove it down and hide from your partner.

• You put every decision through the "Will this make my partner happy?" filter.

Being The Pleaser With Friends and Coworkers

People-pleasers are very closed off with everyone, including their friends. They tend to not share anything deep about themselves, because they're afraid others won't like what's inside. They'll hide all of their personal struggles, personality traits, and opinions. Relationships with People-Pleasers tend to not go below the surface because of this, meaning even though People-Pleasers know a lot of people, they don't have any true friends of the heart. Additionally, People-Pleasers get manipulated and taken advantage of a lot. Their friends get used to always having the People-Pleaser say "yes" to everything, so whenever they need a favor, they know exactly where to go.

At work, a People-Pleaser can get stressed out a lot. They're always taking on extra work, working really hard, and being taken for granted. They tend to bite off more than they can chew just because someone asked for help. Their own work can suffer because they're trying to juggle everybody else's jobs, too. When it comes to the tough decisions, the People-Pleaser often becomes paralyzed with anxiety knowing that they can't possibly make everybody happy. This can be a big problem when there's deadlines approaching and the boss is breathing down their neck.

Saying "No" to People-Pleasing

Once a person realizes they are lovable and don't have to earn that from anyone, they are free. If you're a People-Pleaser, learning to say "no" and loving yourself are key steps to escaping the codependency of people-pleasing. Your partner's attention and affection doesn't make you lovable - you are lovable on your own. Here are some concrete steps you can take to learn that:

- When your partner asks for a favor, say that you need to think about it. This allows you to think about whether or not it's a good idea to say yes.

- When you're meeting your partner for lunch on your break or you have another commitment coming up, set a time limit, so your partner doesn't monopolize your time.

- Don't give a series of excuses for or apologize for why you can't do something your partner wants. They should respect your decision regardless of the reason.

- Make a list about what you really don't like doing with (or for) your partner versus what you actually do enjoy. Get in touch with your feelings, so you can start having a mind of your own and figuring out what your desires and needs are.

- Start saying "no" to the things on your dislike list, so you can still say "yes" to the things you yourself enjoy.

- When a topic of conversation comes up that usually makes you uncomfortable, be open with your partner about your fears, but don't run away from it. (Note: If your partner is abusive and you avoid topics so you don't get hurt, apply this step to your therapist, friends, family, etc, so they can help you).

- Try to do three things just for you every day.

Coming out of a people-pleasing mindset involves rewiring long-held beliefs about yourself. This may require going to therapy alone and spending time focusing on your own dreams and desires. Here are some thought exercises that can help:

- When you do something just for you, take a moment to analyze your feelings. If you feel guilt, use positive affirmation to tell yourself that it's okay to take care of yourself and your needs.

- Visit a therapist who can help you dig up why you feel selfish and bad when you aren't taking care of someone else's needs.

- If you haven't been in touch with your own feelings and desires in a long time, spend time alone figuring out what you really want out of life and your relationship.

- Work on learning that confrontation and hard conversations are all a part of building a strong, healthy relationship.

- Begin living through a filter of "I should treat myself as lovingly and kindly as I treat others."

- Focus on self-acceptance, self-empowerment, and self-love with the mentality that you cannot give the best of yourself to others unless you are a whole person. This can help you get an idea of the bigger picture and what's at stake for your relationship.

Chapter 17 Being Assertive

Perhaps at this point you are beginning to realize what a big challenge you are facing as you work to put your codependence behind you. You know you need to take charge of your personal boundaries, but you just don't have the tools you need to do it. It can seem very scary, but you can keep going through your fear. The first step to reclaiming your personal boundaries is to learn to be assertive.

What Is Being Assertive?

Being assertive means standing up for yourself in a strong, confident way. When you are assertive, you respect your own position as well as the positions of others. You tell people clearly and honestly how you feel, what you think, and what you need.

Assertiveness is very uncommon on both sides of a codependent relationship. The three other types of communication are passive, aggressive and passive-aggressive. As a partner in a codependent relationship, you likely relied on these other forms of communication to try and get what you wanted.

You communicate passively when you let everything happen as it will. You give little or no input into the conversation. When you do say something, you let others convince you that you are wrong. Your partner dominates the relationship and you are merely along for the ride. People who choose to communicate passively usually fear rejection and/or confrontations.

When you communicate aggressively, you push the other person into doing what you want. You are usually hostile and angry, or you complain loudly and nag your partner to quit his addictive behavior. You insist on having your way, no matter how the other person feels. You use punishments, demands and blaming to assert your dominance. If you are an aggressive communicator, you do not concern yourself with the rights and opinions of your partner.

Often, people who are in a codependent relationship become passive-aggressive. They have their own feelings and opinions about family situations.

But they do not express themselves honestly and openly. Instead, they manipulate or trick their partner to do things the way they want them done.

When you choose to be assertive you decrease misunderstandings. Your partner knows what you want, whether he acts to give it to you or not. You do not try to control your partner. You do take away your partner's power over your life.

How to Be Assertive

Being assertive with your partner for the first time is a big hurdle to cross. Once you have established that you are only going to participate in healthy communications, you change the relationship drastically. And, if you want to stop being codependent, that is exactly what you need to do. Here is a step-by-step guide to help you through those first assertive communications.

Step One: Decide What You Want to Communicate

Deciding what to talk about is not as easy as it sounds. If you are in a codependent relationship, you are more accustomed to talking about your partner and what he needs or needs to do. Instead, focus on your own wants, needs, feelings and opinions. Start by talking about just one thing you want to say about yourself.

Step Two: Speak Clearly and Honestly

When you are in a codependent relationship with an addict, it is easy to think first about saying things in a way your partner will accept. Or, conversely, you might be prone to pushing his buttons and provoking him to lash out at you. This time, just think about expressing your thought or feeling in a way your partner will understand. To speak assertively, you have to be honest and give your partner the message that is in your heart.

Step Three: Let Your Partner Own His Feelings and Responses

Right now you might be thinking about how your partner might react if you speak clearly and honestly about your thoughts and feelings. And the truth is that he might get very upset or withdrawn. He might become angry with you and become verbally abusive. You need to know that before you start being assertive.

Just remember that whatever your partner says, does or seems to think or feel, it is something that belongs to him and him alone. You do not have to feel bad for stating your opinion. You do not have to take abuse for expressing your feelings. You have every right to speak assertively.

Step Four: Respect Your Partner's Rights

One of the hallmarks of healthy and assertive communications is maintaining respect for the other person's rights. An addict can become so wrapped up in his addiction that he allows other people to make his decisions and tell him what is right or wrong for him. You might even feel justified in disrespecting his boundaries because he is in no shape to know what he really wants.

But, you can still practice being assertive regardless of your partner's addiction. Speak up and say what you want or need to say. At the same time, give him the consideration of respecting his thoughts, feelings and opinions.

Learning to be assertive is, for most people, a lifetime task. You can begin with just a few assertive conversations a day, and increase them as you get the hang of it. Eventually, you learn to communicate assertively in every conversation. While there will always be the temptation to resort to being passive, passive-aggressive or aggressive, you have the power to choose assertiveness.

Your life will not always be easier, but it will be healthier. You develop a better sense of self esteem as you speak and act assertively. The reverse is also true: when you feel better about yourself, it is easier to stand up for your own needs and wants. And now we come to the heart of the codependent relationship. You need to improve your self-esteem if you want to break free of codependency and move on with your life.

Chapter 18 The essential dictionary to understanding narcissistic abuse

The world of the narcissist is a complex and different one. It is different from how healthy and sane humans operate. That is why insight on how it feels to be a narcissist will help you learn how to relate. In understanding narcissism and narcissistic personality disorder, this chapter lays the foundation.

What is Narcissism Personality Disorder?

When we talk about narcissism, many people attribute it to people who are full of themselves. While this is true in some ways, narcissism is a personality disorder. It is a severe psychological disorder that revolves around attaching excessive importance to oneself. In fact, narcissism doesn't even have to do with genuine self-love. More appropriately, narcissists are in love with a non-existent image of themselves that exists in their head. They resort to falling in love with this image since it allows them to escape the feeling of insecurity that plagues them deep down. However, it takes a lot of effort to keep up with this false sense of majesty. This is why a narcissistic personality involves a dysfunctional attitude and behavior.

This sense of importance is so excessive, and in no way the same as ordinary people. Those with this disorder are characterized by an inability to think of others, let alone put themselves in other people's shoes. This is coupled with an abnormal need for admiration or acknowledgment.

As a result of their excessive need for admiration, they are usually selfish, manipulative, cocky, arrogant or demanding, etc. This individual exists in almost all social circles you encounter in life. Parents, children, romantic partners, colleagues, etc. all manifest this trait. This leads to serious issues, more severe than someone who attaches a little more importance to themselves.

People with this disorder have this false belief that they are better and superior to all others. This belief, however, has no factual basis. It manifests in the way they interact and relate to others. They are drawn to gifted people or those that can act as a source of fuel to them. People with NPD need this association as a supply for their damaged or fragile self-esteem. This is why they are always on a quest for attention as proof their peers hold them in high esteem.

People with NPD also do not take criticism lightly. Even constructive criticism does not go down well for them. They cannot accept the fact that they are wrong or faulty. As a result, they feel humiliated, injured, or attacked when criticized.

In understanding narcissistic personality disorder, it is vital to know the tenets that define the disorder. A few of these are:

- Authority
- Self-sufficiency (believing your strength and wisdom got you here)
- Exhibitionism
- Superiority

- Vanity
- Entitlement
- Exploitation

These characteristics form the foundation of the disturbing personality found in a narcissist. They have a high affinity for accolades while promoting themselves. This only ends up isolating them more even though deep down, they long for approval and inclusion.

Understanding the Mind of a Narcissist

While many people have an idea of what a narcissist is, we are often clueless about what makes them this way. We often wonder what it feels like to be a narcissist! What makes them tick? What is responsible for the excess importance they attach to themselves?

As we strive to understand the concept of narcissistic personality disorder, it can help shed light on what goes on in their mind. With this, we know the thoughts responsible for their excessive self-importance. In understanding the mind of people with Narcissistic Personality Disorder, we should consider some of their characteristics. They display an exaggerated sense of importance with a need for constant admiration, making them appear entitled. Besides, their self-centeredness is alarming, with an excessive focus on themselves. This makes them dangerously envious with a constant need for reassurance. There is also a strong tendency for narcissists to compare themselves with others. It explains why a narcissist gets the urge to put others down or see themselves as more deserving.

This comparison is a vital tool in maintaining the narcissists exaggerated sense of importance. This comparison takes place in the mind, an offshoot of the critical inner voice. This inner voice is a destructive thought pattern coming from painful and disturbing experiences that form our opinion of ourselves, others, and the world around us. This cruel inner voice fuels the negative conversation going on in our head. For many, this mental dialogue can attack, insult, criticize, and is often self-destructive. It can be hostile and also self-soothing.

For a narcissist, however, what is that critical inner voice saying.

In people with NPD, their critical inner coach concentrates mainly on other people, and how to put them down. This is done to make themselves appear and ultimately feel better. If their boss happens to reward a co-worker, a person with this mindset may think: "He's an opportunist; I could do his job better." Or, they deserved that award more. If a narcissist is interested in dating someone, they are likely to think to be in that person's life would only benefit them, and they would be smart to give in.

Not only are there voices of comparison, but there is also the thought of wanting to be unique, an affinity for attention and admiration.

- "You are clearly better. Do something to get their attention."

- "What a fantastic idea, yours is the only worthwhile one."

- "No one knows what is going on better than you."
- "You deserve to be heard."

To a narcissist, this voice could be due to insecurity that is rooted deeply in their personality. It might also be as a result of an exaggerated sense of importance.

Whatever the case may be, why does a narcissist have to listen to these voices? Will they lose out if they ignore the voices?

Many narcissists have admitted that if they do not feel special, they are not okay. Narcissists operate on both sides of the spectrum. In other words, they are either great or they are nothing. They must be the best at what they do, and everyone must notice it, or it's pointless. This can be traced back to the root of the problem. A distortion in their foundation where they learned that just being themselves or ordinary is not accepted, they have to be the best.

An insight into the mind of a narcissist helps understand their action. Even though they appear strong and confident, deep down, they are weak and predictable. This is why a careful examination of a narcissist's behavior shows that their life follows a pattern, making them less enticing.

Watch out for the following patterns.

They Are Cunning and Have Mastered the Act of Earning People's Trust

They always know just the right words to say, how to captivate people. Remember these people are masters of deception and they know how to seem caring and make you feel important, all in a bid to get close to you.

From a distance, a narcissist is playful, exciting, and lively. It is easy to fall in love with them as they are master seducers with a slew of romantic gestures to shower unsuspecting victims.

Once they have you, it's hard to back out. Your life and relationship will likely be subjected to abuse, trauma, and objectification until it ends. They won't show you their true colors until it's time because they know it will just turn you off. This is why so much effort goes into disguising their real personality.

As you proceed in the relationship, you find yourself reluctant to leave. You have a hard time believing your partner is the problem. This makes you always second guess the things you say or do, which would make anyone go crazy.

They Deceive Without Remorse
Honesty is not in the DNA of a narcissist. They can twist any event to a degree that better suits their selfish needs. Bear in mind that they do not think of their lies, as lies. For example, if they claim you are suffocating them in the relationship, they do not mind telling everyone you know that you are too clingy.

Putting others down means nothing to a narcissist. They target your self-esteem with their insults and abusive words so that your subconscious starts accepting it. With time, you start to look up to them for approval. People on the outside won't see it or them for who they are.

They Have a Deep Sense of Insecurity

Even though narcissists love manipulating and putting others down, true happiness is always far from their grasp. This is because anyone truly happy does not need to bring others down. They are a weak, helpless individual with the consciousness that they lack healthy human interaction.

They may not be able to express it, but they know they are broken. Deep down, this person sees the joy and satisfaction from everyday interactions and relationships elude them. Oh, what a lonely place to be.

Rather than looking inward for growth and self-development, they prefer to depend on others for their source of strength. This ultimately forms a pattern of terrible habits.

How to Recognize a Narcissist

Demands Constant Admiration

The same way a motor vehicle engine needs constant fuel to keep running, a narcissist's sense of superiority needs to a steady supply of recognition. This is different from the occasional compliment that is enough for normal people. Their ego must be constantly fed so they like to be around people they can feed off.

They are fond of having only one-sided relationships in which all that matters are what they can get from it. To make matters worse, they see this attention as a right, and react vehemently should the focus diminish.

Lack of Empathy

You do not have to lack empathy to be a narcissist. However, when someone lacks empathy, alongside a sense of exploitation and entitlement, he or she could be a narcissist. Take note of how they react during the hardship of others. Do they appear insensitive to that person's plight?

Some things that demonstrate a lack of empathy are rudeness, violating your boundaries, taking calls during a conversation, etc. It should be noted that these examples alone do not mean someone is a narcissist.

A Sense of Entitlement

In other words, they act like the universe revolves around them. Not only are they special, but they deserve to be treated better than everyone else. They do not count themselves as subject to rules or boundaries. This is why they feel they can push boundaries without thinking of the consequences.

When people with NPD are wrong, every other person caused it, and the law isn't right. You are supposed to put their needs above yours, for instance, only cook their favorite meal or go out for dinner only when they feel like it, etc. Since all they care about is getting what they want, such a relationship will be one sided. And to them, you are just a pawn in place make them feel better about themselves.

Exploiting Others

To a narcissist, people in their life are objects or tools to meet their selfish needs. They are not evolved to the point of identifying with the feelings of others. This makes it easy for them to take advantage of others without remorse. They do not care about the effect their behavior has on others. And if you are bold enough to point it out, expect them to lash out in a very negative way.

If you are unlucky to be in a relationship with one, they will always place their needs, feelings, and wants before yours.

Forms a Pattern of Intimidation, Bully and Belittling Others

You are a threat to the narcissist if you are better than them. People who stand up to them and confront them are a threat. In a means to defend themselves, they resort to ridicule and scorn. They have to put others down in a bid to soothe their ego.

This might take the form of insults, bullying, or threatening to force the person to back down. It can also be in a dismissive way to show that the person means nothing to them.

Excessive Feelings of Superiority

Narcissists are fond of putting others down, talking down on people in charge, etc. because deep down, they know they are inferior. To determine if someone is a narcissist, watch how they treat other people such as the gate-man, waiters, bartenders, etc. They hold people of honor in high esteem in a bid to get on their good side while they are critical to people that serve them.

A narcissist never believes he is wrong and must be right in all circumstances. Even if you argue, they will twist and confuse your brain until you succumb.

Be sure to watch out for more than three traits described above before passing someone off as a narcissist. An individual could manifest any of the signs above and not be a narcissist.

Types of Narcissism

More often than not, the word narcissist is commonly used these days. You hear it in the news headlines, day to day conversation, etc. Besides, many people hold the view that a narcissist is someone who thinks excessively of themselves such that others matter a little to them.

When you consider the way narcissism is used, you will think there is a specific pattern that all narcissism conforms. The reality is that narcissism occurs on a spectrum with healthy self-esteem on one end and NPD on the other. As a result, no two narcissists are rarely alike. They come in diverse personality with various modes of revealing their majesty. Besides, the way they affect self-esteem also differs.

Here are the most extreme types of narcissist you might encounter. They could be of any gender (even though, it is common to the male gender.)

Overt Narcissism

They are loud, have a desire to always be heard, in control, and never wrong. They are the most common. They have this feeling of knowing more and better than others. As a result, whether welcomed or not, they will voice their opinion and expect people to agree and go along with them. Things must always go their way and are not ashamed to say it.

They are bullies that believe in painting others bad to look like the good guy. They lash out at others and humiliate them without guilt. They are known to attack people by mocking and belittling them. They are gifted at coining words to downgrade their victims so they feel useless and worthless as humans.

The Covert Narcissist
On the other hand, the covert narcissist puts up a false image in a bid to deceive people. In other words, they will present themselves as kind, loving, and liberal but don't be fooled. They have mastered the art of manipulation to get what they want.

They are usually found in a position of authority such as politicians, teachers, leaders, etc. Since they are masters at deceiving people, they can pretend and put up any front to get what they want.

The Grandiose Narcissist
This is a type we are more familiar with. The grandiose narcissist considers himself as the most successful, more important than anyone else. He derives pleasure in blowing his trumpet and makes himself feel more relevant than necessary. They do this to make you jealous.

The grandiose narcissist feels his duty in the world is to accomplish great things. Truly, if you meet a serious and hardworking type, the achievement could be in sync with the ambitions. As a result, you have no choice but to admire them.

They love having the spotlight on them so any challenge to outshine them will be met with stern disapproval. They will increase their efforts to ensure you don't surpass them.

The Status Antagonist
These types of narcissists believe they are not worthy unless they receive the validations of others. With little or no sense of self, they strive intensely for power, money, and social status. This social status helps keep their self-confidence and intact. They use their achievement as a measuring stick to judge other people.

They are pretty smart in pursuing their goals and passions. As a result, they strive for headship positions: Chairman and Presidents. They only settle for second in command as a last resort.

The Narcissistic Winner
For the narcissistic winner, everything is competition. They have an extreme desire to compete in everything. This is not about competition in sports, academics, and career. It also involves day to day activities like friendship, spirituality, parenting, etc.

These are the type of people that get jealous when good things happen to their friends. Since life, in general, is a competition to them, they believe they are more qualified for the good things of life. They resort to belittling others achievement in a bid to make themselves feel better.

What Causes Narcissism?
We have passed narcissism as stemming from an inferiority complex and low self-esteem. This, most times, is a result of a discrepancy between the idealized self (standards set by others such as parents) and reality. This imbalance triggers a threatening situation which might be real or perceived, causing anxiety. As a result, they resort to defense mechanisms to try and keep the ego intact.

The narcissist employs denial in a bid to defend against the threat (even though that threat is not real) as well as fact distortion and various other techniques familiar to a person like this. Unfortunately, there is little to no research that has been able to pinpoint a definite cause of such a trait. The bright side, however, is that various studies have linked narcissism to genes and child development.

Genes

Narcissistic personality traits, like other disorders, are transferred through the genes due to an abnormality in the cell. As a result, the connection between the brain and behavior can become faulty. This explains why narcissist does not see anything wrong with their behavior, whereas a rational person would.

Environment

Oversensitive Temperament
Watch out for kids who like throwing tantrums to get what they want. They will cry, mope and sulk in a bid to get you to give in to their demands. These sorts of kids are prone to developing traits of narcissism. These kids believe they deserve special treatment which manifests even at an old age.

Too Much Admiration
When you shower a child with excess praise for a special attribute, it will create a distorted view of self. This is because kids relate this to self-importance. In time, they will expect appreciation for things they didn't deserve. The more apparent this admiration becomes, the more they accept that they are.

Excessive Criticism and Excessive Praise
When criticism is high, there is a likelihood of developing low self-esteem. If this continues, it can trigger specific traits of narcissism as a defense mechanism for self-preservation.

On the other hand, when praise and admiration are too much, the child can still develop traits of narcissism. This is because they grew up with the mentality that they are perfect hence should receive special treatment.

Overindulgence
This is not about disciplining your child for every wrongdoing. But if you give them a pass for every misbehavior, they will have no respect for boundaries. They will have no standards and believe they cannot be questioned for their behavior. These sort of children overly think of themselves as they can do whatever it is that pleases them, with no regard for the feelings of others.

Severe Emotional Abuse
Severely reprimanding a child harms their self-esteem. As they strive to learn who they are, they preserve themselves as they a means for survival. To make sense of what is happening to them, they accept that they are the victims in every case. This translates to a lowered sense of morals which robs them of empathy even when they abuse others.

Emulating Manipulative Behaviors from Parents
A kid will likely follow the parent's behavior rather than do what they are told. As a result of this, kids tend to learn the traits of narcissism from watching their parents. Be careful of how you treat wait staff around your children. Treating these people differently from how you treat your children

sends the wrong message. Your kid will grow up and think it's okay to treat others like they are beneath them.

Who are the Targets of the Narcissist?

If you were abused by a narcissist, remember it is never your fault. As long as you are a human, you qualify as a potential victim of a narcissist. However, it is helpful to know the types of people that narcissists like targeting. This can help you identify any of these traits that may put you at risk and take steps to protect yourself.

Keep in mind that you do not only have to be weak and pitiful for a narcissist to target you. They enjoy going after strong willed people because of the challenge and joy of bringing a certain person down.

People That Struggle with Low Self-Esteem

Many things can cause someone to develop low self-esteem. It could be a devaluing experience, an abusive upbringing, any type of assault albeit physical or emotional and sexual violation, etc. These similar attributes make someone vulnerable to a narcissist. This is because the experiences over time have reconfigured the brain to accept that a person does not deserve affection, decent kindness or unconditional love. These types of people are alien to the concept of friendship and love.

Narcissist love preying on this particular set of people since they will bend their conscious power to them. This is what makes them an easy target for narcissistic abuse.

People Who Love Rescuing Others

If you have a passion for helping, preserving, curing, restoring, and defending others. You hate injustice and love to fight for a cause. You do not mind a little inconvenience to make things better for someone else, and cruelty to animals may set you off.

This is why you are drawn to the narcissist. Even though you realize you cannot cure that person you gravitate towards each other. You approach the interaction or relationship with the idea of making them feel a little better.

Empathy

Narcissists are easily drawn to empaths because only empaths can supply the steady flow of supply needed to keep them going. Since the narcissist lacks empathy, they are attracted to people that can provide the required amount. Empathic individuals are a great source of emotional fuel for the narcissist. This keeps them feeling good as well as relevant.

It is in an empath's nature to try to see another people's perspective on everything. This is an attribute that fuels the narcissist's behavior, which keeps the abuse going. To a narcissist, they know a simple apology is enough to excuse their wrongdoings. The empathic person, who is also always willing to understand their behavior, pardons their shortcomings. They know that no matter how much they misbehave; it is in the nature of the empath to forgive and let go.

Resilience

In a relationship, the ability to bounce back from abuse, fights, and most issues strengthens the partnership. This is why narcissists are attracted to resilient individuals as they quickly get over abuse. Over the years, resilient individuals have built their tolerance for pain. While this is a helpful attribute to keep one going through the storms of life, it can be used to keep them entangled in an abusive relationship.

Since it is in their nature not to give up easily, abuse is not enough to prompt them to pull the plug on the relationship. Despite detecting threats in their environments, they would rather ignore their instincts and fight for the relationship. To resilience people, they might even judge the love they invest in a relationship by the amount of ill-treatment they can put up with.

Highly Sentimental People

Sentimental people who love with all their heart are easy targets to a narcissist. A narcissist can easily employ excess flattery and praise to appeal to these people's needs. During the early stage of the relationship, a narcissist will idealize their victim in a bid to develop trust and appeal to their carving. They will strive to create abundant romantic memories that will soother their victim when the abuse starts.

Narcissists love toying with their victim's emotions. By mirroring their victim, they create a false soulmate effect which leaves their victim addicted to them. All they have to do to get a sentimental person is to manipulate their desire for true love. This is a natural desire peculiar to man but unfortunately, perverted by these unscrupulous beings.

Conclusion

Over the course of this book, we have looked at all kinds of codependent relationships because it's time to stand your own ground and to be the best person you can be. You will win admiration for your honesty and for being caring enough to discuss problems, rather than pretending that your problems don't matter. I have worked with people who suffer from codependency for some years and it never fails to amaze me how pleased these people are when they break the mold and step beyond it.

"I did something for myself today" one lady told me after having looked after her mother for the past 15 years. She had practically given up on life and her mother made no effort to make her feel she had any value at all. In fact, she has moved on and is now able to care for her mother but also care for herself. It isn't selfish. It's human and it's what makes you more complete as a person.

Yet another client lives with a drunk. When they were eventually able to sit down and talk, she was able to encourage him into a program that helped him toward being sober. She was also able to start liking who she was and enjoying her time with her family more than she had for years. She didn't have to make excuses for him anymore. She didn't have to fear the repercussions anymore because she took her stand and her remorseful husband made the changes that he needed to make.

Don't enable people who do not try to improve their lives. Don't put yourself down for not being who they want you to be. Be proud of who you are. That's the most valuable gift you can ever give anyone in the world. Kenny is proud of his wife for her strength of character, whereas in the past, he felt ashamed of what he was doing to her and to the way in which she viewed her life.

There is much happiness to be had after codependence. If you really want to get beyond it, this book holds all the clues. All you need to do is take the steps that are outlined in the book and you will gradually find your way back to health again and back to a healthy state of mind where you appreciate yourself and set boundaries that help others to respect you. This book was written with a lot of emotion because this is a very emotional subject to me and to the men and women I have had to deal with over the years who suffered from the effects of codependency. When you learn to move on and to lay down what are acceptable boundaries, you help everyone – including that person who may have begun to take you for granted.

Thank you for taking the time to read this book. I hope that you have found the information contained within its pages to be of value.

Being in a codependent relationship is hard. It is even harder to muster the courage to change your behavior and end the destructive cycle and move towards a new life.

Through this book you will have discovered what codependency is and how it differs from the normal interdependent closeness between two people. You will have learnt how to establish if you are in a codependent relationship and techniques to help you break free of codependency for good.

I hope you found the chapters on healing and moving on after codependency, uplifting and positive. There is life after a codependent relationship and as you move past these experiences you will find new connections and encounter new relationships while re-building your self-confidence and being truly happy with who you are as an individual.

Remember, the relationship is only codependent if both parties continue the codependent behavior. If you choose not to engage, then you are taking the first step to independence and the path to a rewarding and fulfilling life.

The next step is to implement the strategies in this book to heal from the relationship and ensure you don't step back into old behavior patterns. However, the information contained in the pages of this book will have little value if you don't take action. It will work if you put in the effort.

Thank you once again for downloading this book. I hope it gave you valuable insights and empowered you to feel more confident about breaking the cycle of codependency. I wish you all the best and hope you are able to enjoy more enriching relationships in the future.

NARCISSISM

HOW TO FIND STRENGTH TO SURVIVE AND PROSPER AFTER NARCISSISTIC ABUSE. DISARM THE NARCISSIST, TAKE CONTROL OF YOUR LIFE AND LEARN HOW TO RECOVER FROM A TOXIC RELATIONSHIP

Introduction

On a rainy day back in 2003, two people that had been together since they were 18 years old tied the knot. They were 23 when they were married. The relationship was amazing for the first five years, or at least the wife thought that was what amazing was supposed to be. Little did she know, she was experiencing complex post traumatic stress disorder from living with a narcissistic mother her whole life. She was a people pleaser. So when she had met her husband and his mother was battling cancer, she wanted to show him that she cared for him and would stick by his side.

Married life was blissful for about six months, then it all seemed to spiral downwards. On that Christmas when they married, her husband gave her a puppy. Since that time, he had really distanced himself from her and was rarely home. He would yell at her for going to bed too early, would tell her that she should be waiting up for him to get home from work, or wherever he went after work, and would get mad at her if she didn't want to go out with him. She worked full time at a bank, so she had to go to bed early as she had to be up early in the morning, plus she was attending college online to obtain a master's degree.

Her husband was a chef who worked from sunup to sundown, and he always went out drinking afterward. She was never fond of drinking, and she never agreed with her husband going out without her as she saw it as he was trying to find someone else. If she would mention to him how she did not appreciate that he went to bars without her, she would get yelled at and called names. She grew very insecure the more he was away from home and the more he started to yell at her over ridiculous things.

When she found out she was pregnant two years into their marriage, her husband screamed at her. He yelled at her and told her his sister said that she got pregnant just to keep him around. But at that time, she had already suspected that he was cheating on her with a coworker. When he responded angrily to her announcement, she told him that she did not have to keep him around, but he was her husband and should not be yelling during what should be a happy time.

The wife did not realize it at that time, but she had been emotionally abused for years. Her husband kept drinking and ended up pushing her against the wall one night while she was carrying their child. Over time her self-esteem dropped and throughout the entire marriage she never learnt what was normal or abnormal or even what was considered abusive. So, she stayed in the relationship. Here are some other instances that occurred that she did not recognize:

1. She was told she was crazy and unstable. Eventually, she checked herself in to the psychiatrist to see if that was true. It was not and she was quickly released.

2. She was sent to her doctor to get anxiety medication because she felt emotionally unstable. Her doctor told her that it was not normal for her husband to treat her in the way he did at that time.

3. Eventually she was even physically abused while he was having an affair behind her back. She was grabbed, thrown, shaken, and slapped multiple times.

All of that is abuse, but some people do not recognize the abuse because they are either not educated about it or they are just used to it. It is very important to talk about emotional and physical abuse so victims can take the necessary steps to protect themselves and eventually remove themselves from the situation. Emotional and narcissistic abuse can be devastating to the victim, and it is time to shine a bright light on this issue so victims can be set free.

The main reason for this book is to draw attention to emotional and narcissistic abuse since most victims do not know what it is until it's too late. It is only after they'd been abandoned that they research the abnormal behavior of their abuser. With this book my hope is to reach potential victims of emotional and narcissistic abuse while they are still in the position to change the course of things, to see the signs and tactics ahead of time, to find strength and to make the right decisions for a life full of joy, liberty and true love.

Chapter 1 What is Narcissism?

Let's start by agreeing that a narcissist is a deeply wounded and damaged person and that no matter how damaged and wounded they are, it is not our job to fix them.

As compassionate people, who are also possibly Spiritualists, Buddhists, lightworkers, empaths or any number of other loving souls who see themselves as walking a spiritual path, it can be difficult for us to have a complete conversation in which we only say bad things about someone, anyone! We are always looking for that one saving grace, that single redeeming feature. However, for the sake of our own mental and even physical health, there will come a time when we are forced to admit to ourselves that the person in front of us, the man or woman with whom we have spent so many years or decades trying to fix or appease, is fundamentally beyond redemption. This may be the only way we can finally begin to let go of what is essentially a deeply toxic and potentially life-threatening relationship and begin to move on with our own healing.

One of the hardest things for empaths and other healers to understand, when we find ourselves enmeshed in these connections, is that there might actually be someone or something we can't fix, heal, chant or pray back into goodness. We're so used to being able to make people, situations and things better. We thrive on it. As empaths, making things better makes us feel better. Making things better is our entire raison d'être! How many healers do you know who have experienced such an entanglement and have later gone on to heal and shrug it off thinking, "Oh dear, I hope no one else ever goes through that!" No, we can't just leave it there!! We stop at nothing to ensure that no one else ever goes through it again. We write books and record meditations and courses. We even get prolific on You Tube, even though we despite cameras. We just have a compulsive desire to improve this beautiful world we live in and to bring something of beauty and healing benefit to our fellow brothers and sisters on Earth.

But there will be times when insisting on being the ones to do the healing ourselves, and persisting in this aim despite all indications, might cost us our lives. There are many stories of victims who have either contracted fatal illnesses as a result of the stresses involved in a protracted relationship with a narcissist, or the extraction of their vital life force by the narcissist's vampiric tendencies. And there are many others who have simply given up the fight and ended their lives, when they gradually came to believe that there was truly no other way out.

So, continuing to explore and observe these dynamics from a predominantly psychic and metaphysical perspective, what are we actually talking about when we discuss a narcissist? Purely from my personal, spiritual understanding, and based on what I have observed as a spiritual teacher and energy healer, a narcissist is someone who has become cut off from source and who has none of the usual, functional tools for recharging, re-energising and revitalising themselves energetically. They seem unable to derive deep pleasure, joy or revitalising prana from uplifting situations, pleasant experiences or even beautiful, natural surroundings in the wider world.

Narcissists, in general, seem to lack a life-affirming belief in the goodness of the world, and the things that uplift a normally functioning person will often give them absolutely nothing. They are often joyless and emotionally shut down, putting on a false emotional front, a hollow facade of replicated human emotions, which they have discovered and rehearsed through close observation of well-adjusted people.

They are also closed off from true spiritual connection and devoid of any ability to sustain a belief in the beauty and superiority of anything outside themselves. They cannot recharge themselves directly from Source/God/life force energy/prana/chi/ki (please choose whichever words resonate) because in order to do this, they would first have to accept that something, some being or creation out there, might be greater than themselves, and they are incapable of doing this. It would threaten their own sense of grandiosity far too much.

Essentially, when seen from a purely spiritual perspective, many people would describe narcissists as possessed – the lights are on but there's no one we recognise at home. And it's easy to see how they might be vulnerable to all kinds of unwholesome attachments. A lifetime (or several lifetimes) spent indulging in thoughts which are cynical, vengeful, exploitative and dark will certainly not attract a host of angels.

Those of us who believe in goodness, the beauty of the natural world, the essential perfection of a Higher Plan, the magnificence of the cosmos, Jesus, Buddha, Krishna, Creator, Supreme Being, The unity or all beings, God, fun, creative inspiration or any other purely positive, heavenly and inspiring beauties or deities, can recharge our energies, simply by meditating on these things. We can re energise ourselves with a yoga session or a walk by a lake, time spent laughing with loved ones, making music or spending time in contemplation; the list is endless.

A narcissist, however, has fundamentally evacuated their spiritual being to such a great extent that they are only capable of regurgitating studied emotional responses. They can never let their guard down sufficiently to allow genuine good feelings to flow through them. They are too suspicious of everything and everyone. Therefore, they cannot experience the kind of ecstasy and surrender that plugs us back into the infinite and are only able to suck and drain energy from a secondary source, in other words, another person.

Most books about narcissistic abuse won't really explore the feelings or motivations of a narcissist in any great depth, as they are, quite rightly, much more focused on the recovery and healing of the victim. However, in order to put into a greater perspective, the desperate lengths a narcissist will go to in order to make themselves feel better, let's have a brief look at some of the spiritual differences between an empath and a narcissist and some of the psychological wounds that may have caused them.

Chapter 2 Scoring Narcissistic Traits

Overcoming narcissistic abuse is one of the most difficult things you might ever experience. It takes a lot of effort to find the momentum to jump from the pain that has engulfed your life to a better future. The most natural reaction to abuse is pain. Your life is shattered, your heart is broken, you lose everything. But all is not lost. There are solutions for you, effective solutions that will help you get your life back.

Meditation

Narcissistic abuse leaves victims in emotional trauma. The kind of trauma you experience in such a relationship has long-lasting effects on your life. One of the most effective ways of healing, managing and overcoming the negativity you experience from a narcissist is meditation.

Meditation is useful for virtually any condition that is either caused or exacerbated by stress. Meditation helps your body relax, in the process reducing your metabolism rate, improving your heart rate, and reducing your blood pressure (Huntington, 2015). It also helps your brain waves function properly, and helps you breathe better. As you learn how to relax through meditation, the tension in your muscles oozes out of your body from your muscles where tension resides.

The best thing about meditation is that you can perform it even when you have a very busy schedule. You only need a few minutes daily, and you will be on your way to recovery. During meditation, try and focus on your breathing. Listen to the air flowing in and out of your body. This action helps you focus by following the path the air takes in and out of your body. It is one of the easiest ways to calm down.

As the air moves in and out of your body, try and scan your body to identify the areas where tension is high. Observe your thoughts so you are aware of what you are trying to overcome through meditation. It is okay to feel the overwhelming sensations, but do not judge yourself. Recovery is not a sprint. It might take you a few sessions, but your commitment will see you through.

Do not reject your emotions. Your emotions are a part of who you are. It is normal to react in a certain way to someone's actions or behavior towards you. Embrace the feelings and overcome the negativity. Meditation will help you make the neural pathways to and from your brain healthier and stronger by increasing density of grey matter. You learn to be mindful of your feelings and emotions again, and with time, you break the toxic connection you had with your narcissistic abuser.

Trauma and distress affects your brain by disrupting parts of the brain that regulate planning, memory, learning, focus, and emotional regulation. Over the years, meditation has proven a useful technique in overcoming these challenges by improving the function of the hippocampus, amygdala and prefrontal cortex.

As a victim of narcissistic abuse, once your abuser gets control over your life, you have nothing else but to follow their command. However, meditation gets you back in control of your life. You can reclaim your realities, heal and become empowered to overcome all challenges you experienced under their control.

Group therapy

Group therapy is one of the options you can consider when healing from narcissistic abuse. One of the first things you will learn in group therapy is that you cannot fix your narcissistic abuser. However, what you will learn is how to deal with narcissism.

Most of the time victims are encouraged to walk out of such abusive relationships, because there can only be hurt and trauma from them. Narcissists are ruthless in their pursuit of adulation, attention and gratification. They are aware that what they seek is impossible to achieve, so they delude themselves in the idea that they can make you achieve it for them.

Group therapy for narcissistic abuse is helpful because you get one thing you haven't had in a very long time, support. Each time you hear about the experiences of other group members, you realize you are not alone. The overwhelming feelings you have been going through become lighter, because you learn that there are people out there who can relate to what has been eating you inside.

While group therapy has its benefits, you will have to play your part to enjoy these benefits. Your willingness to heal is signified by the fact that you are taking the first step to seek help. Commit to the therapy sessions by taking a pledge of what you want out of it. Once you are in, participate. It might not be easy at first because you have to open up to strangers, but you will get the hang of it. It is okay to sit and listen to others tell their story at first. Once you feel comfortable, you can open up. Remember that it gets easier over time as you keep sharing. Never hold back. Therapy is a safe place. By sharing your experience, you are not just letting the group in on your pain, you might also be helping someone else in the group open up about theirs.

Cognitive behavioral therapy

Cognitive behavioral therapy (CBT) is a therapeutic process that combines cognitive therapy and behavioral therapy to help patients overcome traumatic events that have wielded control away from them. Cognitive therapy focuses on the influence your thoughts and beliefs have in your life, while behavioral therapy is about identifying and changing unhealthy behavioral patterns (Triscari et al, 2015)

CBT is effective because your therapist doesn't just sit down and listen, they also act as your coach. It is a healthy exchange where you learn useful strategies that can help you manage your life better. You learn to recognize your emotional responses, behavior and perceptions.

CBT is ideal for victims of narcissistic abuse because it helps them understand their emotional experiences, identify behavioral patterns, especially problematic tendencies, and learn how to stay in control over some of the most difficult situations in their lives.

Cognitive processing therapy

CPT is a subset of CBT. It is one of the most recommended methods of treating trauma patients. Victims of narcissistic abuse usually go through a lot of trauma, and they can develop PTSD. When you develop PTSD, you might have a different concept of the environment around you, your life and people you interact with. PTSD affects your perception of life in the following areas:

- Safety

After experiencing abuse, you are conditioned to feel unsafe about yourself and everyone else around you. PTSD can exacerbate these fears about safety. You are afraid you cannot take care of yourself, or anyone else.

- Trust

Narcissists break you down to the ground. They make sure you can no longer trust anyone, or yourself. In the aftermath, PTSD can cause you to not trust yourself to make the right call.

- Control

You don't just lose control over your life, you depend on your abuser to guide you through your life. Narcissism does this to you. Narcissists are happy when they have control over your life because it shows them they have your attention and can do anything they please with you. After leaving a narcissist, PTSD can reinforce a feeling of a loss of control, which makes getting back on your feet a very slow process.

- Esteem

One of the painful things about surviving a narcissist is the way they erode your confidence. Even some of the most confident people who have ever lived ended up unable to recognize who they are or what their lives are about anymore. You shy away from situations that require confidence and astute decision making, which you would have embraced willingly earlier on. Your perception of yourself is a broken, unworthy person.

- Intimacy

Among other manipulative tricks narcissists use, triangulation makes you feel so insecure about yourself and intimacy. You feel insecure because no one understands you, and at the same time, you cannot understand why they behave towards you the way they do. Following narcissistic abuse, PTSD may give you moments of flashbacks to the points when your intimacy was insecure. It can make it difficult to start new relationships.

All these thoughts end up in negative emotions clouding your life, like anger, guilt, anxiety, depression, and fear. Through CPT, you learn useful skills that help in challenging these emotions. The negative emotions create a false sense of being that embeds in your subconscious, making you feel like a lesser being. CPT helps by repairing your perception of yourself and the world around you. You learn how to challenge the abuse and gain a better, positive and healthy perspective of your life.

Yoga

For a trauma survivor, yoga can offer an avenue to healing. The restorative benefits of yoga have long been practiced in Eastern traditional societies for wellness. Yoga helps you establish a connection between the mind and your body. It helps you stay grounded. This is one of the things that you need when you survive a narcissistic relationship.

Yoga has been demonstrated in the past to be effective in treating different physical and mental conditions, trauma-related problems, and stress (Criswell, Wheeler, & Partlow Lauttamus, 2014). By combining breathing exercises, physical movement and relaxation, yoga helps you cultivate mindfulness and become more aware of your environment, internal and external.

Breaking up and walking out of a relationship with a narcissist is just the first step. Healing takes more steps. You need to find your bearings. You need to end the confusion that has engulfed your life to the point where you lack an identity.

During yoga, you will focus on breathing exercises. Breathing is one of the most effective and free ways of getting relief. Whether you are going through a difficult period, emotional upheaval or a moment of anxiety, all you have to do is breathe.

Each time you feel the urge to bring the narcissist back into your life, find a comfortable place where you can sit quietly and relax. Close your eyes and breathe. Focus on your breathing, counting your breaths to take your mind away from the problem. Gentle yoga classes can help with this.

Art therapy

Art therapy is founded in the idea that mental well-being and healing can be fostered through creativity. Art is not just a skill, it is also a technique that can be used to help in mental health. Art therapy has been used in psychotherapy for years. Art allows patients to express themselves without necessarily talking to someone about what they feel.

It is ideal for people who struggle to express themselves verbally. Art can help you learn how to communicate better with people, manage stress and even learn more about your personality. Through art therapy, experts believe that their patients can learn how to solve problems, resolve conflicts, ease stress, learn good behavior, develop or sharpen interpersonal skills, and increase their esteem and awareness (Lusebrink, n.d.)

Art therapists have a lot of tools at their disposal that can be used to help you overcome the trauma of a narcissistic relationship. From collages, to sculpture and painting, there is so much to work with. Art therapy is recommended for people who have survived emotional trauma, depression, anxiety, domestic abuse, physical violence and other psychological problems from an abusive relationship with a narcissist.

The difference between an art therapy session and an art class is that in therapy, the emphasis is on your experiences. Your imagination, feelings, and ideas matter. These are things that your narcissist partner might have conditioned you to give up. You will learn some amazing art skills and techniques, but before you do that, your therapist will encourage you to express yourself from deep within. Instead of focusing on what you can see physically, you learn to create things that you imagine or feel.

EMDR

Eye Movement Desensitization and Reprocessing (EMDR) is another technique that you can consider to heal from narcissistic abuse. It is a technique that helps to reprogram your brain away from trauma, so it can learn how to reprocess memories. Exposure to persistent trauma might see your brain form a pattern which perpetuates the negativity you have experienced for a long time (Mosquera & Knipe, 2015)

Traumatic memories cause victims a lot of psychological distress. EMDR is a unique method of treatment because you don't have to talk through your feelings and problems. The brain is instead stimulated to change the emotions you feel, months or even years after you walk away from a narcissist.

EMDR works because the eye movement enables the brain to open up, making it easier to access your memories in a manner that the brain can reprocess in a safe environment other than the environment in which your trauma was perpetuated. After accessing your memories, it is possible to replace them with more empowering feelings and thoughts, so that over time you dissociate from the pain and embrace more fulfilling responses to the triggers in your environment. Flashbacks, nightmares, and anxiety soon become distant memories as you embrace a new life and free yourself from their hold.

For victims of narcissistic abuse, your brain remembers the painful memories of verbal, sexual, psychological, emotional and even physical abuse. In an EMDR session, you are encouraged to focus on the details of any such traumatic events, while at the same time viewing something else for a short time.

What happens is that while you focus on both the negative memories and a new positive affirmation, your memory feels different. You will also learn self-soothing techniques to help you continue dissociating from the pain. EMDR helps to unchain the shackles in your life and allow your brain to think about experiences differently.

Self-hypnosis

Hypnotherapy has been used successfully to help victims of narcissistic abuse heal for so many years. There are specific conditions that must be met however, for this to work. You must ensure you are in the presence of specific stimuli that can encourage hypnosis. You will also learn how to narrow down your focus and awareness, and finally, allow yourself to freely experience your feelings without making a conscious choice to do so.

Narcissists are not capable of genuine connection, but instead they project their feelings and insecurities about loneliness and abandonment to their victim. How do you get into a trance state for hypnosis? Emotional abuse has a significant impact on your life. Hypnosis allows you to relax effortlessly. Effortless relaxation is one of the last things you might have experienced throughout your ordeal with a narcissist. The moment you are capable of allowing yourself to relax without struggling, you open doors to healing your mind and your body.

Self-hypnosis is a transformative process that restores your belief in yourself, encourages you to learn important emotional tools that can help you recover from abuse, and also help to protect yourself in the future. With each session, you become stronger, and calm. The waves of emotional upheaval you used to experience reduce and you become at peace with yourself and your environment.

Self-hypnosis also gives you a clearer picture of what your life is about. You let go of the negative vibes and embrace peace. You are set on a path to rediscovery. You find more value in yourself than you ever had throughout your narcissistic relationship. As you go on with these sessions, you learn how to take the necessary steps towards healing, and moving in the right direction in life. The most important thing behind self-hypnosis is that you start looking forward to a new life, and you actually believe in your ability to succeed while at it.

Aromatherapy

Even though it might feel like you are at the edge of a cliff and there is no way back for you, it is possible to recover from narcissistic abuse. Many people have done it before and you can do it too. Recovery from this kind of trauma is very sweet. Each time you make progress, you can look back at how far gone you were, and the changes you have made. It helps you appreciate your life, and realize how toxic it was earlier on.

Aromatherapy is one of the conscious efforts you take towards healing and recovering from narcissistic abuse. Think about aromatherapy in the same way you think about exercise. If you feel you are unfit, you exercise regularly. You can schedule three or four training sessions weekly to help you stay in shape.

The same applies to aromatherapy. Narcissists leave you so unfit emotionally. You need to get your emotions in shape so that you can live a happy and fulfilling life. To free yourself of emotional distress, you need to stimulate your amygdala. Smell is one of the best ways to stimulate the amygdala. There is a strong connection between your emotions and sense of smell, a connection that has been there since you were a child.

The sense of smell is closely associated with emotional connections, whether positive or negative. This explains why each time you smell your favorite food being prepared, it reminds you of an event during which you enjoyed it. Smell, therefore, helps to induce comfort, and nostalgia. If smells can take you way back, it can also help to remind you of the traumatic events that you suffered through narcissistic abuse.

Essential oils used in aromatherapy can help you access emotions buried so deep you never realize they are present (Kirksmith, 2004). They can also bring back memories so that you can embrace them and release those that are no longer useful. The difference between emotions and words is that while they both charge through your body, emotions are faster. It might take you a while to listen, speak and read something during therapy and allow your body enough time to process it. On the other hand, your body will respond to emotions faster. This is why most people are prone to making emotional reactions.

The following are some of the essential oils that can help you heal from emotional trauma, and restart a new chapter in your life:

- Basil

- Cedarwood

- Lavender

- Bergamot
- Lemon balm

- Hyssop

- Frankincense

During aromatherapy, you must remember that it is very possible you might not derive the same level of comfort from the essential oils as someone else did. If you don't like the scent of some oil, you might not get positive results from using it.

Chapter 3 Healthy and Extreme Narcissism

One thing that must be very clear in your mind is that recovery from narcissistic abuse is very tricky. It takes a lot of time and effort, and in truth, the pain that you feel inside never goes away completely. Sure, it gets muted by other feelings, and you become stronger, capable of dealing with it in better, healthier ways. And yet, it remains. A chapter of your life that you can't ignore or forget. Going into recovery and expecting to go back to your old self is wrong. This experience changed your life so much that you are simply unable to re-become that person. The old "you" is gone. And that's fine. You now get the chance to reinvent yourself, a new "you" that has become stronger and wiser, as a result of what has happened to you.

In order to heal from complex trauma, a person must work through the phases of trauma recovery (not to be mistaken with the popular "five stages of grief," which are not extremely accurate despite their usage in pop culture).

Stage 1
Also known as "The emergency stabilization phase," in this first stage, the victim is extremely confused. They made the decision or were forced to go "no contact" with their narcissist, and now they are doubting themselves. The memories of the abuse are still fresh in the victim's mind and are in a continuous state of overstimulation - something that is also happening because the narcissist might still be trying to get in contact with you through mutual friends.

For someone that went through daily, severe emotional abuse, being calm and relaxed is a foreign feeling. Their normality re-defined itself as "being abused" while in the relationship, and once that happens it's hard to realize what normality should really look like. The victim still feels as if she/he needs to answer to their abusive partner for whatever they do/say, and that makes them extremely vulnerable.

In this first stage, what a victim most needs are support and reassurance. They need people actively telling them they made the right decision and helping them build back their self-confidence and trust in their decisions.

Stage 2

This is the start of effective recovery. The victim starts getting their energy back, instead of being continuously sucked out of them - something that a narcissist does. The victim's personality and emotions start showing signs of coming back, albeit timidly.

However, this stage is also dangerous. As the victim starts sorting out their feelings, they start experiencing bouts of anger and frustration, both towards their abuser and themselves, for allowing the abuse to happen. If the victim falls into this trap of self-blaming themselves, she/he might slip right back into stage one, unable to move forward through the stages of trauma recovery. The victim needs proper support, meaning specialized individuals, not social media support groups or friends. Relying too much on such forms of support might eventually become a setback in a victim's recovery process. A therapist knows how to properly guide someone through understanding and accepting their feelings - this is the sort of support that a victim desperately needs!

Stage 3

By this point, the victim is doing great as a matter of recovery. They are on their way towards rebuilding their identity, even if their trauma still makes it hard for them to move on. In this stage, the victim might slip into the dangerous act of giving the narcissist too much credit or trying to come up with an excuse for his/her actions. Thoughts like "we are both to blame for the fact that our relationship did not work out" and "he/she is a victim too, is not his/her fault for being this way" are perfectly reasonable for a person that is overly kind and compassionate, but you must understand that they are not true. It is just the good heart of the victim trying to find reasons to justify the actions of a morally abnormal person.

Still, in stage 3, the victim starts building up their confidence, even though they still feel in a strange way compelled to get back in touch with the narcissist. Not for reconciliation, but for an explanation. They want closure, or deep in their hearts they hope that the narcissist has changed (they never do). Be extremely careful when you get to this point in your recovery. You must keep the "no contact" strategy going (unless you have a family with them or something else that binds you two) or you become vulnerable to falling right back into the cycle of abuse.

Don't forget who you are dealing with: a manipulator, a predator, an opportunist. Not a lover that misses you and wants you back. If you get to this point, I would recommend doing some extensive research on narcissists to better understand how they "function."

Stage 4

At this point, the victim is capable to look back at their abusive experience and analyze it in an objective manner, without getting emotional about it. Feelings of anger and confusion are long gone. All that's left is the bare skeleton of a failed relationship that was not your fault.

When you are in stage 4, you are very aware of your emotions, your internal transformation, and you might even help others that are in earlier stages of their recovery. Although you have managed to build back an identity from the ashes of your old self, there might still be times in which you will slip back into negative feelings regarding yourself and doubt your capabilities of making choices. This doubt and tendency to belittle yourself is just another effect of narcissistic abuse, although you may not recognize it as such. Remind yourself that you are not that person anymore - you have grown, and you have gone so far from the vulnerable individual that was just fresh out of an abusive relationship.

This just comes to show how deep and long-lasting are the effects of narcissistic abuse. Patience and resilience are key.

Stage 5

A victim of abuse that gets to this point is able to see things as they are. They know who they are: their limits and their strengths. They are able to assess their own value as humans and individuals, wiping clean from their minds the lies and depreciations of the narcissist.

When you recover from the abuse, you will have a deep understanding of what it means to be in a healthy relationship and how one is supposed to look like. You know your worth, and you respect yourself enough to not let anyone else walk all over you and undermine you. You know how to stand up for yourself and demand to be treated right. Some degree of caution is still advised since narcissists, and other emotional predators are everywhere. You have already proven to be the sort of empathic, kind-hearted person that this nasty type of person is drawn to, so be very careful. It is true that you have become stronger and more aware of how to recognize this type of people before you get entangled with them. Yet, it's better to be safe than sorry.

Your future is in your hands

While it is good to be aware of these stages of recovery, they are still a theory. They tell you how your recovery is supposed to go, they tell you little to nothing about how you are supposed to get there, except for employing the help of a specialized professional to sort through your emotional issues.

During the relationship, the narcissist became the focus point of your life. You had spent all of your time either with them or communicating with them through cute texts and never-ending phone calls. You went on amazing dates that you will probably never forget for the rest of your life. All this happens in the idealization phase, but that stage alone does enough as a matter of isolating you from friends and family and keeping you away from chasing your dreams. Anything else, but the narcissist, became secondary in your life. Your work might have suffered along with your relationships.

But now, your focus should be coming back to your own person. Remember your goals and ambitions! Remember your habits and the things you used to do for fun! Go back to those and re-activate the dopamine - the hormone of happiness, in your mind. You don't need to rely on the narcissist anymore to offer you validation and pleasure. Engage in your favorite activities and take back your happiness in your own hands - something that will make it easier to maintain the no contact rule with your abusive partner.

Here are a few ways in which you can naturally increase your dopamine levels:

- Adopt a diet rich in proteins (turkey, beef, eggs, legumes, dairy) and low in saturated fats (such as butter, animal fat, coconut oil). Proteins are essential because amino acids found in them help with the production of dopamine, while saturated fats can negatively impact the dopamine system.

- Have an exercise routine as it improves mood.

- Make sure that you get a healthy amount of sleep so that your dopamine receptors don't lose their ability to work properly. A good sleep schedule ensures that your dopamine levels stay balanced.

- Take in some sunlight to boost both your dopamine levels and subsequently your mood. Be careful to not go overboard with it as excessive sun exposure could cause skin damage.

- Listen to music - it actually increases levels in the reward and pleasure areas of your brain.

- Have a discussion with a specialist and determine (through some blood work) whether or not your body is in need of vitamin supplements. For example, deficient levels of vitamin B or iron could negatively affect your dopamine production. If you want to go all-natural, you can get Vitamin B from meat, dairy products, peas, leafy green vegetables, and eggs, while iron can be found in fish, turkey, broccoli, and spinach. Consult a nutritionist for more options if necessary.

Besides making sure that your dopamine levels are kept at optimum levels, there are other things that you should look out for when healing a traumatized brain. Firstly, you should know that a brain that has gone through trauma works differently than a healthy one. To put it in simple terms, a traumatized brain has its "thinking center" under-activated because the narcissist fed you what to think at all times; the "emotional regulation center" is also under-activated as it had to be, in order for you to sustain the huge amount of constant trauma; and the "fear center" is overly activated - for obvious reasons. A brain that is in this condition has difficulties with assessing information and with managing emotions, even if the person actively tries to calm down and take it easy when they feel overwhelmed. Getting your brain back to its original state is hard, and it takes a lot of time and repetition. You will require the help of a psychotherapist that specializes in trauma, and who knows how to use evidence-based methods that can produce positive changes in your brain.

Secondly, you will have to make some changes in your regular, day to day life. Learn/practice relaxation techniques, such as meditation, that deactivate the fear center of your brain. It will not only help you relax, but it also gives you the chance to focus on yourself and restore your self-image. It will aid you in forgiving yourself and accepting yourself, which is crucial for recovery. You can also try to practice breathing techniques, other types of self-discovery methods, maybe yoga - it would also offer a chance for meeting new people and getting in tune with your spiritual side.

And last, but not least, in order to help not only your brain but yourself to advance further on this recovery journey, there are some additional changes/things you should try or at least consider doing. It's nothing scary, don't worry. Some of these things will bring you a lot of joy, even if others might be a bit hard to do at first. Smother yourself with self-love, self-respect, and self-care in order to start feeling good about yourself again. You have been through a lot. The narcissist has scooped out an enormous amount of self-worth from you in an attempt to make you a serving slave to them. We need to refill your self-worth and get you feeling good about yourself again and there are many ways we can do that:

• Sit down and create a list of achievable goals, something you can work toward and look forward to. Think of all the things that you wanted to accomplish prior to the relationship or all the interests and passions that you have ignored while you were under the narcissist's influence. There should be at least a few things that pop in your mind. Just be careful to focus on achievable things - be mindful of what you can do and don't try to force your limits. Goals give you a purpose in life, and right now you desperately need one, to motivate you and keep you on track.

- Be physically active even if you are not the type of person that particularly enjoys sports. Besides improving your dopamine levels, physical activity also prompts your brain to secrete endorphins, substances that combat the cortisol that was overly produced due to stress. Choose a type of activity that you would truly enjoy, such as dancing - which has a lot of great benefits to it. However, try to consider first a sport/activity that can be done in teams or with a group of people, as it would be very beneficial for you to socialize. Especially with yoga, where most people are very positive and mindful of other people's feelings. It will help you fend off all that negativity that you have gathered from the traumatic experience.

- Get back in contact with the people in your life. This might be very hard at first because you will have to explain your situation and therefore, "expose" the true nature of your relationship. For you, this will be a bitter-sweet victory as it offers up a cocktail of emotions: shame, anger, relief, and gratitude. But you will be surprised to see that most of the people in your life were already aware of your hurting, but they either decided to not interfere or if they tried, you may have pushed them away. Trust your friends and family. They know you and the type of person you are. They will be there for you to support and love you in your time of need.

- To further expand on this point, be selective with the energy you surround yourself with. Yes, the narcissist may have shattered your boundaries in the past but it is time to rebuild these boundaries from the ground up. It is time to no longer tolerate an ounce of negativity or put-downs from anyone. By surrounding yourself with good energy and vibes only, you put yourself on to the fast track for a healthy recovery.

- Re-engage with your old hobbies that you had prior to the relationship, especially if they are creative or related to the outdoors. Writing, painting, and sculpting might offer you a way to express yourself, helping you re-define your lost identity and maybe get rid of some of that emotional baggage. Video games and reading gives you an entrance into a different world, one in which you can relax and have a good time. Physical activity keeps your body occupied while your mind roams free. Going on walks, hikes or treks gives you the opportunity to be in nature, which is known to be therapeutic for both our minds and our souls. If you don't want to re-engage with an older hobby then start a brand new one from scratch, be it creative or active. Even starting a new business could give you a great opportunity to focus your mind on something both positive and stimulating. Who knows? Maybe you'll even get a new career out of it.

- Escape for a bit from your everyday life. You've been through a lot. It's perfectly fine if you need to go away for some time, in a new exciting place to heal and recharge your depleted batteries. It could be a very refreshing experience to get in contact with a different culture, meet new people, and just explore the wonders that our beautiful world has to offer. Your mind will thrive in a new, exciting environment!

- Laugh as much as you can. Laughter is the ultimate medicine for both your mind and soul. It makes your brain secrete substances that make you feel good and it puts you into a good mood. Go out with your fun-loving friends, see your favorite comedy movies/TV serials, watch stand-up comedy shows, or do anything else that will put a smile on your face.

- Start reading empowering materials. Read self-development books that present motivational stories and good advice. If you feed your mind with positive, empowering materials, which is good-quality food for your brain, you are being proactive in helping your mind heal.

- And last but not least, go splurge on yourself. Get that massage you've always been meaning to get but never made the time for. Get that manicure. Buy that outfit you've always wanted to buy. Try that new hairstyle you've been thinking about getting. Let this be your own stamp of authority that you will not allow yourself to ever be walked over again and your self-worth is not something to be toyed with.

To end this chapter on a good note, here are some "healing affirmations" that you can use as tools to help you move away from the negative mindset that the abuse caused. Use them at the beginning of every morning to boost your mood, hope, belief, trust, and your self-esteem. By using positive daily affirmations, you are re-wiring your subconscious mind which in turn will result in a more desirable and positive reality.

"I am healing one step at a time."

"I am a good person, that deserves love, affection, and respect."

"I surround myself with positive energy only."

"I am worthy of the beautiful things the Universe has to offer me."

"I am open to the beautiful things the Universe has to offer me."

"I love myself."

"I surround myself with people who respect me and my boundaries."

"I am grateful for my friends and family."

"I am putting the past behind me, and I will focus on the present and future."

"I am making a priority out of my recovery."

"I can trust my mind and my instincts to lead me towards making the right decision."

"My boundaries are strong, and nothing can make me overstep them."

"My friends and family will always love and support me, no matter what."

"I choose to become a better version of myself each and every day."

"I continue to learn and educate myself."

"I am improving each and every day."

Chapter 4 Real Narcissistic People

Manipulation is an art that the narcissist has learned to master. Indeed, the narcissist is so skillful at manipulating those around them that the victims may not understand that they have been subjected to a form of mind control as a consequence of being seduced by the charm of the narcissist. Though the narcissist may behave in ways that can (and should) be described as inhumane, they can also possess a deep understanding of human nature or human nature that permits them to say one thing while meaning something else, control the emotional state of others subtly, or to lie.

The man or woman with a narcissistic personality disorder has a requirement to satisfy their vanity, which means that they are engaged in constructing an image of themselves, which may have no resemblance to the reality. Part of being a fully mature human understands that human beings are imbued with positive and negative qualities and are capable of engaging in acts of good and evil. Though the narcissist can engage in acts that are damaging to others and are abusive, they may see themselves as imbued with goodness because of the primary narcissism that they exhibit which prevents them from seeing themselves in a realistic way. What this means is that the narcissist needs you to uphold the image of themselves that they have created.

The narcissist uses you to satisfy their narcissism, and at the same time, they need you to fulfill their codependency problem. The narcissist naturally falls into a pattern of abusive behavior to others because of these needs and because of the lack of empathy toward others that they exhibit as a result of their primary narcissism. The manipulative powers of the narcissist combined with the vulnerabilities that the abused person may have had beforehand (and which the narcissist exploits) can render recognizing narcissistic abuse to the uninitiated a difficult task. Here, you will learn some signs that will help you determine if you have fallen into the clutches of a narcissist.

Sign #1: Your significant other tries to isolate you to retain their control

Relationships can be isolating. In fact, individuals with unique personality characteristics or others who are reserved or just like to be alone can find themselves spending most of their time with their partner and little time with others. Although this is not necessarily dysfunctional, someone with the capacity to hurt you or with the desire to do so can use this isolation to control you. By isolating you, the narcissist can control your sense of reality by exposing you solely to their own perceptions and preventing you from knowing the truth.

The narcissist may tell you that you are unattractive, overweight, or otherwise lacking in value. They know, on some level, that these words will cause you pain, but they do not care because they need to feel superior and they need to keep you dependent. If you find yourself spending more and more time with your significant other and less time with friends and family, then you should take a moment to ask yourself why. This is especially important in situations where you are aware that your significant other is abusive or you feel sad and alone but do not know why.

Sign #2: Your significant other minimizes your successes and emphasizes their own

Vanity is an essential characteristic of narcissistic people. In fact, it is the defining characteristic of the narcissist. Much of the behavior of the narcissist, including the behavior of the abusive variety, stems from the vanity of the narcissist, which prevents them from fully empathizing with you and motivates them to degrade you as part of a need to inflate their image. Some psychoanalysts believe that the narcissist, on some level, recognizes their own inferiority. In particular, Adlerian views of individual psychiatry purport that a subconscious inferiority complex is a primary motivator of human action.

If you notice that your significant other says things to you that minimize your accomplishments, then this is a strong sign that you are dealing with a narcissist. Using this sign requires that you have some understanding of your worth and accomplishments. If you slaved away for a degree while working and your significant other tells you that this is not a big deal because everyone has a college degree these days, they are minimizing your accomplishments. If they then suggest that their college degree is more valuable than yours because of the subject or the school they attended, then they are emphasizing their own accomplishments relative to yours. This emphasis of one's accomplishments is very characteristic of narcissistic people, and it should be regarded as a red flag.

Sign#3: Strong emotions, such as love, are a tool that your significant other uses to blackmail you

The narcissist is aware of the emotions of others; they just do not value them. The narcissist sees their own identity as having more intrinsic value than your own, so establishing an emotional connection with you is often a tool they use for manipulation rather than a genuine indication of how they feel. This is one aspect of dealing with narcissists that can be very challenging. The narcissist can be so charming, so suave that you are not aware of the note of falseness in their words.

Because a narcissist does not value your emotions, they have no qualms about using your emotions against you. The narcissist can use emotion as a form of blackmail, using emotional attention and signs of affection as a means of getting what they want from you. If you notice that your natural signs of affection are met with behavior from your partner that does not seem in accordance with your own, then this can be a sign that you are dealing with a narcissist. Like borderline and histrionic people, the narcissist may not have the typical emotional relays that would permit you to share with them the type of healthy emotional interaction that you would have with someone without a personality disorder.

Sign #4: You may experience bouts of unexpected rage from your partner

The narcissist is inherently selfish. Their self-concept of being superior and their vanity result in a type of egoism that basically forms a barrier between them and others. For this reason, you can experience bouts of rage from the narcissist when you do not give them what they desire. The narcissist does not value you as much as they value themselves, even if you have been in a relationship with them for a long time, so if you fail to give them what they feel they need or what they expect from you, then this can cause them to be very angry.

Although many different things in a relationship can lead to outbursts of rage, the narcissistic relationship is important to point out because this rage is generally unexpected. The rage comes as a surprise because the narcissist generally is not genuine in their interactions with you. Everything that they say, all the behaviors that are visible to you are false and designed to give them what they need from you. It is the rage they feel that is genuine when they do not get what they want or feel they need, and when you experience this type of rage, you should take note.

Sign #5: Your significant other refuses to be held accountable for anything

Although the idea of being above the law or deserving of special consideration is especially associated with the Machiavellian type, this type of perception is also seen in the narcissist. The narcissist perceives themselves as being special, so when they do something, including making a mistake of some kind, it is not the same as when someone else does it. This represents less of a desire to manipulate you into cutting them slack than it does the fact that they are so vain that they do not see their flaws or have learned to overlook those aspects of their behavior that conflict with the self constructs.

If you notice that your significant other does not attach significance to their flaws the same way that they do to yours, then this may be a sign that you are dealing with a narcissist. Because the narcissist is so manipulative, you, too, may have learned to explain away the wrong things that they do. A warning sign here is if you do something, it is harshly criticized and harped on, but when they do the same thing, it is justified or ignored completely. This is a clue that they do not see their flaws as flaws, but yours, they recognize for what they are (or worse).

Sign #6: Your significant other demeans and belittles you

Belittling language is one of the major red flags that alert you that you are dealing with a narcissist. Someone who loves you and values you should not say things to you that cause you to have low self-esteem or which lower your worth. A true partner should endeavor to lift you up rather than put you down because they see the two of you as joined in an important way. The narcissist has no compunctions about putting you down because they do not perceive you as being as special as they are, in a relationship or not.

Sign #7: You feel hollow and ignored

One of the more important signs of narcissistic abuse is feeling ignored, especially when you are sensitive or emotionally vulnerable. This is an important sign because many people do not recognize when they are being manipulated or controlled, especially when this is being done at the hands of a narcissist. Although the abuse of the narcissist may be obvious to the outsider, to the person in the relationship, all the little clues may not be obvious because of the charm of the narcissist or the inherent vulnerabilities of the person being abused.

Sometimes, the only sign that you are in an emotionally abusive relationship is feeling hollow. This type of feeling represents the effects that the words and actions of the narcissist have had on you. It is important to pay attention to this very important, albeit subtle clue.

Sign#8: Your significant other can be cruel, but they are able to turn on the charm when necessary

The narcissist is very calculating. Their words are designed to have an impact on you, whether it is to break you down or to lift themselves up. The narcissist is also aware enough of your emotional state and your weaknesses that they can get a read on the impact that their words have on you. Indeed, the narcissist is very calculating about what they say because they have specific goals concerning you. The narcissist does not act this way with just you but with everyone. They are cut from other people to some degree, so they have learned the value that words can have in helping them get what they want from others.

Therefore, when the narcissist notices that they have gone too far, that they have hurt you to such an extent that the effect is something unexpected, then they know how to turn on the charm to lure you back in. This is thanks to their ability to read you. Just like the person using neuro-linguistic mind control, the narcissist has learned the verbal and non-verbal cues that you send that indicate your emotional state and your receptiveness to this or that. The narcissist is engaged in mind control just as the adept in NLP is as this form of mind control also relies on words.

Sign #9 Just when you have had enough, your significant other finds a way to lure you back in

Although charm is not inherently a dangerous quality, this is one of the character traits of the narcissist that is part of the constellation of quirks that renders them dangerous. Narcissists can be charming because they know that charm is a good way to manipulate people and that they see themselves as better than others, and this comes out in the confidence that others feed into and reinforce. Therefore, when the narcissist notices that they may have gone a tad farther, then they turn on the charm to undo the damage they have done. This change in behavior can happen in a flash, and it is a sign that you are dealing with a manipulative person.

Sign #10: The feelings that your significant other displays toward you change rapidly

The idea of rapidly changing behavior or emotions is very important when it comes to manipulators. Manipulators understand the importance of emotions to control others. As human beings, we naturally seek an emotional connection with others. This is part of our legacy as members of the animal kingdom to be able to form a deep connection with other members of our species, but it also a uniquely human characteristic that we can feel sympathy and have empathy for others.

But the motivations of the narcissistic are less group-focused and more primal—more narcissistic. The emotions of the narcissist change rapidly because their own emotional state is not tied to your own, as it would be if they really felt empathy for you. Their emotional state is tied to their sense of how they can use their emotions to mind-control you and the occasional time when they allow their mask to fall and show you the anger they feel when they do not get what they want. Rapid changes in emotion represent the narcissist switching it up based on how their emotions can impact you. Over time, you should learn to distinguish the real thing from the fake stuff.

Sign #11: You experience emotional ups and downs

The narcissist may be prone to outbursts of emotion, but it is the victim of narcissistic abuse who experiences ups and downs. If you experience emotional highs and lows, it is probably a sign that you are dealing with a highly emotional person or that someone else is manipulating your emotional state at will. The latter is the case with narcissistic abuse because the narcissist basically sees your emotions as a tool they can use to get what they want from you. In a relationship with a person with borderline personality disorder, for example, emotional highs and lows on your part means that the ups and downs of your borderline partner is causing your own ups and downs because you feel empathy for them and cannot help but participate in their emotional whirlwind somehow, even if it is damaging to you.

Emotional ups and downs that do not appear to be tied to any innate feelings on your part are therefore a sign that you are dealing with a manipulator or someone with a personality disorder. In the case of narcissistic abuse, you are dealing with both a manipulator and a person with a personality disorder. Recognizing this key sign is huge in breaking free from this type of bondage.

Sign #12: You are faced with feelings that whatever you do, it is never enough

The vanity of the narcissist requires that you are always less than they are. The narcissist does not see you as being their equal, even though their codependency mandates that you stick around. Your presence serves several key purposes for the narcissist. By keeping you around, the narcissist has someone to meet their practical needs (whether that be money, sex, or housing) and their emotional requirement of validation from you.

The narcissist, therefore, will cause you to feel that whatever you do is not good enough for them because they need to put you down to control you and they do not see you as being their equal. Recognizing the sign that whatever you do does not seem to be good enough for your partner is important in realizing that the narcissist does not truly value you.

Sign #13: Your significant other lies frequently and pathologically

The narcissist relies on manipulation to get what they want and need from other people. Lies are a tool that the narcissist uses as part of their manipulation. Indeed, everything about the narcissist appears to be a lie. Even their persona is a lie. The narcissist behaves in such a way as to give the impression of their innate superiority while deep down, they most likely feel inferior. This inferiority complex is subconscious as the narcissist consciously acts in a way that does suggest their innate superiority over others.

What we would call pathological lying in this context are the deceptive words that the narcissist uses in their interactions with others. They can lie as part of their charm, or they can lie to wound or to demean someone. A narcissist may say that you are unattractive in some important way, while deep down, they do find you attractive or else their vanity probably would not have permitted them to have a relationship with you. Noticing that your partner lies frequently is a sign that something is not right. In this case, your significant other may just be a narcissist.

Sign #14: You find yourself overly anxious or depressed

Anxiety around interacting with a romantic partner is a sign that something is not right in a relationship. In particular, this is a sign that there may be some abuse happening. Your partner should make you feel safe and secure. You should desire to be around them, and you should feel an emotional connection with them. Noticing that you are nervous about meeting your significant other or that you feel another dysfunctional feeling like depression is a sign that something about your partner is causing you to feel this way. This can be a sign that your partner is a narcissist.

Sign #15: You notice that your self-esteem is low

Low self-esteem is a telltale sign of narcissistic abuse. As we have seen, a high self-image for the narcissist means that your self-image has to be low. Because the narcissist generally has a distorted perception of themselves, they need you to reinforce their high self-image, and this usually means putting you down. If you notice that your self-esteem is low in the setting of a relationship, then there's a good chance that your partner might be causing it. Start paying attention to the clues that could be impacting your self-esteem, such as the things your partner is saying or doing.

Chapter 5 Techniques to Handle Narcissists

You might have noticed that in your previous breakups, you would have moved after grieving for a while.

All breakups are disastrous because you pictured a happy ending, but sadly, that did not happen, but you deal with it and move on, but dealing with a breakup with a narcissist is like conquering the Mount Everest, which is the tallest peak in the world.

This requires a healing touch, as it is similar to recovering after a deadly disease.

It can be extremely demotivating to you because every time you take a step forward, you realize you are being pulled backward by two steps immediately. This back-and-forth keeps happening until one fine day when you do not move backward anymore.

One of the most difficult things while healing from narcissistic abuse is the shifting dynamic between extreme anger you feel for what happened and immediately shifting to ruminating about the good times that gain momentum to drag you into dreaming of a happy union.

The mind knows what happened was wrong and hence the anger, but the heart still keeps thinking only about the good phases.

These conflicting emotions between your own heart and mind are what make healing a tedious task.

This cognitive dissonance is the root cause of all the delay in healing, and the most important step is to rid yourself the confusion.

Which means that once your mind and heart start communicating and speak the same language, that is when true healing happens, and you become completely free.

Upon finally accepting all that has happened, you might be shocked, unable to comprehend how a seemingly normal person could torture another person so much. You must understand that narcissists are not normal people like you and I. They have always been like this, and this is their "normal" way of functioning.

All your good traits of compassion, forgiveness, and empathy run so deep within you that all this while you were trying to make sense of the narcissist's behavior and giving him the benefit of the doubt. You are taught about the virtues of forgiveness and showing empathy and compassion to troubled souls, and that is exactly what you did.

Hence, you must not blame yourself because you did everything right. God has finally led you to the path of awakening, and it is your faith and goodness that has brought you to this juncture where you can start the process of healing.

Healing from abuse and learning to walk away is like learning to walk all over again. Look around and observe how toddlers learn to walk. They do not start walking and running immediately, do they? It is a slow process, which involves falling several times, yet the toddler persists and finally can walk.

Your healing journey is similar to that. Consider yourself a child; when you fall, remember, it is temporary, get up, and start again. All this can be exhausting, but remember, nothing worth it comes easy in life, and there are no free lunches either. You have to earn every bit of it.

If you are truly ready to heal, there are a few key points you must consider.

- You must be ready to do through self-introspection—learn about yourself, your childhood.

- You must learn to set boundaries and implement them.

- You must learn what issues you have that allowed you to stay with a narcissist. This is because the narcissist was able to do whatever he did because he saw some issues within you. This is not like blaming yourself, but rather self-exploration to identify the concerns within you. Identifying these will help you tackle them so that you do not let this happen again in future.

- Last but not least, stop expecting the narcissist to take accountability and accept whatever he did. A narcissist will never accept he is wrong, and if he does accept, it is all false promises, and he will never keep up.

This is your journey of healing, and it is best to keep the narcissist out of this for your own good.

You must understand that this is going to be a long process with several stages to your recovery process.

Stages of recovery from narcissistic abuse can be classified into the following:

Denial

This is the first phase in which you will most likely find yourself. In this stage, you conclude that the relationship is over, but you are unable to process it. Against your own better judgment, you cannot help but fantasize about a happy reunion. You run through multiple scenarios of what-ifs, trying to see if you can make things work. So many survivors find it to much to handle as they succumb to the emotional turmoil and return back to the relationship at this stage, however they soon realize that the abuser is never going to change, and the circle of abuse gets even worse. There would be no healing if a victim chooses the fantasy of a perfect loving partner and continues to chase after that instead of choosing to love and protect themselves.

Anger

This is the stage when anger is the dominant emotion. All you will feel is anger—anger at yourself that you let this happen to you, anger at the abuser for causing all the trauma, anger at the world for not understanding you or trusting you, and finally anger at God. This is the stage when a lot of people start disbelieving in the supreme power and turn bitter. You might catch yourself blaming God for all this and not protecting you and guiding you on the right path.

You do this because you need to blame someone. It is a human tendency to try to find something or someone who can be blamed for the situation, and this does not make you a bad person or a bad Christian, but it is also important to remember that anger needs to be channelized in the right manner and not negatively. Your job is to turn this negative emotion of anger into your strength. This is when you must join a nearby gym class or kickboxing classes or take the help of a therapist. Exercise will help you get out all your anger and make you strong.

This is also the phase where because of the anger and rage boiling within you, you want to send angry hate mails to your abuser. Refrain from doing so as this will only help the narcissist understand that you are still thinking about him, and remember all that a narcissist wants is attention, so while you are writing hate mails, the narcissist will be rejoicing thinking that he still has the power to disturb you. Hence, channelize your anger in the right manner.

Bargaining

In this stage, you start bargaining, which is trying to find out ways and means to make this relationship work and give it the happy ending of your dreams. Bargaining and denial go hand in hand, and you could be experiencing both at the same time. It is during this phase that you may think that you have all the power to negotiate and change the narcissist. After all, you have been told that people change and you can change a person. You take this belief seriously and start thinking of ways and means to negotiate with the narcissist to bring about a change. This is also the phase when you may take the help of friends and family to talk to the narcissist.

Depression

Just like anger, depression has many myriad forms. It comes in all shapes and sizes and attacks you. In this face, you are down with hopelessness because you slowly begin to understand the true impact of what has happened to you, and you are left with no choice but to face it. The book Healing from hidden abuse by Shannon Thomas is a great resource for learning how to tackle all the challenges that come at all the different stages of healing from psychological abuse. If you notice signs of depression, please seek for professional help, and if you cannot afford therapy reach out to family and friends and talk to someone. Tell them exactly how you feel and don't be afraid to be direct by saying things as they are. Saying 'I have been feeling down lately' is not the same as 'I have been considering taking my own life'. Depression is a disease and you must try to fight it accordingly.

Acceptance

Congratulations to you for reaching the final stage of recovery and healing. In this stage, you finally accept whatever has happened and make peace with it. It happens very gradually and over some time, and finally, you will get up one fine morning without any depression or soreness. You will suddenly feel light and start feeling positive emotions such as joy, happiness, and above all, peace of mind.

This is the ultimate goal of the recovery process. Once you have reached acceptance, you will realize that the thoughts about the narcissist will not cause a breakdown in you and send you crying buckets. You will realize that suddenly you do not experience panic attacks, flashbacks, or nightmares anymore, and after what feels like centuries, you can sleep peacefully at night. The narcissist does not have any power or control over you, and you are truly free.

It is important to know the various phases of recovery because this will help you understand yourself and be patient with yourself. It will help you normalize the entire process and give you the necessary strength.

You may be wondering if the day will ever come when you will reach the acceptance stage.

It is normal to think this way, especially when it looks like there is no progress being made, but there is light at the end of the tunnel, after all. At the end of this long and daunting journey, you will emerge victoriously and as a better, confident, and assertive person.

There will be times when it will seem like you have progressed to a new stage only to realize the next morning that you have gone back to stage one. The recovery process does not exactly happen in the order in which the steps have been mentioned, though complete acceptance is the last stage. There will be times when you will be going through two or more stages at the same time.

Throughout the stages of recovery, you may experience extreme trust issues and not be able to trust anyone. You can also become paranoid that everyone you meet is a narcissist and has an ulterior motive.

How to Heal from the Narcissistic Abuse

Finally, here you are at the most important topic that is going to change your life for good and forever.

After going through the stages of grief and finally reaching acceptance, it is now important to understand how to heal from the abuse and lead a healthy life full of joy and happiness.

There are two fundamental concepts that you need to keep in mind and implement every single day of your life if you want to heal completely.

- Setting firm boundaries
- No contact or gray rock

Setting firm boundaries. Once you have accepted the abuse that was meted out to you, it is now time for the healing process to begin. Healing of the wounds caused to your mind and soul that cannot be seen by the outside world but can only be felt by you. For the healing to commence, it is important that you build and set firm boundaries.

What Does Building and Setting Boundaries Mean?

Have you ever wondered why homes have fences or apartments have gates? Why does your home have a door? Why don't you leave the door to your home open?

The answer is simple and obvious. It is because you do not want to allow enemies or strangers to enter your premises. It is because you want to protect your space and your privacy.

This is exactly why you need boundaries while healing from the narcissistic abuse as well. If you think about it, the reason the narcissist was able to enter your mind and body and wreak havoc is that you did not enforce boundaries. You let him in with open arms, and he caused the damage.

It is not wrong to love openly, but it is harmful to love without boundaries because without boundaries, there is no protection, so you need to set firm boundaries and communicate the same to the narcissist.

Remember, a narcissist does not care about you or the boundaries that you set. He will do everything in his power to break them and exert control over you because the narcissist's main goal is his happiness at the cost of your destruction.

Even after you have communicated the boundaries, the narcissist will not stop contacting you. He will beg, plead or threaten you to let you into his life. It is here that implementing boundaries comes into the picture. Do not budge and break the boundaries you established and allow them back into your life. Remember, if you do that, you let go of the control you have on your life, as the narcissist will take back the control, in no time.

A narcissist will contact you to test waters and see your reaction. Do not show your emotions to him. You might be seething with rage inside, but on the surface, you must act normal and unaffected because the narcissist cannot tolerate being ignored.

Another way to reinforce boundaries is by learning to say a firm no. It is important for you to understand that no is a complete sentence by itself and does not need further explanations. Learning to say no will help you build self-respect and confidence apart from establishing boundaries that will protect you. This is the boundary you are building to protect your mind and body. It will keep positivity in and negativity out.

It is very important to establish and enforce boundaries because they give you a sense of identity as they define what you want and what you do not want. A narcissist main aim is to damage your identity, and hence, boundaries need to be enforced if you want to reclaim and protect your identity.

Your mind automatically senses danger when your boundaries are being compromised. This is because the body and mind are built in that manner. Remember, all the times when you felt uncomfortable with the narcissist when he was doing something or expecting something from you and your boundaries were being compromised. The uneasy sensation in your body is its way of telling you things are wrong. During the relationship with the narcissist, you learn to silence this voice to keep the relationship intact.

Make a list of all that is important to you. This can be anything from what makes you angry, what hurts you, and what is against your interest or belief system. Keep reminding yourself these, and every time you feel a sense of uneasiness, immediately check which of your boundaries are being compromised. You need to train your brain to work in this manner.

By honoring your boundaries, you will be honoring yourself and thus building your self-respect back. Be explicit about communicating your boundaries, and do not expect anyone to read your mind or the situation and understand. Say what you feel and believe and stick to it.

No Contact

This is often the hardest part of the entire journey, but this is also the second most important part of the healing journey after setting boundaries.

How do you implement no contact?

No contact can be implemented by completely cutting off contact from all possible means of communication. This means blocking the narcissist from all social media accounts and blocking them on the phone as well.

No contact is the way to remove the toxic person out from your life so that you can live a happier, healthier life while trying to rebuild yourself. No contact is the way in which a person is truly blocked from your heart, mind, and spirit.

It is important to establish no contact because this is the only way to deal with from the complex trauma bonds that are established when in a relationship with a narcissist. If you remain in constant contact with the abuser, then you are not giving yourself the necessary time to heal and get better.

No contact will give you time away from the trauma by helping you focus on you, something that you can never do with the narcissist around because they want all the attention.

No contact will help you grieve in peace and focus on yourself and heal from the ending of the unhealthy relationship. It is also established so that the narcissist understands that you have finally seen through his personality, and this will prevent them from coming back into your life.

Full no contact means blocking both in person and virtual world. This means restricting access and not leaving behind any way by which the narcissist can contact or reach you. You must also block the person from calling you and messaging you, even sending emails. This is because the narcissist will try all means to get back to you not because he loves you or misses you but because he misses having a target in his life. You must also avoid the temptation to find out about him through the third party or common friends and family members. It helps to remove triggers such as photographs, gifts, and anything else that might remind you of him.

Always refuse all requests to meet up even for a few minutes because all it takes is a few minutes for the narcissist to manipulate you. It may also mean that you cut contact with any friends you have made through him because he will use them to manipulate you. There are also cases where a narcissist would discard their victim, and block them on all social platforms with no explanation. This can be exceptionally though, especially when the relationship has been going on for years. Now the victim feels that the narcissist owes them an explanation. They feel hurt because no one wants to feel like they don't matter, no one wants to be discarded like trash.

I met Sandra in church, and I was immediately drawn to her because she always looked put together and fashionable. We got close over time and she shared with me how she was able to recover from heartbreak and abuse. In her situation, she wasn't married to the narcissist, but they had been together for about seven years. He had a previous relationship where he had kids. He would shower her with gifts and money, and she liked nice things so she stayed, even though she knew he was having affairs with multiple women. He promised to marry her several times, and on one occasion, they printed out cards, she shopped for a wedding dress, they went as far as paying vendors only for him to cancel just a few days before the wedding. Still she stayed with him. Over the years, she had made her believe that no one else wanted her, and the only thing she was good for was sex. The day he discarded her finally, he moved back in with the mother of his kids, who he apparently had still been with all along. The sad part was she knew nothing about Narcissist until years after. The confusion, betrayal and pain she shared with me, broke my heart.

Chapter 6 What Happens Next

As someone who has gone through the abuse that a narcissist can throw out, it is very confusing where to go next. The narcissist probably had a good hold on you for a very long time, and now that you are back out there in the real world, trying to bring yourself out of some of the isolation that you are dealing with, and back into your true self, there are going to be a few road bumps that happen along the way.

Doing it all on your own is going to be almost impossible. It would be nice if you were able to handle the narcissist and all of the physical, mental, and emotional problems that you are going to face now that that relationship is all done. This is going to be an uphill battle, even if you are able to get some assistance, and figuring out how to deal with all of this is not something that is recommended by most experts for the target.

Whether you are still in the relationship with the narcissist, or you have just gotten out and you are trying to figure out how to lead your life now, you will find that having a good therapist on your side is going to make a huge difference. It can be scary to think about telling a stranger all of the things that went through. You may have already dealt with a lot of people who are mad at you and who don't believe you, and maybe you have been harmed in the past because of asking for help. Since those who are close to you are going to be those who are causing some more of the disbelief and the hurt, so why wouldn't the therapist do the same thing?

The therapist is going to be a specialist that you are able to work with in order to help you to get out of that relationship. It is likely that as a target, you are going to be lost and confused about the whole situation. You are worried about how others perceive them, they feel embarrassed and shame about the situation, and they are still, despite all of this, they are going to still miss the narcissist and wish for the relationship to work again.

When you are looking for a therapist to work with, you first need to make sure that you feel comfortable with them. Therapy is a tough process to go with, and y our therapist is not just there to be your best friend. When you are fantasizing about how great you thought the relationship with the narcissist was, the therapist may have to come in and be a bit harsh to convince you that it wasn't all that great.

With that said, you still need to find someone who respects you and who isn't going to try and take over the conversation, belittle you, or do anything ese that is going to cause you harm along the way. you need to feel that, even if the therapist has to pull you into reality a bit, that they are on your side, that they respect you, and that they are going to be there to actually help you. If they are not able to do that, and you just don't feel comfortable with them, then it is time to find someone else to work with.

If you are working with a therapist and you don't feel like you are getting any relief from those emotional problems in your life, then it is likely that you aren't getting the best treatment that is available. Look for a few warning signs to tell if it is time to get out there and choose a different therapist to work with, such as them not respecting you, then not listening, and more.

The second thing to look for is to find a therapist who has some experience. Dealing with the emotional, mental, and physical signs of something as big as narcissistic abuse is going to be hard, and you want to make sure you go with someone who has the experience to take care of you and actually help you out. For these kinds of cases, it is often best to find someone who has been practicing as a therapist for ten years or more. The longer that a therapist has been practicing in the field, the better the outcome for the client.

This means that if you go with someone who has the right kind of experience behind them, then they are more likely to actually help you. You can seek out someone who has specific experience with the issue, because it can go poorly if you are the first time that the therapist has dealt with that particular issue. But working with someone who knows how to handle your case can make a world of difference.

When you are talking with the therapist, remember that you need to open up, and not be shy. This can be hard after all the issues with the narcissist, but this is the only way that they are going to be able to help you. Remember that you are going to be interviewing your therapist as much as they are interviewing you. You should ask a lot of questions, especially during the first session with them including

1. How long have you been in practice?
2. have you seen a lot of clients with similar concerns as my own?

3. When was the last time you treated someone with a problem that is similar to mine?

And any other questions that come into your head or you are concerned about should be brought up during this timing as well. You want to make sure that you are picking out the right therapist for your needs, and that they are going to be able to take care of you.

The next thing to consider here is whether you are able to afford a therapist or not. If you are not able to afford a psychologist, which would be the best option to help you get through this kind of situation, then you can work with a social worker. These individuals may have a bit less training and experience than the other, but after they are in the field for some time, this is going to become less noticeable because they are going to handle a lot of cases. They are becoming more and more prevalent in giving psychotherapy because the field of managed care is growing so much in recent years.

A couple of things you should note here though. It seems like clients are not really seeing much of a difference between the different types of therapists that they use. The results that are coming in are going to be pretty similar. As long as you find someone who has experience in your field, and someone you are comfortable with, you are going to be just fine working with anyone.

So, the next thing to look at is how you are going to choose a therapist to get started with, no matter what their degree is. The answer of this is going to depend many times on the insurance that you have, if you plan to use this there are some insurance companies and HMOs that are going to first need to talk to their GP and then get a referral from that person, before you are able to find any kind of therapist you will need to take a look at the benefits that come with your own insurance in order to figure out how you need to go about this. If you don't go through the process in the proper manner, it means that you will end up with having to pay out of pocket.

From here, the procedure can be hard. And there is not really an easy way for you to choose a professional, no matter what field you are looking at. If you are in a small area, you may be limited in who you can go with because there aren't a lot of options. In bigger areas, there are going to be some referral agencies who can help you out. Doing a search through the yellow pages can be another way that you will be able to find a therapist who will work for you.

You should also be careful about the qualifications that you find in the therapist. You want to make sure that you find a therapist who is registered and licensed in the state or the territory that they practice in. psychologists, for example, are going to have a valid license before they can list themselves under this category. With clinical social workers, they are going to have more of an "L" in front of the degree. These individuals are not always going to have a license depending on what state they are in, and they are not required to display the licensure in this format.

If you are uncertain about the education and the licensure of the therapist, then go ahead and ask them about it. No legitimate therapist should have a problem with you checking on their educational and professional backgrounds. If the therapist does have a degree of some sort for the field they are practicing, it is usually going to follow their name in any advertisement that you see, and in some states, this is actually a law that they have to follow. If you are going with a therapist, it is best if you find someone who has a minimum of a Master's degree in their field.

With this one, especially since you are dealing with the trauma of narcissistic abuse, you want to make sure that you avoid just regular counselors, ones who have little to no formal training at all. And be careful about any titles that they hold that you are not able to recognize at all. For example, in New York, you just need a high school diploma in order to become what is known as a Certified Addictions Counselor. This may sound pretty impressive, but it is very misleading because there is very little training that is needed in order to get this certificate.

Once you have set up an appointment with your therapist, you will need to go to one of the appointments. You are going to do an Intake Evaluation, which is not going to be the same that you do on all of the other appointments along the way. this one is going to be where you explain what brings you to therapy, what symptoms you are experiencing, and some of your general and family history. This will take a bit of time, and the amount of depth that they go into will depend on the situation and the therapist. There will be a lot of information that the therapist will use to help understand you and your situation a bit more. They may ask you questions about your childhood, education, social relationships and friends, romantic relationships, your current living situation, and your career.

When the therapist is done with this history, they are going to have a much better understanding of who you are and all of the things that are important and will make up your life. They also know what difficulties are there and where they need to go from there. They will then take some time to see if you have any questions. This is a good time for you to see what approach they have, and any other questions that would make you feel more comfortable working with them in the future.

You may be curious as to how long this whole process is going to take. While this sometimes seems like an easy question, it is actually a hard one to go through. This is because each patient is going to vary based on their own backgrounds, how severe the problem is, and a lot of other factors. For mild problems, it is likely that the treatment is not going to be too long, and will just take 12 to 18 sessions.

But if you are dealing with a severe problem, especially if it is long-term or chronic, then it is going to take you a bit longer. Some therapy can last a year or more based on how long it takes to work on the problem. The choice is always yours though. If you start going to the sessions and feel like you have benefited enough after so long, then you can talk to your therapist about ending the sessions. A good therapist may question this decision a bit to make sure that you are positive, but they will respect your decision, and they are going to try and get the process all done in a session or two to help you wrap all of it up.

However, you know that you are working with an unprofessional, or even an unethical, therapist, if they start to attack your decision and they want to keep you in therapy for an indefinite amount of time. if you are dealing with this kind of person, you need to be firm, and decide to leave whether they want you to or not. It is hopeful that you will get a good therapist who will understand when you are done and will work to help heal you and let you go, but there are some therapists who are not going to act in an appropriate manner all the time.

Therapy is a great option to work with when it comes to your overall mental and emotional help after dealing with a narcissist. It is sometimes hard to let go of the pain and the hurt that they caused you all that time, but with a good therapist, and with focusing on yourself for some time, you will be able to make it all better and will be able to get your old life back, making sure that the narcissist is no longer able to take over your life.

Chapter 7 Assessing the Situation Objectively

Victims of narcissistic abuse describe their experience of spending time in a relationship with a narcissist as an emotional, intense, and vicious ride on a roller coaster. When a victim finally breaks away from their control and the grip they've had on their life, they believe the experience and wild "ride" would be over. Unfortunately, it doesn't end immediately and the victim finds that they're wrong in their assessment that it's over.

Recovering from a narcissistic abusive relationship is a process that takes time and has its ups and downs. It takes work, time, and conviction to succeed in putting the poisonous relationship behind you.

Feelings for the Ex

Regardless of everything your abuser had your experience, you can't just turn off the feelings for them like a light switch. This is true for a narcissistic ex because of the manipulation they used to cause strong emotional states in a victim.

When you left the relationship, it was a difficult struggle and took courage to do so. However, leaving the relationship did not squash the loving feelings you believe you still have. Staying away from the relationship is just as difficult because you are feeling lost, have a sense of loss and even grief.

The end of any relationship, regardless of what it is, is like a death and must be mourned. It is no more and there is a certain amount of recognition needed to believe and understand that the relationship is over.

You will fight the longing to pick up the phone and reawaken the feelings and reignite the flame that was the reason you were drawn into the relationship in the beginning. You'll have a desire to go back and work things out, even though you are quite aware that in reality, it's not going to happen in the fantasy way you envision.

This process of desiring to be with your ex again while you relive the cruel treatment you experienced can be painful. You are in conflict and feel confused in just the same way that you were in the relationship (A Conscious Rethink, 2019).

Your heart may feel that you are still loving the person who mercilessly abused you but your mind tells you that it's over, they abused you without a thought about what damage it did to you. You need to keep as far away as possible and never go back.

This is a dialogue that a person who has been subjected to narcissistic abuse and is in the process of trying to recover has with themselves. The dialogue that goes back and forth can go on for a long period of time and possibly will not be resolved.

There are two different views of the same situation. One view focuses on how everything was great between you and your abuser, and the other view concentrates on the reality of what the relationship was and how it turned out in the end.

There are things that you can do to break up this seesaw of emotions and speed up the healing process to end the stalemate and bring finality to the relationships where you have experienced abuse. Here are some that you can follow:

Write down all your beliefs about the relationship that are interfering with your being able to move on.

Here is an example of a victim's list:

- It was my fault I was so badly abused.
- I should have done more to make the situation work.
- They are treating their new love better than me. It must be because that person is better than me.
- I won't be able to find anyone who will make me feel special again.

This list is the emotional, heart based list that a victim will feel about ending a relationship with their abuser. The victim is wishing to have what they once had with their ex when the relationship was in a good period. This is the emotional side that feels the pain that they don't want to face or acknowledge.

The idea that wisdom is the only thing that can be saved from this relationship is too painful for the victim to face. The heart based explanation is attempting to convince the logical, thinking of the victim that there still may be a way for the relationship to work if they could have a do-over. It's unfortunate that this victim is still accepting a share of the blame that is more than they are responsible for in the failure of the relationship.

In your childhood, who determined that you always take the blame? – Victims who believe they are the person to blame for the relationship breaking up had a parent who inappropriately blamed them disproportionately. The victim takes more than their share of the blame for much of what happened in the relationship because of this treatment during their childhood.

This helps to understand that part of what is obscuring the current breakup in a realistic light is that it is a repeat of the recurring childhood blame situation.

Why do you protect your abuser? What does it get you? – Not only does the victim blame themselves out of habit. In order to be able to move forward and away from the abusive situation, it is a good thing for the victim to recognize what they derive from protecting their ex-abuser and applying all the blame on themselves.

Some victims think if they were at fault, they could make the relationship better. They have remembrances of how they felt at the beginning of the relationship— how special and confident they felt. No one else before this relationship made them feel as they did in the relationship with their abuser.

If a victim realized that their abuser is a narcissistic abuser and that they will never get the person or the relationship back to how it was in the beginning, then they have a better chance of getting on the road to recovery.

As a victim goes through the healing process and begins to see the relationship realistically and not through rose-covered glasses, they can write a true statement to the original statements they made at the beginning of their recovery.

These statements are what the victim's mind now believes are true:

- My abuser is to blame for being abusive. I am not to blame. My abuser has a history of being abusive.

- No matter what I could do, nothing I did could change how the relationship turned out.

- My abuser only treats the person well at the beginning of the relationship. This is how they lure the person into being attracted to them

They will eventually abuse the new person when the newness wears off and they have their next victim hooked.

There are many other men/women who find me to be special and attractive. They are attracted to me in a normal way and don't change into the opposite of who they present themselves to be

Disconnecting from Family Members

There is nothing easy in the process of separating from members of your family who are either narcissists or who take the side of the narcissist in your family.

If your parent/parents are narcissistic it is rather challenging to distance yourself because they had a major hand in your upbringing, your past, and continuity and ushered you into the world. The bond you have with them may possibly not be a very strong one because of the narcissistic element in the relationship but as your parents, they will hold a place in your life and your heart.

Your separating from members of your family isn't always because they are the narcissists who abused you. Your narcissistic ex-abuser may continue to keep in contact with your family and may have them believe that you hold the blame for the breakup of the relationship. If there is still contact between your family and your ex, you'll have to let go of both for your own peace and sanity.

Regardless what the reasons for disconnecting with members of your family, it will challenging. Family birthdays, holidays, weddings, and funerals may come and go without your participation. Your own special events may happen without certain family members attending.

Your memories that are good and bad will come to mind every now and again. They will be packaged together with various emotions that can come to the surface and have their affect on you (A Conscious Rethink, 2019).

Isolation and Solitude

Narcissists are masters of isolating their victim and pushing important people away from you to gain and then, maintain control over you. Narcissistic abusers who are your partner will attempt to distance you from family and friends while family members who are the narcissists keep friends and love interests away.

When you've broken free from these relationships, you may face time alone a good deal of the time in the beginning. You may choose to be alone as you begin to rebuild and rediscover who you are and heal from your experience.

There may be times you do want to socialize but your past relationship may have damaged many of your good friendships that you could once count on or have affected relationships with family members who you were once close with.

Gaining your freedom can have healing and disheartening emotions equal in measure. This will continue to shift on that see-saw from one to the other for a time.

Wanting Revenge

A phase that you may go through over the course of recovery is the desire of seeking revenge and retribution on your narcissistic ex-abuser. You may want to have them suffer and feel as you felt while in the relationship with them.

Actually, this is a normal reaction because you are past your vulnerable state to your anger state. No matter how appealing revenge may sound and make you feel vengeance, what you really would be doing is opening old wounds. The stirring of unpleasant feelings and memories will only obstruct your moving forward on the path of being free of your past life and relationship.

Your emotions can't help feeling that your ex deserves a comeuppance but your moving forward and away from reopening your wounds is more important.

Your Curiosity

After leaving a narcissist, curiosity will be another reason why your emotions will be frazzled. You still have feelings for this person, even after all the negative experiences you had.

You'll want to see who they're seeing, where they're going and what they're doing. In this day of social media, this makes it a very easy way to follow up on them and fall into that trap.

Seeing photos of this narcissist from your past can stimulate all kinds of emotional and conflicted feelings that will not do well in your attempts to rehabilitate yourself.

Narcissists have no empathy and don't really care how you're feeling. They have the ability to move on relatively quickly. Having knowledge of what they're doing can make you feel emotionally irrational and have a setback.

Realize that your wanting to have information and knowledge of this person is natural and understandable as it happens in the breakup of relationships under more normal circumstances (A Conscious Rethink, 2019).

Asking Yourself Questions

Why didn't you see the warning signs earlier in the relationship? Why didn't you see the red flags?

This is the time you need to spend asking yourself questions from yourself to yourself, specifically in a romantic relationship. You may take yourself to task and feel ridiculous that you couldn't see what was in plain sight. Now, in hindsight, you can see more clearly but that's not exactly how you view it.

You can swing on the pendulum of finding forgiveness within yourself to browbeating yourself. Each time this happens, you will feel upset and inner confusion and instability.

Another aspect of your path to rebuilding yourself is the question of trust. You will ask yourself if you will have the ability to trust again.

At the beginning of your restructuring, you will feel you'll never be able to commit to another person in a relationship again and envision a life alone. This feeling won't last forever. As you heal, grow and understand that you are a worthy person who people are attracted to, you'll begin to alter your feelings about trust.

You'll be more aware and attentive to any warning signs that will raise those red flags, but your trust level will eventually be elevated to a more normal level.

Zero Contact

You will need to do two things to bring the emotional roller coaster to a halt.

One of the only ways to really move on from a narcissistic abusive relationship and the narcissist is to completely shut down having any contact with them. Only when you've not only shut the door but bolted and locked it and cease having anything to do with them can you begin to heal from some of the pain and hurt you've endured.

The hardest time of your path to healing will be the first few weeks and months. However, as time goes on, the bumps in the road and the roller coaster ups and downs of your emotions will become much less until they are almost fully diminished.

You'll have those odd moments over time when you'll experience something that triggers an old emotion but these moments will be much less and farther between as the years go by (A Conscious Rethink, 2019).

Rebuilding Yourself and Your Life

You've had the narcissist in your past dismantle your sense of self. Now, you face the rebuilding process once you leave the past behind.

The rebuilding process, as well as the healing process, takes some time. It does raise the need for you to face your fears, your demons, and your anxiety. You need to face those demons and purge them. These are the remnants of the narcissist.

They are the wounds and scars as deep and hurtful as if you were cut with a knife. You now have to suture those wounds and heal those scars. They are all the beliefs about yourself that were false—that you were worthless, had no redeeming value, and were led to believe these falsities. The false beliefs that were developed out of your experience. These fallacies need to be dissipated before you can rebuild your new self.

Rebuilding yourself and your life is is not an easy road and there will be bumps along the way. Some days you'll feel like you're making progress and are upbeat about yourself and your new life. Yet, there will be days where you'll feel as if you're treading water and not making progress at all.

You'll have moments of exultation and confidence then quickly see it turn to misery and hopelessness. This journey back to self is like a roller coaster ride but if you hang on, you will see your way through, the bumps will become less and your elation and confident days will begin to outnumber your days of despair

(A Conscious Rethink, 2019).

Healing from narcissistic abuse is difficult because, strangely enough, the victim only focuses on the good times of the relationship and tell themselves if they could have done things differently the relationship could have stood a chance. They imagine that their ex is showering someone else with the special love they crave.

These thoughts are normal at the beginning of the healing process. However, dwelling on this past abusive relationship for an inordinate length of time is unhealthy and needs to be dealt with.

The healing process, as we've noted, is a roller coaster of emotions. Do whatever you can to seek the help of a therapist who will guide you through the maze of emotions.

It takes repeated amounts of the cold reality to counteract the fantasy that was lost with what is now your true reality that is wonderful and irreplaceable.

Chapter 8 Reverse Discourse and Narrative Therapy/ NLP Reframing

How the Narcissist Presents Himself in the World

To a narcissist, there is no gray area, no middle ground. He will not meet anyone halfway, and he is never wrong. There are two states of being in any situation: right and wrong, above and below, superior and inferior. He will always place himself in the better half of these equations.

Look for a superiority complex. This may not seem immediately available, but even during one conversation, signs of this will become apparent. A narcissist feels threatened if he is not considered "the best". Remember that a narcissist is incredibly fragile, like a wounded animal. He can and will strike out at anyone who threatens him: it may not be in a direct, hostile way, but it will be a strike, regardless of whether it's cold and cunning, or overt and boisterous.

Look for signs of an intense need for validation. Oftentimes when people meet someone new, they play themselves down a little, unsure if this new audience will be interested in the topics they might ordinarily talk about. In addition, being more of a "listener" than a "sharer" with someone you just met comes naturally to many people, especially if it's within the context of a professional acquaintance, or at a social gathering where you are not familiar with most of the guests.

A narcissist, however, will break all of the rules. These settings, to them, present perfect opportunities to gain a little extra narcissistic supply. They may inflate stories of themselves to win admiration. They may tell the funniest jokes. They also may discover someone who is the perfect potential victim, and zero in on impressing them the most. If you observe a narcissist in this context, watch for the pause after they finish a story, experience, or joke—they are eyeing their audience, ready and waiting for the validation that must surely come.

Narcissists are bottomless pits when it comes to validation. They may hover and cling to people, filling the spaces of silence with endless conversation, which is always about them. Kind words and positive reinforcement and encouragement often garner no reaction at all—this is not what the narcissist needs, what he is looking for, or even things he knows what to do with. There's a reason that telling a narcissist you appreciate, respect, or love them falls on deaf ears.

It is because a narcissist can't believe that he's capable of being loved.

Narcissists have a completely different definition of "perfect" than the rest of us. Take for example a weekend trip. The weather is nice, traffic isn't too bad, you arrive at your destination with little to incident and check into the hotel. Now perhaps you'd like to stretch your legs a bit, for a half hour or so, before you check out the downtown sights and grab some dinner. Your mood is light, and carefree.

Only the narcissist did not plan on waiting a half an hour. In his mind, you were to immediately hit the streets in search of excitement, have a whirlwind time at the best restaurant and trendiest bar or club, and get back to the room in the wee hours, just in time for some romance. There is no deviation from the plan inside his head. It's either played out to impossible perfection, or the trip is ruined.

What happens after you've selfishly relaxed for thirty minutes is hours of fighting, abuse, and emotional manipulation that could last the entire weekend. What becomes a nightmare for the narcissist's partner actually becomes validating and satisfying to the narcissist: they have their revenge and their satisfaction gained by hurting someone else, making the weekend—in their eyes—nearly perfect.

Other people aren't actually..."real". A narcissist has conversations tucked away in her mind like scripts. Each person is supposed to play their role exactly to her satisfaction. There is no room for people to behave like individuals with minds and ideas of their own. When a person isn't controllable, the narcissist panics. The only way for her to have round-the-clock perfection is to exert absolute, indisputable control over every situation.

This is not a real, or healthy control, of course. Everyone knows that persons in positions of power—be it a Federal judge or a family's head of household—have also great responsibilities, because with power comes the understanding that when things go wrong, the ones in charge have to come up with the solutions to fix things. Only, a narcissist will never "fix" things—she will deflect. Delegation is a fine way to handle a series of challenges rather than shouldering every burden yourself, but with the narcissist, there is no burden she will personally shoulder. Instead, the narcissist will blame and deflect. This might be in a general way, such as towards other drivers, crooked politicians, or people of a certain class or group, but it's more often directed towards the poor soul who is the most emotionally close to the narcissist.

Just as we covered the way babies and toddlers do not yet grasp that their actions might hurt someone, so, in a way, do narcissists. While they know how to hurt people, and take great pride in that ability in fact, they also cannot determine where they end and someone else begins. All of reality is the narcissist, and no one else is actually real.

Narcissists have an imbalanced sensitivity. Just as color-blind people are blind to certain colors—depending if they have red-green color-blindness or blue-yellow color-blindness, not the very rare total color-blindness—narcissists are nearly, emotionally "blind" to other people's pain or emotional distress. What they are hypersensitive to, however, is any perceived slight, criticism, or challenge, and just like our ill-fated couple on a weekend trip, what could merely be a need for a moment of self-care (the partner wanting to relax before going out for dinner) becomes a direct offense to the narcissist, and worthy of retaliation.

What's often terrifying about the narcissist's lack of recognition of basic human emotions is that, depending on the narcissist's mood at the time, a simple statement of "I love you" can be perceived as an attack. There is no room for error. If the partner has a catch in their throat, or is simply tired from a long day, or isn't looking directly at the narcissist—or is looking directly at them—those three words could launch a full-scale assault that might last for days. There is no predictability with a narcissist. The only thing that is certain is that nothing will ever be certain.

Uncovering the Mystery of Narcissistic Reactions

Because a narcissist lacks empathy, this lack causes a systemic failure when interpreting other people's words and actions. A narcissist has trouble reading body language: another red flag is the way the move their own bodies. Their movements may seem overly dramatic, as if they're re-enacting a Shakespearian play. They may raise their eyebrows often or stare a little too intensely after a benign comment is made.

Narcissists have trouble with subtlety. When someone is sarcastic about something, it may throw the narcissist for a bit of a loop and interpret the sarcasm as agreement (causing major problems later when they claim the person was on the same page as them). They might even misinterpret someone joking around as a personal attack, because their egos are just that fragile.

An incredible aspect of narcissism is the fact that no matter how intelligent or learned a narcissist is, he can't get past the notion that his own feelings are because of other people, rather than from the chemical reaction to stimuli in his own brain. Narcissists feel empty, and this extends to their accountability. Other people disrupt, change, and fulfill the narcissist's world. While he must be in control of everything, he has no control over his own happiness, especially when it keeps getting ruined by others.

A narcissistic habit called "splitting" carries over the theme that everything to a narcissist is black and white, right and wrong. They can't attach emotions to any situation that has mixed elements to it, for instance, they will remember an event or period of time as purely bad or perfectly good. They will also switch back and forth from remembering things as wonderful or terrible: a narcissist who is circling back around to revisit an old relationship will dwell on how much he misses the good times, even when there were none to speak of.

A narcissist is deeply afraid, most of the time. This may seem surprising considering how "in control" they appear, when in reality, it is fear that drives and motivates them. A narcissist loathes himself and works round-the-clock to hide his less-desirable traits from the world, especially from those who are closest to him. Therefore unfortunately, the closer he grows to a partner or friend, the worse his behavior is to that person. True love and intimacy are terrifying concepts to him, because those would require he expose his faults and shortcomings, and that is something he simply cannot do, ever.

A narcissist will prove that he will never be able to trust another person, and as a means to distract you, behave in more terrible ways the deeper the relationship gets, if only to distract you from trying to bridge the huge gap that separates the both of you.

Transfer of negative emotions and anxiety. A narcissist is an absolute bundle of raw nerves. They dread each day because they have no emotional center to help them navigate each day. The best way they know how to handle this uncomfortable state is to project, or transfer, these troublesome emotions onto the person who's closest to them. When someone else is suffering or having trouble dealing with day to day life, then the narcissist can feel superior to them.

Narcissists don't feel guilt, but they do feel vast quantities of shame. Shame is at the heart and soul of every narcissist. It's what drives them to constantly act out towards others, and to keep anyone from gaining real access to their psyche. Guilt, however, is just not in the narcissist's vernacular. They are never wrong, nor do they make mistakes, so how could they possibly feel any guilt or remorse?

Narcissists may be serial monogamists. A narcissist simply cannot feel close to someone. If he does, it terrifies him, and fear is a disgraceful emotion to a narcissist. For the narcissist to receive the love and affection someone else might have for them, they would have to be able to empathize with that person. Since they can't, they live in a lonely, loveless vacuum. Because of this, they often move from brief relationship to brief relationship, never satisfied and constantly searching for validation and narcissistic supply. In families, a couple might stay together for years, or even decades, if there are children upon whom the narcissist can take out their anxiety and need for control on.

Malignant narcissists are also sadists. The narcissist enjoys the pain and discomfort of others—it is one of the best distractions from the nightmare that is going on inside them on a daily basis. This is why narcissists frequently abuse their partners and loved ones, by emotional manipulation, verbal insults, and sometimes physical violence or destruction of objects.

Narcissists use manipulation to get what they want from others. Some wait for the right opportunity, while others, such as malignant narcissists, create opportunities rather than bide their time. Manipulation affords the narcissist control of the situation, and is his preferred method of control as well.

Narcissists are ready to fight, 24/7. Because the narcissist is on constant guard from attack, that means also that they are constantly on the defense. Their anger is instant, their rage devastating, especially when they are challenged in any way. No one can rage longer than the narcissist, he is a distance runner when it comes to anger.

Lies, deception, and total lack of a conscience. The narcissist can't be held accountable for anything he says or does because he trusts no one—especially not anyone's observations about himself. In order to have the greatest amount of control over every situation the narcissist finds himself in, he will lie to make himself look as if he was in the right, lie about the words that were said, even lie about the meaning of those words if, say, the victim had the foresight to record the conversation. "I don't see how you could take that as an argument, we were clearly just talking," would be the sort of thing a narcissist would say if you played back an audio recording of him insulting you.

Other Traits and Habits of the Narcissist

The narcissist is the center of her world. While it's vital, important, and healthy to have a strong sense of self, the narcissist possesses this sense to the exclusion of everyone else. While other people often make choices because of how they will positively affect another person, the narcissist would never do that, unless she was in the "love-bombing" phase.

The narcissist does not possess remorse. The narcissist simply is incapable of feeling guilty for his actions or words. Everything he chooses to do and say was right, and perfect—it is always other people's responses and reactions that are the problem. Cause and effect, especially when it comes to emotions, are not part of the narcissist's reality. He is almost navigating on instinct when it comes to other people, and that instinct is to keep him from feeling his own, deep-rooted sense of shame and inadequacy.

You will not be able to depend on the narcissist. A narcissist has only one agenda, and that agenda serves herself alone. If you happen to be a mere acquaintance of the narcissist, then chances are a mere lunch date or meeting to discuss work will go without a hitch: the narcissist will show up on time, pretend to have a normal, healthy conversation, and leave, all without emotional upset or incident.

If you are close to the narcissist, however, all bets are off. The narcissist may wake up in a foul mood and state of heightened paranoia, insistent that you are to blame for recent problems in the relationship. They may stand you up for that lunch date, and neither text nor call to let you know what's happening. If you live together, you may discover upon coming home that your narcissistic partner is no longer speaking to you. If you ever do find out what's eating at the narcissist, it may make absolutely no sense to you, leaving you in a state of bewildered confusion while your partner accuses you of lying and pretending to be baffled.

So, go the chaotic days when there's a narcissist in your life.

Lives life without a care about their own actions. Just as the narcissist is not dependable unless the plans made serve them, so are they unaccountable for their actions. They have a detailed plan concerning what they want to do, and when they want to do it, and it has nothing to do with anyone but themselves. Other people simply do not exist to the narcissist, not in any real sense of the word.

No conscience, or only in limited contexts. A narcissist can exhibit some semblance of conscience, depending on the person and the context. This usually appears in the workplace, and especially if the narcissist has a job where he has the responsibility of caring for others, such as a CNA or a nurse. It may be astounding to see a narcissist show realistic concern for patients, or even children in a daycare or school setting, but the common factor tying all of it together is the fact that this role is part of the narcissist's well-cultivated "persona"; it's what gives them an edge in social settings. Partners of narcissists often find that they are the ones vilified when the relationship ends, because no one else in the narcissist's world could ever believe that the narcissist is capable of harm. The persona has everyone convinced that the narcissist is a loving, caring person.

Curates a convincing persona to show the world. A narcissist is always "on", outside of the home and the relationship. They work on this facade with an energy unmatched, taking up hobbies or making purchases such as expensive boats, cars, or real estate to make themselves look and feel important. They research current events, the best jokes, and cultural bullet points so they sound like the most accomplished person at the party or office get-together. If their partner must attend any of these functions, they are scrutinized to within an inch of their life to appear "worthy" of being on the arm of such a prestigious and likable person.

Full of rationalization for themselves, but not for anyone else. The mind of a narcissist is capable of twisting and bending reality so that any situation becomes a positive example of the narcissist's best intentions, as well as an example of their partner's ineptitude or disloyalty.

Easy to trigger into rage. The constant, delicate storm that is the inner environment of the narcissist is incredibly prone to upset. All one needs to do is challenge the narcissist in any way, regardless of how politely-worded that challenge is. Calling a narcissist on her behavior is incredibly inflammatory, and possibly dangerous.

Keeps a circle of friends who admire them, always at arm's distance. Another aspect of a narcissist's "persona" is the often-ever-changing circle of friends the narcissist has collected. They may be acquaintances from work or connected through other friends or by having mutual hobbies. Most have not been acquainted with the narcissist for very long, because he will have alienated or offended friends along the way. Some, however, have been friends with the narcissist for many years, and these are usually the ones who inflate his ego the most.

Lives multiple, secret lives. Because of the need to keep so many aspects of her personality hidden from different people, the narcissist will exist in numerous, different circles, and nobody from one circle will know anything about the others.

Holds a grudge. It is extremely rare for a narcissist to ever apologize. A grudge is fodder for future punishment and inflicting of pain on their partner. If a narcissist does apologize, it's usually during the "hoovering" cycle, where a narcissist angles to return into a former partner's life.

Rarely expresses gratitude, if ever. Additionally, a narcissist will rarely say thank you to a partner for a nice act or word. What others do to show love is lost on a narcissist—she can't feel deserving of that love, no matter how gently packaged or placed. Her inner, seething, ocean of shame prevents her from receiving any positive or affirming emotion from another person.

Will often express emotions such as sadness with tears to gain sympathy. Part of the narcissist's persona is also the illusion or act that they are capable of a wide range of emotions, just like anyone else. Sadness or so-called "crocodile tears" are just more tools to help them get the reaction that they want, and to make them appear normal in the eyes of their partners and acquaintances.

Heavily controls partner and sabotages their efforts. Once a narcissist gains someone's trust and draws them into their innermost circle, the narcissist exerts his control in every way he can, including making it difficult for a partner to succeed. This may include scheduling important plans on dates that the partner needed to reserve for work or telling them last-minute of a school trip so that they're late in picking up their child. The skies the limit when it comes to narcissistic sabotage. The partner must never be allowed to achieve anything, because that would elevate them to a higher position than the narcissist.

Constantly contradicting themselves. It's not an easy task to manipulate somebody else's reality, and because of this, the narcissist gets caught in many conundrums. This doesn't concern the narcissist however—she simply shifts gears and gaslights her partner, convincing them that she said or did the opposite of what they remembered. Narcissists have no actual, personal codes of ethics. They don't believe in anything but the superiority of themselves. So, if one week they state adamantly that they would never vote Republican, but the next week make critical remarks of the Democratic party, no one should blink an eye, unless they want to be made to feel as if they are the delusional one.

Does not engage in discussion, only dictation. You simply cannot have a balanced, equal conversation with a narcissist. It's said that many people only wait for their turn to speak in a conversation, but a narcissist takes this to an extreme degree. They are adamant that you hear them; they are without a care that they're not hearing you.

The narcissist constantly feels misinterpreted. Taking the unbalanced conversation a step further, the narcissist lives in a constant state of frustration that he is misunderstood, which makes sense, being that he constantly lies, embellishes, and contradicts himself.

Will ignore you when you speak. One rather shocking example of narcissistic behavior occurs when a narcissist is too bored or disinterested to even listen to what their partner is saying. If for instance, the partner is admiring a painting done by a local artist they particularly enjoy, and asks the narcissist to look at the image in the newspaper or on their computer, the narcissist (especially if they feel their partner is making too much of a deal about this artist's talent) may simply continue with their task, or do nothing at all, completely ignoring their partner. When asked why they were ignored, the narcissist may say, "I didn't find it interesting," as if no further explanation or excuse was needed.

Makes you feel tired and emotionally drained in their presence. Narcissists are exhausting people to be in proximity of, unless you're around them in a social setting and you are not a member of their inner circle "elite". If you live with them or date them, however, you will be drained of energy in short time, trying to decipher their odd social cues and behaviors.

Has no interest in solving problems. The narcissist does not believe she causes any problems, so when they arise, they are obviously someone else's to solve.

Chapter 9 Alternative Healing Methods Explained

If you remember from some of the other things that we have talked about in this guidebook, the narcissist is going to be so successful because they are able to use their masks in order to lure the victims in. this mask is going to be known as their false-self. This is a person that the narcissist is going to create in order to support them in creating a positive appearance outwardly, but it doesn't really represent the true person of the narcissist at the time

While those who have gone through a lot of abuse at the hands of a narcissist may have some kind of desire in order to see the true-self of the narcissist as something that is evil and something that is conniving, the reality is that this true-self is going to have a lot more complexities to it than this. This chapter is going to take a look at what we mean when we talk about the true-self versus the false-self of the narcissist.

Understanding the false-self

The first part we are going to take a look at is the false-self. This is the persona in our daily lives where we are going to take a look at the society around us and then see many different admirable figures. These individuals all have a lot of things that we may admire and what to know more about, but they are going to put on a persona for the fans. This allows them to build up their own reputation and can create a brand new image, one that they are able to get their fans to love.

This mask is the same thing that a narcissist is going to work with. The difference here though is that the narcissist is going to use their false-self in order to show everyone else and the true-self is something that the narcissist is going to know about and no one ese can suspect that there are two things going on underneath the surface.

The false self is going to be a mask that the narcissist will spend some time to create, with the sole idea of making sure that they are the best in everything. The use of this self to construct a narrative of their life that is completely false, and they are going to use this narrative in order to make sure that they are able to create their ideal life. Of course, this lifestyle is just going to be achieved through that mask, along with falsehoods, abuse, and deception.

The main point that comes with the false self is that it should give the other people around the narcissist the idea that the narcissist is so much better than others, that they are going through a grandiose life that is amazing, and one that is going to have so many big and wild claims that seem impossible. This false self is going to be useful to the narcissist because it allows them to separate out their true reality of the world, and the delusional life that the narcissist wants to make sure that the world knows about.

The narcissist, along with anyone who is dependent on them, are going to lead their lives with this same narrative. The narcissist is going to take this narrative and then use it to deconstruct and then reconstruct the narratives that their victims have. this really helps the narcissist to bring their falsehood to life in a reality, one that is going to ensure that their desires and needs are always met, without any worry about how this is going to affect the other people.

Beyond the idea that this narrative is false, the biggest problem that comes up in this narrative is that it isn't going to consider anyone besides the narcissist at all. Everyone who is brought in with this narrative is there because it is going to serve the believes and views of the narcissist, and the others are going to be puppets in their storyline.

While it is true that a lot of us are going to spend time creating narratives in our own minds about the way that things are, this turns from normal behavior to a personality disorder when this narrative switches and is only one person serving themselves through the narratives of many, or when they have become so disconnected from the reality of the world that they are dysfunctional, maladaptive, and pathological.

One the false self has had time to form and is functioning well, which is going to happen by the time the individual is in their early adult life, it is going to be able to stifle any of the growth of the true self, and can prevent that true self from operating any further at all. To make this more simple, the narcissist is able to integrate the false self and it will learn how to deny that the true self is even there.

When we are looking at NPD that is full blown, this is going to result in the individual having no idea about the true self narrative. In many cases they are going to deny that this existed in the first place. When they are studied, these kinds of narcissist are not going to have any attachment to who they really are, and they have started to live in the falsehood that they created.

Narcissists are going to be able to develop this kind of false self in order to turn all of the best attributes of themselves, into the person they truly are, without letting any of the bad ones through the door. This may have been because they were punished in excess for their flaws, or because they were admired too much when they were a child. This new version of themselves, the one that doesn't allow for any of the flaws to come out and just the good stuff, is going to make it so that the narcissist turns into the person they wish they were, while ignoring the person they really are. And most narcissists are going to be so effective with this that they will be able to do it, and no longer identify with the person they were as a child.

Not every narcissist will feel the need to change their mask to permanently foster the false self as a result of attempting to get away from any pain or abuse that they dealt with in the past. This only happens to those who were exposed to neglect or abuse when they were younger. For those who were more overly loved as a child, the child is going to start believing that they were special, and this leads to a kind of addiction.

In this case, the person is going to pretty much become addicted to having other people swoon over their best attributes, so, as a response, they are going to adapt to believe that this kind of praise is something that they need to expect all throughout their lives. But, when the narcissist finds that they are not going to receive this same kind of treatment from others in society, they are going to start acting in a narcissistic manner. This allows them to still get their fix of attention, without worrying about how it affects others.

For the narcissist, this false sense is going to give them a chance to split their personality and choose to permanently live in the narrative of one of those splits, usually the one that is not their true selves and the one that allows them to ignore the bad and focus on the good. As a result of this, they truly can lead themselves to believe that the alternative narrative that they are avoiding doesn't even exist. And in some cases, they are going to believe that this narrative never did exist.

Now, there are going to be two main functions that come with this false self for the narcissist. First, it is going to be a kind of decoy. The narcissist is able to use it in order to develop an immunity to indifference, manipulation, exploitation, smothering, and sadism. So, this is going to be something that they developed when they were a child in order to protect themselves.

The second purpose of this false image is to use it as a way to barter the way that they are treated. The narcissist is able to present the false self as the one that is the better self, the one that they believe will deserve a better, painless, and more considerable treatment by those who are near it. It is used in order to alter the attitudes that others have to the narcissist. So, in this way the false self is able to protect the narcissist, but it can also help them to adjust to how those near them are acting in order to make sure the reality of the narcissist is better.

One thing to note before we move on to the true self is the idea that even some healthy individuals will have this kind of false self. This self is going to be a mask that they use as their own persona around the world that they do not know as well. It is a persona that is going to be more polished, and it is going to really show off their good side to others.

The difference is that with a heathy individual, the false self is just going to be shown to those they are trying to impress, or those they don't know all that well. These healthy individuals will still have their true self, one that they are able to share with friends and family members. The only time that this false self is going to start showing up as a big problem is when it is used to suppress the reality of who a person really is, and it can lead to splitting and very false narrative in the head.

The true self

The true self is going to be the part of the person that shows who they really on are the inside. When we are looking at the narcissist, the true self is not really going to die, but it is going to be paralyzed thanks to the false self, and it is not going to be expressed by the narcissist.

In order to understand the true self of a narcissist, we need to first get a good idea of their inner child. This is going to be something that is abuse din a way that they feel that they are not good or worthy enough, or it may lead them to think that only certain parts of them are really lovable. This can make the inner child feel like they are neglected, or at least that there are certain parts that are neglected.

If a child feels that they are neglected completely by their parents, the true self is going to be a part of them that feels neglect, rejection, and hurt. It an also include other parts that are going to cause them a lot of psychological pain. The part of them that is going to be deeply wounded and it is going to result in them feeling that they need to really change up their personality in order to change it all up and make it easier to deal with. When they change the way they are, they come out as a new person, a superhuman, that is meant to protect them from the hurt, and it will make them feel better than ever before.

The result of this is that the narcissist is going to think that they are so much better than all the other people are. Through this, the true self is going to become wounded, and it is going to be silenced. The narcissist is going to go through their life without this true life, and often it is going to be silenced.

If the child was heavily admired by their parents, rather than being neglected, it is likely tat the negative aspects of their personality would be ignored by the parents quite a bit. Because of this, the child was taught that it was fine to deny and neglect these aspects as well. The child would likely be praised a lot and admired for their positive actions and then would be completely neglected for negative ones.

For example, if the person was to score high on a test, they would be admired, but if they had fallen off their bike, then this would be ignored. This is going to make the child feel that they are only going to be worthy of acceptance and love if they are doing their best and winning in life. If there are some less admirable actions that come out, which are things that all of us have, then they are going to choose to ignore these and pretend that they don't exist. These negative aspects are not going to bring them the admiration and praise that they need, so they are pushed down.

Either way, the true self of a narcissist is going to be damaged and wounded quite a bit with a narcissist. They are going to choose to deny this true self because, in their eyes, the true self is going to be responsible for attracting the pain and the trauma that the child had to deal with. When the narcissist is able to deny this aspect of themselves, and they destroy it, as well as replacing it with the false self, the narcissist can become the person that they feel is worthy of a higher degrees of acceptance, love, appreciation, and admiration.

While it is fine to have your own false self to use in order to impress people who you are just meeting and more, the creation and the integration of the false self lead to them not only protecting themselves from the pain of their own abuse but also results in them abusing other people in a different way later on in your life.

The form of abuse that is going to show up during this time is going to lead them to causing harm to others, harm that is not going to look like the kind that they saw in their own childhood unless the narcissism was a learned trait because one of their parents was a narcissist. The difference here is that the narcissist is going to abuse people on te pretense that they are not as good as the narcissist is and therefore they should never have a reason to be ashamed of themselves.

Because the narcissist is not going to accept the true self that they have, and they feel that this true self is going to lead to too much pain, it means that they are just going to take that false self and make it their true reality. The narcissist is often going to deny their true self, even when it seems like it is not that bad and that it would be much better for them to show their own great attributes. In other words, because the narcissist felt that they were not allowed in their childhood to be accepted for their true self, they feel that no one else should be either.

Chapter 10 Your Brain in love, sex and the Narcissist

Perhaps the most difficult thing about taking control back of your life after ending a narcissistic relationship is to change your mindset. You must stop thinking about the pain and must not dwell in the past. Instead, you must try to overcome all the negativity you were exposed to and start looking forward to a brighter future. You must adopt a positive mindset and start believing that things will change for the better. Your natural response to being subjected to narcissistic abuse is a pain. This pain is because of the fact that you are, and your sense of self has been, severely damaged. So, you are certainly dealing with a lot of emotional baggage, which you must learn to handle.

There is the basic dichotomy of two opposing ideas you must deal with- the one where you truly believed that the narcissist you were involved with is your soulmate and the one where your ex is nothing more than an oppressor devoid of all emotions. This dissonance which exists between these ideas can leave you feeling rather confused once the relationship ends. A common emotion you must be experiencing right now will be that of disbelief; the disbelief that your partner subjected you to narcissistic abuse. You might have even believed at some point that your partner loved you! You must be thinking, "How could he hurt me? I thought he loved me!"

One thing you must remind yourself is that all narcissists, regardless of the type of narcissism they have, are not individuals who go from being "normal" only to change their personality when under pressure. It is referred to as narcissistic personality disorder for a specific reason. This is who they inherently are, all the time. A narcissistic partner tends to project their values or perceptions onto you. Your positive traits of empathy, love, compassion, and forgiveness are weaponized against you. Your narcissistic partner used your positive values against you to manipulate you. All these things might have shattered your sense of self. So, it does take some time to recover from narcissistic abuse. Your ability to be compassionate, forgiving, and empathetic to others might make you question the motives behind the manipulative ways of a narcissist. So, you might have given them the benefit of the doubt, time, and again. After a while, your lenient behavior was enabling the abuse and might have even led to its escalation. Instead of trying to resolve it, your kindness along with your willingness to rationalize the ill treatment only perpetuated the troubling cycle of narcissistic abuse.

So, you have finally accepted the harsh reality and managed to escape from the clutches of the narcissist. What now? Now, it is time to start your healing process. Initially, you might feel like you are trying to swim upstream when the current is against you. There will be times when you feel like you are drowning or feel tired of trying. However, remember that it merely feels that way and you are making progress. Every deed of kindness toward yourself, regardless of how big or small the act is, it will help heal your body, mind, and soul.

After a while, all the small steps of self-care you take will help you heal fully. It will take time and conscious effort, but the results will be worth your while. Once you are fully healed, you will not feel like you are being sucked into an endless pit of despair. Instead, you will learn to be kinder and more loving toward yourself. In this section, you will learn about different things you can do to overcome the narcissistic abuse and regain control of your life.

Setting Boundaries

A narcissist has no respect for the boundaries that others might have. Your narcissistic partner might have displayed an utter disregard for your boundaries and might have even walked all over them. However, it is time to understand that setting boundaries is the first step to recover from narcissistic abuse. Not only will it help you heal, but it will also reduce the chances of being targeted by other emotional manipulators again. To start the process of healing yourself, you need to establish a protective boundary around yourself. The best thing you can do at this stage is to try to put as much distance between yourself and the narcissist as you possibly can.

Any and all memories related to the narcissist and your relationship will trigger pain along with other unpleasant emotions that can harm any progress you make. So, for your wellbeing, it is a good idea to sever all ties with the narcissist. You can even block the said individual on your phone, email list, and social media accounts. You need to get rid of everything that might remind you of the narcissist. It is time to get rid of all the traces of the narcissist from your life. The age-old saying, "out of sight, out of mind" is perfect in this situation.

If maintaining physical distance is not an option for you, then you can use a method referred to as the grey rock to establish a protective wall around yourself. The premise of this concept is quite simple; whenever you need to interact with the narcissist you need to unfasten yourself emotionally as well as mentally from such interactions. You might experience a wave of boiling anger within yourself, but keep it contained and don't allow the narcissist know that they can still affect you. You are free to allow your emotions to come through when you are in a safe place. Feel free to cry, scream, shout, or do anything else which will make you feel better.

If you aren't sure how you are supposed to set boundaries, then the first thing you must do is start learning to say "no." When you can say no and can stand by it, it will help develop the self-respect and self-confidence you lost while with a narcissist. Think of your boundaries like the firewalls you have on your laptop to protect it from any virus. It will not only help you keep safe but will also help you heal. It is time to start being selective about all those you let in. You can choose who you allow entering your space; after all, your mind is your sacred space.

Another simple way in which you can start establishing boundaries is by saying no. By learning and practicing saying no, you can work on developing your self-respect as well as self-confidence. Your boundary is like a firewall that keeps all malware out while protecting what's within. You must become selective about all those you let in; after all, your mind is a sacred space.

Remove All Toxicity

In the past, when you were with a narcissist, you might have done everything you possibly could and then some to please or even appease the narcissist. You might not have realized, but this can take a severe toll on your mental wellbeing. You unknowingly subjected your body, mind, and soul to a lot of toxicity, in your bid to "understand" and "empathize" with the narcissist. Narcissists always know that they have absolute control over their victims. Not just that, but they also violate and exploit this empathetic trait as and when they see fit.

Now, it is time to remove all this toxicity from your system so that you can once again think rationally. The best way is to externalize it. A simple way to go about doing this is by maintaining a dairy to make a note of all the things you were put through. You can talk to your loved ones and the friends you trust about your hardships. If you want, you can also join therapy or a support group to deal with the aftereffects of the narcissistic abuse you experienced. Joining a support group is a good idea since it helps you connect with others who have experienced all that you did. By externalizing all the harm that you were subjected to, you can remove any confusion you experience so that you can start thinking clearly one again. After you get rid of all the negative and toxic slush from your mind, you will feel lighter and better. Another option is to start engaging in physical activity to remove the toxicity.

You Must Acknowledge

You must acknowledge that you were subjected to narcissistic abuse and were the victim of a narcissist's manipulative ways. Only when you accept a problem will you be able to solve it. You must accept the fact that the narcissist was not only a toxic individual but also hurt you consciously without the trace of any remorse or guilt. You must understand and accept that you were not only manipulated and tricked but were the victim of abuse. Your resilience, along with your ability to withstand pain, was weaponized against you. Not just that, you must acknowledge that the narcissist manipulated and twisted all your positive traits and used them to perpetuate the abuse. All your positive traits were used to harm you. Your ability to understand, to love, and be empathetic was used as ammunition against you. The narcissist managed to trick and outmaneuver you while you weren't even aware that you were a pawn in the narcissist's dirty game with the odds stacked against you. Understand that all this was not your fault. You never asked for any of it and were merely a victim. You must understand you were victimized, and it is time to forgive yourself.

Time to Realize

Now, it is time to realize and acknowledge that some part of you knew that you were in an abusive relationship. Regardless of how faint this understanding was, it did exist, and you must acknowledge it. However, you decided to silence that feeble voice in your head, which kept telling you that something was wrong. Now, it is time to accept a little responsibility and rationally dissect what you experienced. No, this isn't the same as blaming yourself. Maybe you felt that something was terribly wrong during the starting stages of the relationship. Perhaps you felt that certain things that the narcissist told you never really added up. You must perform the post-mortem analysis of the relationship you were in to understand what went wrong. Narcissistic abuse doesn't take place overnight, and it is a slow but steady process. You might have noticed several red flags that you chose to ignore because of your love or empathy for the narcissist. Now, it is time to carefully analyze each of those red flags you ignored in the past. Were there any reasons as to why you ignored your intuition? Why did you silence that tiny voice in your head that told you something wasn't right? Did you do all that to salvage your relationship? Or were you blinded by the charm and all the lies the narcissist told you? Did the narcissist's words and acts of so-called love fill some void in you that you weren't aware of?

If you never got a chance to experience unconditional love, especially in your childhood and formative years, it is quite natural to seek someone who can fill that void. However, this does make you quite vulnerable, especially to the advances made by an emotional manipulator like a narcissist. Emotional predators like narcissists are exceptionally good at smelling any trauma that others suffered in their past. They are drawn to vulnerable individuals the way sharks are drawn to blood in the water.

It is time to start believing and listening to your intuition. The more you follow and trust your gut, the stronger the intuition will become. It can be a little difficult to start trusting your gut, especially after enduring narcissistic abuse, but it needs to be done. You were subjected to trauma, but you survived. However, in this process, your psyche was scarred. The PTSD you might experience will make you rather sensitive to your environment. It will take a while before you can start distinguishing between real and imaginary threats. If you feel like you are facing this problem, then it means you need longer to heal. Also, if you want, you can be free to be extra cautious while you recuperate. It is better to avoid any questionable situations as well as individuals. It is perfectly all right to maintain your distance and don't let anyone else tell you otherwise. You must do what is best for you, and if right now, that means being extra cautious, then be cautious.

A Little Self-inquiry

The time you need to overcome and recover from the narcissistic abuse is an opportunity for you to concentrate on your growth. It is a chance for personal growth since it enables you to understand your vulnerabilities. Take a long hard look at all your possible vulnerabilities. This will not be an easy or pleasant task, but it must be done. This is the primary reason why people never do this: to avoid the unpleasantness of having to look at their vulnerabilities. If you want to overcome the abuse, regain control of your life, and want to prevent any exploitation in the future, then you need to know your vulnerabilities. Did you know that whenever an app is developed, ethical hackers are used to testing the app for different vulnerabilities? It is done to ensure that the app is safe for use and it cannot be hacked. Likewise, by performing a safety check, you can understand whether you have any existing or potential vulnerabilities. Once you are aware of all this, you can start taking steps to eliminate all such vulnerabilities and shield yourself from emotional predators. A simple way to do this is by conducting a little self-inquiry. The narcissistic abuse you were subjected is your wakeup call. Your vulnerabilities make you susceptible to manipulation. If you don't want to be manipulated ever again, then you need to understand your vulnerabilities. Common vulnerabilities are the need to feel loved, secure, and the desire to be acknowledged. These manipulations can leave you open to manipulation if you leave them unaddressed.

Healing

If you want to start healing yourself, then it is time to take a stroll down your memory lane and revisit your formative years. It will give you a better sense of understanding and will help get rid of any unresolved issues. Not just that, it will help strengthen a strong relationship with your inner self. The narcissistic abuse you were subjected to harmed your inner child. You need to help your inner child heal if you want to make a full recovery. You can understand the primary cause of any fears or insecurities you harbor when you connect with your inner child. Reconnecting with your inner child doesn't mean you need to start acting childish or immature. It means that you need to spend some time and reconnect with the child-like persona that exists within you. It is about reestablishing the bond with a part of your psyche, which is innocent and pure. There are different ways in which you can start healing your inner child. You can start spending some time saying loving and positive things to your inner child. You can communicate with your inner child by maintaining a written record of all the things you want to tell it. Spend some time doing things you used to like doing in your childhood. Rediscover your forgotten hobbies. You can also spend some time going through your photo albums to rediscover any happy yet forgotten memories. Spend time and recreate those experiences that were dear to you while growing up. Cherish and nourish your inner child.

Focus

There will be instances when you feel like you are drowning in your past. The cognitive dissonance, along with the trauma bond you formed with the narcissist, causes this negative feeling. If you ever feel like this, it means you need to spend more time to understand and process your emotions. Instead of allowing your past to destroy your present, you need to give yourself the time and the opportunity to analyze your past thoroughly. It is a continuous process you must be involved in if you are interested in overcoming the abuse you suffered.

Until you can heal yourself, you must practice mindfulness. Understand that whatever has happened is in the past and you cannot make any changes to your past. However, you have the power to stop it from ruining your present and your future. Whatever happened has happened, but you can control the way you react and respond. Learn to stay in the present and start living your life. Whenever you feel like your past is getting a hold of you, you need to be mindful, and consciously stop yourself. Ensure that you have a sense of purpose and direction in your life. You must look forward to bringing positivity back into your life. Don't dwell in the past and instead learn to move on without looking back.

Trust Yourself

Call it your intuition, sixth sense, or your gut feeling. That tiny voice you keep hearing in your head, which is trying to communicate with you. The voice that starts ringing alarm bells when things don't feel right. If you want to recover fully from narcissistic abuse, then it is time to listen to that tiny voice you have been ignoring all along. The problem is that it can be rather difficult to hear that little voice unless and until your mind is calm. Only when you drown out all sorts of mental chatter can you hear what the voice is trying to tell you. Most humans tend to have overactive minds and tend to place too much emphasis on their thoughts. You must understand that neither your thoughts control you nor they define you. Instead, you must be able to exert control over your thoughts. Once you can get rid of any mental chatter, you will be able to focus on your intuition. Find a quiet spot for yourself, close the door, turn off your phone, and start concentrating on your thoughts. Take a couple of calming and relaxing deep breaths. Concentrate on the way you breathe. You can call it meditation if you want, but this simple breathing exercise will help you feel infinitely better and give you the ability to control your mind. Once your mind is calm, you can start concentrating on your instincts.

Please start paying attention to what your instincts tell you, especially when you are meeting someone for the first time. Your body is quite adept at understanding the different vibes it gets from others. It isn't a full-fledged science, but it will certainly help you get a read on the situations and people around you. Please start-paying attention to the way you feel as soon as you meet them. The first and instant reaction of your body even before you have the time to think is your intuition. It will essentially enable you to understand whether someone makes you feel comfortable or not.

Science usually associates all these feelings with the tiny brain present in your gut, which is known as the enteric nervous system. This system comprises of a network of different neurons which process information immediately. Before you can even form a conscious thought, you must think about what your intuition is telling you. What is the first reaction you experience upon meeting someone? Do you feel calm, anxious, nervous, or uneasy? Does the situation make you feel at ease, or does it make you feel uneasy? Whenever you notice tiny alarm bells going off in your head, please don't ignore it. If something feels amiss, it is probably because that's the truth- something is amiss indeed. Alternatively, you can wait for more information before you make any decisions.

Your body keeps giving you messages about your wellbeing, the decisions you make, and those around you. Start paying attention to all the signals your body keeps giving you. For instance, it can be something as simple as resting when you feel tired, crying when you are sad, and eating when you are hungry. It can also mean noticing the effect others have on your energy levels. If you feel tired and quite dejected around some people, then it means they are not doing you any good. Notice the way others make you feel and use it as a compass to decide whether you want them in your life or not. If someone zaps you of all your energy, maybe it is best that they go!

Learn to be Patient

You need to be patient with yourself. The process of recovery takes time and effort. It isn't something that you can rush through. The emotional abuse you were subjected didn't happen overnight, so you cannot expect the recovery to be an overnight process. There will be times when you feel like you are staring at a dark abyss of endless despair; you might feel frustrated with yourself or even get depressed. If you experience any of these things, it means you must focus your attention on healing yourself.

It is time to regain control of your life and get back on track. It is time to put an end to the control the narcissist has on your life. You are the only one who can decide your destiny and don't relinquish this control. Start healing yourself by following the practical tips discussed in this section.

Chapter 11 Effects Of Narcissistic Abuse

Narcissistic abuse can have long-lasting effects on the target of this abuse. These are effects that the narcissist can sometimes be unconscious of or, at the very least, insensitive to. The narcissist does engage in abusive acts because they have a purpose, such as to satisfy their vanity or to manipulate you. But it is also true that the narcissist may not fully understand the effects that their behavior has because they are so self-obsessed and they are not able to connect with people deeply the way that others can.

The idea that the narcissist may not be fully conscious of the effects of their abuse is not mentioned to justify the actions of the narcissist. This aspect of narcissistic abuse is touched on here to emphasize just how out of touch the narcissist is. The narcissist perceives themselves as being set apart from others, so it is almost as if you are a different form of life than they are. Just as the lioness lacks empathy for the wild beast that she slaughters in the savanna, so does the narcissist lacks empathy for the loved one whose emotions they aim to crush because they are unable to escape their inflated self-concept.

The abuse that the narcissist inflicts on others has been touched on in other areas of this book. Narcissistic abuse can include manipulation, blackmail, gaslighting, and belittling. Much of the abuse is emotional in nature, but some forms of abuse can be physical, mental, or designed to isolate. In this chapter, we will explore how narcissistic abuse impacts relationships. We will see that the emotional abuse of the narcissist can leave the individual feeling disconnected, isolated, weakened, and alone.

Emotional Abuse

Emotional abuse is such a powerful tool because it can leave a person weak, vulnerable, and incapable of breaking free without knowing why. Human beings naturally seek emotional connections with other human beings. Although the narcissist is generally unable to form a lasting connection with other people because they do not sincerely value others, they do recognize the value that emotions have in forming a connection, and they are able to use their understanding of emotions and human behavior to their advantage.

For example, in a type of mind control called neuro-linguistic programming or NLP, the practitioner of this art can use cues such as involuntary movements, spoken words, physical proximity, and touch to control the thoughts and perceptions of the person that they are using their tricks on. They can use touching (such as placing a hand on the other person's arm) to induce rapport formation with the other person. They can also use eye contact and subliminal messaging to introduce thoughts in the other person's head.

Although most narcissists have not studied NLP, they also behave in this way. The narcissist knows how to behave to get people to like them and what to say to manipulate them. The emotions of the narcissist may be cut off and inaccessible to their significant other, but they understand emotions well enough to permit them to use the emotions of the other person to their advantage. They know when you are sad; they know when you are happy. They know when you may be feeling confident or when you might be feeling particularly dispirited. The cues that you send the narcissist reveal your emotions to them, and they are tools that permit them to abuse you.

This emotional manipulation can have several impacts on a relationship. It can lead the other person in the relationship to have low self-esteem or experience bouts of emotional whirlwinds, where their emotions are up, down, or uncontrollable. This type of emotional abuse can cause you to feel that your emotional needs are not being met in the relationship, even if the narcissist occasionally says or does things to indicate emotional closeness. This emotional manipulation can also lead you to feel sad, even sadder than you were when you were alone.

Isolation

One of the goals of the words and deeds of the narcissist in a relationship is to isolate the other person. This isolation serves two purposes. One, it places the other person in a situation where they are too weak and emotional to leave the relationship, which gives the narcissist someone to continue to abuse for their vanity. Two, this isolation serves the narcissist's codependency need. They may not value you, but the narcissist still needs you on a certain level. They need the validation that comes from being able to belittle you and abuse you. They need to be in a relationship with someone who agrees to be less than them because it satisfies the inflated self-image that they have created for themselves. Therefore, one of the biggest impacts that narcissistic abuse can have on a relationship is to isolate one of the partners effectively and prevent them from being motivated to leave.

Disconnection

The emotional abuse and isolation of narcissism can leave the target feeling disconnected. Human beings form connections by having meaningful interactions with others. This allows the emotional needs of the individual to be met while the corresponding emotional needs of the other person also are met. This type of emotional bonding lies on a spectrum with empathy. Empathy is a way of being emotionally connected with other people without the need for words.

Because the narcissist is false in their display of emotion, and they use words to deceive and manipulate, the other person in the relationship feels disconnected rather than connected with their partner. They may notice this together with exhaustion or confusion, and this is all related to the inability to form a real connection with a narcissist. Also, the other person in this relationship becomes disconnected from the other important people in their life and society as a whole. This disconnection is perhaps more important because it can discourage the individual from leaving the relationship (and thereby reinforcing the isolation). Working on forming connections with people outside of the relationship with the narcissist is actually an important step in breaking free.

Interacting with a Narcissist

Much care has to be taken when it comes to interacting with the narcissist. Just as any manipulator uses the information that you give them to their advantage, so does the narcissist. In fact, wearing your heart on your sleeve with the narcissist is tantamount to giving your checking account information to an escaped identity thief. Providing the narcissist with private information merely gives them a vantage point from which to formulate their plan of attack.

For example, the narcissist understands that human beings use verbal and non-verbal communication to form bonds with one another. We tend to like people that we perceive as having similarities with ourselves or sharing common ground with us. The narcissist knows this. If you unconsciously express an interest in something by smiling, laughing, happily tapping your foot, et cetera, the narcissist makes a mental note that you like that particular thing. They can be so adept at collecting information about people even if they might not be conscious about it.

Therefore, the next time you have a conversation with the narcissist, you may be surprised to learn that they like the same TV shows that you do, or their favorite food is medium rare steak just like you or they love the same classical composers that you do. They chuckle at the same sort of things you laugh at, or they turn their head slightly at an angle when they are interested in something just like you do. It seems that God has sent you the soul mate that you were praying for in this person, right? Wrong.

The narcissist has studied you like the high school chemistry textbook. They noticed when you smiled when an image of steak showed up on a TV commercial. They saw the way you laughed when "The King of Queens" popped up on TV as you were flipping through the channels. They notice the way that you run your fingers through your hair with your right hand or the particular angle you hold your head when you are interested or excited. They see the way you tap your foot when you are anxious, like when the waiter is about to bring the bill at a restaurant. They have been studying you, and they now know how to form a rapport with you, enter into your psyche, and mind-control you.

Protecting Yourself from the Narcissist

To protect yourself from the narcissist, you need to understand the tricks that narcissists use to manipulate and mind-control people. You should be warned. The narcissist is very skillful at forming a rapport with people and controlling their emotional state, so it is not always easy to protect oneself from the narcissist. In fact, protecting yourself from the narcissist can be tantamount to resisting the manipulations of Rasputin. In the end, the only way the Russian aristocrats could find their way out of that situation was to shoot him.

All jokes aside, books are not written about narcissists for nothing. If you have been paying attention, then by now, you have realized that the narcissist has been taking notes on the quirky things that you do. They know what your interests are, what makes you emotional, how you display your emotions, what your sensitive areas are, and how you are different from other people. Therefore, the first and most obvious line of defense against the narcissist is learning to hold your cards a little closer to your chest when it comes to your interactions with certain people.

Just as you would not wave around a stack full of cash while walking past the methadone clinic, you should also not be so forthcoming with your emotions when dealing with someone you suspect might be dangerous. Your emotions are an important part of who you are, and when you allow someone in, to the point where they know what your gesture means, how to copy those gestures, or how to induce them to manipulate and confuse you, then you have given them the keys to the kingdom. The cold, hard truth is that narcissists know how to control you because you have taught them how to control you. Being a little more reserved can go a long way.

In protecting yourself from the narcissist, it may help to take a page from the neuro-linguistic programming handbook. Individuals trained in NLP know how to study the gestures of other people and how to use certain words to form rapport instantly and induce mind control. NLP mind control can be hard to break, just as narcissistic mind control can be. If you want to protect yourself from narcissistic abuse, then it may help to keep some of the following in mind:

- Do not let the other person touch you during a conversation.

- Be conscious of changes in subject or words that do not fit in what is being said.

- Be conscious of gestures that mimic yours or seem overly similar.

- Be wary of vague or nonspecific language.

- Watch for averting of the eyes or moving them unpredictably.

- Develop an intuition about what things make you uncomfortable or emotional, and follow that intuition.

These are important steps in protecting yourself from the narcissist. They represent a critical first line of defense when it comes to interacting with narcissistic people. Protecting yourself from narcissists also entails developing some confidence. Your self-esteem should be high enough for you to notice when you are emotionally abused and recognize that you do not deserve to be treated this way. Other steps that you can take in defending yourself include learning to doubt the negative things the narcissist says about you and learning to question the intentions of the narcissist when they suggest this or that. Remember, the narcissist is not thinking primarily about you but about themselves. Finally, establishing physical distance between you and the narcissist so that you are not exposed to their tools of manipulation can help, too.

Conclusion

While recovering from narcissistic abuse can be prolonged, it's possible to move forward into a more beautiful life than could have ever been imagined. There's light at the end of the tunnel should you choose to run toward it. Leaving an abusive situation takes more courage than may ever be fully understood by those who've never had to live through it, but one must muster the courage to reinstate the self-confidence, strength, and sense of independence necessary. Going no contact, or maintaining very minimal contact with the abuser should minor children be involved is absolutely essential. Finding a higher power and developing a solid support system, believing that one is not alone in the struggle is the key to finding this courage.

Abusive narcissistic relationships forever affect the way a survivor views the world, and what they'll bring to future relationships. They'll inevitably be left with an entirely new perspective and appreciation for life. They'll learn to truly self-love, perhaps for the first time ever, after the relationship has ended. They'll be more cautious when entering into new relationships and be more apt to identify red flags sooner. These are blessings in disguise that need to be embraced.

Often, victims are left with the lingering effects of PTSD, and it's essential that therapeutic help is sought and the advice embraced to heal. Following the steps of an established recovery system, such as a twelve-step program, provides the best prospect in finding peace by rediscovering oneself and practicing internal healing. Modifications can be made to best serve the individual's unique situation and aid in recovery from narcissistic abuse. It's absolutely necessary to make amends with the past to effectively move forward.

Having questions without answers, regrets, and feelings of guilt are all very common. Each step in the grieving process should be fully embraced and completely felt by the victim, with the aid of a supportive network so they can ultimately move into acceptance. Only when they've accepted the past and present for exactly what they are will they be able to create an effective future. Once they've developed self-love and those aspects of self they lost amid the abuse they'll be able to enter a solid, meaningful relationship with a new partner. Rushing through the healing process does no good, and can skew the survivor's perspective. They may not see things for what they truly are. Codependency often prevails and victims re-enter abusive situations out of habit, continuing the cycle.

Knowledge is power, and it's the belief of this author that those who have had the debilitating experience of living with a narcissist and have successfully circumvented the situation have an obligation to share their stories. First-hand knowledge is especially powerful, and through the advice of survivors, others can be saved. Therefore, it's my hope that survivors can band together to promote awareness and provide support to those who need it most.

Remembering where we came from helps us to appreciate those who are living the hell we escaped, and motivates us to create waves that will initiate change. We must first be the change we wish to see in the world. Life is a miracle, and each day is a blessing. Go forth and live fully!

NARCISSISTIC ABUSE

THE COMPLETE SURVIVAL GUIDE FOR HIGHLY SENSITIVE PEOPLE, OVERCOME YOUR CHILDHOOD MANIPULATION AND LACK OF EMPATHY. RECOVER YOURSELF AND TAKE REVENGE FROM YOUR TOXIC EX

Introduction

In Greek mythology, Narcissus was the most handsome man who ever lived. Everyone who saw the young hunter fell in love with him, but Narcissus was incapable of loving anyone. One day, on a hunting trip, a nymph named Echo confessed her love to him. He rejected her so cruelly that she shriveled up and disappeared, leaving only her voice behind. Later, Narcissus happened to see his own reflection in a pool of water and was so captivated by his own beauty that he stared into the pool until he wasted away.

All of us, at some point, have known a narcissist. A narcissist is a person with a distorted and ultimately false self-image, just like the reflection that Narcissus saw in the pond. The self-image of the narcissist is overblown—smarter, more competent, and more beautiful than any normal person. Despite what seems to be egotistical self-admiration, the narcissist desperately needs approval and validation from other people. In the end, he doesn't really believe his own self-image. The narcissist feels an uncontrollable compulsion to be loved and praised and will seek out relationships for the sole purpose of getting this need met by any means necessary.

Types of Abuse

There are many different types of abusive behavior, but most abuse fits into one of four major categories.

Physical abuse is any form of physical violence or restraint. This includes not only obvious behaviors like punching, kicking, or shoving—but it's also comprised of less obvious behaviors such as holding you in place to prevent you from leaving or punching a hole in the wall to frighten and intimidate you.

Sexual abuse is any violation of your sexual boundaries or autonomy, including the use of pressure and manipulation to get you to consent to sexual contact.

Neglect is the failure to provide care when it is the person's responsibility to do so. For instance, parents who don't provide adequate food and clothing or who don't set healthy rules and boundaries to keep the child safe may be neglecting the child. Narcissistic parents often neglect their children, as they see their children primarily as sources of the love and admiration that they need rather than as individual human beings who need to be cared for and protected.

Emotional abuse refers to words and behaviors that harm the victim's psychological well-being, such as verbal abuse and manipulative behavior. Physical and sexual abuse is often combined with emotional abuse, but emotional abuse can also occur on its own. Emotional abuse is subtler and harder to define than physical or sexual abuse. If someone hits you or touches you without your consent, then they are obviously abusive to you—but it's much harder to say when words and other behaviors cross the line. Despite being subtler, emotional abuse can be just as harmful as other forms of abuse—or even more so.

Recognizing Abusive Behaviors

Abuse can sometimes be hard to recognize because a lot of abusive behaviors occur on a spectrum with less extreme behaviors that are not necessarily harmful or malicious enough to be considered abusive. Almost everyone has said or done something passive-aggressive or manipulative when frustrated. Almost everyone has said something insulting or overly critical when angry. These behaviors are not ideal, but they aren't always an example of abuse.

Thus, how do you know when someone is abusing you? You have to make a judgment call based on the big picture of your relationship with the person, and how pervasive and destructive the behaviors are. One or two incidents in isolation might not constitute abuse, but if you suspect something about the relationship is toxic, you should look for the warning signs. Potentially abusive behaviors include harmful words, manipulative actions, taking advantage of you, ignoring your boundaries, isolating you from your support networks, undermining your goals and dreams, trying to control you, and dishonest behavior.

Harmful Words

People can use words to hurt each other in dozens of different ways, from excessive criticism to insulting comments. Verbal abuse can look like anything from over-the-top rage to a coldly calm expression of disdain and contempt.

An abuser may say things to put you down, accuse you of doing things you didn't do, blame you for things that aren't really your fault, compare you to other people in a demeaning way, interrupt you whenever you try to express yourself, or give you commands like a drill sergeant. Shaming is one of the most common forms of abusive behavior from a narcissistic parent.

Sometimes, verbal abuse can be subtler than this, like disagreeing with everything you say or making so many demands that you constantly feel inadequate. Other times verbal abuse isn't subtle at all and may even include threats or openly bullying behaviors. Verbal abuse can also include putting you down in front of other people, spreading unflattering stories about you, or encouraging other people to make fun of you or exclude you in some way.

There are so many different types of verbal abuse that it would be impossible to list them all, but they all have one thing in common. The abuser gains more power in the relationship through harmful words, and the abused person feels smaller and smaller for as long as the abuse continues.

How can you tell whether something constitutes abuse or not? The important point to consider here is how malicious the behavior seems. For instance, there's a big difference between an occasional sarcastic comment and a pattern of constant, demeaning sarcasm. How do you usually feel when you talk to this person? If your conversations often leave you feeling worse about yourself, you may be a victim of verbal abuse. If the person seems to be putting you down to feel better about themselves, this could be part of a pattern of narcissistic abuse. Whether the person abusing you is a narcissist or not, verbal abuse can cause tremendous damage to your self-esteem and well-being.

Manipulative Actions

Manipulative behavior can be hard to recognize because manipulation is indirect. For example, a manipulative person might offer to help you with a problem but then try to get you to feel guilty or excessively obligated to them for accepting their help. Alternatively, they might use guilt or shame to get you to do something for them.

They may seem kind and warm until you don't do what they want you to do, at which point they become cold and distant. They may withhold attention or affection so that you will pursue them, constantly forcing you to guess what they really want from you. They might use gossip and jealousy to play two friends or two siblings or two love interests against each other, a divide and conquer strategy known as "triangulation." As with verbal abuse, manipulation takes many forms.

The person being manipulated often feels like the bad guy in the situation, because that's exactly how the abuser wants them to feel. So, how can you recognize when you're being manipulated? Manipulation causes "FOG," a combination of three potent emotions—fear, obligation, and guilt. Fear that something bad will happen if you don't do what the other person wants, a sense that you owe them something for some reason, and the feeling that you will be a bad person if you don't go along with it. The result of FOG is that you doubt your own judgment, even though your instincts are telling you that something is wrong with the situation.

One of the most insidious types of manipulation is known as "gaslighting," in which the abuser manipulates you into distrusting your own memories and second-guessing your own ability to tell reality from illusion.

Taking Advantage of You

An abuser may take advantage of you financially by spending shared money without your consent, taking money out of your bank account, selling things that belong to you, or running up debts in your name. Financial abuse allows the abuser to profit by using your financial resources as their own, but it also tends to leave you impoverished and financially dependent on the abuser for your own survival.

The same dynamic can occur in any relationship where the other person has total control over the household finances, even if they aren't actually dipping into your bank account or writing checks with your name on them. Without financial independence, you're a lot less likely to leave the relationship—and the abuser knows that.

Financial abuse can also be combined with other forms of abuse, such as emotional blackmail. For example, most people are happy to help family or friends in need if the situation comes up. An abusive person will take advantage of the kindness of a friend or relative by guilt-tripping them into helping again and again whether they really need it or not. How can you tell the difference? By looking out for FOG. If you feel a combination of fear, obligation, and guilt about the request, then you should ask yourself if you are being manipulated.

Ignoring Boundaries

Manipulators and abusers will ignore your boundaries and destroy your sense of independence because they don't respect your right to establish boundaries in the first place. For an abusive narcissist, the other person in the relationship is only there to fulfill their needs, and they feel justified in doing whatever it takes to keep the person attached to them and dependent on them.

For example, a narcissistic parent might read a child's diary, or a narcissistic boyfriend might read his girlfriend's text messages. An abuser might go through your things without asking permission or walk in on you without knocking when you have the door closed. In general, one of the warning signs of an abusive relationship is when you try to set boundaries, and they are repeatedly ignored.

An abuser might ignore a request for more space or refuse to accept a break-up or a rejection. It can be dangerous to think of this as a simple failure of communication. Any time a person ignores your boundaries, you should consider this a serious warning sign.

Isolating

Most people have a support network of family and friends—the people we confide in and whose opinions we trust, the people we would call if we needed help. To an abuser, all these people are a potential threat. Your old college roommate might tell you that your new boyfriend sounds a little controlling. Your brother might let you crash on his couch for a while if you suddenly decide to move out. Your friends might say supportive and encouraging things that contradict the constant criticism you're being subjected to.

To prevent any of these things from happening, an abuser will systematically undermine your other relationships to leave you as isolated and dependent as possible. Behaviors intended to isolate you can take many forms, such as expecting you to constantly account for your whereabouts or suddenly "getting sick" and needing support from you when you were planning to spend time with friends. It can even involve deliberate character assassination, such as telling friends or family members lies about you.

If someone in your life is acting as a gatekeeper, making it hard for people to see you or talk to you, this may be a sign that they are trying to isolate you from your usual support networks.

Undermining

An abuser may sabotage and undermine you in various ways to keep you from achieving an independent sense of success and happiness. For example, they may "forget" to pass on an important message, or they may say embarrassing things to humiliate you in front of your friends or coworkers. It can be hard to recognize sabotaging behavior because the abuser can pretend it was all just an innocent mistake or a misunderstanding.

If you start to suspect an important person in your life of intentionally sabotaging you, step back and look at the big picture. Our loved ones are supposed to support us and help us achieve our goals and dreams. If someone you care about has a consistent pattern of getting in your way rather than helping you out, it might be sabotage.

Another form of sabotage is to compare you unkindly to other people. The abuser's goal is to undermine your self-confidence and chip away at your self-respect. The topic of comparison may probably be your looks or your cooking or how much money you make, but the message is always the same—that you don't measure up.

Why would anyone want you to feel worse about yourself? Remember, the narcissistic abuser needs an endless supply of love and praise and doesn't really believe you'll stick around of your own free will. By tearing you down, the narcissist can make you completely dependent. If someone is telling you that you are stupid or useless, that other people don't like you, or that you couldn't possibly live without them, ask yourself why they would want you to think that.

Control

In a healthy relationship, both parties have an equal level of power. Shared decisions such as whether to buy a new home or where to go on vacation are made through discussion and compromise. Both partners have the right and ability to make individual decisions, too, such as whether to spend time with friends or spend small amounts of money.

In an abusive relationship, one partner has all the power, and the other partner is effectively under their control. Major decisions are all made by the dominant partner, who also seeks to micromanage every little detail of the other person's life.

An abuser may limit the time you spend with your friends or expect you to account for every penny you spend. They may want to know where you are and what you are doing at all times. They may expect you to clear everything you do with them ahead of time and accuse you of dishonesty or infidelity if you do not.

Sometimes, the abuser establishes control through outright dominance and bullying. Sometimes, control established through subtler and indirect forms of manipulation such as sabotage and undermining. Either way, if you start to feel like you can no longer make your own decisions and have no equality in the relationship, this is a warning sign that you may be under the control of an abuser.

Dishonesty

Abusers and narcissists often accuse their partners of being unfaithful or dishonest but feel no obligation to be faithful or honest themselves. The narcissist typically sees himself as being superior to others and may, therefore, feel that the rules don't apply to him.

In addition, the narcissist is constantly looking for a new source of praise and admiration, and no one is more likely to supply this than a new person who doesn't know what the narcissist is truly like. For this reason, narcissists typically can't sustain a committed relationship for very long before they start looking around for a new source of the admiration they crave.

Projection is one of the defining characteristics of the narcissistic abuser, meaning that they will project their own negative feelings and behaviors onto other people. The narcissist tells you that you are worthless because he secretly feels worthless and accuses you of being dishonest and unfaithful because he is dishonest and unfaithful.

The Narcissistic Abuser

Narcissistic abuse can include any or all of these abusive behaviors. So, what makes any particular abusive behavior narcissistic?

It all comes down to the abuser's motivation. Not all abusers are narcissists. For instance, a sociopathic abuser is not motivated by the need for admiration or praise, but only by the desire to get whatever he wants out of the situation without regard for others. A sadistic abuser gets pleasure or amusement from causing suffering. Some abusers are motivated by a pathological need to control every aspect of life in an attempt to manage their own intense feelings of anxiety and fear. Some are mentally ill and unaware of how their actions impact the people around them.

Whatever the reason for the abuse, the abuser is always responsible for their own actions. The victim is never at fault for the abuse. To the victim of abuse, it may not matter much whether the abuser is motivated by narcissism or sociopathy or something else. Getting free of the abuse is what really matters.

However, recognizing patterns can sometimes be a crucial step in learning how to break out of them for good. If you've been the victim of narcissistic abuse, understanding what happened and how it happened can help you move on. It may help you avoid a similar situation in the future, or it may help you avoid repeating the pattern by abusing others.

The narcissistic abuser is motivated by a deep sense of shame and self-loathing, leading them to create a mask or an imaginary version of the self that is far superior to other people. Because the narcissist secretly knows that this imaginary self isn't real at all, they need constant reassurance in the form of love and admiration from others to sustain the illusion. The narcissist abuses others to prop up this false self, using tactics you can learn to recognize.

Chapter 1 What is the Narcissistic abuse?

Many people are unaware of the dangers that come with having a narcissistic partner. It's not a pleasant experience at all as narcissists are egoistic, abusive, manipulative, and they result in all sorts of emotional blackmail and torture on their targets.

People that are narcissistic in nature suffer from Narcissistic Personality Disorder because they lack empathy and the true understanding of emotions. Also, it can be very confusing to deal with narcissistic partners as they can be kind to you today and hate you tomorrow. They usually find it difficult to choose either to love you or hate you. Due to this, many people in relationships with narcissists find it challenging to understand their continuous hot and cold pattern of love.

In this chapter, we will be taking a more in-depth look into the way the narcissist acts when in love. This will help you determine if your partner is a narcissist, and if you need to get yourself out of this toxic relationship.

The Love Circle of Narcissists

Most of the time, it's often too late to realize that you're dealing with a narcissist. So, having a clean break becomes difficult. Some people would have spent a long time together with the narcissist and may as well get married and give birth to kids. Some also get attached to the toxic relationship and become addicted in spite of all the trauma that they might have experienced by being with a narcissist.

In fact, through the many scheming's of a narcissist, some people may even believe they aren't good for better things and do not deserve the best. These people have been abused continuously and devalued to think they're worth nothing, and with time, they come to share in this belief.

How Does a Narcissist Love?

The narcissist acts differently from normal individuals when in love. Below, we will be looking into their pattern of love to point it out.

Throwing Bait

When you come across a narcissist at first, they are usually the best pretenders. Narcissists begin most relationships with kindness and show of affection. They'll shower you with love and praises. They'll appear very kind to you and will do everything to ensure you fall at their feet.

At the beginning of a relationship with a narcissist, you might have been very sure that you were with the right person at last. It appears too good to believe, and you don't even wish for it to end. You may have been showered with praises, appreciation, gifts, validation, outings, and dinner that convinced you that you're with your true love and life partner.

This first stage is referred to as the love bombing stage. At this stage, the narcissists will try all they can to prove to you that they have a genuine love for you. As soon as you believe this, they're happy to get you hooked and replace the earlier show of love with any form of abuse, dehumanize and devalue you. While doing this, they do not accept they are wrong or become responsible for their actions. Instead, they'll blame you for all that happens because you're not a reflection of their unrealistic idea of who you should be or who you are. Soon, you only remember the good times as you fight every day.

However, narcissists may sometimes appear to love you by bribing you with outings or gifts, but this doesn't last. Before you're able to breathe the fresh air of renewed love, you're back to your intense fight and another round of degradation. The feelings of worthlessness return after this and you're back to where you are

Their reason for doing this is because of their belief in transactional relationships and enjoyment of uncommitted pleasure. They are always after their satisfaction and happiness and the need for them to boost their self-esteem. Narcissists believe relationships are games, and winning should be the only focus. They are concerned about winning the game and nothing else. However, once they have been able to bait you in, they begin to show their true colors by being manipulative.

They Are Manipulative

Many narcissists are able to convince someone to go into a relationship with them because of their energetic and engaging character. They also possess the ability to manage, understand, and express emotions due to their possession of emotional intelligence. With this, they're also manipulative and win people's admiration and love. They are manipulative and will do everything to ensure you feel insecure by discrediting you to make you feel inferior. They do this because they're aware of your fragility and insecurity.

They believe in bragging about commanding respect and seeking gratification. They are also social and are able to create a great first impression when you first come in contact with them. Some narcissists appear to be great lovers due to their ability to express love, romance, flattery, and unending promises of staying committed. Also, they lie to convince their partner of the deep love they have for them and express it through material things.

As soon as they're able to get a partner, narcissists begin to lose interest in intimacy and oftentimes find it difficult to keep a relationship for six months and above. Most times, they place power above intimacy and loathe vulnerability, and they consider this a weakness. They prefer to dominate others because they believe they're superior to orders. As a result of this, they prefer to avoid closeness. Therefore, the best way to meet their needs is to flirt with multiple partners.

The after-effects of a relationship with a narcissist can lead to a dramatic end. The breakup will be sudden, and the ex becomes overwhelmed and bewildered by the unexpected end of the relationship. They feel betrayed, used, discarded, crushed, and confused. However, if they continue with the relationship, they would have seen or discovered the narcissistic nature of their partner.

Sometimes a narcissist may be pragmatic in his approach, so he's in relationships to focus on his goals alone. He may have positive feelings towards a friend or people with a shared interest, though. In marriage, he lacks the motivation to keep a healthy relationship as he wouldn't be able to keep up with the façade. When this happens, he looks for different ways of preventing closeness by acting angry, cold, and critical.

It becomes difficult to challenge him as a result of this as doing so will result in issues. Although, narcissists may satisfy the needs of their partners when they feel like, they usually devalue their partners and look for somewhere else to lift their already inflated ego. However, in most situations, narcissists would rather stay in relationships and would hardly discard a partner so long as they remain useful to them.

Why Do Narcissists Prefer to Stay?

Narcissists prefer to stay because of their narcissistic nature. They need to always prove a point to people they meet and having you will make their life more comfortable and improve their status. Also, narcissists aren't after your happiness or the happiness of others. With this, it will become difficult for them to have a fulfilling and loving relationship. They'll always find someone new but aren't ever truly happy.

A narcissist will always look for someone to devalue in order to feed his ego. As a result of this, he enjoys blaming others for every fight and arguments. Even when they're wrong, they find it challenging to apologize or be remorseful. Everything will be centered around you, and you can't win the argument.

You may be wondering why they prefer to stay and abuse you constantly in-spite of all they say about you and the amount of hatred portrayed. Well, here are a few reasons why a narcissist will always prefer to stay than leave.

You're the Assistant They Wouldn't Want to Lose

Who would help around the house? Who would get the groceries, clean the mess, and oversee the general running of the home? Narcissists prefer staying and enjoying all these benefits and more. That is, they're only with you because of the benefits that come with being with you.

They are Happy to Make You Feel Worthless

Narcissistic partners prefer to stay because they derive joy in seeing you become sad. They do this without letting their friends and coworkers find out, and some even find it difficult to believe it when they do find out. Some narcissists are that good at hiding such behaviors.

Losing You Means Failure to a Narcissist

A narcissist does not like to admit being a failure, and leaving you would undoubtedly make them realize that. So, they would rather be with you and unleash all the abuses on you. Also, they always look forward to seeing you fail and validating their claim that you're worthless and useless.

They Like it When You Depend on Them

A narcissist likes it when you are so dependent on them for everything. They achieved this by first showing you kindness, love, and affection and then gets withdrawn as soon as they gain your attention. They become moody and disconnect themselves from anything that interests you. With this, you'll be forced to depend on them as their attitude has a negative effect on your behavior.

Even when you decide to walk away from a narcissist, they'll always come back. The goal of this is to tell you they've changed, but they only do this to enable them to control you like they used to before. They believe they're the best and will not settle for unacceptance. A narcissist believes he shouldn't be detested but desired and they will do everything to ensure you're back together. If you forgive a narcissist the first time, they will always look forward to controlling and manipulating you.

Chapter 2 Identifying Your Inner Strengths

Inevitably when we are in a relationship with someone, we create bonds with them. When we create an attachment to someone that is a narcissist we inadvertently dig a hole for ourselves. Despite the ill treatment we receive, finding our way out of the hole and into a place of recovery can be nearly impossible.

You might be constantly asking yourself why. Why can you not just let this person go? Why can you not just try to move on? Why are you struggling with not getting closure? Why do you stay when they are not connected to you like you are to them?

Some of the only ways we can process these ideas are to remember that a narcissist does not behave or act like a normal person, and our inclination is to fix that. We want to fix what is broken in them so that they can love us.

A narcissist can not be fixed by our hands, though. No matter how hard we try, it is not within our power to remove decades of trauma and repressed feelings from our narcissistic partner.

When we acknowledge that we can not help them, why do we still struggle with letting go? Once you do let go you will go through feelings where you only feel like half of yourself and not whole. You might be so attached to your partner, even when you are not near them or when you see them with another person. Then you will lean into asking yourself why you cannot remove your partner from your life. These questions lead to psychological reasoning for your suffering.

The condition where you cannot let go of your abuser is called trauma bonding.

Before I go into any more detail, I want to clarify a point here. Trauma bonding, while associated at the time with Stockholm syndrome (TSS), has inherent differences. TSS occurs mainly in situations that become life-threatening. The victim in TSS cases is at the mercy of their abuser's will.

Trauma bonding relates more to our dilemma with attachment to our partner. This stems from the emotional trauma we experienced with our narcissist - betrayal, neglect, and manipulation. Trauma bonding happens during passive-aggressive manipulation tactics like sex, temper tantrums, and other forms of control that your narcissistic partner might have used.

Your partner knows that the best way to make sure that you are a constant stream of support to their needs and desires is to create a trauma bond with you. They do this with a method known as seducing and discard. Your narcissist is cunning and they understand that they need to get you totally dependent on them in a way that you no longer fight or resist them. Without any real or formal training, your narcissist knows exactly what to do to make sure that you remain their enabler.

You need to be conditioned to be trauma bonded, and so using two sources of reinforcement your narcissist begins this process by continually hitting you with their reinforcements again and again. This reinforcement method has been termed by psychologists as "arousal-jag." This refers to the excitement that happens before the trauma occurs (arousal) and the peace that is felt after the surrender (jag).

Think about how your partner treats you. Do they participate in conditioning you this way? Are you living in denial about what they do to you? Your narcissist is adept at creating trauma bonds, after all, they have been doing it all their life.

'Arousal-jag' reinforcement involves giving just a little bit to the victim and then taking it away. This is repeated over and over again at well-timed intervals. Narcissists practice this method all the time with their victims. It can be done in a disappearing and reappearing act or the difference between their silence and chaos.

During this reinforcement, your partner can create his own connection however it will be to the excitement they feel and to to the victim. And to be clear, it is not just you. Your narcissist will also feel a connection. The difference is that their connection is to the excitement alone and not to us.

Does this make sense to you now? Are some of the behaviors that your partner does making more sense to you?

The trauma you experience is going to be portrayed in your partner's betrayal and neglect. The excitement you feel before this occurs is built up in the process with your partner devalues you. This is when we are aware that our partner is going to leave us. We become attuned to their behaviors and we can make intuitive decisions based on our narcissist's actions at this point. This will display itself in you like anxiety. This is the chaos that your narcissist is creating. You are mentally preparing yourself for the silence.

See, whether you like to admit it or not, you are now caught up in their game and bonded to the trauma they have subjected you to. We are addicted to their pattern of behavior now, no matter how much we might hurt from it ourselves.

When our narcissist leaves us with only the silence, we miss all of their previous behaviors.

This demonstrates that you are addicted to the self-destructive cycle of falling in love with a narcissist. We crave the connection when our narcissist leaves, and they time it well. Just when you get to the point of coming to your senses or banging your head against the wall your narcissist partner will walk back in the door and scoop you back up into their trap. Now they will give us the second reinforcement. The peace that happens after they have abandoned us. Your partner will time his periods of reinforcement to make sure that your bond to them is strengthening with each reinforcement. The way this conditioning works is that you will become accustomed to letting the narcissist do as they please and asking less than the minimum from them.

You will find bliss in this second reinforcement. The peace of surrender is what solidifies your addiction to your bond. You will become addicted to your partner (the narcissist), the makeup sex, the disappearance of your anxiety, the rush of calm that overtakes your body, and then the happiness that you feel when you realize that once you can breathe again, the cycle begins all over again. Yes, you read that right. You will be happy that you get to experience this cycle again, in fact, you will become addicted to this happiness. Play it over in your head until you are familiar with your narcissist's seduce and discard methods. One of the first steps to realizing the vicious cycle that you are in is to just realize what they do to put you in it. This step can be hard because you want this cycle to continue at first, but you need to recognize the unhealthy behavior involved in trauma bonds.

When you try to move on you can find it hard to keep no contact with your previous abuser. You can even struggle to move into healthier new relationships. This is because you were addicted to your partner's system of narcissism and chaos and the eventual reprieve from the created chaos. We find it hard to generate this same excitement in a new partner, and the intensity of the relationship seems to dull in comparison to your former narcissist.

Due to trauma bonding, we end up forgetting what it is like to be in a normal and healthy relationship. Excitement stops having good and bad connotations to us, we just know we want to experience the excitement. We find that at the end of your relationship, we enjoyed the chaos and destructive attitude as much as our narcissist did (of course this is due to the conditioning).

I urge you to reflect on your relationship at this point. If you managed to get out, reflect on what it was for you. If you find yourself still trapped in a relationship with your narcissist, reflect on what you are experiencing right now. You should be able to see where your partner started creating a trauma bond with you. There are avenues that you can take to heal yourself.

If you are still trapped in a relationship, begin looking for your way out. You may want to stay and make things work with your partner, but remember that they need to want to help themselves first. If they can not or will not you need to remove yourself before you are unable to quit your addiction to the trauma.

Chapter 3 Self Control & Self-Responsibility

Tactic Narcissists, accustomed to desensitizing someone to inappropriate or abusive behaviors, are manipulating a person to agree or settle for one thing that's in conflict with the norms of law and society or codes of behavior that are basic to them. During this stage, victims begin to form excuses for his or her Narcissist. The cycle of abuse has become standard for the victim and it is no longer the fault of the Narcissist. The victim perceives the abuse as 'normal' and despite pleas from others will excuse the Narcissist's behavior, even defending the Narcissist's actions.

This stage is often frustrating from an outside perspective. The victim is largely attempting to rationalize this new view of the world and they're looking for another type of coping mechanism. Once the victim is unable to do this, they start convincing themselves that it is their obligation to assist the Narcissist in achieving his goals. Still, on some level, be it subconsciously or consciously, the victim is aware that things are amiss. At some point, the victim of Narcissistic abuse can reach a mental break. The surreptitious, subtle, underground currents of ill-usage are generally neglected even by the victims themselves until it's too late.

The fostering and improvement of environment and intimidation, feeling of fear and instability, can all be a part of the Narcissist's several abuse patterns and circles. Typically victims don't understand that the mental abuse is even occurring until they're already too much into it or it is explained to them directly and simply. By the time that victims realize what's happening, the abuse has become so 'normal' that the victim becomes confused by taking the abuse away. It's as if the victim craves the Narcissist, whereas actually, it's simply that the Narcissist has been coaching them to possess bound responses right along.

A psychological defense reaction wherever someone "projects" their own undesirable thoughts, feelings, or actions onto some other person is to hunt final decisions from their own conscience. For example: If Narcissists accuse the victim of cheating, there are good chances that he is the one who is cheating. "Attack is the best defense" can be a classic Narcissist move. In other words, they 'flip the script,' and adjust the talk to their own needs. The Narcissist's fears or actions become projected onto their victims and altered into the victim's wrongdoing rather than the Narcissists. This can be terribly confusing from a victim's stance. At this point, the victims are already reeling from jumping through hoops. They are seeking their Narcissist's validation and they are walking on eggshells, so to speak. But the Narcissist can quickly change the script and suddenly throw accusations in the victim's face. There can even be some kind of penalty. Narcissists use this as a bearing technique. But once they can't keep up with their mask the victim might want to leave.

A Narcissist is compelled to gain the admiration and adoration he thinks he deserves from others. It builds them up and it is viewed as confronting to their false sense of superiority and title.

Maybe one of the toughest things for victims to realize is that they're not alone. And we are not talking in the sense that this happens to multiple Narcissistic partners or lovers, or if you want to name them differently. The thing is, the Narcissist will use this kind of behavior on anyone they find fit to fulfill their requirements. Despite a victim's best efforts and intentions, they're not the sole victim of their Narcissist. The Narcissist will go from person to person in order to satisfy their need for attention. And sometimes even if a victim offers her life, it won't be good enough for the Narcissist.

A Narcissist can't stand not having the attention of others; in fact, he can become depressed and feel down because of it. This kind of depression is usually followed by rage and destructive behavior.

The Narcissist isn't the sensitive and empathetic person who will take on the emotions of others at the expense of their own emotional well-being. He will do just the opposite. Empathy is a human characteristic the majority of healthy mental adults feel. It helps us see and feel how people around us feel and will make us do something about it. For example, empathy is feeling sad when you see a homeless person sleeping in the park during winter. Or when you see a sad movie, you tend to feel sad too. Since Narcissists lack empathy, some would argue that they find empathic victims to be more malleable targets for their deceptions.

Roots Of Narcissistic Personality Disorder And Abuse (The Family Model)

There are a large number of studies on Narcissistic Personality Disorder. However, it's still unknown what causes it. As it happens with most personality disorders, the cause of this personality disorder is not simple. Still, it is said that Narcissistic Personality Disorder may be linked to environment, genetics, and neurobiology. When it comes to the environment, some psychologists believe that the cause of Narcissistic personality disorder can be a mismatch in parent-child relationships. Narcissistic personality disorder can develop if that relationship between the parents and the child is either excessive adoration or excessive criticism. The other possible cause is genetics. Some studies say that it is possible that Narcissistic personality disorder can be inherited. And last but not least, there are studies that say that Narcissistic personality disorder can be a consequence of the altered connection between the brain, behavior, and thinking.

Even if the precise causes are unknown, there are risk factors that can increase the possibility of Narcissistic personality disorder development. It is said that Narcissistic personality disorder will more likely affect men rather than females, but that it isn't uncommon that the women develop Narcissistic personality disorder. As explained in numerous studies, Narcissistic Personality Disorder often begins in early adulthood. There is a healthy dose of Narcissism that a child can show at that age and that it doesn't mean that they'll develop a Narcissistic Personality Disorder. Having this kind of personality disorder causes complications on multiple levels including school, work, and relationships. Some people who are dealing with Narcissistic personality disorder tend to be depressed or anxious, or they start abusing drugs or alcohol.

So, as we already said, the exact cause of someone becoming a Narcissist is unknown. But what most mental health professionals believe is that Narcissism comes from a combination of factors coming together and that's the reason why the person feels this way they feel. This mostly means that these combinations include psychological factors and social interactions with the parents of the person. They add their biological vulnerability too. Many researchers believe that Narcissism begins in childhood. There are even some theories that say that Narcissism can be caused if the parents feel that their children need to be special or talented because the parents weren't successful and they want to boost their own self-esteem through the children. On the other hand, some researchers believe that Narcissistic personality is a result of trauma parents caused and abuse that they inflicted on the child when they were young. This kind of disorder starts showing up during adolescence, or in early adulthood when the traits are fully developed and starting to become more permanent. The transition to the adult world of this child fails and when you add environment and genetics, they all add up to form Narcissism. There have been some indications that Narcissism can appear across families and that it could be due to genetics. But most frequently it is just the way that the person was raised. If the person had a Narcissistic parent, that parent didn't bond well with them as a child. If that is the case, then the child will most likely become a Narcissist too.

Risk factors of Narcissism can be different, as we already explained. There are; however, some that are most likely the cause of all types of Narcissism, or Narcissistic Personality Disorder. This is a rare condition that affects about one percent or less of the general population. Some studies show that it is more likely to affect males than females, although it is not impossible for females to develop this disorder as well. Narcissistic personality disorder will most likely develop during adulthood, although some teenagers have traits of Narcissism that may not be diagnosed until later on in their lives. Risk factors that could cause Narcissism are also parental derision for having needs and fears when the person was a child, or a lack of affection and praise from the parents when the child is small. The events that can cause Narcissistic Personality Disorder are also emotional abuse and being neglected during childhood. Also, in some cases, it can go the other way. If there is excessive praise from peers, family members, or parents, the child can develop this disorder as well. If the Narcissist begins to get what he wants every time and if they are praised too much for the things they do, they are going to start expecting this kind of treatment all the time. Children can become Narcissists if they had unreliable and unpredictable care from their parents, or if they have spent a lot of time looking around to get the attention that their parents couldn't provide. If the child had excessive admiration as they were growing up, they didn't have realistic feedback on what is right or wrong, nor they learned how to counteract exaggerated admiration.

Often it is this kind of situation that influences the development of Narcissistic Personality Disorder. These are a combination of the factors that will cause the Narcissist to develop personality traits that are perceived as this disorder. They often received too much praise, and that's why they expect it all of the time from everyone that they meet. Or, in another case, the person probably had trouble getting attention when they were young and now expects others to provide them with the validity that they want.

A couple of genetic studies have been done to determine if there is a genetic potential in developing a Narcissistic Personality Disorder. These studies described two different things they used to try to understand the genetic origin of Narcissism, together with studies on identical twins and examining the human genome. When they analyzed the twin studies, the researchers examined identical twins who had been separated at birth and lived in different houses. To point out, this research was based on the premise that the identical twins share the same genes, and so if the researchers determined that there are some personality traits that are the same, they should be attributed to genetics. They have been able to determine that there is a certain gene that is connected with personality disorders. The study published in 2006, talks about a gene called tryptophan hydroxylase-2 that may be the root cause of personality disorders including Narcissism. On the other hand, some researchers have shown that if the child is neglected or abused, it can lead to the development of Narcissism or other personality disorders. It has been proven many times that adults who have gone through child abuse have a higher probability of developing Narcissism or some other personality disorders. There is one more issue that is considered one of the causes of Narcissistic Personality Disorder and it is called social conditioning. People with Narcissistic Personality Disorder are often taught as kids that they need to expect special treatment from others. They learned that they can expect this without helping out others or do anything of value. Even in our modern media, we see information about how people should always work to achieve better things on a daily basis but when it comes to a Narcissist, they have negative counter-reaction if they don't get the attention they think they deserve. They are raised with this idea that you should be able to get what you want for nothing and it is, in some cases, the core idea of forming some traits that come with Narcissism. Even if the individual had a normal childhood, sometimes the social conditioning influence of the media can be a trigger for bringing out some personality disorders, even Narcissism.

In this comparison, Narcissus represents a parent and Echo represents a child. Psychologists Freud and Mahler made a developmental theory in which they stated that their model is about the parenting system. As they further explain, this parenting system can't mirror anything but itself and its own needs (in our case Narcissus). In this system, the child exists for the parent only to meet those needs (in this case the child represents the Echo).

The family model that we are discussing here is not about pathological Narcissism, but about a system of relationships that develop personal traits that we associate with Narcissism. Those personal traits are usually lack of empathy, self-absorption, detachment, putting them first, etc.

The origin of the term Narcissistic family has a root both in history and sociology. We already mentioned Ovid's and Freud's brands of Narcissism to illustrate certain concepts. There are many references through professional literature that explain the concept of mental illness as a continuum. There are personal characteristics described through these studies that help us look at an individual's tendency toward self-centeredness and establish if it is a Narcissistic Personality Disorder or that there is a just a degree of healthy Narcissism that contributes to self-protection and creativity. Being self-centered and having strong fantasies of power may result in big success and wealth to some people. Apparently, distinctions between healthy amounts of self-admiration and Narcissistic personality disorder are not always easy to make. It is difficult to determine the line between the good amount of Narcissism that helps the person become a favorite of the gods and the "unhealthy amount" that it is hated and destined to become a patient.

In the book The Mask of Sanity, written by American psychiatrist Hervey M Cleckley, we have a chance to analyze the relationship between two brothers. One is eccentric and self-absorbed and the other brother is well-balanced. What Cleckley tried to do with this book is to bring the audience a closer look at one of the types of psychopathic personality. She initially defined it like a relatively high-functioning and aggressively Narcissistic persona that is concealing an antisocial and latent psychotic core. This kind of behavior is also connected to APD (antisocial personality disorder).

It is established that the primary difference between Narcissistic and antisocial personality disorder is one of a degree. Both of these disorders have traits of each other; pathological Narcissism has some antisocial traits and APD typically demonstrates Narcissistic tendencies. Even the diagnostic boundary between these two types of personality disorders isn't totally clear. That being said, the psychoanalyst Otto Kernberg introduced the term "malignant Narcissism". Greenberg describes this syndrome as a certain destructively aggressive behavior manifested through combined traits of Narcissistic, paranoid, and antisocial personality.

When we talk about Narcissistic family systems, many cases illustrate dramatically abusive families that are relatively easy to diagnose. There are a number of examples of these overtly Narcissistic families. Those are usually the families that are dealing with drug and alcohol abuse, families that deal with incest, families that deal with assaultive behaviors, etc. Some therapists; however, have given them their own label. So instead of the family dealing with alcohol, they'll use the term alcohol-troubled families, for the families that are dealing with incest they'll use the term the incest family, and so forth.

There are many metaphors used to describe the Narcissistic family, but we'll use the one that is common. The Narcissistic family is compared to the good-looking apple with a worm inside. The comparison continues with the person biting the apple and discovering the worm. Even though the rest of the apple seems fine, the person loses appetite since there was a worm inside. That's what happens with the Narcissistic family. Mostly the things are "just fine" but there is no emotional connection. The parents aren't meeting their children's emotional needs because they're not focused on meeting them. The difference with the Narcissistic parents is that they are not supportive, nurturing role models for their children; they are the mirror that reflects their own needs. Furthermore, they expect that their children should be the ones to react to those needs and meet them. When the child is raised unable to trust in the stability and safety, it means that that child will distrust its own feelings, its perceptions, and self-worth. The children that are raised as "an Echo", don't have skills that are necessary to live a satisfying life. When it comes to the classification of Narcissistic families, there are two categories: overt and covert Narcissistic families.

Chapter 4 Reprogramming the self-talk

Narcissistic abuse can break down a person's self-esteem, eroding the very person they thought they knew. If you have suffered from narcissistic abuse, you may one day look in the mirror and not see someone you know. You may see someone, dead-eyed and resigned looking back at you were once, you saw someone filled with hope and joy.

The abuse endured from a narcissist can leave lasting damage, made worse when the victim struggles to escape, and it may escalate if the victim tries to escape. Amidst the emotional manipulation, the narcissist toys with the victim's mind in ways that most people would never even consider. The results can be a person with extensive damage to their emotional states and self-esteems that are long-lasting and difficult to heal without assistance.

The Harm of Narcissistic Abuse

The harm of narcissistic abuse can be difficult to spot if you do not know what to look for. Each of these effects is debilitating on their own, but when they all come together, the victim of narcissistic abuse is left reeling, mind racing in an attempt to make sense of the serious manipulation and distortion of reality that has occurred and feeling entirely off-balance. The results of narcissistic abuse create such characteristic results that it is often referred to as narcissistic abuse syndrome.

People who have suffered from narcissistic abuse frequently suffer from echoism, mental health issues as a result of long periods of time in which they were the victim.

Echoism

Have you heard the story of Narcissus and Echo? In this story, Narcissus was a handsome man who was hunting with a group in the forest. The nymph, Echo, sees Narcissus on his way through the forest and immediately falls in love. She had just been cursed to only repeat back what is said to her, so despite being quite enamored by Narcissus, she could not call out. When Narcissus eventually called out, and she answered, she was rejected by Narcissus. She was so heartbroken that she faded away, leaving behind only her voice to echo the sounds of other people.

The victim of narcissistic abuse becomes like Echo, fading away. Though the victim's physical body remains present, the personality and everything that made that individual unique and him or herself fades away. Self-esteem falters, desires fade away, and the victim finds him- or herself entirely consumed with one purpose: Serving the narcissist at all costs.

When echoism occurs, you no longer feel like yourself. You feel as though who you are was stripped away from you, and you simply exist in the world rather than thriving. You are just as much a shadow, a voice on the wind, as Echo became when she allowed herself to love Narcissus. Your needs are put last. Your thoughts and feelings are quashed and replaced with whatever will serve the narcissist best. Your individuality is destroyed. You are told that you are not good enough, that you will never be good enough—and you believe it.

Mental Health Issues

Along with echoism, suffering from narcissistic abuse also brings out mental health issues. People who have suffered from this abuse find their mental health strained due to constantly trying to survive. They are constantly met with cortisol, adrenaline, and norepinephrine as they are perpetually living in stress. They are unable to truly relax, constantly feeling as though they are attempting to make a life on thin ice that may shatter beneath them at any point in time—which they are.

The narcissist's unpredictability and tendency to react violently and abusively teaches the victim to always be on alert, always searching for signs that the narcissist might explode again. The victim feels as though the only choice is catering to the narcissist's every whim to avoid an explosion.

Those who live with this kind of abuse tend to develop some of the telltale mental health issues of anxiety, codependency, depression, and oftentimes also post-traumatic stress disorder.

People who lived through narcissistic abuse find themselves questioning whether they can perceive reality accurately. They think that their needs and wants are meaningless and must be sacrificed for the narcissist, and they frequently are very down on themselves. They do not see their own value, instead of settling into a state of depression while constantly on edge about when the narcissist's abuse will strike next.

Thoughts of Suicide or Self-harming

All of those mental health issues come with an increased risk of self-harm and thoughts of suicide. Stressed and abused by the narcissist, afraid to so much as breath without permission, and feeling hopeless toward anything ever getting better, some victims of the narcissist will turn to thoughts of suicide or self-harm in order to cope. They may feel that death would be a release from the narcissist's abuse, and especially if they are feeling trapped with no escape, such as if they do not have a support network or access to the means to leave, they may feel as they have no other choice.

Self-harm does not always look like cutting or physically leaving injuries—it can sometimes occur through self-medication and feeding addictions. The victim may turn to drugs or alcohol in order to cope with the stress from the narcissist, frequently drinking too much or seeking out dangerous and addictive drugs. This sort of self-abuse can result in addiction, physical illness or injury, or even death. However, the release the victim feels in the moment feels worthwhile, and the victim risks serious addiction in the future to get that small, albeit dangerous, reprieve from the pain and numbness.

The Traits of Victims of Narcissistic Abuse

Victims of narcissistic abuse typically present with a series of traits, not unlike that of the narcissist and the codependent. While sometimes the codependent and the abuse victim are one and the same, that is not always the case. Keep in mind that not every abuse victim will have any or all of these traits, and sometimes, someone with several of these traits has never been abused or mistreated at all. Keep these as a general guide as to what to expect to see in situations of abuse, but do not treat it as a hard-and-fast rule.

Dissociation

Dissociation occurs when the victim starts to distance him- or herself from any emotional states. It becomes easier to hide behind a veil of numbness than to face the abuse, and the victim retreats within him- or herself. This is a common sign seen in post-traumatic stress disorder or individuals who have suffered from some sort of trauma. While this is beneficial when trying to survive some sort of short-term or acute trauma, it is not a state that is healthy to live in long-term. No one is going to be happy or healthy living numbed and dissociated.

Distrustful

When constantly surrounded by abuse and manipulation, it becomes easy to grow distrustful. While you may continue to trust the narcissist, such as if he is gaslighting you and making you doubt yourself, you grow doubtful of your own ability to understand the world around you as well as your ability to trust other people. If you do escape the narcissist, you are likely to have troubles trusting other people or opening yourself up to future relationships. You may distrust anyone who dares to voice any sort of concern about your situation, finding it easier to live in denial than to confront the abuse head-on.

Fearful

Along with being distrustful, you may grow fearful as exposed to narcissistic abuse. The narcissist's explosive reactions and tendency to over-react has taught you to constantly be on edge, worrying about the narcissist's reaction, how his reactions may be perceived by other people, and what will happen to you. This fear leads to the constant production of stress hormones that keep you unable to ever truly relax.

Paranoid

Due to a combination of distrust and fearfulness, you may become paranoid. You think that you are untrustworthy, or unable to see situations clearly. You become paranoid that you are being taken advantage of, or that people are trying to manipulate you, though this thought is typically directed toward everyone but the narcissist. The narcissist may be whispering in your ear that others are simply jealous of what the two of you share and that anyone who dares say anything against the narcissist only wants him for themselves.

Self-sacrificing

The narcissist wants his victims to surrender themselves fully to his whims, meeting his needs whenever necessary and forsaking their own. You oftentimes do this as a survival mechanism to placate the narcissist, but over time, you learn that your own needs are unimportant. After extended periods of time being unable to assert yourself or meet your own needs, you eventually forsake them all together, instead of finding purpose and temporary relief at meeting the needs of the narcissist as you recognize that a content narcissist is a narcissist that is not likely to lash out of you. Of course, that contentment is short-lived.

Blaming yourself

During this, you may blame yourself, feeling as though it is your own fault. Especially with stigmas on abuse being the fault of the victim and with the narcissist whispering that it is all your fault in your ear, you internalize this. You may think that you could have been smarter or stronger to get away from the abuse before it escalated into something more. You may think that you have brought on the abuse yourself, deserving the abuse due to your own incompetence or insufficiencies. You may think that you, yourself, are just unworthy of love inherently. No matter the reason, you find yourself directing blame inwardly in an attempt to make sense of the situation, despite the fact that abuse is never the fault of the victim.

Self-sabotaging

Along with blaming yourself, you may get to the point of self-sabotage. Your self-esteem has been so damaged and twisted that you believe every word of what the narcissist says about your worth. You begin to act accordingly. If you are not good enough at cooking, for example, you may stop caring, thinking it does not matter anyway. This means that you may not pay attention to measurements because your food will come out poorly anyway. In a more extreme example, you may believe that you are incapable of earning enough money to sustain yourself, and after internalizing that, you never aim for jobs that will pay you enough to live off of. Because you never apply for jobs that allow you to live by yourself, you remain dependent on the narcissist.

Protecting their abuser

Perhaps the one nearly universal trait of abuse victims is the urge to vehemently protect the abuser. The victim is likely to protect the abuser, oftentimes still feeling loyal to the narcissist, or feeling in love with the person they thought the narcissist was. You may deny that the abuse was as bad as it may have been, or when someone tells you that the abuser is not a good person, you may point out all the ways you see the abuser as a good person, such as pointing to how he took you on a nice vacation and showers you with love when you are in the idealization stage in your relationship. This is enough for the victim, but it becomes clear to those around the victim that the relationship is not normal or healthy.

Why Victims Struggle to Leave the Narcissistic Abuser

Ultimately, victims struggle to leave their abusers for several reasons, ranging from being unable to, lacking resources, to not feeling ready. Remember, oftentimes, the victim does love the narcissist; the victim is entirely capable of loving other people, and that is taken advantage by the narcissist.

Lacking closure on the relationship

Healthy relationships involve respecting one another and treating each other with compassion. In these relationships, if they fail, they can trust each other to not make life difficult after ending it. They trust that the other person will not harass, stalk, or threaten them, and this makes it easier to let go and know it is truly over.

In a narcissistic relationship, however, there is no such closure. Ending a relationship is fraught with uncertainty and fear that the narcissist will retaliate. The narcissist is likely to return back to the victim repeatedly in an attempt to hoover things back to status quo, and the victim never feels as though the relationship is truly over, even though the victim may want it to be.

Believing that the abuse was their own fault or that they do not deserve better

During the constant abuse and manipulation, the victim begins to internalize what is said. The victim begins to believe that the abuse was her fault, seeing herself through the eyes of the narcissist, and she feels she does not deserve more or to be treated with basic human respect. Her own self-esteem is shattered, and she accepts the abuse or the blame for the abuse without fighting back, especially if they believe that they could have tried harder to avoid the abuse in the first place.

Ending the relationship means acknowledging the abuse

Sometimes, the victim is not ready to end the relationship because ending it means directly acknowledging that the relationship was harmful in the first place. The victim is not ready to face the trauma that has been suffered and instead attempts to minimize and deny the abuse, saying it was not that bad, or that things could have been worse. They may experience abuse amnesia—essentially forgetting the abuse when times are good, and times of dissociation when the abuse is bad, leaving them feeling like they lack an emotional connection at all to the situation.

Lack of support due to the shame and social stigma that surrounds abuse victims

The victim is frequently blamed, and is said to have deserved what happened. This leads to a lack of support to help the victim escape, even if he is ready. He may not have anyone to turn to for help or guidance, and anyone he tries to turn to instead looks down on him. Instead, he is stuck in the situation, unable to get out.

They are not yet ready

Sometimes, the victim is simply not yet ready. Only when the victim reaches rock-bottom, the point at which she says she can no longer do this anymore and that she has finally had enough can she really leave. Ultimately, love and manipulation may have made her stay, but the love and manipulation can only go so far. Until the victim is ready to acknowledge the abuse and face it head-on, nothing anyone can say or do will convince her to leave.

Chapter 5 Redefining your Inner Circle

Narcissistic abuse is the worst form of abuse that can be inflicted on someone, yet one that is highly misunderstood by the public. You may still be wondering why it is paramount to raise awareness about narcissistic abuse, especially in romantic relationships, while most people have not even heard about it. Research and statistics about this unfortunate phenomenon are hard to locate because of it being understudied. However, a closer look at staggering figures showing just how many people are associated with narcissism which signifies the need to educate everyone regarding this phenomenon. The Institute for Relational Harm Reduction and Public Pathology Education found out in its analysis that the probability of people suffering from the Narcissistic Personality Disorder is 1 out of 25, notes Miller et al. (2010). Further, each narcissist will impact on 5 people at least, those whom they lure into romantic relationships. Further, this figure is considered conservative because there are unidentified kids who are victims of trauma; hence they are exposed to the idea of being narcissists.

Worse yet, most people never realize when they are getting into a relationship with a narcissist until it is too late, and they have suffered a lot. A romantic relationship with a narcissist exposes people to a lot of trauma and confusion once it ends since a narcissist manages to control what you do by engaging you in a friendly way. Yet the chances of encountering a narcissist in life are more than 70 percent since they are in society with us and they are always identifying targets.

There is need to pay great attention to narcissistic abuse because unlike physical abuse, the former does not leave clearly visible marks. Understanding the concept of coercive control is important, which is a relatively new concept for most of us. This phrase describes the kind of abuse that narcissists inflict on their partners because it does not entail physical abuse, but the aspect of the victim being isolated from their support system and being made reliant on the abusive partner, who uses the victim for their advantage. It happens when one begins to monitor your moves and takes away your ability to see your friends, and before you know it you are reliant on them alone for all social contact.

In fact, this is one of the reasons why most people do not consider it a reasonable form of abuse and don't understand the need to raise an alarm until the damage is done. Describing something without proof has always been challenging and people fail to realize and acknowledge its presence and effects. Also, it is challenging to describe categorically what narcissistic abuse is and to get people who have never experienced it concerned about it. People tend to feel like they are too strong to be tracked and controlled by a narcissist. Instead, they hold a myth that it is only the weak-minded and codependent types of individuals who are taken advantage of. Unfortunately, this kind of mentality is what gives most people a false sense of protection.

Therefore, this is why it is recommended that you should involve your family and friends, let them know about the disorder and how detrimental it is to a person's life. This can help you to further pinpoint other people who may be suffering from this abuse without knowing it.

It is important to let other people realize that is it not okay at all to be abused. Remind them that life is precious and that no one is warranted to stand in the way of enhancing their autonomy. Remember, there are various reasons that people stay in abusive relationships, including the threat of harm or for the sake of maintaining the social status, or for the hope that things will change for the better. Leaving from a relationship where one is heavily invested is not an easy thing to do. In fact, based on your own experience as a victim, you can tell that it took a lot of efforts and self-empowerment to get out of this. Therefore, you will be careful with your reactions towards the excuses other people give as to why they are unwilling to leave their abusive relationship. If at any time you make them feel embarrassed, they will get defensive and refrain from sharing with you. Therefore, you must use tactfulness to engage with them and be the most understanding person they can rely on. It is distressing to see your friend or loved one be abused. Yet they are always defensive when their partner is bossing them around. Rather than making them avoid you, be gentle and do not judge them.

Also, you should make it clear that even though the wounds are not visible, narcissistic abuse wounds counts as abuse. Let them know that someone can appear so loving yet not wish the best for them. Narcissistic abuse is often disguised as great love, yet it is a series of evil deeds. It is a form of abuse meant at downgrading someone's identity and making them see the world through another person's perspective and value system. It is the mixture of imitation love and emotional coercion that confuses one and makes them lack a way of interpreting their abuse. Therefore, let your family and friends realize that abuse that is emotional still counts as abuse.

Further, tell them how they can swiftly alleviate themselves from the abuse of the narcissist. Rather, it is the use of tactfulness of gaining a strategic advantage over the narcissist by observing their weaknesses and working around them. It is about being the smarter person, acknowledging that the narcissist will never care about your need and using effective techniques to tell them off. For instance, it would be unwise for a victim to panic and react with anger towards the narcissist once they realize that they are being abused. This would attract an even harsher reaction from the narcissist and the result would be injuries and great harm.

If possible, form a campaign and target people whom you feel are being abused yet are afraid to acknowledge it or get help. The worst thing about narcissistic abuse is that the victim hardly notices that they are being used, and they will continue holding on and hoping to get the initial spark of the relationship, without realizing that that was their narcissistic partner's bait to get them hooked. Therefore, it is important to call out the attitude of holding on even when you are hurting too much. Offer them a shoulder whenever they need someone to talk to or to cry with. Tell them that bad experiences happen to sharpen us and empower us to be better people in the future. Also, show them how to start improving themselves instead of giving up and concentrating on the amount of time and energy they have wasted in the abusive relationship. Most importantly, teach them about forgiving themselves and being kind to themselves for having allowed the toxic person to take advantage of them: that they did not deserve such treatment, but that self-forgiveness is the first step toward healing and regaining full control of their lives.

Chapter 6 Rebuilding Self-Trust

Manipulation is an art that the narcissist has learned to master. Indeed, the narcissist is so skillful at manipulating those around them that the victims may not understand that they have been subjected to a form of mind control as a consequence of being seduced by the charm of the narcissist. Though the narcissist may behave in ways that can (and should) be described as inhumane, they can also possess a deep understanding of human nature or human nature that permits them to say one thing while meaning something else, control the emotional state of others subtly, or to lie.

The man or woman with a narcissistic personality disorder has a requirement to satisfy their vanity, which means that they are engaged in constructing an image of themselves, which may have no resemblance to the reality. Part of being a fully mature human understands that human beings are imbued with positive and negative qualities and are capable of engaging in acts of good and evil. Though the narcissist can engage in acts that are damaging to others and are abusive, they may see themselves as imbued with goodness because of the primary narcissism that they exhibit which prevents them from seeing themselves in a realistic way. What this means is that the narcissist needs you to uphold the image of themselves that they have created.

The narcissist uses you to satisfy their narcissism, and at the same time, they need you to fulfill their codependency problem. The narcissist naturally falls into a pattern of abusive behavior to others because of these needs and because of the lack of empathy toward others that they exhibit as a result of their primary narcissism. The manipulative powers of the narcissist combined with the vulnerabilities that the abused person may have had beforehand (and which the narcissist exploits) can render recognizing narcissistic abuse to the uninitiated a difficult task. Here, you will learn some signs that will help you determine if you have fallen into the clutches of a narcissist.

Sign #1: Your significant other tries to isolate you to retain their control

Relationships can be isolating. In fact, individuals with unique personality characteristics or others who are reserved or just like to be alone can find themselves spending most of their time with their partner and little time with others. Although this is not necessarily dysfunctional, someone with the capacity to hurt you or with the desire to do so can use this isolation to control you. By isolating you, the narcissist can control your sense of reality by exposing you solely to their own perceptions and preventing you from knowing the truth.

The narcissist may tell you that you are unattractive, overweight, or otherwise lacking in value. They know, on some level, that these words will cause you pain, but they do not care because they need to feel superior and they need to keep you dependent. If you find yourself spending more and more time with your significant other and less time with friends and family, then you should take a moment to ask yourself why. This is especially important in situations where you are aware that your significant other is abusive or you feel sad and alone but do not know why.

Sign #2: Your significant other minimizes your successes and emphasizes their own

Vanity is an essential characteristic of narcissistic people. In fact, it is the defining characteristic of the narcissist. Much of the behavior of the narcissist, including the behavior of the abusive variety, stems from the vanity of the narcissist, which prevents them from fully empathizing with you and motivates them to degrade you as part of a need to inflate their image. Some psychoanalysts believe that the narcissist, on some level, recognizes their own inferiority. In particular, Adlerian views of individual psychiatry purport that a subconscious inferiority complex is a primary motivator of human action.

If you notice that your significant other says things to you that minimize your accomplishments, then this is a strong sign that you are dealing with a narcissist. Using this sign requires that you have some understanding of your worth and accomplishments. If you slaved away for a degree while working and your significant other tells you that this is not a big deal because everyone has a college degree these days, they are minimizing your accomplishments. If they then suggest that their college degree is more valuable than yours because of the subject or the school they attended, then they are emphasizing their own accomplishments relative to yours. This emphasis of one's accomplishments is very characteristic of narcissistic people, and it should be regarded as a red flag.

Sign #3: Strong emotions, such as love, are a tool that your significant other uses to blackmail you

The narcissist is aware of the emotions of others; they just do not value them. The narcissist sees their own identity as having more intrinsic value than your own, so establishing an emotional connection with you is often a tool they use for manipulation rather than a genuine indication of how they feel. This is one aspect of dealing with narcissists that can be very challenging. The narcissist can be so charming, so suave that you are not aware of the note of falseness in their words.

Because a narcissist does not value your emotions, they have no qualms about using your emotions against you. The narcissist can use emotion as a form of blackmail, using emotional attention and signs of affection as a means of getting what they want from you. If you notice that your natural signs of affection are met with behavior from your partner that does not seem in accordance with your own, then this can be a sign that you are dealing with a narcissist. Like borderline and histrionic people, the narcissist may not have the typical emotional relays that would permit you to share with them the type of healthy emotional interaction that you would have with someone without a personality disorder.

Sign #4: You may experience bouts of unexpected rage from your partner

The narcissist is inherently selfish. Their self-concept of being superior and their vanity result in a type of egoism that basically forms a barrier between them and others. For this reason, you can experience bouts of rage from the narcissist when you do not give them what they desire. The narcissist does not value you as much as they value themselves, even if you have been in a relationship with them for a long time, so if you fail to give them what they feel they need or what they expect from you, then this can cause them to be very angry.

Although many different things in a relationship can lead to outbursts of rage, the narcissistic relationship is important to point out because this rage is generally unexpected. The rage comes as a surprise because the narcissist generally is not genuine in their interactions with you. Everything that they say, all the behaviors that are visible to you are false and designed to give them what they need from you. It is the rage they feel that is genuine when they do not get what they want or feel they need, and when you experience this type of rage, you should take note.

Sign #5: Your significant other refuses to be held accountable for anything

Although the idea of being above the law or deserving of special consideration is especially associated with the Machiavellian type, this type of perception is also seen in the narcissist. The narcissist perceives themselves as being special, so when they do something, including making a mistake of some kind, it is not the same as when someone else does it. This represents less of a desire to manipulate you into cutting them slack than it does the fact that they are so vain that they do not see their flaws or have learned to overlook those aspects of their behavior that conflict with the self constructs.

If you notice that your significant other does not attach significance to their flaws the same way that they do to yours, then this may be a sign that you are dealing with a narcissist. Because the narcissist is so manipulative, you, too, may have learned to explain away the wrong things that they do. A warning sign here is if you do something, it is harshly criticized and harped on, but when they do the same thing, it is justified or ignored completely. This is a clue that they do not see their flaws as flaws, but yours, they recognize for what they are (or worse).

Sign #6: Your significant other demeans and belittles you

Belittling language is one of the major red flags that alert you that you are dealing with a narcissist. Someone who loves you and values you should not say things to you that cause you to have low self-esteem or which lower your worth. A true partner should endeavor to lift you up rather than put you down because they see the two of you as joined in an important way. The narcissist has no compunctions about putting you down because they do not perceive you as being as special as they are, in a relationship or not.

Sign #7: You feel hollow and ignored

One of the more important signs of narcissistic abuse is feeling ignored, especially when you are sensitive or emotionally vulnerable. This is an important sign because many people do not recognize when they are being manipulated or controlled, especially when this is being done at the hands of a narcissist. Although the abuse of the narcissist may be obvious to the outsider, to the person in the relationship, all the little clues may not be obvious because of the charm of the narcissist or the inherent vulnerabilities of the person being abused.

Sometimes, the only sign that you are in an emotionally abusive relationship is feeling hollow. This type of feeling represents the effects that the words and actions of the narcissist have had on you. It is important to pay attention to this very important, albeit subtle clue.

Sign#8: Your significant other can be cruel, but they are able to turn on the charm when necessary

The narcissist is very calculating. Their words are designed to have an impact on you, whether it is to break you down or to lift themselves up. The narcissist is also aware enough of your emotional state and your weaknesses that they can get a read on the impact that their words have on you. Indeed, the narcissist is very calculating about what they say because they have specific goals concerning you. The narcissist does not act this way with just you but with everyone. They are cut from other people to some degree, so they have learned the value that words can have in helping them get what they want from others.

Therefore, when the narcissist notices that they have gone too far, that they have hurt you to such an extent that the effect is something unexpected, then they know how to turn on the charm to lure you back in. This is thanks to their ability to read you. Just like the person using neuro-linguistic mind control, the narcissist has learned the verbal and non-verbal cues that you send that indicate your emotional state and your receptiveness to this or that. The narcissist is engaged in mind control just as the adept in NLP is as this form of mind control also relies on words.

Sign #9 Just when you have had enough, your significant other finds a way to lure you back in

Although charm is not inherently a dangerous quality, this is one of the character traits of the narcissist that is part of the constellation of quirks that renders them dangerous. Narcissists can be charming because they know that charm is a good way to manipulate people and that they see themselves as better than others, and this comes out in the confidence that others feed into and reinforce. Therefore, when the narcissist notices that they may have gone a tad farther, then they turn on the charm to undo the damage they have done. This change in behavior can happen in a flash, and it is a sign that you are dealing with a manipulative person.

Sign #10: The feelings that your significant other displays toward you change rapidly

The idea of rapidly changing behavior or emotions is very important when it comes to manipulators. Manipulators understand the importance of emotions to control others. As human beings, we naturally seek an emotional connection with others. This is part of our legacy as members of the animal kingdom to be able to form a deep connection with other members of our species, but it also a uniquely human characteristic that we can feel sympathy and have empathy for others.

But the motivations of the narcissistic are less group-focused and more primal—more narcissistic. The emotions of the narcissist change rapidly because their own emotional state is not tied to your own, as it would be if they really felt empathy for you. Their emotional state is tied to their sense of how they can use their emotions to mind-control you and the occasional time when they allow their mask to fall and show you the anger they feel when they do not get what they want. Rapid changes in emotion represent the narcissist switching it up based on how their emotions can impact you. Over time, you should learn to distinguish the real thing from the fake stuff.

Sign #11: You experience emotional ups and downs

The narcissist may be prone to outbursts of emotion, but it is the victim of narcissistic abuse who experiences ups and downs. If you experience emotional highs and lows, it is probably a sign that you are dealing with a highly emotional person or that someone else is manipulating your emotional state at will. The latter is the case with narcissistic abuse because the narcissist basically sees your emotions as a tool they can use to get what they want from you. In a relationship with a person with borderline personality disorder, for example, emotional highs and lows on your part means that the ups and downs of your borderline partner is causing your own ups and downs because you feel empathy for them and cannot help but participate in their emotional whirlwind somehow, even if it is damaging to you.

Emotional ups and downs that do not appear to be tied to any innate feelings on your part are therefore a sign that you are dealing with a manipulator or someone with a personality disorder. In the case of narcissistic abuse, you are dealing with both a manipulator and a person with a personality disorder. Recognizing this key sign is huge in breaking free from this type of bondage.

Sign #12: You are faced with feelings that whatever you do, it is never enough

The vanity of the narcissist requires that you are always less than they are. The narcissist does not see you as being their equal, even though their codependency mandates that you stick around. Your presence serves several key purposes for the narcissist. By keeping you around, the narcissist has someone to meet their practical needs (whether that be money, sex, or housing) and their emotional requirement of validation from you.

The narcissist, therefore, will cause you to feel that whatever you do is not good enough for them because they need to put you down to control you and they do not see you as being their equal. Recognizing the sign that whatever you do does not seem to be good enough for your partner is important in realizing that the narcissist does not truly value you.

Sign #13: Your significant other lies frequently and pathologically

The narcissist relies on manipulation to get what they want and need from other people. Lies are a tool that the narcissist uses as part of their manipulation. Indeed, everything about the narcissist appears to be a lie. Even their persona is a lie. The narcissist behaves in such a way as to give the impression of their innate superiority while deep down, they most likely feel inferior. This inferiority complex is subconscious as the narcissist consciously acts in a way that does suggest their innate superiority over others.

What we would call pathological lying in this context are the deceptive words that the narcissist uses in their interactions with others. They can lie as part of their charm, or they can lie to wound or to demean someone. A narcissist may say that you are unattractive in some important way, while deep down, they do find you attractive or else their vanity probably would not have permitted them to have a relationship with you. Noticing that your partner lies frequently is a sign that something is not right. In this case, your significant other may just be a narcissist.

Sign #14: You find yourself overly anxious or depressed

Anxiety around interacting with a romantic partner is a sign that something is not right in a relationship. In particular, this is a sign that there may be some abuse happening. Your partner should make you feel safe and secure. You should desire to be around them, and you should feel an emotional connection with them. Noticing that you are nervous about meeting your significant other or that you feel another dysfunctional feeling like depression is a sign that something about your partner is causing you to feel this way. This can be a sign that your partner is a narcissist.

Sign #15: You notice that your self-esteem is low

Low self-esteem is a telltale sign of narcissistic abuse. As we have seen, a high self-image for the narcissist means that your self-image has to be low. Because the narcissist generally has a distorted perception of themselves, they need you to reinforce their high self-image, and this usually means putting you down. If you notice that your self-esteem is low in the setting of a relationship, then there's a good chance that your partner might be causing it. Start paying attention to the clues that could be impacting your self-esteem, such as the things your partner is saying or doing.

Chapter 7 Speaking your Trust

We all want a good relationship. It's very distressing to learn that a person you trusted to be a narcissist or a psychopath for life. It is shocking and shocking as what you thought was far from the truth.

A narcissist doesn't behave like a typical human. If you want to get what you want, you always use mind games. Such games are like hidden tornadoes in which you don't know.

Why do they first use these games? Okay, they want you to risk anything that's special to you. You want your entire self and reputation to be lost. There is no place for dignity and independence. They want you to give up and go under their control and be what they think you are.

Such mind games take your natural self, confuse you to choose your own beliefs and lies. You want to be a fully controlled marionette who does whatever you want. It's classified as mental slavery.

#Mind Game No 1' You Must Learn How To Trust Me' They are friendly, confident, and supportive at the beginning of the relationship. You are in this person and are very involved in the life, fears, thoughts, and concerns of an individual. You should play a victim to think he is your partner's heart.

Unfortunately, narcissists love to know the vulnerabilities of the victim. You know everybody has specific vulnerabilities. You must learn to exploit a victim. In other words, you collect information about yourself. It is referred to as supply narcissistic. The bad news is that what you feel or think doesn't really matter. They are happy and satisfied when you end up feeling angry and hurt. You think you're drawn under.

They say, "Oh, you're sad about that issue. Anyway, it's all your fault!"

Note, narcissists are never responsible for themselves and their acts. We are incredibly defensive and ashamed of you.

Each game is invisible. Narcissists are just cowards and never say what they expect.

From them, you never hear:' Hello Mary! Can you tell me all about yourself as I take notes? I plan to use it later against you. After you have hooked and accepted how pleasant and friendly they are, they judge you. You'll not be as smart and competent as I am.

You'll find some criticism like,' Why did you do it? I don't think that you ought to have said this way.' ' No! No! No! No! No! No! You're wrong! You're wrong! I can do that better than that. I can do better than you. You ought to do this like me because I'm always right! We want to let you know that we look much better at life than the average person. You have no choice but to trust and listen.

The real narcissistic essence is that they love when you're scared of them.

Fear Installment: It is your way through fear of power and controls you. One day you might be able to tell them the truth. You'll go crazy to be even more scared of you. They groom you to be obedient and reliant on them through fear. You know that people are afraid of terror. That is why they use it until you give it up and give it up.

This mental game forces survivors to lose their identity. You no longer share your real feelings and opinions. They do everything to avoid retribution.

Isolation: They continue to isolate you after they have heard about you and your weaknesses. The goal is to monitor you entirely. It helps them hold a higher position. You are segregated from others. You want to lose supporters and strong allies.

Such people will say about you many times without you even knowing about it. Somebody can love your job. When you succeed, the narcissist hates. Within one minute, he will expose your weaknesses and dark secrets to others to ruin and undermine your abilities. He will do possible thing to prevent people from trusting you too much.

It sabotages other people's relationships with you. They begin to disappear from your life over time. You are totally isolated and entirely dependent on your abuser.

Weaknesses' Narcissists love to reveal and maintain your personal flaws. In the beginning, you trusted me with a game of attitude. You told him your secrets, your shortcomings, and your mistakes of years ago. So, any time you want to score points, you're going to remember your mistakes. You want to decrease your interest and damage you.

Each good you do in life will be destroyed by him. Note, narcissists hate to see people fulfilled, happy, and successful. You just collect information about your victims. If you expose yourself to something wrong, you use this mind game. You must dwell on your adverse effects from the past. It helps to become innocent victims.

Blameless Victim: The narcissist is always blamed for others. We play a role as victims to prove that they have good intentions. You never admit how you screwed it up. We still apologize for blaming other people who blew them. We need someone else on whom they can pin their mistakes.

Rules and Regulations: When referring to offenders, they use' you will' imperative forms,' you have to' imperative. The narcissist sees life as a significant regulatory body. Others should meet their obligations even if they don't want them.

It is critical that these tricks are realized. You can battle a narcissist, but it's a meaningless game because he's never going to stop the abuse. In this case, what can you do? You're too valuable to waste your time. Concentrate on yourself, face your fears, pain, and worries. Choose a better life without toxic people for yourself.

Why is the Victim not leaving his or her abuser?

In the case of a woman, people usually ask it not to abandon her abusive husband, but the opposite happens so often. Or it could be a person who does not break the relationship with an abusive family or a family who acts as a proxy for a narcissist. Whichever-why does the violence target not leave?

Each abuser asks the same question to himself! Truth is stranger than fiction, but the fact that this is manipulative is this: it is "normal" when abused, but the family target or abused partner is Normal. Only they were humiliated and exploited in such a way that they felt powerless to change the situation.

Truth be told, if they were in her shoes, people who say, "Why won't she leave him?" wouldn't leave them.

People vary in how much violence they need to leave. In other words, some will go faster than others. But they all take far more abuse than anybody thinks a person might. Why? Why? It's an intuitive counter.

Ancient art is connected to your abuser. This is the Inquisitor's art and the torturer's art. A black art that acts like sorcery. The Inquisition and the KGB had this in an artistic way.

The most important thing is that this is what NORMAL people do. The abuser creates a bumpy world in which all normal human reactions reverse.

How long? How long? How much it takes to make you face facts and see how bad he or she is that person you love with all your heart. Is bad. It's evil. An impassable idea, isn't it? You still think it is going to improve, even though you know that he returns your love as much as the snake will return your love. Has he played you just for a fool? The idea that is unimaginable. Denial. Denial.

The abuser still faces and leaves finally, only to return over and over again. They did not enter the "hunt" abuse relationship, and people who say this are simply ignorant or narcissistic. Deliberate or voluntary misuse is contrary to the laws of nature. It burns blood every time someone says it about a person who is abused.

The victim hates and tries to prevent violence. The dilemma is that narcissists are intentionally difficult men, so avoiding narcissistic disorder is the only way. Even if the abused partner or the abused family survivor wants to get away, it takes more than just the desire, knowledge, and skills to escape finally. The victim may think the information you give is some kind of assessment planned by the abuser, depending on how much power the abuser has so that they don't acknowledge the data or, worse, voluntary to the abuser. It results in more violence and alienation.

Look at the situation in which you are now. Happiness is an attraction. With all your soul, you love this guy-an an overwhelming appeal to him. But with an explosion of abusive tactics, he responds to your affection and creates an overwhelming repulsion that desperately try to hide, but he resents you and senses it, subjecting you even more violence.

To her rapist, she's here on her knees and clings to him for dear life with the naïve hope that she can train the demon inside. The more he refuses her aggressively, the more she sticks. There's something to share.

It seemed he was extremely dense. But he really wasn't. The coercive methods used against all innocent partners are destructive and social, and private responses are to them. We're wrong to say what we would do if it were us because it's never going to be us. You may be the victim of a partner or family member, but in every situation, the dynamics will never be the same.

Nevertheless, despite being told by their abuser, no abused partner or target should ever feel guilty for the assault. To share in the culpability of violence, she would need to do so, and just being with an aggressor does not cause abuse. All the victims are complicit and frustrated because they believe the lies, do not see the deception, do not know the truth, and are guilty of abuse for far too long. But this is the culpability caused by the violence. It is these "guilt trips" which carry abusive relationships with many abused people. The survivor learns later or sooner that she is just as unfeeling and cold as her abuser, and the violence eventually drives her out of her head if she doesn't come from the reality of denial and eyes.

It is ridiculous to see their feelings of regret and sorrow as partially judging what the perpetrator did. It is insane. It's not just being with someone that justifies being abused. Loving someone doesn't make you guilty of allowing your abuser. Feeling compassionate and empathic does not encourage the abuser to exploit you. The failure of the goal to leave does not take away one bit of the guilt and responsibility of the offender. That is what the perpetrator wants all of us to think about. The abuser always leads to conflict, turns around, and puts the blame on her feet.

Chapter 8 Taking New Risks

Most people are open to the idea of meeting a partner and having a healthy, loving relationship. This is what most people aim towards, and even if it isn't your final aim in life, most of us enjoy the process. What we don't enjoy is meeting someone who is unable to have that kind of healthy relationship.

A narcissist finds it extremely difficult to maintain healthy, loving relationships. The reason isn't clear, and it can vary from person to person; it could be because they experienced a lack of affection when they were a child, it could be because they've been hurt before and as a result they are using defense tactics, or it could be because they exhibit very jealous traits which make it borderline impossible for another person to live with. Of course, there is also the rest of the narcissistic spectrum of traits to take into account, which makes it very difficult for someone to maintain a relationship in a healthy way, with someone who has NPD.

When we meet someone we like, we know that there is a chance we are going to get our heart broken, and whilst we hope that it won't happen, we know that it is a possibility. We try not to let this bother us and simply move on with the fun side of a relationship. The problem is, a narcissist doesn't have the right amount of empathy or trust for a relationship to be anything but chaotic and emotionally damaging for the other person. As a result, many narcissists end up alone in the long-run. Most partners eventually leave, because they simply can't take it anymore; it can be a mild reason, or it can be something more severe, such as emotional abuse and gaslighting techniques.

We've mentioned gaslighting a few times already, but if you're not sure what it is, we're going to cover that in more detail in this very chapter. Whilst gaslighting isn't only found in narcissist relationships, it is quite common in this type of union.

We also know that there are more male narcissists on the planet than women. In that case, it's more likely that the male partner will be narcissistic towards the female, but that shouldn't lead you to believe that it is never the other way around. Just as there are many relationships which involve emotional abuse from the female partner to the male, there are also female narcissistic relationships too, either same-sex or female to male. People are people at the end of the day, and a narcissist is a narcissist whether male or female.

What most people don't understand about relationships with narcissists is how it actually got to the point of being a relationship in the first place. Surely if someone is being treated badly from the start they would leave before emotions got involved? Let's explore that in more detail.

A Wolf in Sheep's Clothing

One way to describe a narcissist in a relationship is like a wolf in Little Red Riding Hood. The wolf was clever and dressed up as someone Red could trust, i.e. her grandmother. By doing that, he appeared to be something he wasn't. Many narcissists do this without even realizing it.

When you first meet a narcissistic in a potentially date-like or attraction situation, they will be on their best behavior. He or she will be as charming as can be. Nobody really knows why this is the case, but it is thought to be down to their deep-seated desire to be liked and approved of. When they see someone they like, their desire is to potentially 'own' that person. Not in the actual ownership sense, but in a 'look what I managed to attract' kind of way. It sounds terrible, but that is how the mind of a narcissist operates at the first signs of attraction.

When a man or woman meets someone, who is on their best behavior, charming the socks off them and complimenting them on everything they say and do, it's hard not to become enamored. It's also worth pointing out that certain types of narcissists, especially the toxic ones, tend to focus on those who are a little emotionally weak or vulnerable. This makes the first stages of attraction far easier to navigate; someone who is quite vulnerable is probably going to overlook a few red flags, compared to someone who is strong and has a high level of self-worth. In that case, a person is far more likely to walk away at the first sign of an issue.

Once that first flush of attraction begins, the narcissist will keep up the wolf in sheep's clothing act until their partner is totally hooked. By that point, all bets are off. By that point, the true colors start to show.

This is why so many men and women end up in relationships with narcissistic partners. They have been tricked by an illusion.

Of course, not every narcissist is like this; we are painting a picture of the very worst type of narcissist here. Having said that, it is a common way for people to become close to those who do have narcissistic traits. In addition, it could be that an empathic person, or someone who has a natural tendency to want to help others, see the damaged side of a narcissistic and wants to make them 'better'.

You cannot make a narcissistic better. You cannot change them and heal them, but it doesn't stop some people from trying. One of the most toxic combinations in romance is a narcissist and an empath, and it is for this very reason. We're going to cover that particular subject in a little more detail shortly.

Signs You Are in a Relationship with a Narcissist

If you're in a relationship currently and you're looking at your partner and thinking 'you might be a narcissist', or you simply want to know what to look out for in the future, let's check out some of the most common signs that you are indeed in a relationship with a narcissist.

- He or She Hijacks Every Conversation - If you're out on a date, or you're simply chilling at home, and he or she always turn every conversation around to themselves, you're looking at narcissism territory. Narcissists love to hear their own voice and they love to talk about themselves and what they've done. If you manage to get a word into the conversation, then it's likely that whatever you say will be ignored or thrown to one side. When you start talking, they will probably interrupt you and turn everything back to themselves.

- Showing Off on Dates - Whilst it's nice to be wined and dined if you notice that your partner goes out of their way to basically show off when they take you out, it could be a narcissistic nod. Do be careful with this one, because it could equally be your partner trying to woo you! A few signs to look out for include tipping far too much, not tipping at all, treating the waiter with disrespect, or ignoring advice on wine/food from the waiter and telling them that he/she knows better.

- Always Breaks Promises and Oversteps Boundaries - If he or she is always borrowing things and not bringing them back, maybe borrowing money, or simply avoiding the need to recognize your personal boundaries, then that is a narcissist sign to look for. A narcissist doesn't have respect for anyone else's thoughts or feelings, because they have very little empathic ability. They also don't know much about personal space, so if you find that they're always 'in your space', that's something to look out for too. If they make you a promise and barely keep it, again, red flag.

- Everything is Your Fault - They make you a promise or say they'll do something and when they don't do it, they turn the blame onto you. For example, perhaps you were supposed to meet for coffee after work but he or she didn't turn up. A response could be 'what do you expect, you didn't remind me!'. They might be cooking dinner and burn it, and it will be your fault because you distracted them with something you said.

- They're Always Looking in The Mirror - Whilst many men and women have slight vanity issues, narcissists are literally in love with their own appearance. If you notice that your partner is always looking in the mirror, always changing their hair or dress sense to look good and gain approval from others, then narcissism could be on the cards. A narcissist has to be the best, look the best, and be admired, and they place a huge amount of importance on appearance over everything else.

- Your Opinion Isn't Worth Anything - If you're having a conversation about something and you voice your opinion, a true narcissist will belittle that view and tell you that you're stupid/your opinion is stupid/tell you that theirs is better. Trying to get a narcissist to agree with you is a blatant waste of time and oxygen.

- They Have to Have the Best - Possessions and the way others see them is vital to a narcissist. For example, if you're trying to buy a car together but you're on a budget, a narcissistic would rather go down the finance route and land themselves in debt to drive the latest Mercedes, than go for something lower in status quality, but within budget.

- They Matter, You Don't - A narcissistic partner will expect you to forget your wants and needs and focus entirely on theirs. If anything, your wants and needs never registered on the scale! You will, therefore, need to drop everything for what they need, and they will not show any thanks in return.

- Arguments Often End in Them Sulking or Running Away - Narcissists do not handle rejection or criticism well, in fact, it will end in them either sulking and starting another argument or running away/becoming emotionally detached. This can extend to a certain type of emotional abuse also because by belittling you in the middle of an argument, they make themselves feel better about the criticism you've given them (probably rightly).

- They Often Act Out of Jealousy - Narcissists are often quite jealous and this is even more so in a relationship. If you notice regular bouts of jealousy, then that is a narcissistic red flag to be aware of.

How many of those signs you see in your relationship depends on whether or not you can truly class your partner as narcissistic. Don't go throwing the label around just because you can tick off one or two! Remember, in order for a narcissist to be diagnosed with NPD, they need to tick five or more of the traits from a rather short list, as outlined in the diagnostic criteria. We can't give you a definite number of these signs to tick off, but you would be looking at half or more, over a constant period of time, before you could categorically decide either way.

Is There a Future for a Relationship Touched by Narcissism?

Ah, the million-dollar question. We cannot say yes, and we cannot say no, it really depends on the couple and the amount of narcissistic involved.

What one person is happy to put up with, another person would run away from. What you need to do, however, is ask yourself whether you're truly happy and whether you see a future for the two of you. Never stick with a narcissistic person if they are making you feel unhappy, belittled, or questioning your own self-esteem or sanity. The problem is, that questioning your own sanity is part of the whole gaslighting issue we've mentioned so many times already.

Many men and women stay in narcissistic relationships because they aren't sure whether or not they're imagining it, or whether it's really happening. Deep down, they know something isn't right and they know that they shouldn't be dealing with the way things are, but they love that person, and they don't want to give up on them. Whenever their partner shows their bad side, they quickly show their good side not long afterwards; by doing that, they're keeping the person right where they want them - not leaving.

In terms of whether there is a future or not, perhaps we should instead be questioning whether there is a healthy future or not. There is a difference between a general future and a healthy one. A relationship where one partner is constantly belittling and dragging down another isn't healthy, whether they're doing it because of a personality disorder or not.

There aren't that many narcissists who remain in relationships for that long. The reason is that in the end, the other partner really sees the light and finds the strength to leave. This doesn't always happen, and there are instances where a future could be on the cards, provided the narcissistic partner is able to realize that they are doing and get help. It does happen, but it doesn't happen often.

Whilst we might be painting a bleak picture, it really is a case of looking at your individual circumstances and deciding what is right for you. There is no right or wrong answer here.

The Narcissist and The Empath

There is one particular toxic mixture that we need to talk about in more detail. This combination of people is a highly damaging and extremely incompatible one, but it is also a very common union you will find. We are talking about a person classed as an empath and a narcissist of any type.

For this to be a damaging combination, the narcissist doesn't have to be a toxic or malignant type, they can be classic, vulnerable, or a combination of types. The problem here is that an empath is an extremely sensitive person, someone who is hurt easily and who wants to help. A narcissistic possesses very little, probably zero, empathy and as a result, the two cannot understand each other. You might wonder in that case how they come together in the first place, but it is a union which is surprisingly common.

The bottom line is that an empath wants to help, and they are attracted by the charming nature of a narcissist when they first meet. Whilst empaths usually have extremely good instincts and can normally spot someone acting out of character from a long distance, a narcissist is extremely good at getting past that defense mechanism. As a result, the empath finds themselves totally enamored with this new person in their lives. They then start to see chinks in their armor, e.g. the vulnerable side, the side which needs constant reassurance. The empathic side of their nature then wants to help, and almost wants to 'fix' the narcissist.

As we've explored already and will certainly delve into in more detail later in the book, a narcissist cannot be fixed, as this is an ingrained part of their personality which requires professional assistance in order to change the disordered pattern of thinking. What eventually happens is that the empath is belittled and emotionally damaged by the narcissist's lack of empathy and general behavior. It's also likely to be the case that an empath will struggle to leave the narcissist because they will keep turning on the charm just at the moment, they think the empath is finally going to summon up the courage move on.

Empaths are extremely sensitive, as we have already said. They do not understand how someone can use emotions for manipulation and they are extremely easy to hurt. Therefore, the thoughtless actions of a narcissist can cause extreme upset and hurt to an empath.

Of course, the same could be said for any type of emotionally sensitive person. In many cases, narcissists actually seek out vulnerable and sensitive people, because they are far easier to manipulate. This is particularly the case with toxic and malignant narcissists, who almost seem to get a kick or some kind of enjoyment out of causing distress and upset to another person.

Unfortunately, the only way to get around this particular problem is for an empath to see the light and leave. For many people, however, that is extremely difficult and pulls on every heart string possible. Even when someone does bad to an empath, they still try and see the good in them.

When it's Time to Leave

Whilst it's not impossible for a relationship touched by narcissism to succeed over time, there are far more instances when the union will ultimately fail. It is likely to be a long and protracted process, because of something which we're going to finally get around to discussing next - gas lighting.

The person in the relationship with the narcissist will question themselves endlessly and wonder whether they really are being treated badly, or whether they are imagining it. The narcissist will turn everything around on them and make them feel like it's them that is to blame. For a person who is quite sensitive or emotionally vulnerable, this type of treatment can cause them to stay in a relationship which is damaging and unhealthy for far too long.

A person leaving a narcissistic relationship will probably go back a few times before finally breaking contact. A narcissist is unlikely to just 'let it go'. As we've mentioned previously in this book, many narcissists want to have the best of the best, and they collect things as possessions. In some ways, their partner is an extension of that. When their partner chooses to leave them, they see this as a failure and a huge rejection. They will react either with anger, or they will attempt to charm them back, reverting to the 'old' version which initially attracted the person to them in the first place. In many cases, this can be enough to get their partner to return to them because they still have deep feelings underneath it all.

Many partners who leave this type of relationship require a large amount of support afterwards, and some even require emotional counseling. Depending upon the type of treatment they have been subjected to (far worst in the event of being close to a toxic or malignant narcissist), the empath may find it extremely difficult to have trusting and healthy relationships in the future, without some kind of therapy or support into the future.

As you can see, narcissistic relationships aren't just damaging for the narcissist (because many ends up missing out on genuine loving unions as a result of their inability to have healthy relationships), but also for the partner too. Leaving it difficult, and in some cases, it can be a process which takes months, if not years.

It's often the case that they know their partner is narcissistic towards the end. This is usually the catalyst for making them think they should leave. However, when gas lighting begins, the difficulty really turns itself up a notch or two.

Chapter 9 Let go of the fight to win and the your need for Justice

Another way that empaths are commonly described is as highly sensitive people. This is a fairly accurate representation, since empaths are incredibly sensitive to the world around them. However, it is not just the emotions and energies of the people around them that empaths are sensitive to. This chapter will explain highly sensitive people and how electromagnetic fields and other stimulation affect them.

What Are Electromagnetic Fields?

Electromagnetic fields exist around electrically charged objects, as a physical manifestation. This field has the power to affect any of the charged objects that are within the field's reach. Electromagnetic fields are a fundamental force of nature, because the field produced by an object can project itself indefinitely through space.

A field is created when a magnetic field and an electric field come together as one. A stationary object produces the electrical element of the charge and the moving charges, or currents, create the magnetic element of the field. The force that is put out by this field determines how far it reaches. The power of this electromagnetic field is often determined by the Lorentz Force Law, which states that the velocity of a charged particle will experience a certain force when acted on by electric and magnetic fields. We will leave things here to keep them simple, as once you delve deeper into physics and quantum physics, things can become complicated.

How Electromagnetic Fields Relate to Empathy

Electromagnetic fields are another external element that empaths are sensitive to. The reason that electromagnetic fields relate to empaths is because the heart and brain emit electromagnetic fields. A study published by the Heart Math Institute tested the electrical field of the heart and brain using an electrocardiogram, finding that the heart had 60 times greater amplitude than the brain and that the heart's magnetic component was about 100 times stronger. Because the signal from the heart does not travel through the tissue, it can be tested and measured several feet away. This study used a Superconducting Quantum Interference Device (SQUID) manometer.

The conclusion of this study was that the rhythm of the heart has certain patterns depending on the emotion that is being experienced at the time. Additionally, the rhythm and signal from the heart are felt in all the cells of the human body. This can change sound pressure, blood pressure and the electromagnetic fields that are emitted. The study also concluded that for this reason, when people experience the same emotion, it works as a global synchronizing signal. This signal carries the frequency of a person's thoughts and emotions across distance.

This study is important because it explains the phenomena that empaths may experience when they sense the emotions of someone who is not in their presence. There have been many anecdotal incidents where empaths have sensed the emotions of close friends or loved ones when they were hundreds of miles away. The only explanation from this is that empaths are so receptive to the signals put out by those that they love that empaths can sense their emotions across long distances.

To understand how this works, let's call the loved one person "A" and the empath person "B." Person A is feeling a strong emotion. The rhythm of their heart beats creates an electromagnetic field that projects out like a beacon. Person B is highly sensitive to person A's field because of their close relationship. Because person B is receptive to the signals that the 'beacon' is sending out, they can sense person A's emotions across long distances.

The key to this phenomenon are the magnetic waves put out into the electrical field. Unlike electrical currents that require a conductive substance, magnetic waves can pass through anything, even solid object and maintain their trajectory. They are broadcast across long distances and the human heart constantly puts out these energies, so there is an eternal broadcast system of electromagnetic waves that affect how an empath may feel or act.

People do not put out the only electromagnetic field that empaths are sensitive to. The sun, moon and Earth all produce their own electromagnetic fields. This explains why empaths are physically and emotionally affected by these orbiting bodies. Empaths also experience emotions when listening to music or when watching television. For this reason, someone with an empathic nature should always use discretion when choosing what type of emotion that they want to experience.

Highly Sensitive People: From Childhood to Adulthood

Science proves that some people are just more sensitive than others. In one famous study, Jerome Kagan studied the reactions of 462 healthy babies as they were introduced to unfamiliar events. These babies were exposed to tactile, auditory and visual stimulation. It was found that around 20% of the group were more stressed than the others, reacting more seriously to the stimulation. Doctor Elain Aron is another supporter of this idea of highly sensitive people, believing that it goes beyond the simple introvert/extrovert explanation under Jungian concepts.

One of the greatest hardships that empaths face is growing up as an empath. Overly sensitive children may cry more than others and their parents may be frustrated, unable to keep up with their child's needs and eventually telling them that they must grow tougher skins. Teachers do not recognize over-stimulation as a problem that causes scattered attention, but instead tell the child to focus more. It is not necessarily the parent's or teacher's fault, as they are likely uneducated on these types of matters, however, it creates a difficult journey for the child. This is especially true in stressful households, such as one where the parents fight or one of the parents is absent. Child empaths may also have trouble making and keeping friends, because friends do not always understand that they need to step away and regroup sometimes.

When all these problems come down on the shoulders of a child, it can be disastrous. They may feel as if there is something wrong with them or that they are a burden on those around them. Empathic adolescents may see others around them acting and responding differently than they do, but cannot understand why they are not able to deal with life in the same way. Empathic children and adolescents often try to suppress their outward reactions, but this just overloads the nervous system and the mind, and makes them seem even more frazzled.

Some parents may even choose to medicate their children. While this can be effective, it does not solve the core of the problem. It just covers up a child's empathic nature. The child will still have trouble developing personal relationships, now because they cannot feel to make that connection with the outside world.

Even once empaths enter adulthood, they may struggle with being an empath. Before empaths know of their empathic nature, they often question themselves, their capabilities, and their ability to function in normal society. As soon as that label of empath is defined, however, adolescents and adults can take steps toward wellness. They can start looking for help in the form of books and articles, as well as groups for empaths who are trying to find the balance in life, the perfect level that exists between under-stimulation and over-stimulation. It is within this balance, that empaths can control and realize their true abilities.

Why Understanding the Physiological and Biological Causes and the Sensitivities of Empathic People is Important

Have you noted some of the same behaviors in yourself or gained a deeper understanding of why you are an empath? By this point, you may be wondering why it is important to understand all this. You may even be eager to start learning how you can control it. This chapter will give you that explanation and provide closure to all that you now know about why you are an empath. As you have learned, being empathic is rooted deep within you and it is not something that you can change. Therefore, you must learn how to control it so that you can lead a happier, more fulfilled life.

Why the Empathic Experience is Different than a Conscious Experience

Take a moment and consider the way that you would learn a new skill. To keep things simple, imagine how you would learn to throw a ball if you had no experience, as if you were a child. To learn that skill, a conscious decision is made to undergo that learning experience. Even people who are naturally inclined at sports would need to first make the conscious decision to pick up that ball and practice.

Once the decision is made, by either saying or thinking, "I want to learn how to toss a ball," the physical manifestation of the want is made. A child would start to practice throwing the ball, aiming for a target or another person. Even though the practice period may be shorter for some than others, it is always the same progression of making a conscious decision and then physically manifesting what you want into existence.

When an empath experiences emotion, it is not a learned skill. In fact, it never occurs as something conscious and willing. A child cannot decide to be an empath and then physically manifest it in their lives. This is because an empath does not make a conscious decision to feel an emotion. When you are an empath, the experience begins uncontrollably, deep within your subconscious mind. This is the reason that people who do not know they are empaths may seek medication or question what is wrong with them. They may not have healthy relationships, because they seem to lash out in anger or feel great sadness at times and cannot explain it.

You see, within the mind of an empath, the physical manifestation of the emotion that is being experienced occurs before the conscious decision to feel it. Empath's minds quickly analyze a person that is in the vicinity and then mirror their emotion, before the empath has decided that they want to feel that way. The first step to learning to control these emotions is accepting that what happens first is beyond your control. After acceptance, know that the next reaction is up to you. Once you realize what is happening within your own mind, you can start to take the steps to control it.

The section that follows will teach you those necessary skills to begin controlling your empathic nature. As you embark on this journey, know that it is a long one that requires strength and willpower. You will not be able to block out the emotions of all those around you overnight, nor will you immediately start to push the emotions of others out of your mind the moment that you experience them. Trust, however, that these abilities will come with time.

You are truly gifted as an empath and it is going to take this training for you to see it. As you read into the next section, be prepared to challenge yourself and overcome obstacles. This will not be easy - but if you want to be in control of your gift instead of it controlling you, then the long process will be well worth it when it pays off in the end.

Chapter 10 Release the immediate pain and feelings of loss

The experience of falling in love can be indescribable. You cannot tell why, cannot explain how you just feel irresistibly drawn to someone as magnets do. Little do you know when you actually get allured into leaving your goals and wishes, and even your will for what suddenly turns feeling much less like love. People are drawn onto love much more by some invisible forces than what they think, feel, and see. This strange force of attraction seems to work so naturally that the parties tend to flow along and think it is okay and in fact go their way to justify how it happened.

Codependents are naturally passive members who automatically take on the role of the follower in the relationship. On the other hand, narcissists are naturally assumed and the leadership role, deciding how and where to direct the relationship. The narcissist and the codependent, on a conscious level, feel they are matches as soulmates. However, underneath, there lie deeper and darker feelings of anger, frustration, resentment, and pain. These feelings reflect the emerging dysfunctional patterns that eventually show up.

Narcissists and codependents are brought together by psychological forces that function subconsciously, reflexively, and repetitively leading them into a long-term relationship in which they consciously experience each other irresistibly desirably. And these forces get stronger and stronger with time. The attraction is normally overwhelmingly strong for codependents. They become addicted to it. They are compelled to seek closeness with their partner with the view to soothe the intense emotional pain that has been with them since before.

People fall for unmatched romantic partners for certain characteristics of familiarity, which are actually dysfunctional relationship patterns, not so perceived at the start. The relationship we experience with our parents laid certain patterns which form the instinct that we use to judge our romantic relationships. There exists an instinctive sense of calmness, familiarity, and safety that underlines interactions between people who are having a romantic company based on a preformed and matched relationship template.

The two become infatuated or obsessed with each other, and typically involuntarily experience this as a strong desire for reciprocation of feelings, though not necessarily sexual. Lovers express each other depending on their relationship orientation. The others-relationship orientation focuses mainly on giving love, care, and respect, while the self-relationship orientation focuses on receiving care, respect, and love.

Couples often play within such a relationship in a manner that they balance their orientations and subconsciously keep an equilibrium that is autonomous, lacking in health and dysfunction. Things are not good, but they are not bad either. Compatibility in relationships is not fixed. While our personalities may differ greatly but the human spirit and psyche are capable of achieving compatibility.

It begins with developing understanding. Codependents have a deficit of self-love. They sacrifice themselves for others. Their circumstances from childhood seem to progress from attachment trauma with their caretakers, then core shame when they fail to regard themselves as worth beings, then pathological loneliness as they become withdrawn from the world, and finally addiction to relationship at a stage where they desire to find with themselves by searching for that in their partners hence not loving themselves at all - self-love deficit disorder.

By understanding the human magnet syndrome, codependents embark on their recovery journey towards self-love abundance. They need to focus on understanding and breaking away from their addictive pathological relationships. Mastering the power and control tactics used by narcissists, setting, and observing sound selfoboundaries, addressing their subconscious traumas, and moving from disregarding to embracing their self-love will help to consciously transition into self-love abundant relationships. It is not normally an easy road to travel and may take time, but such is how the biggest payoffs are worked toward.

The Codependence Dilemma

Codependent Men

Only a few men discuss their relationship problems with their friends and family. They internalize their hurts, live in denial, suffer silently, and are addicted to numbness to their needs and feelings. Rather than attract attention, they try doing the right things, being good sons, siblings, husbands, and fathers, to the extent of abandoning their duties of making a living for themselves and their wives and children and meeting their needs as well. Codependent men think that spending time away from their wives is being selfish, and that way sacrifice themselves.

Men are viewed as strong and as not having the need to express their feelings or needs and can be shamed for it. Hence they turn to addiction to cope, mainly by living in denial of their needs, suppressing their feelings, and losing control.

Men who grow up in dysfunctional families do not find safe to express their feelings and needs. It is easier to ignore criticized feelings and denied or shamed needs. Age-inappropriate duties during a man's growing are evidence of ignored childhood. This could be because the parents lacked control, irresponsible or immature in some way. Growing up amid chaos and conflicts in family forces one to exercise self-control in order to survive. This very self-control could lead you into an inactive life, avoiding extremes and seeking to live on the lowest edge.

Men who think their wives are codependent, are most likely codependent themselves too. Oftentimes codependent men embrace needy, demanding, jealous, or critical women. These men end up being dependent on the approval of their wives, whose demands, expectations, and manipulations can be trapping. Abusive, or ever demanding or unappreciative women are kept by codependent husbands. Their men cannot set boundaries and live in fear of emotional vengeance and refutation, including being denied sex.

Paradoxically too, very emotional wives can provide a sense of aliveness that compensates for the coldness that their codependent husbands harbor within. This can cheer up a man in the start showing him as powerful and sensitive to his wife, who needs extra care or attention or gifts. Long after he has conformed to her expectations, assured of her loyalty, he realizes it never gets enough satisfying her. She could simply be desperate or addicted to something and will keep desiring more of it all the time.

Workaholic men try to justify themselves for time alone, but leave their need for nurturing, freedom, respect, appreciation, etc. unmet. There is the caliber of men who stick around their wives physically but withdraw into emotional bubbles then become resented for feeling trapped or controlled. The wives are no cause in this case, but the man's own codependence tendencies.

Naturally, a wife who often wants more intimacy from her man brings him to therapy. She wants him to open up and share his feelings freely. While the man is fully capable of communicating his feelings, setting healthy boundaries, and being just assertive, he reacts to criticism and demands by fighting back, withdrawing, or endlessly apologizing for sufficient reasons.

Some codependent men endure abuse from their wives because they know they will not be believed by authorities calling their wives abusive. Occasionally, their wives do or threaten to lie instead, accusing their victim partners of the violence. The man then chooses to keep it secret, silently suffering from the inside.

Addicted Men are codependent. Whether it is alcohol, drug, gambling, food, sex, or work, that is what they turn to for modulation of their attitude and self-esteem.

Codependency in Women

More women than men are codependent. The following are some of the reasons for it.

Biologically, women thrive on relationships. They are more sensitive to feelings, and they bond more easily and deeply. Under stress, they seek to care for children and make friendships. Men prepare for attack when stressed. Women prepare to love and be loved instead.

Women are more emotionally involved with their parents and, therefore, husbands. Losing a relationship is most painful to them. Threats of separation create a lot of anxiety for them, and autonomy is not something they naturally prefer.

Generally, also, women are subordinate to men in terms of handling money, entitlement to rights, and access to power. They have learned to be compliant in these ways. They endure more trauma and abuse than men, hence acquiring lower self-esteem by default.

Men are generally more drawn toward independence and autonomy than women. Women are more restricted and do not have more natural willingness and power to fight for their certain freedoms. Women are also granted less opportunity for independent life progress.

Overcoming Childhood Emotional Negligence

Childhood emotional negligence happens when parents are unable to respond to their child's emotional needs adequately. This sets up a child for codependence growing up into adulthood. Most codependence cases arise from this childhood emotional negligence or at least stem from events that happen in one's earlier days of life. So how should one handle this when they realize it?

1. Acknowledge how it occurred and how it affected you

Ask yourself whether the negligence was on the part of one or both parents. See whether they were struggling with something themselves, or whether they were just selfish to you. Think of whether they neglected you actively or passively, and whether they portray generosity or meanness in the course of it. Then acknowledge how that has affected you in your adult life. This will help you to shift from shame and self-blame and validate your experience.

2. Realize that you still have your feelings

Your emotions are with you. You might only have been cautious earlier to protect yourself and tried to suppress them, but they are still accessible. You can reach them and use them to manage them.

3. Recognize your feelings

The emotions that you grew up with actually are the opposite of what you need to feel. With care and attentiveness, whenever you detect your emotion, ask whether it resembles what you learned growing up and reach for the opposite of it. Where you feel vulnerable, you are strong. You are not unworthy, you have high self-esteem, etc. Honor your authentic feelings and intuition. You are right to trust your feelings and act according to them.

4. Grow your tolerance

Learn to sit with painful or strong feelings while focusing on acting not by them but by your sober judgment. This how you begin to overcome the negativity you have already been carrying by now.

5. Monitor your changing likes and dislikes

Write down your daily happenstances of likes and dislikes and detail them just adequately, however big, or small. This will start to guide you on how to make yourself happier under given any circumstances.

6. Develop and practice self-compassion

You are most like kinder to others than to yourself. But start to realize that you have rights equally as the others. Do not be harsh on yourself for your mistakes and failures. Handle yourself with care, as you do to others. Build your self-love.

7. Be sensitive to anger

Anger is the one emotion which, when blocked or over-expressed, will eat you up. Find a way to release it moderately, and you will soon be soothed and empowered against it.

8. Learn to be assertive

This is important when you have to deal with emotions of anger. Let people know your needs, feelings, and opinions. Do not hold back. Respect yourself by speaking up, and you will be respected too.

Characteristics of a Mindful Relationship

Let us begin out by describing a healthy relationship using a few, some even subtle details.

1. You know each other's best friends of either gender and can point out positive things about them, including their importance in your partner's life.

2. You are playful with each other.

3. You think your partner has constructive ideas and actually regard them positively, even trying them out.

4. You admire more in your partner and wish to take on more of their values for your better being.

5. You know your partner has valuable facts and points, though you may not be agreeable to all of them.

6. You always think of each other even when physically distant and away.

7. You find total trust in your partner.

8. You find your partner more attractive relationship-wise than themselves or others do.

9. You admire the growth your partner has exhibited ever since you met and are happy about it.

10. Your partner is optimistic about your successes and becomes enthusiastic when you achieve more in your life.

11. You see the positive things about each other first before pointing on what negatives that need change or improvement.

12. You think about your past together and are happy and find them admirable even in the current moment.

13. You know your partners' favorite book and what it is about, as well as what it says about them.

14. You know your partner's goals, objectives, and aspirations in life.

15. You still remember with fondness some new and challenging task you went through some time in the past.

16. You kiss every day.

17. You are comfortable telling your partner about your worries and vulnerabilities and can listen to their bit too – and share on how you can help each other in such moments.

18. You have a love language between yourselves and are aware of personalized gestures that fit for each other.

19. You know the embarrassments your partner has come through from their childhood.

20. You know the proudest moments from their childhood.

21. You rarely show contempt in your partner, e.g. by rolling your eyes, sneering, swearing them, or labeling or calling them names.

22. You know the positive traits that your partner inherited from their parents.

A healthy relationship is worked at. It does not happen by itself or by default. The couple can mindfully work together to elevate their relationship status in the following ways.

Couples who like disconnecting from their gadgets and be in the moment with each other by focusing and looking onto each other exclusively when they are together are mindful of their relationship. They listen actively to each other with eyes, ears, body, and heart. They cease what they are thinking and listen to what their partner has to say. They listen with curiosity and ask questions in order to get every detail and make their partner know they understand.

You create time to think of the moments you make each other happy and feel gratitude for them. Feeling grateful sets your minds and hearts for more happy moments to come. You enjoy moments of silence together. You do not always have to be talking to connect. You still hear each out without in your silence. You do not react to each other with anger. You consciously factor each other feelings in exchanges and take steps to maintain a rational tone and thought process through hard conversations.

You envision your future interactions together and set out goals and targets on what you are going to do in the course of time to get their someday. Such goals include each other's growth or fun moments to come. You also engage in caring actions to make each other feel good and happy about themselves and have made a commitment to do specific special things on a regular basis, e.g. buying flowers or holding hands.

Mindfulness in relationships includes daily appreciation. You take your turns every evening to be grateful for what each of you has done or said or thought or is planning. You take time to explain the details of it and how that makes you happy or feel special or loved in each other's care. Do spend time to gaze in each other's eyes and notice how stronger your bonds will grow with time.

Whenever you first see each other, after a few hours or even minutes away, embrace before saying anything until both of you come to a point where you feel you are relaxing. It feels good relaxing in each other's arms first thing before you think of the next concerns, great or small. Breathe together. Hold each other closely like in an embrace any slow down your breaths and take breaths together, counting say to ten. It is relaxing and reassuring.

Converse mindfully too. You talk to each other with open minds and without judging each other in a way or the other. Be present throughout the conversation; however, deep or humorous the conversation gets. Mindfulness in relationships invokes feelings of compassion too. Consider how much your partner has endured reaching where they are in life as well as many sacrifices they have made to be with you in spite of their demanding careers or extended family needs.

Practice mindfulness meditation together. Meditate together. Find one from YouTube, or download onto your phone and play it as you together take in the exercise. It creates a connection point between the two of you that is deeper than anyone could possibly explain. Mindful touching is good for both of you. Create time to be touching each other in an intentional manner. Be fully present and purposeful with what you are doing.

Finally, always think before you speak. Think about what you want to say, and make sure you are clear with what you want your partner to know and the kind of response they could give or associated action. Beware of your feelings and emotions, too, and make sure you package your communications in a way that is easily receivable, understandable, and actionable. Whatever the communication, you must seek to foster the strength of your bond than end up at the exchange alone.

Chapter 11 Release and heal the connection to the Narcissist

Before we address some advice for dealing with a narcissist and the aftermath of abuse, it is important that we outline some of the key indicators that you are indeed suffering from narcissistic abuse syndrome.

The first and foremost signal to yourself that you are suffering from dealing with a narcissist in a toxic relationship is the persistent feeling that you are alone. If you come home each day and see your boyfriend, eat meals with your boyfriend, sit in front of a TV with your boyfriend, then go to bed next to a boyfriend, but still feel like you've spent the whole day alone, it's because you might be dealing with a narcissist who is only presenting to you a mirage of the relationship you thought you were living. There is an absence of feeling underneath the actions that leave you feeling lost, confused, and very lonely. If you feel this constantly and are unsure of where the feeling came from, this may be a sign of narcissistic abuse syndrome.

If you are constantly struggling with the feeling that you are just not good enough for anyone, especially your boyfriend/partner, then you may be suffering from narcissistic abuse syndrome. Narcissists are very good at tearing down their victims' self-esteem and convincing them through both subtle and not-so-subtle strategies that they are messing things up, constantly making mistakes, etc. They may make fun of you and laugh at you or mock you and make you feel small. This abuse leads you to believe that you are worthless and that you would never be good enough for anything you want to accomplish in life.

You may feel suffocated by the relationship itself as your narcissist partner attempts to hijack your personal life and everything that existed before he/she entered your life. It is a trademark strategy of exercising control to isolate the victim from those he/she once trusted and loved. It is the narcissist's goal to make him/herself the only person you lean on for anything kind of support.

Another sign of narcissistic abuse syndrome is the realization that you've become a different person in terms of belief systems, morals, principles, or other characteristics which were once at the core of who you are. If your partner has managed to change these essential things about you and they don't seem right, it is a sign that you've got some toxic forces at work doing everything they can to make you into a different person that serves the purposes of only the narcissist.

Narcissists often utilize outright name-calling in an effort to belittle and gradually break down a victim's sense of self-worth. This practice may not be overt in the beginning, but instead, be framed as a kind of joke and kidding by the narcissist. He may say while giggling, "You're just overreacting because you're too sensitive." Comments like these may seem innocent at first, but over time with persistent use, these things can be internalized by the victim until the accusations became a reality for them. They may start to believe these things which at first they didn't feel were affecting them in any damaging way.

Finally, the cycle of something called "hurt and rescue" can take such a toll on a victim as to lead to life-long emotional anxieties and struggles. With this technique, the narcissist introduces stress through an event or an argument or an accusation and then gives the victim the silent treatment for a certain amount of time. They may use a tactic other than the silent treatment, but whatever they choose to do, the object is to relieve that stress or silence it for an amount of time. The silent treatment, when used in this way, triggers a fear of abandonment that is innate in pretty much every human being out there. This makes it an inescapable strategy to induce pain, as long as the victim feels attachment and emotion for the perpetrator.

The rescue stage entails the perpetrator coming back and relieving that fear of abandonment, but now, the victim has learned to be afraid whenever the cycle starts again, anticipating that period of staged abandonment, or silence.

Over time, this technique becomes a powerful strategy for control and manipulating behaviors because the feelings associated with abandonment can be so strong and hurtful. Each one of us is hardwired to crave attention, love, and affection, so when someone offers this then abruptly takes it away, we learn to do whatever we need to do to avoid having that attachment leave us again, even if it means apologizing for something we didn't even do, much to the narcissist's delight.

When you feel sure you are dealing with a narcissist in a romantic relationship, you need to seek support in getting out and away as soon as possible. Educate yourself on the tactics used by narcissists to keep that feeling of attachment in you and do everything you can to resist it and break free. Remind yourself again and again that it's all been an act and nothing you were feeling attached to is real.

If you are dealing with a narcissist who is not a romantic partner but still an unavoidable part of your life, your best defense is going to be constant awareness and alertness to any schemes and manipulation the narcissist may be trying to employ on you. It would be unwise to start an all-out war on the narcissist since his whole being is centered on crushing others and he will surely be able to invest more time and emotional energy into hurting you than you will in hurting him. Besides, you're not that kind of person!

Even though you may feel anger, letting your guard down and losing control is exactly what the narcissist wants you to do, so do not give him the satisfaction.

As always, strength in numbers is a good rule of thumb to follow. If you are feeling vulnerable or susceptible to a narcissist in your purview, recruit others to support you and help form a barrier. Let the narcissist know that you are too smart to fall for his schemes and that you are not going to give an inch. Create a thick skin around yourself and prepare for some demeaning insults designed to rile you up. You don't have to give in to these. Form your support group and move on with your life. When the narcissist sees that you've all but become immune to his charms, he will look elsewhere and leave you alone. Be on the lookout for others whom he may be targeting and be sure to let them know what's going on if you think they are also in danger. This will probably trigger a defensive response, but the key is to maintain your composure and remind yourself of your reality and your standing. Don't buy into the narcissist portraying himself as more than what he is. Inside, he is just an insecure little boy trying to validate himself through other people's praises. He does not have power over you or those you love. You are stronger than this person because you know the strength and power of genuine love and affection.

Chapter 12 Speaking your truth to the family and community

Exploitative and lacking empathy, narcissists are masters at manipulating others. They frequently have several tactics they employ in order to manipulate their targets, and the most effective and common of the tactics will be provided in this chapter. Through reading these tactics, you will find yourself better prepared to recognize when a narcissist or other person is attempting to manipulate you. When armed with the knowledge, you will be able to step away from the mind games altogether in order to avoid falling into the narcissist's manipulative traps.

Mirroring

Perhaps one of the most important of the tactics employed by narcissists is mirroring. In this, the narcissist creates a persona that she believes will be desirable to others. This persona is created to hide behind that enables her to pretend to be someone she is not. After all, her true self as a narcissist would be largely undesirable to all and would mark her as a social pariah. Because of this, she seeks to create a persona.

This is done by reflecting or mirroring back the person the narcissist is trying to win over. This can be done through picking up mannerisms or quirks that the other person exhibits, or deciding that her favorite food, color, television drama, animal, and preference in music are the same as yours in order to make you seem more common. She sees you as being someone to envy, and because of that, she attempts to mimic as much about you as she can. She wants to be whatever it was within you that attracted her attention in the first place. While some degree of mirroring is normal in human behavior to create rapport between each other, narcissists take this to an entirely different level. The narcissist wants to make it seem like you and she has more in common. You will naturally be attracted to people with similar likes, interests, and preferences as yourself, so she aims to become the ultimate mirror to attract you.

The reason for this manipulative behavior is because narcissists fail to develop their own stable sense of self. Because they lack that sense of who they are and are so fragile and fractured, they seek to mirror others. If someone is attracted to the narcissist for some reason, he or she must be worth mirroring, and the narcissist does just that. They create their mirror image in hopes of earning what the other person has, and to fake a relationship. Since the narcissist lacks the capacity for empathy, the closest thing she can do is mirror the other person, essentially erasing her own self in favor of seeing the world as someone else.

Projecting

Projecting is essentially mirroring, but it works the other way around. Instead of pretending to be someone else, the narcissist projects himself onto the other person. Typically, the projection is something true about the narcissist that the narcissist is desperately trying to deny, so he instead projects that part of him onto other people. That allows him to live in denial that he is the problem and allows him the reality he believes.

These projections are typically either positive or negative, depending on the narrative the narcissist is trying to portray, and there is rarely anything in between. The narcissist is usually projecting some of his own behaviors or his feelings toward himself onto other people in order to cope with the feelings or behaviors. For example, consider a narcissist who accuses an employee of trying to steal credit for work he did when in reality, the narcissist has been stealing credit for ages. Likewise, if you are in a relationship with a narcissist and he has a tendency of engaging in demeaning or abusive behavior, he may be quick to call you abusive if you ever upset him.

This tactic has a particularly useful benefit to the narcissist: When he projects negatively, he almost immediately puts the other person on the defensive, which detracts attention from his own transgressions. Because the other person suddenly feels the need to prove that the narcissist is wrong, attention is on the other person, and the narcissist is free to continue on his way, never changing his behaviors. This leaves the other person feeling as though he or she is walking on eggshells while focusing intently on proving the narcissist wrong.

This behavior is also often exhibited by narcissistic parents on their children. They project onto their children, creating either a scapegoat or a projection of a golden child. The scapegoat represents everything wrong with the narcissist and serves as an outlet for all of the self-loathing that narcissists frequently internalize. If the narcissist is sensitive about intelligence issues, he may insist that the scapegoat is stupid and incapable, no matter how smart the scapegoat may be in reality. In contrast, the golden child is everything the narcissist loves or wants to be. The golden child can do no wrong and is oftentimes spoiled and coddled. The golden child frequently feels pressure to obey the parents at all costs in fear of losing the golden status, while the scapegoat constantly vies for any scraps of affection or acknowledgment. The scapegoat never receives this, and ultimately spends time uselessly trying to better his or her parent's opinions. Both the scapegoat and the golden child are seen not as people, but as blank screens for the narcissist to project onto, and because of that, neither gets the opportunity to grow and flourish.

Playing the Victim

Especially for vulnerable narcissists, playing the victim is one of the most effective methods to manipulate others. Oftentimes, these narcissists will try to get something they want, and when denied, they turn things around to make themselves the victim. For example, if a narcissistic mother-in-law wants more access to grandchildren and you hesitate, she may cry to her own child that the grandchildren know their other grandmother so much better, and say how much of a shame it is that they will never get the chance to know her before she dies. She may also point out how the grandchildren's other parent must clearly hate her for restricting access so much, and that if she is such a big burden, she will no longer bother trying to see the kids. Oh, and be sure to let them know how much she loves them and wishes she could see her grandchildren more.

This entire diatribe is spewed in order to make you sympathize with her and feel as though you have to give her what she wants in order to make her feel better. She words things in such a way that makes it seem as though she is the victim when in reality, the reason that she is restricted from the grandchildren is that she would not stop stomping over boundaries and lavishing the children in candy while telling them to keep secrets from their parents about things they did.

Love Bombing

Despite how pleasant love bombs may sound, they are quite manipulative. They seek to create a sort of addiction to the one showering you in affection. In many of the non-familial, non-workplace relationships with narcissists, love bombing is a frequent favorite tactic. Narcissists rely on this tactic in order to create and bolster feelings of love and attachment to them in order to manipulate their targets into being more receptive to abuse in the future. It is meant to make them look more desirable to the target and draw the target in closer. As the love bombing continues, the target craves contact with the narcissist, focusing on the good feelings earned when being showered with gifts.

These gifts could be anything, ranging from thoughtful little trinkets that show that the narcissist was listening to you when you were talking, too expensive, high-end items you feel wrong for accepting, especially so early into the relationship. He may invite you on exotic vacations or take you on cruises, and even if you resist initially, he will insist that you accept.

As time passes, the love bombing increases in frequency, and you may find yourself reflecting on the situation, trying to decide if the gifts are overbearing or thoughtful and romantic. He wants you to develop a close attachment to him, and these trinkets are nothing if they will award him your affection and loyalty.

Triangulating

As implied by the name, triangulation involves three different people. Typically, it is the narcissist in the middle of a situation with two others. When engaging in triangulation, the narcissist creates a conflict intentionally between the other two people. This usually involves giving each person a slightly different story that puts the other person at fault. This encourages conflict between the two other people and allows the narcissist to sit back and watch the chaos without any blame. As the two bicker and fight, they are too focused on each other to focus on what actually happened, and a wedge is forced between the two of them. This is especially useful when a narcissist needs to sever an alliance or friendship.

For example, imagine a case in which there is a friend group consisting of the narcissist that we will name Allie for easy reference, and a friend named Brittany, and a friend named Callie. Both Callie and Brittany have a crush on the same person, who we will call Dave, and each has confided this crush in Allie, though they have not told each other yet because they know the other person also likes Dave. Callie and Brittany are great friends and Allie is the new person in the friend group. One day, Callie is hanging out with Allie alone, and she makes mention that Brittany had told her that

Callie is interested Dave, but Brittany wants him too and had planned on telling Callie that Dave hates how she looks so she would not try to pursue him. Immediately, Callie feels annoyed at the situation and she tries to keep her distance from Brittany because she feels hurt and betrayed. Meanwhile, Allie hangs out with Brittany, who casually mentions that Callie has been keeping her distance and that she hopes Callie is okay. Allie tells Brittany that Callie had been planning on telling Brittany that Dave does not like her or how she talks in hopes of deterring her from pursuing Dave.

This leaves both Brittany and Callie upset at each other and unwilling to speak about the situation. Because they are both so overwhelmed with their feelings of betrayal, neither think that they should stop and consider why the other would ever do such a thing, and they each hang out with Allie individually. Allie is happy because she no longer feels as though she needs to fight with another person to get her narcissistic supply.

Gaslighting

While all manipulation is wrong, gaslighting is especially heinous in its own way. Gaslighting involves convincing the other person that he or she is perceiving reality incorrectly, causing doubt in his or her sanity. The name for this type of manipulation comes from the play published in 1938 called Gas Light, which involved a man convincing his wife that the lights in their home are not dimming every time he goes to an area of the home that is blocked off and turns on the light. When she questions him about the lights dimming, he insists that they never did, and she begins to doubt her own sanity.

Narcissists employ this when they want to deny the existence or occurrence of something that they know would ruin them. For example, the narcissist will deny any claims that she had said something cruel, telling her target that in reality, he had said those cruel things to him. Over time, with plenty of unwavering insistence from the narcissist, the target begins to believe her. As soon as this begins and he starts to doubt his own perceptions, he becomes more easily manipulated, as all she has to do is remind him that he is wrong and things happened another way. Over time, he takes that as evidence that he is losing his sanity, and trusts her at her word. He begins to doubt everything that happens and everything that he believes happened because he feels as though his own perceptions are no longer trustworthy, and he will default to whatever the narcissist says.

Intimidating

When all else fails, the narcissist will resort to intimidation. This can be physical or verbal and can range from veiled threats hidden behind plausible deniability, such as saying that you will not like what happens if you do not obey, to overt threats such as threatening to hurt you or take your children away if you do not stop and listen. He will use everything you told him in confidence to hurt you or threaten you into obedience, and may even resort to punching doors, throwing dishes at walls, or engaging in other risky and dangerous behavior to prove that he is deadly serious in hopes of scaring you into submission. He may even physically hurt you to teach you a lesson. He wants you to fear the consequences of disobeying or denying him what he desires, and like you are better off putting up with the narcissist's behaviors instead of attempting to leave because it is easier to stomach.

Insulting and Belittling

Similar to intimidating, narcissists will frequently insult, belittle, or demean anything that you do. Narcissists thrive on making other people miserable as it boosts their own egos, and he loves to validate his own existence and skills by making you doubt yours. He will often fling insults at you, and when you feel annoyed by it and call him out, he will laugh it off and tell you it was a joke that you should not take so seriously.

By laughing and claiming it was a joke and that you are being too sensitive, the narcissist is making you feel insecure. You feel bad for being offended and feel bad that the implication of being bad at something was enough to make you feel offended, leaving you striving to do better and more in hopes of pleasing the narcissist. For example, if the narcissist claims that you are awful at playing his favorite video game and that you are not good enough to play with him, even casually, you may seriously work toward becoming better at the game in order to win the acknowledgment that would come with learning to play better. Unfortunately, however, the narcissist is never satisfied, and no matter how hard you may try to please him, he will never be wholly satisfied with who you are. There will always be something else to insult, and even if there is nothing left, he will make something else up instead.

Lying and False Promises

Narcissists have a tendency to lie if it suits them. If they do something that upsets you, they will lie and say they did not mean to hurt you and they will never do it again. These false promises keep you clinging to hope that the future will be better, when in reality; the narcissist has no interest in changing or bettering his behavior. So long as the narcissist was thorough enough in the love bombing stage, the target is so enamored with the idea of the person he was in the early stages that the target will overlook those transgressions. Unfortunately to the target, however, that persona was little more than an act and as soon as it was no longer needed to win over the person of choice, that persona was discarded.

The narcissist may apologize and attempt to do better if you make it clear that you are done with the abuse and mistreatment and that you are leaning toward ending the relationship altogether. His promise might not mean much, but when you see him bringing back that person you fell in love with, you may be more willing to overlook it. You want to believe that the narcissist is a good person and can change. Unfortunately, that change is only temporary and will not last. Because the narcissist lacks empathy and does not see how it could possibly benefit him, he sees no reason to go beyond the bare minimum to keep you interested in him.

FOG (Fear, Obligation, Guilt)

Narcissists frequently let their victims get lost in the FOG in the relationship. Just like how in real fog, it is impossible to see or navigate safely or effectively, navigating the FOG is incredibly difficult. When lost in FOG, you struggle to see that some of the behaviors are dangerous or unhealthy, and your ability to evaluate your relationship is clouded and obscured. FOG stands for fear, obligation, and guilt, and narcissists love getting their victims stuck and lost in it.

When you are afraid of a relationship or situation, you are much more likely to be obedient simply due to self-preservation. Narcissists know that and they want you to be afraid. Fear is a response to danger, and you react in whatever way will make that danger disappear, even if it means going along with things you never wanted to do.

The obligation is not necessarily as negative as fear: We feel obligated to people we love and feel loyalty toward. When we love or are loyal to someone, we feel a certain sense of duty to make sure they are happy, safe, and protected. The narcissist preys upon these feelings of obligation and showers you with gifts and affection to win your affection. Once he has won that spot in your inner circle of friends and family, he knows he can start to tap into your feelings of obligation and use it as a way to manipulating you into doing things in the name of love. After all, if you loved him, you would be willing to do it because you know how much it means to him. In non-romantic relationships, this could involve a relative asking for money or help with childcare with a reminder that family always takes care of its own, or a friend reminding you of that time she bought you something to get you to pay for an expensive meal.

The guilt is employed when the narcissist can see that you are resisting giving in to the sense of obligation. At this stage, the narcissist will blame you for any negative consequences. If he cheated on you because you were unwilling to spend time with him, it is your fault for driving him to that loneliness and had you only been willing to give him whatever he had been asking for, he would not have felt the need to go feel validated with someone else. The person who needed help with childcare may blame you if he loses his job due to not having someone to watch the children.

FOG is frequently employed when the narcissist is grasping at straws. This is a bit more of a long-term manipulation tactic that requires plenty of effort to maintain, as the narcissist must always have something that can be held over your head. This could be the narcissist threatening to take custody of children, or a family member withholding inheritance money.

DARVO (Deny, Attack, and Reverse Victim and Offender)

Yet another acronym, DARVO stands for denies, attack, and reverses victim and offender. This is a common reaction when narcissists feel called out. This technique has three steps that follow in a specific order. First, the narcissist denies the claim against him. Next, he attacks the accuser with a statement intended to put the accuser on the defensive. Lastly, he reverses the victim and offender by painting himself as the victim. This manipulation tactic puts the accuser on defensive and removes attention from him.

For example, imagine confronting your narcissistic friend about never being there for you. You may see the following dialogue:

You: "You are never there for me when I need you."

Friend: That's not true. But remember when I fell and broke my foot? You never came to help me. No matter how hard I try, I am never good enough for you and you never want to help me when you feel like I'm an inconvenience."

You can see how, in this dialogue, the narcissist twisted the situation around to benefit her. She denied, and then attacked you with an accusation of not coming to her help when she needed it, and then made herself the victim.

The Silent Treatment

Perhaps more than anything else, narcissists fear a lack of attention. The ultimate lack of attention, to a narcissist, is the silent treatment, and when you have done something that the narcissist is not happy with, she is quick to dole out the silent treatment to make that unhappiness as obvious as possible. Knowing that the ultimate insult to the narcissist is the silent treatment, that is how she goes about showing her displeasure. She seeks to because you distress by ignoring your very existence, looking past you and refusing to even acknowledge you are there. You may not even know why it is happening, but you are left confused and hurt by the exchange or lack thereof, and when the silent treatment is ended, the narcissist comes back as if nothing ever happened. This is especially hurtful in romantic relationships, as you are suddenly dropped, and you do not even have an explanation for why or an idea of whether it is your partner looking for space or ending the relationship entirely. You are left in a sort of emotional limbo as you wait to see if the narcissist will ever return to you.

Chapter 13 Speaking your truth to the family and community

After the storm, when the waves of the emotional seas calm down a little bit, and you can feel a new attitude and outlook on your life, you may still have a lot of work to do to help yourself recover from your awakened awareness of the situation. If you are someone who has chosen to stay in your relationship with your partner because you want to heal yourself from within that dynamic, then some of this chapter will not be as helpful for you.

When you are in a narcissistic abuse situation, the best recourse is to remove yourself to gain insight. Surviving a narcissistic relationship and staying with a partner who suffers from this personality disorder can be a very one-sided battle that you will fight alone, and you will have to decide what is most important for you in your relationship with yourself.

Breaking away from the patterns of the narcissistic abuse cycle is best achieved by letting go and moving on, as you read in Even if you have ties that keep you together, like children or other matters, you can still succeed and thrive after the storm has calmed and you have moved forward and onward. To fully heal from the cycles of abuse, the toxic patterns of narcissistic partnership, and the emotional manipulation you endured, you will have to do a lot of personal growth work to support your choice and remove any doubts in making the right choice. Being mentally manipulated for some time is not without its damaging side-effects, and it could take some time for you to end the emotional upheaval you experienced.

The person you were involved with may still try to convince you that you have something special and that you are making a huge mistake, or you may find yourself head over heels with another partner soon after you end your relationship, who also happens to be a narcissist, but you weren't able to see the red flags because of how close you still are to those behaviors, thoughts, and emotional patterns.

This chapter will serve as a motivation for you to heal the patterns of narcissistic abuse and relationships so that you can seek out a healthier relationship with yourself and someone else in your future.

After You Walk Away
After you walk away from a narcissistic partnership, you may go through several feelings of doubt, uncertainty, "but what-ifs," and all sorts of highs and lows that will want you to question whether or not you have made the right choice. You will always have to work out your version of what happened in your relationship with your partner, and they are not going to be willing or able to face the trauma you experienced. Your narcissistic partner won't even care that you are or were in pain or that you felt emotionally abused, and so anything that comes up and suggests that you are doing something wrong or making the wrong choice by leaving your partner is just more of the toxic reality of being a victim of narcissistic abuse rearing its head.

The following guidelines will help you stay focused on getting through the hard parts of walking away and how to continue healing the patterns of the narcissistic relationship and cycles of abuse.

1. Process your emotions.

Spending time with your feelings, honoring them, labeling them, and acknowledging your experiences and the events of your relationship will help you manage the reality of what you experienced more efficiently and effectively. When you can explore what happened from a distance, instead of from the confines of the relationship, you will have a clearer perspective. You can even try to imagine how it would look if it happened to someone else, like a friend or a colleague, to help you see more objectively and process your feelings from a variety of angles.

Using a journal or notebook, seeking counseling, and asking for support in a group can also help you process your emotions more effectively so that you don't have floods of feelings or doubts about your process as you change course and create a new life for yourself.

2. Keep it personal and try not to generalize.

It would be very easy to become cynical and embittered about anyone in the world after an experience of narcissistic abuse, and creating a shield of armor to prevent further issues can be even more damaging. The tendency might be to generalize the situation to say, "all women are control freaks," or "all men are manipulative masochists," but that is simply not the case or the answer to your healing dialogue. Take time to reflect on the situation as a personal experience and not the assumption of all society, all men, all women, or all of anything.

3. A little self-compassion goes a long way.

You may no longer be offering yourself compassion. How could you be after living with a narcissist who is the antithesis of compassion and empathy? Pitying yourself or being overly critical of your experience will keep you locked in patterns of self-abuse, the learned behavior of emotional manipulation you gained in your relationship. The antidote to those feelings is self-compassion, which could take some practice at first, but a little goes a long way and will add up over time, supporting you in a much healthier way.

Be kind and try not to judge yourself too much. Be understanding that you are not a fool for getting involved with someone like that; they are incredibly charming and warm when you first get to know them and incredibly skilled at convincing you of anything. You are not an idiot or a fool. So, just be kind and understanding in the face of the narcissistic aftermath.

Recognize that thousands of people find themselves in these circumstances and that you are one of many people who were a victim of narcissistic abuse. We all have lessons to learn, and we are all working with ourselves and the people in our lives to figure it all out.

4. The high-road is the road to take.

Reacting to your narcissistic ex is not always easy to avoid, especially when they are provoking you and looking for a fight just to prove a point. Take the high road in every situation. It may feel awkward and uncomfortable at the moment because you have to put with their antics, but you will find a sense of relief, calm, and responsibility for your emotional agility when you choose the path that reflects a more grounded, resourceful, and wise individual.

Everything in recovery and moving forward is a stepping stone. It may feel like a long-haul, but every choice that you make every day to help yourself let go and move forward healthily is what takes you to the path you truly want to be on, as you create a happier and more fulfilling life for yourself.

Know the Flags

A great way to keep yourself out of the patterns of narcissistic coupling and abuse is to make sure you know and understand what all of the flags are.

If you are recovering from this type of a relationship, you will be much more likely to spot a flag from a mile away, but even still, narcissists can be incredibly cunning and slippery and are willing to do whatever it takes to convince you they are 100 percent compatible with you.

Researching your experience and finding out all of the specific experiences as you process, journal, and speak to a therapist will help you prevent a future narcissistic relationship. Watch out for the following flags as you meet new people and embrace new romances:

- Idolizing you in front of friends and family to an extreme degree
- Love-bombing
- Whirl-wind getaways in a very short time
- Promising things and not sticking to those promises

- Having manic episodes of extreme love expressions (think Tom Cruise jumping onto Oprah's sofa)
- Excessive sexual needs
- The subtle devaluing of your efforts or feelings
- Not taking the blame for anything
- Never apologizing
- Expecting your love without offering much in return

This list is just the beginning before things get worse, and you don't want them to get worse, so heading it off at the pass with these first few red flags is a good plan. Some relationships that are healthy and stable start with a powerful and romantic bang, however, some excessive love demands can lead you toward knowing that you are dealing with a narcissist and this book is your answer to making sure you understand how that looks.

Seek Help
You are not alone, and many people have experienced or are experiencing what you are going through. Don't be afraid to ask for help and find a support system to offer you what you need to stay balanced, secure, and self-confident in your choices and journey forward.

It has never been your fault that the person you are in a relationship with doesn't understand their disorder or issue, and even if you were capable of enabling it for a long period of time, you are certainly capable of healing from it and learning how not to repeat the same patterns over and over again.

Help is always available and all around you. If you cannot get to a public support group, or feel comfortable talking to friends and family about it, go online and look for more resources. Find an anonymous group to join if you want to protect your identity. Ask other people what it was like for them and how their recovery process is going. You will learn so much by simply reaching out for help and letting it clear your fears that you are somehow at fault for your experience.

As you move forward, use this chapter to help refresh your decision. All it takes is awareness and courage, as you let go of the narcissistic relationship. Empowering yourself to enjoy your life more through a balanced partnership is what any person deserves, and you are on the right track to getting there. Heal the patterns so that they are broken and cannot be repeated by offering yourself kindness, staying personal with your journey, process your emotions regularly, take the high road, know the red flags of the narcissist, and seek help whenever you feel like you need support.

You are on your way to becoming the confident, happy, and balanced person you always knew you are and could be. Learning to survive the narcissistic relationship may seem hard at first, but you have all of the tools that you need to accept your story and begin the healing journey.

Chapter 14 Relationships With A Narcissist

Codependency and narcissism are two sides to the same coin. They both lack healthy senses of self and they both struggle with defining who they are, bringing a whole barrage of issues to the table. Ultimately, codependency and narcissism are two different reactions to similar situations. Whereas the narcissist learns to be overtly selfish, the codependent learns to be overtly selfless. However, they are not always strictly opposites, and in some cases, the two can overlap to some degree; someone can exhibit codependent behaviors in certain situations while behaving narcissistically in other contexts. For example, someone could be very codependent in a marriage or relationship, seeking out to cater to their spouse's every whim, but be quite narcissistic with other people, such as friends or strangers. Though narcissism and codependence are both quite different, their root cause is the same.

What is Codependency?

In many normal relationships, we develop dependent relationships. This means that we prioritize our partners and rely on each other for love and in times we need support. The relationship is mutually beneficial, and neither person worries about expressing their true emotions. In a dependent relationship, both people are able to enjoy time spent away from the relationship while still meeting each other's needs.

However, in a codependent relationship, the codependent feels as though his only worth comes from being needed. He will make huge sacrifices, martyring himself out in order to ensure that the other person's needs are met. He only feels worthy if he is able to be needed. He exists solely for the relationship and feels as though he is worthless outside of that relationship. The relationship is his only identity, and he will cling to it at all costs, and within that relationship, he will ignore his own needs and wants, feeling as though they are unimportant.

Someone with codependent tendencies will struggle to detach from his partner because his entire sense of self is wrapped up in aiding that other person. It may get so bad that it begins to negatively impact the codependent's life. The codependent relationship can become all-consuming, taking over the person's life in all areas. Other relationships can weaken and fail as the codependent focuses solely on the person with which the relationship is held. Career potential may be lost, or the codependent may be fired when the relationship begins to interfere with the quality of work. Everyday responsibilities may be shirked in favor of catering to the enabler, the person with whom the codependent is in a relationship. Overall, the entire relationship is built on the faulty ground and is dysfunctional.

Causes of Codependency

Like NPD, there are many external factors that are believed to cause a codependent personality to develop. You may recognize these as being quite similar to what was discussed as causes for NPD earlier within the book. This is because both codependency and narcissism are similar personality flaws, stemming from the same root cause of damaged self-esteem.

Poor Parental Relationships

Oftentimes, people who have developed a codependent personality have grown up repeatedly having conflicts with their parents throughout childhood. Their parents may have prioritized themselves, or somehow otherwise denied that the child's needs were important. By repeatedly downplaying the child's needs, the child internalizes that those needs are not important enough to meet. After all, if the child's parents could not be bothered to tend to them, they must not matter. The child learns to prioritize his or her parents instead, and feel greedy or as though a selfish decision was made when trying to commit to self-care. Oftentimes, this kind of relationship between parent and child happens because the parent has an addiction problem and would do anything to feed the addiction, or the parent never matured past the selfish stage of development as a child and focuses solely on him or herself. Because of all the time spent focusing on the parent's needs, the child never develops the independence and identity necessary to be successful in life. Feeling incomplete when not needed, these people frequently seek out other enablers that will allow them to continue living in this fashion.

Living with Someone Dependent on Care

When a child grows up around someone else who requires frequent or around-the-clock care beyond the realm of normal, whether due to severe illness, injury, or some sort of mental illness, the child's needs may go unmet in favor of meeting more pressing ones. As the child is pushed aside in favor of the person who needs the care, the idea of the child's needs become less important to become internalized. The child may also engage in some of the care for the dependent person as well, causing his needs to be put on the backburner as he takes care of the person who literally cannot care for herself. While living with a family member that requires extra care does not necessarily cause codependency to develop on its own and many people can make it through the caregiving stage without issue, in certain circumstances and with certain personality types that are predisposed to codependent tendencies, it can become an issue. It becomes an issue in particular if the child is younger during the time there is someone dependent on care and the parent of the child has a tendency to focus entirely on the dependent instead of spending the time the child needs to grow and thrive meeting the child's needs.

Abuse

It is no surprise that abuse, regardless of physical, emotional, or sexual, leaves lasting harm on a child. While some children go on to abuse others, others may fall into a pattern of codependency. A child who is exposed to repeated abuse eventually begins to develop a coping mechanism in which she suppresses her feelings. She begins to ignore and cast aside the pain that is felt as a result of the abuse, and this ultimately teaches her to ignore her own needs later in life. This leaves her only caring about other people's needs while neglecting her own.

Abuse victims also have a tendency to seek out people with similar tendencies as the abuser as this is what is familiar. They know how to live through the abuse and understand that the relationship will often revolve around the codependent behaviors. Abusers and narcissists love codependents, as codependents will tolerate vast amounts of abuse that would make other people balk.

Key Features of Codependency

Oftentimes, codependency manifests in ways that are incredibly recognizable. Though every person is different and the behaviors will change depending on the relationship, there are several behavioral patterns associated with codependency. Knowing how to identify these will enable you to recognize when you or someone you know is exhibiting codependent tendencies. If you feel as though you yourself may be codependent, seeking the professional opinion from a trained psychologist would be a great place to start on your journey toward understanding yourself.

- Exaggerated Sense of Responsibility: Codependents frequently feel as though the weight of their loved one's actions is on their shoulders. They feel as though they are directly responsible for the actions of their partners, children, or anyone else with which they are codependent.

- Confuse Love and Pity: Codependents think that pitying and desiring to help someone is the same as love. They think that every time they feel compelled to rescue someone, they are doing it out of love instead of out of compassion for another human being.

- Doing More Than Their Fair Share: Codependents have a tendency to bear the burden of work, even when the share is more than unfair. They feel as though they have to take the burden in order to support or protect their enabler, who typically is more than happy to allow the codependent to do so, even when it may be detrimental to the codependent to take that added burden.

- Sensitive When Good Deeds are Unrecognized: When a codependent feels as though her efforts have gone ignored, she is likely to feel hurt or as though she was not good enough. She will try to further martyr herself in order to get the recognition she craves to soothe her low self-esteem and prove that she matters.

- Feeling Guilty When Caring for Self: Any time the codependent engages in acts she may see as selfish or unnecessary in the grand scheme of things, she will feel guilty. After all, her needs ought to be met last, and if she does anything other than that, she is behaving selfishly, and that is absolutely unacceptable to her.

- Rigid: Codependents do not tolerate change. They often seek out things that are familiar for this reason, which leads them to constantly seek out other enablers in relationships, even if those enablers prove to be abusive.

- Cannot Set Healthy Boundaries: Codependents see no boundaries between themselves and their enablers. They have no sense of self that is outside of the relationship or apart from the enabler. Because they fail to set boundaries, the relationship eventually consumes their lives and leaves little room for anything else. This lack of boundaries also leads to needs going unmet.

- Needs Recognition to Feel Whole: Without recognition for good deeds and caring for others, codependents feel unwanted and unimportant. They require people to recognize their actions in order to help bolster their fragile self-esteem.

- Need to Control Others: Codependents, feeling utterly responsible for the actions of their enablers, also seek some level of control over the relationships. Because the codependents always do everything possible for the enablers, they develop that control they desire, and the enabler allows them to have it. Without control, the codependents feel unable to help.

- Fear of Abandonment: With their sub-par self-esteem and feeling as though they have no sense of identity beyond their relationship, codependents are terrified of being abandoned. They will do anything in their power to keep the relationship going.

- Poor Decision-making Skills: Oftentimes, their dysfunctional opinion and view of their relationships make the codependents make bad decisions. These could range from refusing to leave a dangerous situation because they want to stay with their partner, or refusing to meet their needs, even if it makes them sick or gets them hurt.

- Difficulty Communicating: Codependents struggle to communicate their own needs and wants because they are so caught up in the idea that they do not matter. Even if they hate something, they will refuse to say it if they think it would be detrimental, even slightly, to the other person.

- Unhealthy Dependence on Relationship: Codependents exist solely for their relationships and enablers, and that dependence on their enablers crosses the line into the territory of dysfunction.

- Untrusting: Oftentimes due to so much dysfunction in childhood, codependents tend to distrust those around them, especially those who insist that their needs should be met or that try to point out that their relationship is unhealthy.

- Confrontation-Avoidant: Codependents avoid confrontation at all costs. They have developed their tendency to avoid their own needs due to wanting to avoid confrontation, and that tendency to avoid confrontation has extended well into adulthood. The codependent will do anything to avoid a conflict, especially with the enabler.

Codependents and Narcissists

As you have read about codependents and their tendencies, it should become obvious that codependents make the ultimate target for the narcissist. They meet each and every line on the narcissist's guide to choosing a target, and they are the ultimate victim for the narcissist. In a partnership between a codependent and a narcissist, the codependent gives endlessly to the narcissist, who needs the attention to feel loved, and the narcissist gets to give the codependent the gift of being needed. Both the narcissist and the codependent get their dysfunctional needs met. While this may seem like the perfect arrangement, it still encourages two people to live incredibly unhealthy lives. The codependent never have basic needs met and still has broken self-esteem and lacks an identity. The narcissist never gives back in the relationship and continues to live in the delusion that the narcissist is the only one that matters. The narcissist's own self-esteem and disordered thinking are not fixed through being catered to. This leads to an interesting relationship in which both the narcissist and the codependent enable each other.

Furthermore, this relationship leads to the codependent wanting to live through the narcissist. When the narcissist is not appreciative of the codependent's behaviors, which he will never be because he does not recognize other people's needs, the codependent may feel slighted or unappreciated.

Over time, these patterns may lead to resentment, but the codependent will continue trekking through the relationship, martyring her to him because that is what she feels is the right thing to do. The narcissist typically will begin to exploit the codependent more and more over time, seeking out more narcissistic supply without ever returning the sentiment with any appreciation that the codependent needs. The codependent eventually reaches a point of giving up, but despite this, neither partner is likely to leave. The narcissist loves the easy access to narcissistic supply and having someone willing to cater to his every whim, and the codependent wants to feel needed, even though there is no appreciation reciprocated. Even if the relationship teeters toward abusive, neither partner is likely to leave, nor does the relationship become even more toxic and dysfunctional.

Conclusion

Thank you for making it through to the end of Narcissistic Abuse. Let's hope it was informative and able to provide you with all of the tools you need to achieve your goals whatever they may be.

The next step is to share what you have learned with anyone else in your life or your family's and friends' lives who you think may benefit from the information on narcissistic abuse offered in this book. As I've said many times throughout this text, the most important weapon you have against narcissistic abusers is knowledge and learning how to spot them before they have a chance to harm you. If you or someone you love has experienced narcissistic abuse firsthand, I hope that the information and advice in this book have offered some degree of comfort and help as you move forward past this awful experience. People suffer each and every day at the hands of narcissistic abusers, and it is more important now than ever before that we all help spread the knowledge and tools available to defend ourselves from potential abusers. It is possible to escape, even if you've already fallen victim. Don't underestimate the power of the human mind to overcome even the most hurtful of emotional experiences. As you wake up each morning and take steps toward recovery each day, I hope you remember the encouragement and the tips offered in this book. Also, don't be afraid to get creative and realize new ways that are personally helpful that you may be able to share with others who may share in your unique experience. There are many different ways survivors can choose from on their paths to recovery. The key is to believe in yourself and trust in your instincts and gut feelings fueling you forward and past any and all symptoms of narcissistic abuse.

EMOTIONAL AND NARCISSISTIC PARTNER ABUSE

HOW TO STOP THE AGGRESSIVE NARCISSIST AND FREE HIMSELF FROM THE PSYCHOPATHIC PARTNER, TAKE BACK YOUR LIFE FROM A TOXIC RELATIONSHIP AND HEALING YOUR HEART FROM EMOTIONAL ABUSE

Introduction

Once we enter a human space, we actively and unconsciously tap into and are affected positive and negative by the feelings of others around us. This natural propensity to in synch psychologically with the other people around us is what psychologists call psychological contagion.

Instinctively we respond to the emotional tone of those around us, and all ordinary people are, to some degree, susceptible to sensitive touch.

Mental contagion and empathy the most favorable form of the emotional disease is the foundation of human empathy virtue. We need to be in emotional harmony with others to comprehend, support, and function effectively in the human social world.

The compassionate observational skills of people make them more responsive than most to the nuances of the feelings of other people. It causes them sometimes to hate others because the mass of emotional signals is all too overwhelming. But even one-on-one relationships can be a challenge for a person to read and answer the subtle, sensitive questions of others.

As HSP's own emotional reactions are intense, rapid, and difficult to shake off, they often get caught in the feelings of others. Getting attuned to the rawness of other people's emotions, like emotional contagion, can be painful and upsetting.

The danger of Codependence Because unhappiness, frustration, or misery of others is so unbearable for someone with a high degree of sensitivity, and it is easy to understand why people would be tempted to cooperate and manipulate social situations in order to keep others emotionally equal. If the need to ensure that people around them never get angry or upset, there is a risk of developing mutual dependence.

Co-dependents feel accountable to others. We feel anxious when we learn about others who are suffering and do everything, they can to ease their burdens. The tendency of co-dependents to think about others impacts their own lives. It's easy for people who depend on others, but that leads to resentment. "Stay ahead of the other's emotional curve. Because a person with sensitivity can understand what others feel so emphatically and because they're often quite skilled at recognizing and naming feelings, they're sometimes in a peculiar position to have a person. The willingness to engage in direct and open discussion of difficult subjects is an essential communication skill, both as a quality and as a practice. It is easier to tolerate some of the distress you experience may be an emotional contagion arising in others instead of in yourself.

Chapter 1 What Is Narcissistic Abuse?

Energy protection is a critical competency for all people and a vital competency for coaches but is especially essential for those of us who are incredibly energy-sensitive. As coaches, we must consider our own energy system and make ourselves more mindful of the energetic interactions between us and our world and the people in it, and of course, the active exchange between ourselves and our coaching customers. This knowledge helps us to understand the forces with which we communicate every day and how they affect us and others in our surroundings. Nothing is as contagious as energy—we all influence each other across the full energy field, and if we understand the power of our energy, we will make better energy decisions for washing, refilling, and preserving our energy. When you feel exhausted after a customer interaction, there is probably an energetic explanation for this. Many coaches are also extremely sensitive to energy but do not know the flow of energy in their communications and coaching interactions. That is why the setting of boundaries is so important to us all.

Let me be specific; you have a private boundary structure, and you have been developing it for a lifetime. But it may be attached and ready to protect you like a smoke alarm or disconnected, suspended, or unable to warn you of danger by its wires. Without healthy boundaries, you can not thrive, and everything begins with you. You're doing what you love. When you understand where you stop, and others start, when you take full control of your life, become your best friend, you naturally establish better boundaries. Your border system describes you clearly, determines what you want, and won't allow in your life. You make conscious decisions for yourself. It lets other people know who they are, what they want, and what they can give.

Boundaries have three purposes: defending you, maintaining you, and encouraging your presence. And let me make it quite clear that you are not closed to life because boundaries actually allow you to feel safe to open up your field of energy. Borderline starting out with how you appear in your body, it starts off with signals that others take up in an intuitive manner — to begin by thinking about what you look like (hair, jewelry, clothes, shoes, conformity or non-conformity, trends, etc.) — the way you sound (words, speech patterns or laughs, tone).

Talk about what matters to you, your beliefs, your convictions. You always know when someone crosses a border because there will be an internal alarm. Your instincts and your conscience, your moral and ethical compass, your honesty, and your emotions are precious here. Being in your body will allow you to understand what is happening to you, and if you believe a limit has been through, decreased, or just frustrated. Tables. Lists.

Finally, how can you activate your borders when an alarm sounds and borders are challenged? What can you do? There was a mistake.

This helps clear agreements with others, so you have clarity about what is and will not happen, so that if an alarm sounds easy to remind you of your previous contracts. Trust yourself to defend your limits with words such as "No, that's not my style." "I am sorry I don't go in the direction I want to go to." Be clear about your commitment to your goals. And have your limits-think of the signs your presence is genuine and appropriate; step confidently to demonstrate an enthusiastic and yet calm awareness of your intention. If you do this, you and your energy will be trusted. You have to speak, though, to enforce the limitations, and I will talk to a stereotype for a moment-if you are woman, responsive, empathetic, you only hear me when you often say that no one can be a full word.

Boundaries are then the first energy protection level. And since I'm sure you can tell limits, self-awareness starts. You must learn yourself indoors and outdoors. Once you have discovered yourself more thoroughly and become aware of your own power, you will step into the second level of protection to defend and protect your life. You must be fully in your physical body to do practical energy work and influence energy around you, and you must feel that your body is firmly connected with the world. You must be able to breathe calmly, consistently–if you can't, then you tend to be inaccurate in your perception.

Let's take a look at yourself–three questions:

- Are you well-grounded?
- How much are you in your body?
- Is your breath rhythmic and calm?

Check-in and alert yourself. Trying to remain in them with a steady breath, they all really wanted to be confident.

Do your inner work and even know the enemy inside. Your side of the moon. Why because you sometimes get negative energy from outside, because an alarm sounds internally-sometimes those feelings are yours. I've had many customers try to avoid their own problems by accusing the energy fields of everything. Unpleasant, "bad" emotions are signs of the false. However, most people think this means something is wrong if the whole answer lies inside, and we project it onto other people. As coaches, we must be mindful of our predictions. It could be your thoughts, not anything outside of you. It can be a warning that you say flawed ideas to yourself if you have negative emotions. You're thinking the wrong way.

Pick up your thoughts. Order your thoughts. Replace thoughts, beliefs that make you feel less fulfilled with those that make you happier. This obviously means that it's not beneficial to hide your feelings, to stuff them inside you. It's all burying the problem. You must learn to understand what you feel, what you hear, and what thoughts these feelings make. You must then learn how to change perceptions because it is likely dangerous to focus on these negative emotions rather than to repress them! If you are living on negative emotions, you will attract them in your lives. Non-violent communication from Marshall Rosenberg is an excellent resource for learning how to recognize and transform your feelings.

Remember that your own portable space is your energy field-more than just an abstract range. It is an energy field that flows and surrounds you, an extension of your own feelings, mind, and spirit-it's your consciousness ' living force field.

Think about how much space you need physically around you, and how much energy do you start feeling when you communicate with others? You can expand and contract your energy field. In fact, you will probably do this unconsciously all the time.

Inside and outside, learn yourself. Love yourself enough to set clear limits.

Take care of yourself to do any energy work; you need to be balanced and in good health.

Get clear of your boundaries and put them into practice-not in a rigid manner but in a consciously flexible way, live with them and evolves when you find what works and what does not enhance your energy awareness, the energetic exchanges between yourself and others-play with your own personal space and protection techniques Be aware of the massive energy trapped, whether it's yours or someone else, and practice removing it. Your own energetic burden is essential. As a coach who is interconnected with the earth's energy field, you need to know what energy you feed into the world. Because every feeling, every thought you have, is a vibration, which is making in the world more of itself! And we've got sufficient negativity. You are a resonance force field.

Sensitive: can someone be overly sensitive to trapped emotions?

Several people are described as overly sensitive and empathic. And while this leads to many benefits, there are many difficulties as a result of this method. We can feel like sponges that absorb anything and everything in a setting.

For other people that are sensitive, but maybe not to the same degree, they can take everything to heart. One expression, look, or a lot of voice, and you can feel overwhelmed emotionally.

If the world was suitable for this kind of person, their lives would be much more comfortable. And yet, in many cases, it is best suited to people who feel enthusiastic and disconnected. Here you are not in touch with your feelings, let alone sensitive, and you can't feel them.

Therefore, even though both of these extremes are questioned, feeling dumb is more suited for today's world. This does not mean that it is absolute truth and that sensitive individuals have no position or can not succeed. What is usually concerned is the business environment and areas where people are out of touch.

In these kinds of environments, it is not always viewed as unusual to become emotionally cut off and to wear masks; it is often perceived as natural and as life is. On this basis, one could infer that being sensitive is a bad thing, and something must be modified in some way.

This could lead to some kind of personal harm, and one could feel a sense of shame for being like it. Because they don't suit the way most people are, they may decide that being like other people that are not responsive would be more comfortable. And while in some situations it may be better to be like people who are not so sensitive, there are many advantages one would miss.

One thing is to criticize oneself and another to receive criticism from others. You may obtain all sorts of tags from others, and if they are not sensitive, it would be easy; because they do not know how painful it is to be.

And if you have not experienced anything or are not very empathetic, you can hardly really understand what someone else is going through. Some things others could say: you are too sensitive; what they said was just a joke; you have to grow up; you shouldn't take things so personally; just let go of it and don't get it worked up.

Logic Now, these opinions that come from the mouth of another may sound logical and even support them, but that's all about it. If it were as simple as internalizing these beliefs and becoming less reactive, indeed, that would be the case.

But it's not so easy. So no matter what the mind of another person comes up with or what one feels of himself, it doesn't have to change something.

The Other Alternative Many people will be sensitive at one stage and eventually end up insensitive. And this can make them critical of vulnerable people. These people might remind them of what they refused, and perhaps they used food, alcohol, drugs, or some kind of muscular building to tone their sensitive side. So in most cases, they went from being extremely emotional to feeling very little.

Or you can go from one extreme to the next; sometimes, you feel extraordinarily reactive and sometimes. This could focus, for example, on what is happening in this person's life.

Examples For those who are excessively sensitive, it can affect all aspects of their lives or only specific areas. One could not deal with criticism from others, be it negative or positive, and be provided with the best of intentions.

Relationship breaks may be another area that wipes this person out and overwhelms them. Loud noises or large crowds in places full of people could be another boiling point.

Powerful, Loud, and regulated people may cause problems. You should do everything you can to stop any conflict or confrontation and find it difficult to stand up for yourself. Watching the news or living in the circumstances could be too much for people to manage.

Explanations Now, there will be as many explanations why someone is too sensitive. Next, the nervous system is different from someone who lives differently. One thing that can cause someone to have no control over their excitement is if their emotions and feelings are trapped.

And as they are trapped in your body, the nervous system can affect yourself and cause you to have a higher level of excitement, either at certain times or in the way of life. These could be adults and go home when you were a kid and an infant.

This could be because of an incident that was extremely traumatic or an accumulation of minor events that, for instance, caused pain. And since they stay in your body, you have very little say in how you feel; it is an involuntary reaction and not a conscious decision.

Awareness This is not to say that by releasing those trapped emotions and feelings, you lose your sensitivity. But it could mean that their enthusiasm would calm, and the nervous system reflects this transition. Therefore, even if one is still sensitive, they might not be too sensitive any longer. It could also lead to better limits to protect their delicate nature.

A psychologist or a healer will support you in this process, helping you to confront and relieve your feelings and emotions.

How cultural sensitivity and labeling affect people with intellectual handicaps

Cultural sensitivity is defined as knowledge of cultural differences. Getting mindful of these differences also has an effect on training and behavior. Examples of cultural sensitivity include attending cultural events or religious centers, changing the environment of the individual, or discussing life experiences in connection with the culture of the person. Labeling involves representing someone positively or negatively in a short word or phrase. For instance, the name of a person can harm the self-image, the categorization of a person without his permission, or indirect recognition in a group (using an incorrect term to describe an individual).

To staff, physicians, health professionals, and family members, cultural sensitivity and branding are critical to be aware of. It is essential to recognize the importance of a person's culture. Culture forms your personality and part of your environment; culture can even affect challenging behavior. It is also essential to recognize that diversity affects interaction and involvement. For instance, a person may not be used to be around different cultures or races. This is particularly true in view of the ever more diverse patient population in America and the health status differences between people of different ethnic, racial, socioeconomic, religious, and cultural backgrounds. An individual needs to respect differences in other people, including practices, behavior, opinions, beliefs, interaction styles, traditions, and institutions, to appreciate diversity. One of the significant components of cultural insensitivity and labeling can be the language barrier. For example, a person may speak in English but prefer to talk in Spanish or vice versa.

Active treatment, which also involves active participation, takes place when people are engaged in positive activities. Participation improves when both workers and individuals embrace cultural standards. Conversely, the belief that all members of an ethnic, linguistic, or religious group share a common culture is incorrect. The larger group can share everyday historical and geographical experiences, but individuals may share nothing in the group. The way a staff handles the actions of a person in a new environment is essential to the tolerance of culture — for example, an individual from another district, state, or even country. Adapting to your situation only helps you to feel more comfortable. The primary and most important aspect is education. Education. It is crucial that workers are willing to learn more about customs or characteristics of cultures to better connect with their individuals; not everyone was born or raised in the same place. Simple things like to learn a few Spanish words to better communicate with your Spanish speaker can go a long way.

One of the biggest hurdles in the implementation of person-centric planning is when people do not understand each other. Whether from a different race, ethnicity, or history, disabled persons deserve the same rights and opportunities that we have. Labeling can also be disrespectful and can destroy people's relationships. In addition, we as employees need to educate others about the acceptance of cultures. Person-centered planning takes place specific to the goals or goals of each individual. Engaging in more cultural activities increases employee knowledge and relationships.

There are many ways that a healthcare clinician, worker, and family member can communicate with a person in culturally sensitive ways. A cultural director, a staff member, or a clinician should see all patients as individuals and understand that their views, background, beliefs, and vocabulary influence their expectations of the provision of medical care, acceptance, and enforcement of a diagnosis. If you're from the West Indies, it won't be enough to coordinate community inclusion tours to local West Indian restaurants. It is imperative to maintain and develop a relationship with the family. Talk to the family what the person likes, what does he or she do for fun? How does he or she take part in family roles? Members of the support group should also understand their own cultural values and draw parallels where possible, listen to your people about past experiences, and how they grew up in a different country? What they miss? What they miss? Therefore, be aware of the fact that people can communicate in voice, language, or body language differently. Avoid labeling and refrain from saying' I don't understand,' and identify prejudices and stereotypes that prevent them from effectively communicating with patients from different cultures. One of the most critical mistakes that staff can make is to equate the religion of an entity to some person or another. Your guy, for instance, wants lunch at the Spanish Restaurant, but the staff says they don't like Spanish food because it is easier to have two fats, fried chicken and black-eyed peas! Think of the impact of this comment and how the person would feel if you judge their decision. However, he or she always has compassion for the individual. What if you were able to react to this, how would you react? How would you preserve your lifestyle? Open to everything!

The Psychometric Practice and Psychic Children

One of my skills as an empathic sensitive is the psychometry of artifacts. Like all spiritual gifts, this one allows the reader to acquire specific perceptions of emotions and thoughts. The stronger of the two cognitive systems, Emotions seem to get through a little more directly, but they can seem somewhat confused and disjointed. On the other hand, thoughts can be softer and simpler but can be a little harder to pick up if the person in question does not have a high level of focus.

The recipient must learn to become a passive recipient for psychometry to function. That is, he or she who reads should make every effort to release preconceived notions or expectations so that information is correctly received. Say, for example, giving you a costly watch. On the surface, you would think that the owner was somebody with great resources and a lot of money. This assumption is based on a social filter or expectation based on surface appearances, which could very probably be a false premise.

The best practice is to take the object instead of basing the readings on surface appearances without any implied representation. Enable the energy of the object to move without preconceived restrictions to prevent it from being modified. Even if you receive the power, try not to make any personal assumptions about the acquired images. After all, no one is entirely faultless, and, just as we want to be respected despite our faults, let him read the same courtesy.

It is, therefore, necessary for a reader to create a neutral point of reference for any reading. It is straightforward to establish a neutral reference point, but it can be one of the hardest tasks to accomplish successfully. As with meditation, with the exception of purpose, the same principles apply. In this scenario, you intend to find a position where you can neither control nor be controlled in a passive mode. When you come to this state, remember how you feel, so that later you can re-enter the country when necessary.

Chapter 2 What Causes Narcissism?

Narcissists are surprisingly hidden. They are masters at disguising themselves in public, blending in and working their manipulative magic behind the scenes. They do not want to be called out for what they are, and the majority of them take necessary effort to hide their abusive tendencies behind plausible deniability. Snide comments are disguised as jokes. Words meant to shatter you, demean you, and control you, are hidden behind a façade of concern for you or your wellbeing. The worst part is, people tend to fall for it. People inherently want to trust others, and they often will take other people at face value. They seek to take advantage of this, using it to continue to operate behind the scenes as they seek what it is, they truly want.

Identifying a Narcissist

When you are trying to identify a narcissist, you may as well be trying to prove the existence of something so sneaky that it will take some serious effort on your part. People around you probably deny that there is anything wrong with the person who has been abusing you, or they announce that you must be delusional. Because narcissists are so charming, so capable of identifying how they present themselves to others, and such good manipulators, you may find yourself on a wild goose chase if you do not know where to start or how to identify one. When trying to identify a narcissist, try the WEB method. WEB stands for Words, Emotions, Behaviors.

Watch their words

When attempting to identify a narcissist, the first step is identifying words or ways of speaking that are indicative of a narcissist. Their words typically take either extremely positive or negative connotations; they show a lack of empathy or they are manipulative words that paint the narcissist as a victim.

- Positive words: Positive words are used to draw in the narcissist's target. They will word things incredibly positively, seeking to hook the target to the narcissist and allow for future manipulation. These words can be seen as seductive, as they essentially seduce the narcissist's targets into submission. These are words like:
  - I love you so much!
  - You are the best person I have ever met!
  - Wow, you are so good at your job, and you deserve the world. Let me give you everything you deserve.
  - We will go to great places in this world if we stick together!
- Negative words: Negative words are a direct contrast to the positive. Negative words are used to disparage or tear down the narcissist's target. These are typically weaponized to directly harm the target and browbeat the other person into submission. Negative words may look like:
  - Wow, you are completely incompetent.

- You never do anything right.
- Look at that idiot over there—he didn't recognize the greatness in my proposal I made for the new job.
- You know, you could be a much better person if you'd only listen to me. Maybe you'd do something the right way for a change.

- **Uninterested words:** These words show a lack of empathy, or that the narcissist does not care about other people. He may halfheartedly listen to what is being said but shift the topic as soon as he has the chance to do so. Particularly if you are complaining about something that happened, the narcissist may voice how he had it worse. Any concerns or discomfort you may be feeling are disregarded altogether.
  - Maybe you should have tried harder. I faced a similar situation, but I managed to get through okay because I actually tried.
  - Yeah, that sounds annoying, I guess, but it could have been worse. I had to deal with this before. Let me tell you how THAT was hard.
  - Okay. What do you want me to do about it?
  - I don't really care. Can you help me with this thing over here?

- **Victimizing words:** The narcissist sees himself as superior, just by virtue of his personality, and because he is superior, he feels he can only fail when he is an innocent victim of happenstance, and the failure had nothing to do with himself. The narcissist often uses words that will portray himself as the victim when talking to others, or even in his own internal monologue. He may say things like:

- o That was so unfair. I should have been the one promoted for the job. Everyone knows I'm better than the other person anyway.
- o That was not my fault! Someone else interfered. I would have been fine if they hadn't shown up.
- o How could you do that to me? I didn't deserve that.
- o Why are you trying to hurt me? I may have made a mistake, but look at how you responded! You're treating me so poorly.

Watch your emotions

The next step to identifying the narcissist in your midst, after listening to the words said, is to watch how you feel around him. If you feel like what the narcissist is saying is too good to be true, then it probably is. Even though at the moment, you may feel the greatest joy you have felt in a long while, particularly due to their long soliloquies about how much they love and cherish you, such a strong response may feel as though it could not possibly be real—because it is not.

If you find yourself feeling incredibly negatively about yourself, whether inadequate, unsuccessful, unworthy, or even anxious and as though you are walking on eggshells, you should look at the relationship closer. While everyone feels down about themselves sometimes, it should not be a regular occurrence. If you notice that your feelings seem to oscillate with the suspected narcissist's own word patterns, you should probably move on to the next step in trying to identify the narcissist.

Watch their behaviors

Paying attention to what the suspected narcissist is doing separately from what he is saying will help you identify whether he is a narcissist or not. Narcissists typically say lots of things in rapid-fire sequence in an attempt to keep you distracted from the problematic behaviors. This is a manipulation tactic—you are so focused on the words that you miss the abusive or insensitive actions happening right under your nose.

Particularly, you should pay attention to see if the narcissist is easily frustrated or angered when things do not go quite according to plans. Narcissists typically lack flexibility, and when they feel as though their control over the situation has been thwarted, they lash out at others. If the narcissist responds through snapping at you instead of rationally approaching the situation like an adult, you may have a problem. Likewise, if you noticed that the narcissist does insensitive things, such as taking a coworker's lunch out of the fridge or cutting in front of people waiting for a coffee, you may be able easier identify the narcissist.

Lastly, the narcissist has a tendency to blame others for anything that goes wrong. Watch to see if the suspected narcissist is constantly blaming other people even when everyone knows that the narcissist is the one who has made a mistake. This is a telltale sign of the narcissist.

Diagnosing Narcissistic Personality Disorder

Narcissists are not just people who are annoying to be around. True narcissists actually suffer from what is known as a narcissistic personality disorder (NPD), and it is a recognized mental health disorder that has a pervasive impact on the individual with the disorder and how he or she functions through life. Ultimately, the DSM-5 has identified several traits that are shared amongst narcissists. They must meet at least five of the nine presented traits to be clinically diagnosed, but even those who do not meet clinical diagnostic criteria may still be quite toxic to be around. Proceed with caution when you have identified a narcissist, as the traits he likely has can make it quite difficult to interact healthily. The traits of NPD all fall into one of three categories: A lack of empathy, an innate, insatiable desire for attention, and delusions of grandeur. The nine traits are depicted in the following graphic, as well as detailed, in-depth here.

Grandiosity

The most obvious of the traits is the grandiose nature narcissists everywhere seem to have. The narcissists believe that they are better than everyone else, and treat it as if it is an inherent fact, needing no more justification than any other inherent facts, such as the sky being blue or that hearts beat to keep people alive. The narcissist simply is better, stronger, smarter, faster, and generally superior to those around him. He believes that he is perfect exactly the way he is.

This belief of perfection then entails that the narcissist believes that he is infallible: He can never be at fault because perfection is never wrong. This means that he could never possibly be wrong because being wrong would deny his inherent superiority and perfection. He insists that everything he does is intentional and serves exactly the purpose he needs it to, or that some external, uncontrollable force sabotaged him. He did not fail due to a lack of skill, but rather because of happenstance, or because someone else messed up so badly that not even his perfection could save the situation.

Obsession with fantasies of power or success

Because narcissists assert that they are better than everyone else, they are preoccupied with the idea that they should have the power, success, status, and anything else they desire to prove it. Their perfection should go hand in hand with power and success, as far as they are concerned, and they obsess over obtaining it. The narcissist will do anything possible to convince others that he deserves it.

Unfortunately, the narcissist's own standards are unrealistic and oftentimes entirely unattainable for the average person. Very few people get to live the dream the narcissist has, and this means that the narcissist's beliefs of perfection and fantasies of power are constantly being challenged. This keeps the narcissist in a state of constant dissonance, in which he believes one thing but gets something entirely different. He struggles to accept this, and it often leads to denial, manipulation, and narcissistic rages.

Delusion of uniqueness

The narcissist, as a perfect individual with fantasies of power that he believes he has or should have, also believes that he is perfectly unique. No one is on par with him, and therefore, no one can ever understand him, his desires, or his logic. He will use this in two ways: It works to deny when people question his motives, as he can just assert that there is a method to his madness, and anyone who fails to see the method is simply too dumb to understand it, or he can use it to justify that the other person is not special like he is, and therefore is inferior in some way. If the other person is inferior, there is no reason to concern himself with the other person's belief as it is irrelevant and not at all educated. After all, if the narcissist is really so special and unique, he must be superior by default.

Because the narcissist is special and no one can ever understand him, he is also able to play the perfect victim. No one understands his plight, and no one understands how he suffers. This means that no one can dare judge him for his behaviors or criticize him because he has it so much worse than anyone else, and no one else understands how badly he feels. Never mind the fact that other people have likely been through incredibly similar situations, or worse, just through sheer numbers of people. Most likely, there is always someone who is in a worse state than the narcissist, though he will never admit that.

Further, the narcissist will use his uniqueness to deny any sort of relationship with people he deems as inferior. He will refuse to associate with people who do not relate to him and may even choose to only shop at certain stores, wear certain brands, or eat certain foods that align with his superiority.

The never-ending desire for attention and admiration

The narcissist seeks to constantly be inundated with love, attention, and admiration. He needs this to justify his own existence, and while he may not consciously feel as though his superiority needs justification, he does justify it in comparing himself to others, even if that justification is delusional in the first place. He craves the attention of other people and will do anything he needs to do to get it, whether it is manipulating others, forcing himself to be a victim, or inserting himself as the center of attention when he should not be. No matter the situation, the narcissist has a plan to ensure that he gets the narcissistic supply, the sort of mental energy sustenance that he requires to feel secure in himself.

Entitled

Entitlement naturally follows with the previous traits of the narcissist. He believes that he deserves what he wants simply because of who he is, and he never wants to put in the effort. He will expect other people to cater to his whims, or he may simply wait for what he wants to be brought to him on a silver platter. Regardless of how it works out, the narcissist believes that he deserves it all with none of the work.

He expects to win despite having never proven he is skilled at whatever he is doing. He expects the promotion he does not qualify for. He expects to get the girlfriend he wants without putting in the effort or recognizing that she has free will and can decide whether she likes him or not. He expects the house, the prestige, the money, the power, and the general success at all of his endeavors simply because he deserves it. He believes he should have it, and that is enough.

Manipulative and exploitative

Narcissists do not perceive the world the way normal people do. They see everything through a distorted perception of reality, and they believe that their distortions are the truth, no matter how much people may point out that they are mistaken. The narcissist then feels as though he has to force everything around him to line up with his skewed perceptions, and he will manipulate others in order to browbeat them into line. He will gaslight others, believing the words that come out of his mouth so thoroughly that the other person begins to believe them too. He will tell people that they are incompetent, inferior, undeserving, or generally at fault because he believes it, and he will manipulate the listener into believing it as well. He will disguise himself with a persona in order to make himself seem more desirable and to exert the aura of perfection he believes he has in order to manipulate others into believing his reality. When people do not bow to his demands and see the world through his eyes, he will choose to instead threaten or exploit them into obedience instead. The manner he manages to get what he wants is of little consequence to the narcissist, so long as he ultimately gets his way and his delusions are upheld.

Lacking Empathy

Narcissists lack basic empathy. They are unable to really relate to how others are feeling, and because of that, they struggle to care about how other people are doing. They do not feel motivated to stop harming others, even when their behaviors are destroying another person. They do not care enough to feel guilty about the manipulation tactics they use. They do not see a reason to meet other people's needs. All of these behaviors lead to an individual who is not suited for life in a smoothly running society. The narcissist seems to go against the grain when in social groups, stepping on others and using them to his advantage rather than creating a way for everyone to benefit. The only person he cares about being successful, happy, or cared for is himself, and every action that he will do will be in his own interest.

Envious of others, while also believing others are envious of the narcissist

The narcissist frequently envies other people, particularly if they have what he wants. They may have worked hard for what they have, but the narcissist does not care. The narcissist wants to get it too but expects to have it handed to him. He instead wallows in his own envy of the other person before eventually twisting it around in his own mind, changing the narrative into the other person envying him instead. For example, if he looks enviously at someone who has managed to get a promotion, he may then tell himself that he did not want the job anyway, and that the other person will be jealous when the narcissist is on vacation and getting off work on time every day while the other person attends to newfound responsibilities that came with the promotion.

Arrogant

Due to their beliefs of superiority and uniqueness, the narcissist frequently separates himself from people that he sees as beneath him. He frequently comes across as arrogant to nearly everyone because of this haughty demeanor he uses when asserting his superiority. He only bothers showing any signs of respect to people who are equal or superior to him, and so few meet that standard that he has set that he frequently just comes across as arrogant to all.

Chapter 3 Who is The Narcissist?

One of the most difficult things for victims of narcissists is learning to let go. When someone is dear to you, it is normal to see the best in them. You try to get them help, try to understand them and hope that someday they will change. Unfortunately, this is not always the case.

Narcissists do not seek help. They believe they don't have a problem. If anything, in the mind of a narcissist, the person who thinks they need to change their ways is the one who needs to embrace change. It is so traumatizing, watching someone you love dive deeper into the abyss like that.

If you cannot change someone, at best you can learn how to cope with them. Remember that in as much as you might hold them dear, your first priority is your personal safety and peace of mind. In learning how to handle a narcissist, you can counter their manipulative motives and prevent yourself from becoming a puppet.

The first step is to learn how to identify a narcissist, which we have done. Next, you learn how to identify their manipulative traits, and what to do in order to counter their outbursts. In a relationship, it is very difficult when you realize you are living with a narcissist. The best solution is always to keep a healthy distance from a narcissist, especially if you know they can overpower your resolve.

Four-point framework for dealing with a narcissist

There are several ways of handling a narcissist. Before we look into them, the following are four of the most important things you should always keep in mind when dealing with a narcissist.

1. Positivity

Life throws many curve balls at you all the time. It never gets easier. To get through anything, you must embrace positivity and change your outlook about life. Narcissists will drain the life out of you, and by the time they are done with you, all that's left might be a shell of your former self.

People who maintain a positive approach to life generally live happier lives than most. Your happiness is one of the things a narcissist will go after. When you are happy, to them it means there is something else in your life responsible for your happiness, something other than them. Since your life must revolve around them, they will do everything they can to take away your happiness.

Narcissists will do random things to disturb your peace. They also monitor you to see the effect. It fills them with joy when you lose focus and are disturbed. They respond by pushing your limits further until you break.

Staying positive will help you learn how to handle a narcissist. They have an endless barrage of insults and ill behavior that they can hurl at you. Instead of bowing to the pressure, be positive and show them that you are not affected by the things they do or what they say. If you are persistent, they might soon realize that it is impossible to break you, and they have to make peace with it.

Positivity is not just about handling a narcissist, it is also about your mindset. You need to stay sharp because a narcissist will never give up on testing you. You can condition your mind to think positively, filter negative vibes and focus only on things that bring joy, meaning and satisfaction in your life. This will help you become aware of, and impervious to narcissistic manipulation.

2. Healthy boundaries

One of the top recommendations when dealing with a narcissist is to set boundaries. This helps, especially when you realize you are in an unhealthy relationship. The challenge with setting boundaries is that in most cases, people don't even know what their boundaries are. It is very difficult to change something you don't know you have.

Setting boundaries depends on your previous experiences and upbringing. It might be easier for some people to establish boundaries than others because of such predispositions. It might take some learning, but if you are persistent, you will get it right.

First, you need to learn what you are about. What are your boundaries? You must acknowledge your feelings. Boundaries are only effective when you know what you are protecting, hence what you are shielding yourself from (Newland, 2008). Does someone's comment make you feel terrible? Do you feel drained when you are in their presence? This is a good place to start.

Learning about yourself helps you evaluate your actions and choices, and recognize how you feel. Most people have leaky boundaries in their relationships, and at some point they give up altogether. In such a relationship, you become so engrossed in your partner's life that you substitute your life for theirs. Relationships are about two unique individuals coming together to form a healthy unit.

Take some time to rethink your life. Reflect and check in with yourself until you are aware of the difference between your partner or the other party to this interaction, and yourself.

Second, how do you know when your boundaries are crossed? Once you are aware of your feelings, you know when you are hurt. That is the point your boundaries are breached. Ask yourself how was your boundary breached? Here are some examples.

Scenario 1:

"Your partner always promises to take you out and meet their friends and family, but it never happens."

Scenario 2:

"Someone in your life is always asking for money, promising to pay back but they never do."

Scenario 3:

"A close friend or family member keeps calling you in the middle of the night or messaging about their problems, but they don't seem interested in solving the problems themselves. Each time they call, you cannot fall asleep after the call."

Each time these events happen, something breaks inside you. You feel disappointed, unloved, cheated, unappreciated and so forth. You already know what matters to you, and how you feel when those feelings are not appreciated. Now, you know how your boundaries are breached.

Third, you focus on how to reset boundaries. You are in charge of your life, and to borrow a common phrase in many establishments, Management reserves the right of admission!

Why should you put up with someone who has made it clear they don't respect anything you say? Having realized the things that hurt you and how, the next step is to confront the problem. Address the person who keeps breaching your boundaries without a care.

Here are some examples on how to handle the scenarios above:

Scenario 1

Tell your partner why it bothers you that they haven't kept this promise. Tell them to stop making the promise altogether, and act on it once and get it out of the way.

Scenario 2

Remind them that since they have failed to honor their commitments, you will not lend them more money until they pay back what they owe.

Scenario 3

Tell your friend or family member that you understand their pain, but it is draining the life out of you. Ask them to seek professional help, and if possible, stop answering the calls.

By addressing these issues, you make the other person aware that they are hurting you, and they need to stop.

Fourth, you must learn how to ground your boundaries. Establishing boundaries is one thing, but maintaining them is not easy either. If you have weak boundaries, your partner will recognize this and can manipulate you into feeling guilty through backlash. However, the most important thing is that these boundaries are there for you.

You must respect your boundaries before you expect the same of someone else. Grounding your boundaries is more about awareness and strengthening your resolve. Meditation, deep breathing, chakra are some of the techniques you can use to enforce your boundaries.

While enforcing your boundaries, don't forget your emotions. They are valid. Trust in yourself. You are not wrong to set your boundaries. This is healthy, and everyone must respect each other's boundaries if you are to be happy together. You have individual boundaries and couple boundaries. Each of these boundaries are unique, and it is their independence that makes your relationship healthy.

Fifth, talk about your boundaries. Talk about it. Let your partner know you have boundaries and they have persistently crossed them, and you need them to stop. Fair warning, this might not always go well. If your partner retorts, argues back or lashes out at you for having boundaries, perhaps it is best you walk away and take care of yourself. It is clear that you are not a priority to them.

Backlash is usually one of the signs that someone does not acknowledge or respect your boundaries. Arguing with them about it is an acknowledgement of their disrespect, which opens room for unhealthy compromise. Boundaries are simple. If someone doesn't understand them, the best they can do is ask you to enlighten them about your boundaries and need thereof. This can help them understand you better, and why you need the boundaries.

Boundaries must come with consequences. People will always push your boundaries, at times just to see what happens. Decide on appropriate consequences and communicate them clearly. Setting consequences is the ultimate way of embracing your boundaries. Make this about you. After all, the purpose of boundaries is to honor your commitment to your inner peace, not to judge or satisfy another person's choices and actions.

Finally, take care of yourself. If the discussion about your boundaries did not go according to plan, don't spend your time worrying about it. Step outside, exercise, run along the beach, go for a walk or something. Do anything that will prevent you from spending a lot of your energy worrying about what transpired earlier.

3. Personal detachment

Narcissists will always project their flaws to you. They blame you for things that you have nothing to do with. They will undermine you and break your spirit. A good solution for this is to retreat and embrace a different approach so that you learn how to deal with their tirades.

Learn how to ignore their personal attacks. Don't take anything a narcissist says personally. When you do this, it is easier for you to handle the situation better. The last thing you want to do is pick up an argument with a narcissist because they will never listen to you. At best, let them know you don't agree with their position, and leave it at that.

Any encounter with a narcissist is most likely about them, and never about you. In order to identify and reject these attacks, you should understand your self-worth, believe in yourself, and shun any criticism that they might level against you.

4. Contextual evaluation

What is the situation at hand? Take time and learn the context before you respond to a narcissist. Some of their outbursts are not because they are narcissists but because of circumstances which eventually make them embrace the narcissistic personality.

A good example is when you are offered a promotion over your colleague who has a narcissistic personality, and was eyeing the position too. Working together might not be easy. Your colleague will easily resent you for no reason. They will highlight your mistakes and wonder how you got the job instead of them.

Even if your colleague is not usually a confronting person, they might develop a condescending attitude towards you. In any argument or disagreement, they will throw words like "so you think you are better than everyone else," to vent and air out their frustration. It is always wise to assess the context of these tirades so that you know what you are dealing with and why.

Tips for dealing with a narcissist

A lot of things might run through your mind when you encounter a narcissist. It is normal that you might be engulfed by the desire to flee the situation. While self-preservation is important, you should also have it at the back of your mind that narcissistic personality disorder is a real mental problem, and if possible, encourage the individual to seek medical attention.

Besides those who have NPD, there are individuals who portray narcissistic characteristics. It is quite helpful if you know how to handle such people. This helps in managing your expectations, and creating a safe environment for you to interact with them without their narcissistic tendencies taking over. Below are useful ideas that will help you manage the situation better:

- Acceptance

One of the first things you have to do is realize that this person is who they are. Accept them. There is no version of themselves that you can create in your mind that will change their behavior. Many victims of narcissistic abuse suffer because deep down they hold onto a fallacy that someday, the abuser might change their ways. The only thing that might happen is your life changing for the worst.

- Deny them attention

Narcissists are attention hogs. Since they thrive on attention, why not shut them out? These are people who will do anything to be recognized. The attention might be positive or negative, but they will still thrive off of it. If you give them all the attention they need, the only thing that happens is that you end up sacrificing what is important to you, to satisfy them. Attention seekers like these will never respect you. They never see you in the same way you see them.

- Establish boundaries

The trick is not just establishing boundaries, but creating very clear boundaries. Communicate. Talk to the other person about what you feel when they do something that exceeds your boundaries. Set consequences and make sure they are aware of what it will cost them the next time they cross your boundaries.

More importantly, hold them accountable for their actions. You have to be steadfast in your approach to dealing with narcissists. A narcissist will try to find the easiest way to get back control from you. While you set these boundaries, they might feel you are moving further away from them, which is infuriating. Instead, ensure you communicate the boundaries to them in a healthy way. Do it in a manner that does not feel like they are being attacked.

There are sacrifices you can make for people who are dear to you, like these ones. However, at the same time you must also be aware that some people might never change. If this is that kind of a person, then your personal safety and peace of mind comes first, and the best thing to do is to walk away. It does not matter if they are your parents, siblings or lovers; walking away might be the only way you stay alive.

- Retaliation

When you figure out how to handle a narcissist, do not assume they will take it kindly. Expect retaliation. Some mind tricks might be coming your way, so brace yourself for impact. One of the common responses to your boundaries is that they will also give you a list of their boundaries or demands. Be careful because what might seem like a counter offer to your boundaries might be a manipulation tactic.

It is common for a narcissist to state their terms in such a way that you feel guilty about your boundaries. They need you to go back to the drawing board and rethink your strategy. They can even make you feel like you are pushing them away. If you fall for this trick, you give up control of your life. Watch out for the sympathetic pleas, because in most cases, they are anything but sympathetic.

- Stand your ground

The last thing you can expect from a narcissist is that they will admit they made a mistake, or take responsibility for hurting you. Instead of owning up to it, it is easier for them to make you bear the responsibility for their actions. This is why you must always stand your ground. Be strong in your resolve because you know what is right. Do not give in to the manipulation. Theirs is an inflated ego that you can never truly please. Accepting the blame will only create more trouble for you in the future.

- No promises

You might have learned this about your partner already, their promises never materialize. You cannot keep up that unhealthy cycle. Instead of worrying about what happens next, insist on immediate action. If they promise you something, make sure they do it right away. Hold them accountable for it and insist on action.

The reason why you need to do this is because most of the time, promises from narcissists are nothing but a means to an end. Whenever they make a promise, there is something they want from you. Once they have it, the promises become a distant memory.

The Narcissist's False Self And True Self

Not all relationships are toxic and imbalanced, and even so, a majority of relationships, even platonic or work-related ones, will develop patterns. Patterns are evident in our daily life activities: the pattern of your workday, the pattern when you come home, the routine with your spouse or partner about who cooks and who cleans after supper, or the routine or pattern of when you go to sleep and your nighttime rituals.

All patterns begin somewhere and develop or change over time, and in any relationship, you have in your life, a lot of patterns will change while many stay the same. If you tend to date men or women who have certain tendencies or attributes, in this case, NPD, then you will already be comfortable with these patterns, and perhaps, not realize that you are repeating the same patterns over and over again by being drawn to similar types of people.

Patterns are the life grooves that get worn into our consciousness and mental state. They are the basis of how we think, react, feel, and treat others and ourselves. Patterns, like bad habits, can be broken and will only require that you acknowledge what the patterns are in the first place so that you know what needs to change.

As with any relationship, typical narcissistic relationships will follow a general pattern that causes the partners involved to exist in a repetitive cycle. Otherwise, the pattern is the general rule of thumb for how the narcissist will operate in every relationship. The usual pattern has three stages, including idealizing the partner, devaluing them, and finally discarding them. It is an emotional rollercoaster, and it can repeat itself, depending on how many times you are willing to go on this ride without facing the truth of what is going on.

Let's explore the stages so that you figure out what stage you might currently be in with your partner, or if you can recognize a common theme in your relationship from these patterns.

Idealize

In the first stages of the romantic partnership, a narcissistic person will create a reality with their partner that involves a feeling of infatuation and otherworldliness, almost as if it was destiny that the two of you came together. The sensation is of true love and a beautiful and inspiring courtship coming into being. Some people have described this part of the stage as intoxicating or like being on a drug and the high lasts for weeks, months, and occasionally longer than that.

It is not abnormal to feel the love high in the beginning stages of any relationship, and it is greatly common for couples to inspire this feeling in each other as they get closer and form the love bond. In the case of the narcissistic relationship, the following stages offer a broader explanation of how it is different than other love relationships in their blossoming stage.

People who have reported being in narcissistic relationships have described the "idealize" stage like finding a soulmate and are on a cloud of beautiful life possibilities with their partner. The sensation is that you will never fall apart and that you are meant to be together. This connection is offered greatly by the narcissist who will "drug" their partner with loving words, dedications, praise, courting rituals, intense sexual relations, regular vacations or trips, promises of creating a future life together, and the admonishment of being the most important and special person they have ever met.

It sounds amazing, doesn't it? And who wouldn't want to have such a whirlwind romance right from the get-go? Isn't that what every romantic comedy is selling to you? The "love bomb" phase of the relationship feels like a dream come true, and the reality is that anyone who experienced something like this would probably have a hard time being skeptical, especially when they are being promised the world and that love will last forever.

The next stage creates the platform for understanding the true nature of the narcissistic relationship after the "honeymoon" phase has worn out their ability to gain "narcissistic supply."

Devalue

As the relationship enters a more realistic and comfortable rhythm, the intensity may not be as extreme, and some aspects of the connection may start to wane or grown faded. There are moments of disagreement and possible attempts to confront the narcissist about their attitude or behavior, with a reaction that is not what you might expect from someone who is so deeply in love with you, as they demonstrated before.

The large, red flags on the tropical paradise, love island you created together start to paint another picture of reality. It happens slowly and subtly and can sometimes even feel stealthy, cunning, and deceptive. The objective of the narcissist is to devalue their partner in covert ways to attain a level of emotional superiority, in effect, causing their partner to establish an urge or desire to rekindle the level of affection that they had experienced in the first stages of becoming acquainted with each other.

The narcissist quietly bullies while their partner, or the victim of narcissistic abuse, works tirelessly to bring the sensuality and love back into the courtship by falling for the game and asking the narcissist what they can do to change or "fix it."

In a lot of situations, a person might see these red flags and not feel attached to the narcissist, choosing instead to let the relationship naturally dissolve into the final stage (discarding). However, in many cases, the partner of the narcissist will want to remind themselves of how magical the opening of the affair was and that it must be true love, and therefore, worth seeking out solutions to whatever issues are arising.

The patterns will continue in the "devaluing" stage, as the narcissist will not want to comply with any kind of growth and will create emotional and mental (occasionally physical) abuse in the form of gaslighting, putting down their partner with verbal comments, avoiding or withdrawing emotional or physical intimacy as a form of punishment, disappearing for periods of time without word, withholding seduction or affection, and blaming their partner for anything that might be an issue with them (projecting).

This stage can continue for a while, but eventually, if the partner of the narcissist is not complying with their demands, needs, and expectations, then they will be discarded and cast off.

Discard

If the partner of the narcissist cannot provide them with adequate narcissistic supply, then they will be discarded without emotion or need for debate. If the partner asks for a kind of compromise, honesty, relationship counseling, healthy boundaries, or mutual exchange, then the narcissist will likely determine that they are no longer with the "perfect partner." What they want is someone who can always feed their ego without the demand for anything else in return, and so, if you are not able to meet these demands, you are no longer a viable partner for the narcissist.

Keep in mind, as you read this that it is totally and completely normal and healthy to ask for reciprocity, balance, comradery, communication, and compromise in your relationships. These qualities and attributes, however, are not commonly practiced by the narcissist and so you will be throwing bricks at a brick wall for no good reason if you ask them to compromise or see your side of things.

In a codependent partnership or a situation between a narcissist and an empath, the relationship can be a lifelong pattern(idealize, devalue, discard - over and over again) that will never fully reach a full discarding of the relationship. However, the act of discarding can occur as a result of not meeting the narcissist's needs, and it will be an emotional discarding and punishment that can only be rectified by the partner of the narcissist succumbing to the emotional needs and demands of the narcissist's ego.

Either way, the discarding stage can feel like a huge shock to the victim or target of narcissistic abuse, because it began with such passion, love, and admiration. How can such a loving and amiable person become so different and not even care about your special bond? The answer is that they never truly cared and they were simply looking for someone to feed their ego and offer them narcissistic supply. If you can't meet that demand, then you're out.

Unfortunately, this can happen all of the time, especially if you don't know what patterns or flags to observe when you are getting involved with someone. The key is identifying the patterns in the devaluing stage so that you don't end up shocked, confused, and alone with a stack of insecurities and neuroses about yourself that you were convinced of having by your narcissistic partner.

The effects of this pattern over time can be exhausting and detrimental to you. If you have already engaged in this type of pattern before and you keep going through it with certain patterns, stop blaming yourself for the relationship ending after such a whirlwind start. Odds are, it's not your fault and whatever your narcissistic partner told you about yourself is not true.

Chapter 4 Narcissistic Personality Disorder

hew, there were a lot of symptoms to cover! But nevertheless, we think that it's extremely important to get know each and every one of them, and most importantly, to see how they are manifested in the real world. "Real world? you might ask, "but you've talked so much about some fictional characters and literature! What's real in that?". The thing is, although literature isn't necessarily correct in the literal sense, some characters and situations described in good literature seem as truthful as the chair you're sitting on.

But now that we're finished, we will pass on to other topics that will take everything we've said so far and put it into a wider context. Already, we have mentioned some wide-scale consequences of narcissism. Wars, corrupt ideologies, murders, these things can all happen as a result of untamed and uncontrolled narcissistic traits.

Terrorism

Terrorism is the modern day's plague. It can take many forms, but, of course, the most shocking and appalling ones get the most media coverage. And these cases of terrorism are linked with narcissism. And this is not a coincidence. In big media coverage and fame, narcissistic terrorists seek and find the admiration they need. Or, as Brad Bushman has put it "As ego deflates, the aggression inflates."- It is not much different with admiration. The more they long for excessive admiration, the more extreme their methods become.

We'll analyze only a few cases, starting from the Columbine School Shooting.

The two perpetrators of that horrible misdeed, Eric Harris and Dylan Klebold, were only teenagers at the time. They murdered 12 and injured 21 people, most of them were children, Eric and Dylan's former classmates. One, of course, has to ask: "Why?" and unfortunately, there isn't a simple answer. For instance, various researchers concluded that Dylan Klebold exhibited major signs of depression- "Dylan wanted to die and didn't care if others died as well."

But Eric Harris' story is different. Besides being a psychopath, Eric Harris most probably had reached an almost delusional level of grandiosity and superiority complex. By killing and injuring countless persons he wanted to show his power and might to the world. Unlike Dylan, he "...wanted to kill others and didn't care if he died in the process." It's obvious that in Eric, we have the deadly combination of psychopathic and narcissistic traits. Also, he considered himself as the mastermind of their deadly plan and regarded this "feat" as his work of art. So Klebold simply wanted to end his life, while Harris clearly wanted to show his greatness to the world. His delusions where so overwhelmingly vivid that he would rather lose his life than let them pale in the light of reality.

Harris' private journal is of great importance for our conclusions. In his journal, he mostly talks about his "right" to do anything he wants, and that anyone who dares to even try and take this "right" away from him will be annihilated. For instance, speaking about a minor theft he committed previously, Harris writes about this little incident and says that if he wants to take something, he has an absolute entitlement to that object. Finally, it is alleged that shooting was Harris' idea in the first place. However, this statement is often contested, but one thing is clear- Harris was probably much more enthusiastic about the shooting than Klebold, and it is not impossible that he coaxed Klebold into committing this horrible crime.

Let's analyze another case, probably the worst shooting of all times- Breivik's attacks in Norway. Being a lone wolf attacker, Anders Breivik is an even better example of how terrorism and narcissism are inextricably linked. Breivik first detonated a car bomb in Oslo's center. Oslo is the capital city, so all eyes were turned towards the city's center. And this was a perfect diversion. Shortly after the detonation; Anders Breivik, armed to the teeth headed for the island where the youth division of Norway's Labor party camped. As soon as he disembarked from the boat, he started shooting everywhere. Epilogue: 69 teenagers murdered, 110 injured, 55 seriously wounded. Add the casualties of the car bomb that exploded earlier to that- 8 people died, while 209 were injured. If you do the math, you will see that Breivik affected lives; 396 teens. This is why it's so important to talk about this disorder. If everyone knew just a bit more about the signs and symptoms of the disorder, men like Breivik could be stopped before they commit their horrible crimes. But let's get back to our current topic.

Although it looks as if Breivik's main motives were purely political, this most surely isn't the case. Or even if political motives played a role, it was a minor and minuscule one. The chief thing is that Breivik, by adopting extreme far-right views, got the opportunity to regard himself as a "warrior", or "saver", someone who will singlehandedly stop the Islamization of Europe. Needless to say, this kind of thinking doesn't come without extreme fantasies of grandeur. Breivik thought that Europe is no good with the current politics, and he wanted to be seen as a savior, almost as a messiah, someone who would save the country from the ongoing scourge. He could be described as a Nazi. He also openly praised the Srebrenica massacre, as in this little Bosnian town, some 8 thousand Muslims were massacred by the Republic of Srpska army. This all happened prior to the massacre Breivik himself committed. Let's leave the rest to the expert, Brad Busman: "The gunman was diagnosed with narcissistic personality disorder, along with several other mental disorders. Narcissistic tendencies can also be seen in his manifesto, where he rewrites his life history by fabricating his supposed accomplishments (e.g., being part of one of the toughest gangs, being a prominent graffiti artist with works all over the city, being a high-ranking Freemason), and describes himself as a revolutionary leader, an international political leader, and a patriot with a large number of followers."

As was the case with Sergey Nechayev, political attitudes and opinions were only a charade for deep, relentless egocentrism. This is at the same time why we mentioned Nechayev's story in the first place- to show how narcissists exist through centuries and influence history.

We'll give a short list of other shootings that shook the world:

1. At Simon's Rock College of Bard, MA, in 1992. The gunman took the lives of two while wounding

4 people. A psychiatrist concluded that the attacker suffered from narcissistic personality disorder, and had an inflated image of himself.

2. In 1997, a massacre happened at one Mississippi high school, where 1 was killed and 7 more injured. Here, there was no question - three psychologists, independent from one another, concluded that the attacker suffered from NPD.

3. At Case Western University, Ohio, in 2003, the attacker killed one and seriously wounded two students, after which he was overpowered by a SWAT team. A psychologist, who spoke with the gunman on numerous occasions which totaled to 11 hours of observation, concluded that the Case Western University attacker had narcissistic personality disorder.

4. At Arapahoe High School in Colorado, in 2013, one student was killed, although it could have been much worse as the perpetrator brought 125 rounds of ammunition, a shotgun, and few Molotov cocktails. Fortunately, he didn't succeed in setting fire to the school. A school psychologist believed that the attacker had NPD.

The relationship between narcissism and violence

Over the years, a lot of authors supported the thesis that low self-esteem leads to violence. It's obvious that with this stance, we're not going to get anywhere with our explanations of narcissistic violence. A lot of more recent studies showed that narcissism is indeed linked with violence and aggressive behavior, and this link is far from being weak. The newest research suggests that individuals with inflated egos are more likely to exhibit aggressive behavior towards others. More specifically; it is the instability of their inflated self-concept that leads them towards committing such atrocious crimes. This is sometimes called threatened egotism. Narcissists are the most dangerous when their fantasies and unrealistic representations are brought to question. To defend these fantasies, some people resort to extreme measures. Eric Harris, whose personality we've tried to describe as concisely as possible, for sure acted in the goal of protecting his egotism. Is there a better way to affirm one's might, one's "lust for life" than by taking those same characteristics from others.

Here we come to an important point. The more threatened the ego, the more likely is a person to act aggressively. And this statement has important consequences when deciding how to deal with narcissists.

Let's say that you realized that your dear friend is actually a covert narcissist. It's obvious that he's fond of you, and up until now, you've met on a regular basis. There are few alternatives you can choose to try and deal with this problem. Of course, upon realizing the true nature of your friend, you will most likely either try to help him or break all contacts. Both alternatives are pretty dangerous. If you opt for the first one, you will be faced with an almost insurmountable hurdle. By being direct and honest, you will most likely cause a brusque and harsh response. In other words, you'll threaten the egotism of your friend and bring yourself to an inconvenient position, open confrontation, verbal abuse, or even physical violence are just some of the things that come to mind.

On the other hand, you might opt to break all contacts altogether. This alternative is not much different from the first one, at least when it comes to your friend's response. Like any human being, your friend would be hurt and would suffer emotionally. But, unlike other, normal human beings, your friend will project all the pain, everything that goes on in his mind onto you. His ego being shaken by the rejection, he'll seek to foster it by hurting you personally. By doing this, he will affirm that the problem isn't within him, but within you. And this kind of response should always be expected. Because, if your narcissistic friend didn't begin to insult and attack you, what is left for him to do? To question himself? and finally destroy the remainders of his shaken ego? Never.

As already mentioned, some narcissists would rather die than change their overinflated self-images. Eric Harris stands as a reminder of this bitter fact. Breivik, on the other hand, was different. He didn't kill himself after his deadly spree has ended. He continues to live, probably without a trace of repentance and penitence. Breivik is, in a way, the true narcissist. He wanted to live and see the consequences of his actions.

Don't think that we're just speculating here. There are experiments, done by an expert in this field (the aforementioned Bushman), that show just how dangerous narcissists are. In his experiment, Bushman first caused anger in his subjects. After doing this, he gave them the opportunity to express their anger- either towards an innocent person or towards a person who insulted them. As expected, narcissists were most likely to express their anger, and they were the most aggressive towards the person who caused their anger. Have this in mind the next time you're dealing with a narcissist. Most importantly, the seriousness of the insult was in relation to the intensity of the wrath. So, our statement - The more threatened the ego, the more likely is a person to act aggressively- has been experimentally proved.

Narcissistic abuse syndrome

Narcissistic abuse is a thing. It happens, and it has serious consequences for the well-being of its victims. This syndrome is relatively unknown, especially when compared to other stress disorders, like Posttraumatic Stress Disorder, that has been in the center of attention since the first Vietnam War veterans returned to the USA. And this is why we want to describe and the narcissistic abuse syndrome (NAS). Note that there are several slightly different terminological solutions- we refer to the disorder as narcissistic abuse syndrome, but it is often referred to as narcissistic victim syndrome, or even narcissistic victim abuse syndrome. These little differences aren't that important. What is important is the problem itself.

This syndrome refers to any kind of abuse committed by a narcissist. It mostly concerns emotional abuse but isn't confined to this particular type. There are many subtypes of this syndrome, of which parental narcissistic abuse syndrome is the most well-known one. In this case, the parent becomes excessively controlling and autocratic. We all know that type of parent that has already planned the next 20 years of a 2-year-old child. They overburden their children with innumerable obligations, like sports, instrument playing, school-related activities, etc. This might not be that big of a problem, only if narcissistic parents weren't so aggressive when their child fails. Just imagine being a child who is constantly dragged from one activity to the other. After your swimming class, you rush to piano lessons. And, as if this wasn't enough of a drag, your parent(s) gets extremely angry at you when you aren't the best one in your group.

The situation is a bit different with adult-to-adult relationships. Besides our main antagonist, narcissist, another type of individuals steps into the game- dependent persons.

By finding a dependent person, a narcissist gets all the admiration he needs. On the other hand, the dependent person finally finds someone who will take control. By choosing a narcissistic individual, not only will they find someone who will control them, but also someone who will enjoy doing this. Needless to say, these relationships rarely have a happy ending. It is much more likely that it ends up in a cycle of abuse, where the dependent person formed a bond so strong that abuse isn't seen as a problem. They will endure anything in order to retain their traumatic bond.

A little disclaimer; Narcissistic abuse syndrome is something that has only recently begun to be researched. So there still is a lot to be learned about this syndrome, from a scientific point of view. We won't give lists of symptoms or anything like that, as there still isn't a list of symptoms that has been scientifically validated. Rather, we will only mention the most important signs of narcissistic abuse syndrome.

Probably the most important thing about NAS is the fact that victims rarely mention their real cause of problems in therapy. They will often come to therapy and complain about something that doesn't have even the remotest connection to the abuser. They will come and say: "I feel a bit depressed lately.", or "My husband told me that I need to get some help." They will usually blame some irrelevant factors. But, little by little, a good therapist will begin to know what he's dealing with.

Second thing, if the therapist tries to confront the victim with the real cause of problems, even if his confrontation is only a mild and careful one, he will encounter strong resistance. People with narcissistic abuse syndrome will seldom, if ever admit that the person whom they idolize is bad. They may something like: "Yes, my husband is sometimes a very nervous and anxious person. But even when he does bad things, I know that he didn't really want to do them. He's not that sort of person". In statements like these, there is a lot to be analyzed. For example, you probably noted how the victim said "nervous" and "anxious". These are classical euphemisms for aggressive and abusing behavior. Of course, it's much easier to say that someone is nervous than saying that he is aggressive, especially when we idolize that person. Secondly, in statements like this last one, we can see how the victim, while admitting that their abuser can be bad, don't believe that this badness is his inherent characteristic. The bad behavior is perceived as something that just "doesn't go with his personality." However, there must be someone to blame. And it is not rare to see the victim of narcissistic abuse blaming herself for her husband's misdeeds.

Furthermore, victims are often filled with feelings of shame and guilt. They suffer, but they don't know why. As mentioned, there must be someone to blame, and if the victim blames herself, what are the most logical emotions to ensue- of course, shame, guilt, low self-esteem, etc. This only makes the situation even worse, as the person lacks the power of will to face her present and future struggles. What do we mean by "present and future struggles"? Well, for starters, we supposed that a vast majority of people who suffer from narcissistic abuse syndrome aren't aware of the real cause of their troubles, at least in the initial period. This initial period of the disorder can be of lesser intensity when compared to the latter phases of the disorder. By "present struggles", we wanted to say that the victim first has to know the real truth. That is the first and sometimes the most important hurdle on the way towards recuperation.

Future struggles come when the person finally becomes aware, and when idolization of the abuser begins to pale. This is probably the most challenging phase, as the person has to face the fact that she devoted years of her life to the man who actually despises her and has continually hurt her over the years. Memories of past traumas that have been repressed up until now all come to the surface. The victim finds herself overburdened by vivid, relentless visions of traumatic events. These memories also haunt their dreams. Victims' lives become completely absorbed by the past. Everything they do, every little thing they own, everything points to their wound that looks as if it will never heal. Despair, sulk, depression slowly enter the victims' lives. Finally, people who suffer from narcissistic abuse syndrome may have problems with forming new interpersonal relations. After all, they have been hurt so bad, it is reasonable to be suspicious and on alarm every time a new person appears. So, not only does the victim suffer emotionally, but she is also unable to find support in others.

There are other peripheral symptoms. Depressive people might have some cognitive difficulties- problems with attention, short and long-term memory. Work performance might decrease severely. In short, the whole life, every little aspect is influenced by the abuse they endured. Luckily, this is not something that stays for good. When treated, victims of NAS get back to their usual levels of performance, which is why it's very important to appropriately treat this disorder.

NAS is quite similar to PTSD. For example, we've mentioned that people with NAS have nightmares and cognitive deficits, which is also the case with people who have PTSD. Moreover; people with PTSD avoid situations that have some connection to the traumatic event. For example, a soldier who was severely traumatized during the war may avoid seeing his fellow veterans. He may avoid movies with war-thematic. Similarly; the individual with NAS may avoid any situation that will remind her of her abuser. Mutual friends, places they have visited together, the house they lived together, even their kids, all this might remind her of her abuser.

There are other similarities. Recurring thoughts, memories about the initial trauma happen in both disorders. Vivid, almost life-like "flashbacks" of the traumatic event, although one of the major symptoms of PTSD might as well appear in NAS. Especially in cases when the person is surrounded with objects that remind her of her abuser, these flashbacks are highly likely. And they feel like going through hell all over again. Also, people with PTSD and NAS experience extreme sensitivity and reactivity to unexpected, sudden stimuli. This shows how defensive they become. They are so traumatized they always watch out for threats. It's obvious that this hypervigilance is something extremely exhausting. Imagine being 24/7 on the alarm; always being afraid of some unexpected disaster. You don't sleep, eat, or smile. Nothing stays the same. Hell on Earth.

Let's see how Patrick Carnes, counselor, and famous best-selling writer, systematized traumatic response. He discerned 8 major groups of symptoms:

1. Reaction- we've mentioned some of these symptoms. They are usually seen in PTSD when people avoid situations that might remind them of their trauma. Recurrent memories, thoughts, and images of the trauma itself also fall within this group.

2. Arousal- this is an obscure part of trauma, and rarely debated. We could say that this is a "pleasurable" part of trauma. In other words, victims of narcissistic abuse, although severely traumatized, sometimes experience positive emotions in relation to their abuser, which, of course, makes the situation even more confusing for them.

3. Blocking- cognitive problems, depression, indifference, lack of motivation, and numbing. These and other symptoms represent a way to adapt to the horrible consequences of the abuse. It is sometimes much better to completely "turn off", and become numb than to continuously think about the trauma. So, once again, the term maladaptation is pertinent.

4. Splitting- when a person goes through extreme abuse and trauma (such happens during a war), the reality can just become too much. It becomes impossible to block unwanted thoughts entering the mind, even with depression and numbing. So a person has to resort to another means- making up her own fantasy world. It slowly becomes obvious that the real, harsh reality is completely dissociated from the fantasy world, there are no overlaps.

5. Abstinence- this is a somewhat more constructive way of dealing with abuse. It is not unusual to see the victim become completely immersed in her work. When this happens, victim closely resembles individuals with obsessive-compulsive personality disorder. For example, they begin hoarding money, without any special goal or intention. The victim exerts herself and works long hours. Social functioning may suffer as a result. The victim just doesn't have enough time to hang out with other people, and even if she did, she feels awkward in the company of others and isn't sure how to behave around other people.

6. Shame- there was already much talk on shame and guilt. Simply put; when victims reflect on the years of their life that passed in utter suffering, they cannot shake off the impression that they were extremely stupid, submissive, or even that they are to blame for the unfortunate events that happened.

7. Trauma repetition- it is not unusual to see the victim returning to her abuser. This is the so-called vicious cycle of abuse. As mentioned before, the relationship between the abuser and his victim is almost always an ambiguous one. Yes, there is a lot of bad stuff going on, but sometimes, the victim may feel some positive emotions in relation to her abuser. And her dependency, her belief that the abuser "finally changed" and "got back to his senses" is what gets her to forget everything bad that happened. And we all know what happens after.

8. Trauma bonds- it is not unusual to see the victim still cherishing some positive emotions towards her abuser. For example, William Faulkner, although a good writer, was a very difficult man. He drank profusely and was particularly aggressive at times. His lover, Meta Wilde, often had to endure Faulkner's fits of rage. But she never left him, always returning even after severe physical abuse she suffered.

Chapter 5 Narcissistic Manipulation Tactics

The Cycle of Abuse

The key to understanding narcissistic abuse is to understand what the narcissist is looking for in a relationship. Narcissists are always looking for someone to admire them, someone to reinforce the ideal self they've created. This feeling of being admired and praised is called "narcissistic supply," and everything the narcissist does is done for the purpose of either maintaining one source of narcissistic supply or cultivating a new source.

In parent-to-child narcissistic relationships, the narcissistic parent treats the child as a permanent source of narcissistic supply and does everything possible to prevent the child from ever becoming an independent person through guilt-tripping, belittling, and other abusive behaviors.

In adult-to-adult narcissistic relationships, the narcissist comes on strong in the early stages with an idealized and ultimately imaginary version of his real personality. The ideal self isn't real, so the narcissist won't be able to keep up the façade. The true self slips out, and the narcissist does something abusive and damaging. When the mask is restored, the victim is once again shown the idealized self. This emotional roller coaster can result in something called "trauma bonding," where the victim actually gets emotionally closer to the abuser as a result of the abuse. Even though the victim may want to believe that the idealized version of the narcissist is real, and the abusive behavior is the exception, the truth is the exact opposite.

In the end, the narcissist will seek out a new source of narcissistic supply, discarding the old relationship as if it never meant anything. In some cases, the narcissist will hover in the background rather than completely disappearing. By going away and then coming back, the narcissist can keep the victim from ever moving on and ensure his own access to the narcissistic supply.

The Five Stages of Abuse

The cycle of abuse can be divided into five stages, marked by different types of abusive behavior—some of which will not appear abusive at first. The first stage is gaining trust, in which the abuser idealizes the victim and acts loving, kind, and sweet. In cases of narcissistic abuse, this is when the narcissist will present only the false or idealized self.

The second stage is over-involvement, in which the abuser works his way into every little detail of the victim's life. Healthy boundaries are slowly eroded until the victim can no longer tell what a boundary violation is and what is not.

The third stage is rulemaking, in which the abuser sets the terms of the relationship through jealous and controlling behavior. This is presented by the abuser as an expression of their love for the victim, but the level of jealousy and micromanaging extends far beyond normal relationship insecurity.

The fourth stage deals with control, in which the abuser gains power over the victim through all kinds of abuse and manipulation. Most of the obviously abusive behaviors don't occur until this stage when the victim already has a diminished ability to recognize and respond to what is happening.

The fifth stage is trauma bonding, where the abuser once again presents the ideal self for a time to draw the victim closer again.

Methods of Control

Once you understand that the abuser's manipulative and controlling behaviors are part of a pattern, it should be easier to recognize specific abusive behaviors for what they are. The narcissistic abuser's methods of control include:

- Superficial charm
- Love bombing
- Nagging
- Ignoring
- Punishment
- Guilt Tripping
- Emotional Blackmail
- Isolation
- Mind Games
- Gaslighting
- Blaming the Victim

Superficial Charm

"Superficial charm" is the narcissist's version of courtship behavior. The narcissist is slick and likable, but there is nothing behind it because the charming behavior is only an expression of the false self the narcissist has created. Narcissistic parents may use superficial charm when interacting with anyone outside the household, such as teachers or social workers. In a dating relationship, the narcissist uses superficial charm to gain the victim's trust.

Narcissists in the early stages of a relationship may appear to be unusually romantic, attentive, and complimentary. They may seem to idealize you or to have a lot in common with you—perhaps too much to be completely believable. One tactic of psychological control is "ingratiation," in which the abuser gains your trust by deliberately mirroring your likes and dislikes.

In reality, these behaviors are all part of the act. It isn't easy to tell the difference between superficial charm and genuine good-will, but if your instincts are telling you that something is off, then you should slow down and pay close attention to other red flags such as "love bombing."

Love Bombing

The term "love bombing" originally referred to as a recruitment tactic used by some cult groups. Potential members of the cult would be drawn in through intense displays of positive attention and affection combined with strong pressure to join the group. Later on, mental health counselors started to use the term to describe a similar tactic often used by narcissistic abusers.

To a lonely person looking for love and affection, a sudden and over-the-top display of love can be like a drug. It feels so good that you just want more. The narcissist knows this and uses the "love bomb" to draw the victim in. The intense positive attention is combined with pressure to commit quickly, escalating the relationship to a higher level much faster than most people would usually be comfortable with.

The combination of affection and pressure creates a sense of anxiety, as the victim doesn't want to miss out on the chance at "true love" by resisting the narcissist's wishes. The pressure to commit is also a test, in which the narcissist is trying to find out whether the target will set a firm boundary or not. When the victim gives in to the pressure and agrees to a commitment, the narcissist is already in the second stage of abuse—the stage of over-involvement.

Of course, it can be hard to tell whether someone is love bombing you or genuinely falling in love with you. The main difference is consistency. Love bombing is shallow and is always followed by devaluation. From being idealized, you become the object of contempt and derision. Real love isn't like that, but the only certain way to tell the difference between the two is to wait and see. That's why it's so important not to get carried away and escalate the relationship too quickly—especially if you're feeling pressured.

Nagging

Superficial charm and love bombing are both types of positive reinforcement, in which you are rewarded with positive attention for doing what the abuser wants you to do. Nagging is a type of negative reinforcement in which you are pressured to do what the abuser wants you to do.

Nagging isn't always abusive. Parents nag children to clean up their rooms, and children nag parents for candy or screen time. As annoying as that can be, it doesn't constitute abuse. Abusive nagging happens when you try to set a healthy boundary, and the abuser wears your boundary down with repeated requests. Like many other kinds of subtle manipulation, nagging always has plausible deniability. If you call out the narcissist for pushing your boundaries, she can always claim that she was "only asking" and accuse you of being oversensitive.

In a healthy relationship, some decisions are shared equally between both parties, and some decisions are yours alone. You may be the victim of abusive nagging if the other person is always pressuring you to agree to their wishes on shared decisions or to let them influence decisions that should be yours to make. Nagging is a common tactic in narcissistic parenting but is also used by narcissists in other types of relationships.

Ignoring

Ignoring or shunning is another type of negative reinforcement. This includes "the silent treatment," withholding affection, and so on. It can be as overt as simply refusing to speak to you or acknowledge your presence, or as covert as a vague but persistent atmosphere of emotional coldness and rejection.

Ignoring goes hand in hand with love bombing even though the two may seem to be opposites. First, the abuser gives you the addictive drug of intense affection and admiration—then, she cuts it off completely if you don't do what she wants. Desperate to get the feelings back, you quickly cave in under pressure—and the abuser gains more control.

Some narcissists will alternate positive reinforcement and negative reinforcement just to leave you off-balance and emotionally dependent. This tactic is known as intermittent reinforcement. Through acting cold and dismissive one moment and extremely sweet the next, the abuser creates a situation where the victim is constantly chasing after them and trying to win their approval and affection back.

When the abuser starts being sweet again after ignoring or being cold to you, the relief can be so intense that you actually crave their affection even more than before. This is one example of trauma bonding, where the abuse brings you closer to the abuser in a profoundly toxic way.

Punishment

Ignoring and nagging can both used as types of punishment, along with other behaviors such as yelling, swearing at you, or dramatic emotional displays. By flipping out and making a huge scene when you don't do what he wants, the abuser makes you reluctant to go against his wishes in the future.

One of the most dramatic and frightening types of punishment is "narcissistic rage," where the narcissist responds with total fury to even the slightest hint of criticism. The narcissist may lash out with intentionally vicious personal attacks, escalating in some cases to property destruction or physical violence.

Narcissistic rage has two sides to it. On the one hand, the narcissist's self-image is a fragile veneer covering a much more profound self-loathing. Any criticism destroys the illusion, forcing the narcissist to confront the intolerably painful reality. To this extent, the rage is real.

On the other hand, the narcissist uses her rage to intimidate and manipulate the victim, by creating such a horrible scene that the victim will feel very reluctant ever to criticize the narcissist again. From this perspective, narcissistic rage is just a tactic of manipulation and control.

Sobbing, playing the victim, and threats of self-harm can also be used as forms of punishment. It can be hard to tell whether a person is intentionally trying to punish you or is simply feeling emotional. As always, the key is to see if there is an ongoing pattern. If there is a heavy price tag whenever you fail to do what the other person wants, then it's probably safest to assume they're doing it intentionally.

Guilt Tripping

The guilt trip is one type of punishment behavior. This behavior is especially common when dealing with a narcissistic parent, but it can also be found in other relationships.

The person who is trying to guilt-trip you accuses you of not really loving them, not caring about their problems, or of having done something to harm them in the past. Once they can see that you are feeling guilty, they give you the chance to be absolved of your guilt, but only if you do what they want. For instance, a narcissistic parent may guilt trip you into spending time with them instead of a friend, which also has the effect of isolating you.

Guilt-tripping only works on a person who cares about being loving and kind. It's painful to be told that you aren't a good person, so you're strongly motivated to do whatever it takes to avoid that. Unfortunately, this makes you vulnerable to manipulation.

Of course, if you were really such a terrible and uncaring person, then no one could make you feel guilty in the first place because you just wouldn't care. If someone wants you to feel like a bad person, you should ask yourself what they want from you. If it's something you wouldn't normally do, then they may simply be trying to use your guilt to get past your healthy boundaries and gain control over your decisions.

Emotional Blackmail Tactics

There are four different types of emotional blackmail tactics, as identified by the therapists Forward and Frazier in their study of the topic.

The first type is the threat of punishment, which includes several of the other tactics discussed in this chapter. For example, "Have sex with me, or I'll give you the silent treatment for the next three days," or "Add my name to your bank account, or I'll call off our engagement." The threat of punishment doesn't have to be explicitly stated; it can just as easily be implied.

The second type of emotional blackmail is the threat of self-harm. This is also a type of guilt trip because the obvious implication is that you are responsible for what happens next. "If you break up with me, I'll kill myself" is the clearest example of this tactic.

The third type of emotional blackmail is based on a display of self-pity. This is another type of guilt trip, in which the abuser does something nice for you but makes a big deal about the huge sacrifice they're making. For example, "I cooked you your favorite dinner even though I have a terrible headache." The idea is to put you in their debt so they can have more leverage over you.

The fourth type of emotional blackmail is to imply that you'll get a reward of some kind if you do whatever the other person wants you to do. This is different from a straightforward exchange of favors because it's used to pressure you into doing something you don't really want to do. In one way or another, it doesn't feel like an equal exchange.

Emotional blackmail tactics can be used for different purposes. Sometimes, they are used to get you to do something little that you might easily have agreed to anyway. Sometimes, they are used to get you to agree to something you're uncomfortable with, but that is still fairly minor in the big scheme of things. Sometimes, they are used to influence your life decisions, such as where to live or whether to go to school. In the most extreme scenario, emotional blackmail can even be used to convince you to participate in criminal behavior.

Isolation Tactics

The narcissistic abuser may use any of these manipulation and control tactics to isolate you from the other people in your life. For example, if you make plans to see a friend for coffee, a narcissistic partner may nag you to change your plans, or give you the silent treatment when you get home or accuse you of not wanting to spend any time with him. He may use emotional blackmail, saying, "Of course I don't mind if you go out with your friends, all I want is for you to be happy. It's just that I've been feeling so depressed."

Whatever specific tactic the narcissist uses, the end result is the same—you find it so difficult to make plans with your friends that you gradually stop doing so, and the narcissist increasingly becomes your only source of emotional support. This not only makes it less likely that you will decide to leave, but it also feeds into the narcissist's own need to be the center of your world.

Mind Games

Abusers often play mind games to keep their victims disoriented and passive. For example, an abuser may set you up to fail by giving you a task without the time or resources needed to complete it successfully. If you accomplish something you're proud of, the abuser may minimize it or refuse to acknowledge it. The abuser may repeatedly remind you of past failures or mistakes, or may "shift the goalposts" so you're always trying to catch up with an ever-changing set of expectations. He may use a one-sided story about your relationship as a type of propaganda, leading you to accept a distorted view of past events. This is also a type of brainwashing, where the abuser seeks to alter your ability to process reality and form your own opinions about it.

Gaslighting

If you bring up issues in the relationship or things that have hurt your feelings, the abuser may try to convince you that you are simply irrational and that your concerns have no validity. This is known as "gaslighting," the process of making someone doubt their own experiences and memories so they will not question or attempt to resist abuse.

For example, a narcissist who's cheating on you may try to convince you that you are irrationally jealous and controlling. A narcissist who is keeping you isolated may try to convince you that you are a paranoid and suspicious person. Gaslighting tactics are meant to make you feel crazy, so you attribute your legitimate concerns about the relationship to your own mental health issues rather than the other person's behavior.

Blaming the Victim

Gaslighting often goes hand in hand with blaming the victim. The abuser may accuse you of abusing them, or of somehow provoking their abusive behavior. The most common form of "blaming the victim" is seen in cases of domestic violence, where a partner hits you but then blames you for making them so angry in the first place.

In some cases, the narcissist can even convince other people that they really have been wronged and that their victim is "the real abuser." The narcissist's superficial charm can sometimes fool people, leading them to accept a twisted and one-sided interpretation of events. These people can then be manipulated into siding with the narcissist or participating in a smear campaign against the victim of the narcissist's abuse. Victims have coined the phrase "flying monkeys" to describe people who have been manipulated into helping a narcissistic abuser, just like the flying monkey soldiers of the wicked witch in The Wizard of Oz.

The Big Picture

Some actions are clearly and unambiguously abusive, such as hitting the other person. Far more often, a toxic relationship has many complex aspects to it, and it's not so easy to say whether a partner is intentionally unmannerly or not.

The big picture is what really matters. Abuse isn't about being passive-aggressive or guilt-trippy on a few occasions—it's an ongoing pattern of control and manipulation. The narcissist isn't just acting out in a moment of weakness but using you as a means to an end. That end is a deep need that can never be satisfied, and the roots of that need to go back to childhood.

Chapter 6 Learning The Language Of Narcissist: Who Abusers Use Anything And Everything Against Their Victims

If you do have to walk away from a narcissistic partner, friend, family member, etc., then there are a few things you need to know about 'after the event'.

It's this simple - a narcissist is not likely to shrug his or her shoulders and say, 'okay then, see you', and then let you walk away with nothing else occurring. It's far more likely that they will revert to their best behavior and try and lure you back.

There is one very good reason for this - because they hate rejection and take it very badly indeed. When you walk away from a narcissist you are rejecting them as a person, no matter how badly they treated you. They will not see all the emotional abuse and manipulation that came your way, in their eyes, they treated you like a king or queen. Instead, they will see you walking away, and it will rile them, or cut deep into their self-conscious depths. The next step could be one of two things:

- They will either become angry and resentful and probably bombard you with messages and social media posts about how they're better off without you and you're this, that, and the other (more abuse)

- Or they all become the epitome of charm once more and try and remind you of all the good times

If you find scenario one coming your way, ignore and block. This is simple pride getting in the way. In this case, they see you as rejecting them, they see you as making a mistake, and they're turning the whole thing on you. Of course, you know better. Block their number, block them on social media, do not go anywhere you know they will be, and go and stay with a friend for a while if you're worried, they're going to turn up at your door. Eventually, they will become bored and grow tired with no response. Sad, but true.

Scenario two is also common, and this is how many people in narcissistic relationships end up going back time and time again. The only answer here is to stand firm and remember why you left. If you can stick with your tried and tested support group, then even better. These people will remind you when your resolve might be wobbling, and it will at some point. You did have good times, and you were with them for a reason. Remember, if you've been a victim of gaslighting then it might also be that you're unsure of your next step because you're still suffering from the after-effects of this type of emotional abuse. Your friends and family will need to hold you firm in this case, but again, block numbers and social media access. The less they can contact you, the easier it will be for you to make large strides into your future.

What to Expect:

- Begging

- Pleading

- Bargaining

- Blame games

- Insults

- Eventual silence

If you think you're out of the woods then the silence comes, don't be so hasty. If they see you in the street quickly afterwards, bargaining and pleading is likely to start again. Breaking away from a narcissist takes time but know that it will be a process you'll be pleased you embarked on.

Dating After Leaving a Narcissist

Once you are over the 'getting away from a narcissist' process, the future will seem brighter and far clearer. It's important to give yourself the time to grieve the relationship properly, and not to jump straight into another union in order to try and block out the upset that occurred previously. This is a common scenario, but more common is trying to avoid another relationship altogether.

Remember that you cannot judge a future partner based on what you went through before, but it's entirely normal if you do. For this reason, seeking out counseling or therapy after leaving a narcissistic partner is a good idea. By not dealing with everything that happened, you are actually putting your future at risk. Many people who have emerged from narcissistic relationships are so scarred by what they went through emotionally, they don't want to ever get close to another person again. As soon as a new partner starts to show even the tiniest hint of something which could be akin to narcissism, they run.

The fact is that we all show slight signs of narcissism from time to time, but that doesn't make us narcissists. We can all lack empathy sometimes, we can all belittle someone without meaning to once or twice, and we can all act in ways we wish we hadn't. The difference is that we will apologize and see the error of our ways, whilst a narcissist won't. Do not make the error of labelling everyone with the same tag or tarring everyone with the same brush.

The best way to dip your toe back into the dating world after emerging from a narcissistic relationship is to do so slowly. Try this:

- Give yourself time to simply be. Don't attempt to do anything, don't try and feel anything and don't push yourself to move on; simply spend time on yourself and try and unpick the events in your mind and deal with them. If you need to gain someone else's perspective, or you need to seek out professional help, now is the time to do so.

- Focus on yourself. Next, it's time to seek out things you enjoy and be kind to yourself. You spent so long with someone being unkind to you, it's likely that you've forgotten how to do things for yourself and to enjoy them. Find a hobby you've always wanted to try, go to a night class, go out with friends, spend Sunday mornings being lazy, read your favorite books, eat your favorite foods, and get out into nature.

- Focus on your health. Next up, after your self-focusing time, turn your attention to your health. A healthy body and mind are the best types of revenge! Whilst revenge shouldn't be on your mind, being a better version of yourself after a bad experience certainly feels great. Eat healthy foods, make sure you get plenty of exercise, get plenty of sleep, avoid stress, and make sure that you challenge your mind on a regular basis. You will notice how much stronger you feel.

- Enjoy your life. Once you start to feel better, and it may take considerable time in some cases, simply start to enjoy your life. Don't make it your sole aim to meet someone, and don't even think about dating; if it happens, it happens. There is plenty of time for all of that.

- When you're ready, simply be open to the possibility. The point is to try and meet someone who is worthy of your time and attention and who can give you what you didn't have before. The point isn't for someone to complete you or heal you. When you think you might be ready, simply be open to meeting people, but don't place huge importance on it. People who have come out of narcissistic relationships can sometimes be needy because they're so desperate for it not to happen again. By following these steps and placing importance on building yourself up once more, this is far less likely to happen to you.

- Do not tar them with the same brush. Again, if you do meet someone and you start to date, don't tar them with the same narcissistic brush as your ex. This is a vitally important step. True narcissists are very, very rare, and that is something to remember. It's highly unlikely you're going to meet someone with NPD twice in your lifetime, and whilst it's possible that you might meet someone who acts a little narcissistic on occasion, this isn't at rue narcissist and therefore won't bring the same types of problems.

- Know the signs. Do not run at the first sign of a problem but always hold your requirement for respect and understanding high up on your list. If someone starts to treat you badly, address the issue and stand firm before walking away. If being in a relationship with a narcissist will teach you anything, it's not to allow the same thing to happen again.

If you're reading this and thinking 'there's no way on Earth I'm even attempting to date again, I'm good by myself', it's time to question why you feel that way. Are you saying that because you truly don't want a relationship and you would rather be alone and spend your time traveling, making meaningful connections with friends, etc? Or, are you saying it because you're scared of going through the same thing twice?

Some people don't want to be in a relationship and that's fine, provided it's for the right reasons. If you're avoiding romantic connections simply because you're scared, that's something to address early on. You will probably find that your feelings change over time, but avoid being closed off to possible connections, simply because your past experiences are clouding your judgement.

Remember, you deserve to be loved, no matter what you might have been forced to believe in the past.

The Future for a Narcissist Who Refuses Help

We've talked a lot about the future for a person who was in a narcissistic relationship, but what about the future for the narcissist themselves?

It doesn't paint a great picture if the person isn't willing to seek help. In that case, it's far more likely that a narcissist will end up jumping from destructive relationship to destructive relationship, and if they do end up in a long-term union, it's unlikely that their partner will be truly happy and fulfilled. That person is far more likely to be simply 'putting up' with the narcissism.

If a narcissist ends up in a relationship which yields children, the sad truth is that their children are quite likely to develop narcissistic tendencies as a result of being open to them during their early years. Whilst there isn't a certain answer in terms of what causes NPD, there a definite suggestion that childhood experiences have a very firm link towards someone developing the personality development in their adolescent and then adult years.

Narcissists also have a habit of becoming quite bitter over time. This is partly because people have come into their lives and then left them, and they can't see why; of course, they will project the blame onto the other person and won't see their role in them leaving. Many narcissistic traits, therefore, worsen with age, as more experiences are racked up throughout life.

As you can see, it's quite a bleak picture we're painting and that is the sad truth about life as a narcissist. People will only stand being treated a certain way for so long before they eventually pluck up the courage to leave. Whilst some may never get to that point, these relationships are likely to be empty and lacking in true love and respect.

For these reasons, the biggest price a narcissist pays for their actions over time is loneliness and a lack of truly meaningful relationships in the end. For a narcissistic, however, the most loving and deep relationship they have is with themselves.

Are Modern Social Elements to Blame?

You're almost at the point where you know everything there is to know about Narcissistic Personality Disorder and the traits and issues which go alongside it, but we also need to explore one possible area before we sign off. Are modern social elements to blame for the rising number of narcissists in the world?

Remember, true narcissists are quite rare, yet it's a term that we hear on such a common basis. For that reason, perhaps narcissistic tendencies are becoming more common, and we have to question why that is. Is it down to the social pressures we are forced to deal with? Is it down to social media? Is it because of pressures to be the best, look the best, and own the best?

It's probably unfair to lay the blame of narcissism at the feet of modern society, but you have to wonder whether it has played a hand. For instance, social media has made us all so much more aware of other peoples' lives, and our appearances. Social media influences are always telling us that if we want to be the best, we need to look the best, and that means using this product. We're bombarded with people taking selfies and full body photos, without realizing that they've been photoshopped and filtered to within an inch of their lives. Most of what we see these days simply isn't real. Is it any wonder that we have such high and unrealistic expectations of what we're supposed to be, what we're supposed to look like, and what we're supposed to aim for?

We aren't entirely sure what causes NPD, so could it be the things we're exposed to in modern life? Of course, much of NPD is thought to be down childhood experiences, but what influences those experiences? What causes a person to act a certain way, causing trauma to another, which could then lead them to develop a specific type of personality disorder? It's hard to pinpoint, but you have to consider the possibility if nothing else.

Whilst we may never entirely understand what causes NPD, and there will always be a certain amount of stigma attached to it, trying to be the best is always a fruitless task. Perhaps instead we should simply be aiming to be ourselves.

In terms of future generations, perhaps it is our responsibility to ensure that children are raised to be happy with who they are, without the need to continually compete and reach certain unrealistic goals. By doing that, we will raise a generation of youngsters who are well-mannered, respectful of others and fulfilled. Surely those are major boosts towards avoiding personality disorders and the types of trauma which may contribute towards development.

Conclusion

And there we have it! We've reached the end of our book about narcissism, and by now you should be far clearer about what it is and what it really means.

After reading this book you should bandy around the idea of narcissism far less and appreciate that it is actually a truly rare personality disorder which shouldn't be misinterpreted. A person who is a little jealous or unkind once or twice in their life isn't a narcissist, they're simply having a bad day; provided they realize this and apologize to those they offended or hurt, there is no harm done. If however, that person doesn't see a problem with their actions, you could be dealing with someone who has an NPD touch.

Whilst a narcissistic cannot actually 'help' what they do, that doesn't mean that you should stick around and put up with it if they're not willing to seek out help to change. Leaving a narcissist behind isn't easy, but it is entirely necessary in order to live a happier life in the future.

The sad thing about narcissism is that whilst we're always talking about it in a negative way, the person who is truly affected is the narcissist themselves. This person is going to end up lonely unless they seek out steps towards a brighter future. This doesn't happen often however, because most narcissists don't realize there is anything wrong with them, and they assume that everyone else has the problem, not them.

Points to Take Away from This Book

Now you've read everything we've had to say about this rather confusing, yet fascinating subject, what are the main points to take away from the book?

- Narcissism is far rarer than most people think, with just 1% of the population affected on the whole

- True narcissism means being diagnosed with Narcissistic Personality Disorder (NPD)

- Men are far more likely to be narcissistic than women, however, that doesn't mean that female narcissist don't exist!

- A narcissistic is defined by a sense of the grandeur of one's self, inflated ego and self-importance, and a need to be the center of attention, but the traits are quite far-reaching beyond that

- Narcissistic behavior can be mild, moderate, or extremely severe

- Many narcissists use emotional abuse without even realize it, e.g. gas lighting

- There are several types of narcissists, including classic, vulnerable, and toxic

- Toxic or malignant narcissists are extremely damaging and are closely linked to psychopaths and sociopaths

- Many narcissists end up alone in the end, because they refuse to see a problem with their actions, and blame everything on those around them

- A person in a relationship with a narcissist is likely to be subjected to various levels of emotional abuse and manipulation, and will probably find it very hard to leave

- Empaths and narcissists are the worst combinations on the planet

- Treatment for Narcissistic Personality Disorder (NPD) involves therapy, counseling, behavioral therapy and challenging mindsets, and can take a considerable amount of time

- There is no known cause for NPD, however, it is thought to stem from childhood, and could be genetic

- Underneath it all, narcissists are fragile and lacking in self-confidence, with a need for constant validation

- Narcissists take rejection extremely badly

- In order for a person to receive treatment for NPD, they need to realize the problem for themselves, and this cannot be done for them. For this reason, most narcissists are never diagnosed and never treated

- It is impossible to fix or change a narcissist without them seeing the error of their ways and understanding that they have a personality disorder which requires treatment

- Finding the strength to leave a narcissistic relationship can be extremely difficult, and many people need to seek professional help afterwards, e.g. therapy and counseling

- Gaslighting is a very common tool employed by narcissists, which involves manipulating the thoughts and emotions of another person, causing them to question their own sanity

- You should never feel guilty or bad about needing to leave a narcissistic relationship - it's important to focus on yourself

There is a huge amount to talk about on this subject, and we've covered the main areas in detail, whilst reiterating the key points several times. Because narcissism and emotional abuse are so closely linked, this is a subject which requires a lot of press space. There is no fun in being in a relationship with a narcissist, just like there is no fun in a friendship with a narcissist or being closely linked in a working situation. All you will deal with is constantly belittling and their inflated sense of grandeur. Despite that, it's also important to realize that this person isn't a 'bad person', they're someone who is suffering from a personality disorder, which actually links very closely to other mental health problems.

By knowing all you can possibly know about narcissism, you can take the right steps towards managing a situation which is touched by narcissism in your own life.

The takeaway point from this whole book? If a narcissist tells you it's your fault, it's really not. Never feel guilty for putting yourself first.

Chapter 7 The Essential Dictionary To Understanding Narcissistic Abuse

Empathy is thus rather beneficial. However, in cases where an empath is not able to cope with all the feelings and emotions received and precepted from others, empathy may feel like a burden too heavy to withstand alone.

It may be easier for you to cope with what you are experiencing through empathy if you could first identify the type of empathy that defines you and describes you the best, even though empaths can have all of the three defined types.

Take a look at the types of empathy and try to find yourself in description and definition:

Cognitive Empathy

Cognitive empathy is strictly related to the theory of mind as referred to by psychologists and behavioralists. Cognitive empathy carries the ability to understand others by understanding their mental state and their mindset. Empaths that have increased cognitive empathy can somewhat predict what the other person would say based on understanding of their mind and their character. Cognitive empathy draws roots from the ability to deduct what the other person might say or think based on their previous "performance" as perceived by a cognitive empath. Psychologists refer to this social ability as to "thinking about thinking", where the empath with this ability is drawing conclusions on what the other person is thinking, or is capable of, based on determining their mindset, mental state, knowledge, emotions, desires, and even beliefs. It is not only that cognitive empathy allows you to guess what others might think or be able to do based on what you know about them, but it also allows you to understand why is that so – why is someone doing what they are doing based on all factors that you are able to perceive. Needless to say, cognitive empathy represents a rather valuable social skill.

The reason why cognitive empathy as a social skill is referred to as "the theory of mind" lies in the fact that as a person with strong cognitive empathy, you may only presume or predict what the other person would say or what is the other person thinking, or is able to do based on what you know about them and their personality, making it a theory more than a fact. Cognitive empathy is otherwise rather useful as a social skill as it may help you generate an appropriate social response based on what you are perceiving within your mind theory. Cognitive empathy is a rather crucial aspect of our social interaction as we are maturing and can be nurtured and improved already in the early age when your mind and emotions are yet to be defined and developed alongside your character and your personality. As we are growing up and maturing, the importance of understanding other people's mental state becomes very important in relation to how we are responding to other people's actions and reactions, as cognitive empathy helps us understand how someone's mental state may influence their actions. Resolving conflicts with other people also requires understanding how others might feel and how others may act based on their personality and various factors related to their mind and emotions.

Affective Empathy

Affective empathy is perhaps a type of empathy that may take the best out of an empath in case you are not sure how to respond to the way you are feeling about other people's emotions. The definition of affective empathy states that this type of empathy represents the ability to understand how others feel, so you can act in accordance with their emotions. This sensitivity can also backfire, as an empath who has increased affective empathy might be actually physically affected with what other people are feeling. While sympathy and compassion allow us to associate with other people and express our understanding for other people's emotions by being there for them and providing emotional and mental support, affective empathy actually affects empaths to feel the same way others do once they get emotionally involved. This state relates to the explanation we have previously provided on the topic of what empathy actually stands for, explaining the case as a product of emotional experiences that don't belong to us but can be mirrored by our brain receptors where the brain creates an emotional response to other people's distress the way it would generate an emotional reaction in case you would be the one going through that same situation someone else is going through. That is how affective empathy makes an empath feel the same way the other person does, while also carrying the ability to feel the emotions of others as their personal emotional distress. Still, affective empathy is yet another type of empathy that represents a social skill, as it allows us to feel concerned for other people based on the emotions we perceive.

Somatic Empathy

Somatic empathy, as you may guess by the name of this type of empathy, relates to actually feeling physical effects triggered by how you perceive that other people feel. With somatic empathy, the body of an empath may have a physical reaction to an emotion that other people are experiencing. For instance, as an empath who has increased somatic empathy, you may feel nervous when you notice that someone else feels the same way, or even when you know that the person you are connecting with is nervous about something. The same goes for any type of feeling – anger, sadness, disappointment, happiness – somatic empathy represents the ability to physically experience other people's emotions, which can also be rather overwhelming for empaths who are unable to control the way they are experiencing other people's emotions. The somatic nervous system will make the same response to other people's experiences just as it would be the case if you were the one going through that specific case, which is how somatic empathy is defined. Even though empathy represents an important social skill, regardless of which type of empathy is stronger, experiencing other people's emotions physically and emotionally may be exhausting for empaths who give in, or better said "feel in", which is the exact definition of the word "empathy" derived from the German word Einfühlung. Empathy as a term has been studied for around a century by far, however, the word empathy can also find its origins in the Greek word empatheia roughly translated to "in feeling".

How Can We Benefit from Empathy and Why Is It Important?

What needs to be understood is that empathy is indeed a crucial social skill and should be present in every human being – while some people may lack sympathy or compassion, being unable to care for others, these people can still have empathy and understand emotions – the only difference would be that they just don't care how others feel, which may lead to isolation and psychosocial deviations. We are after all social beings, which means that we rely on the company of others just as much we would be unable to survive without being connected to at least one person. Since early ages, when we are still growing up and learning, we also learn how to behave around other people and how to be able to generate an adequate social or emotional response when it is noted that there is a lack of appropriate reactions. For example, two children are playing and they are not getting along well because they both want the same toy at the same time – as they are yet growing up, they don't understand the concept of making compromises and may even have problems with sharing as little children are often acting selfishly. Both children are crying but neither of them is yet able to understand how the other well as their empathy is yet to be developed. This is where an adult has to balance everything and explain how the two children should act appropriately. However, there is an exception to every rule, so there are children whose character will allow them to empathize already in the early age even though social skills might not be entirely developed at that point. This type of children usually grows up to be highly sensitive to other people's emotions, which can sometimes be harmful for their own good.

Talking about the importance of empathy, you also need to note that some people may use their empathy as understanding how other people feel in order to manipulate those people, which is immoral the least to say, but is proving the fact that even people who are not compassionate and fail to sympathize with others can also have empathy. Empathy is thus a crucial part of the way we connect with others, as well as the way we connect.

The way we connect through empathy is actually a benefit that comes hand in hand with this social skill. Not only that people are able to empathize with others, but we can even experience emotions of fictional characters we see in movies and books, which allows us to experience emotions that we otherwise wouldn't be able to, making empathy an important part of emotional intelligence.

What is important to you to know as a highly sensitive being that has an increased capacity of feeling what other people feel, is that despite occasional hardships that may arrive with overreacting to what others are feeling, empathy is truly a gift. That gift allows us to be what we are born to be – human beings that can connect and coexist in a most poetic way – by feeling other people's emotions, which altogether describes the role and importance of empathy.

Precisely thanks to empathy, you are able to create bonds and healthy relationships with others, having the ability to connect on emotional level and to understand others as well as understand your own emotions and how these emotions affect your actions.

How Empathy May Affect Empath's Everyday Life?

Empathy, as we emphasized more than once, is a crucial social skill that helps us establish relationships with other people and connect by understanding our own emotions and other people's emotions. Being an empath is healthy and even necessary based on that definition. But, what about the case of overactive empathy?

How to tell if you are being overactive in empathizing to the extent where your empathy is affecting your everyday life in a negative way?

There are signs that you may pick up in your own reactions to other people's emotions by that may indicate that you might be an overactive empath, which may harm you mentally, spiritually and psychologically.

There are people who are sensitive to how others feel, which can sometimes go beyond their control, which is why protecting themselves from negative influence of other people's emotions comes in as a crucial point of survival. Since you have come this far with the book, you are probably having a hard time with balancing the effects that different people leave on you with their own emotional experiences that are easily soaked in by your sensitive nature. That is how empathy may affect your everyday life, leaving you stranded on how to protect yourself from negative effects that different emotional experiences may imprint on your own map of emotions.

Starting from feeling overwhelmed to actually being able to feel physically exhausted, the inability to control the effects that empathy may be leaving on you may make your life far more difficult to the point where overactive empathy feels like a curse, which is less likely the case with people who are able to balance the way they are receiving and perceiving different emotional experiences that don't originally belong to them.

The fact with overactive empathy is that it leaves the person affected by it vulnerable to other people's emotions making it difficult for an overactive empath to control the way these emotions are received and experienced. Whenever you, as an empath, receive a combination of emotions or a strong emotional reaction appearing at other people, you actually become open to the effects of these emotions. In case you are able to balance this emotional reaction and your response to it, you can use your sensitivity in form of empathy to help others by understanding them, that way also creating bonds and significant relationships. However, in cases where you are more likely to give in to overactive empathy, your emotions are being directed towards the other person with a purpose of helping them feel better, while you are receiving and keeping negative emotions. Overactive empaths may flourish in the presence of love, joy, happiness and positive emotions, as well as among people who know how to appreciate their sensitivity. However, in case an empath with increased sensitivity is exposed to people who may take advantage of their empathy and sensitivity, an empath may feel exhausted, tired, depressed, and even physically ill.

This sort of environment may cause you to retreat and become an introvert as an overactive empath as you would want to avoid the feeling of despair and fatigue that other people may leave on you with negative emotions.

Another case scenario that may affect your life in a negative way is feeling empathy and giving out your positive energy to people who do not deserve to be empathized with. Let's face it – as much as there are people with empathy who want to help others, there are manipulative people capable of horrible feelings, and perhaps worse – horrible actions and reactions. As an empath, you need to try and distance yourself from toxic environments in order to be able to balance emotions you are picking up with your own emotional response, and we are going to show you how this can be done further in the book.

Empaths with overactive empathy also tend to take over other people's problems alongside their emotions which is because empathy allows us to feel the need to help others and feel compassion for problems that aren't even ours to solve. Helping others is a wonderful thing that connects us with other people, but in case you don't own your empathy and the empathy owns you, you won't be able to distance yourself from completely taking over the problems of others. Without boundaries between your own life and other people's lives, you may become easily overwhelmed and even neglect your own problems, which over time becomes debilitating for your personal life.

Even though you are blessed with overactive empathy, that doesn't mean that you should throw your life away and focus on everyone else's feelings and problems but yours.

Overactive empathy may also turn your relationships upside down and lead to codependence, making the way you are connecting with others unhealthy for you. Without setting up boundaries between you and the people you care for, you are preventing them from facing their problems on their own, taking over the role of bringing change into other people's lives instead of allowing them to make changes by themselves with a little push from your side. These sorts of scenarios may create a rather unhealthy environment for you as a highly sensitive person, while your emotional involvement will definitely take its toll over time.

Empaths who have problems with balancing their sensitivity may also be suppressed to energy drainage as you can easily be pulled into feeling other people more than you feel yourself. If you are investing yourself in others, who is investing in your own emotional state?

It may be the case that you are also able to pick up the atmosphere from different places and allow this experience to overwhelm you. Has it ever happened to you that you just walk into a building, come to a visit to someone's house, or pay a visit to someone at a hospital and you can just feel that something isn't quite right? You may feel anxious, sad, and even uncomfortable and scared in case you allow these settings to overwhelm you.

In some cases, empaths may feel physical distress such as headache, nausea, and develop problems of addictions to food alcohol and even drugs as a way of helping themselves cope with what they are going through, while other people's emotions would continue to take more from their sensitivity.

There are so many factors that can affect the quality of your life in case you don't learn how to set boundaries and control the way you feel about different emotions, places, energies and people, which is why we will try and teach you how to avoid falling in despair and gaining control over what you feel.

Is Empathy a Weakness?

In our culture, sensitivity may be considered to be a flaw, and the sad truth is not different when it comes to natural selection – the strongest survive. However, empathy and the sensitivity to other people's emotions doesn't need to be a weakness even though your empathy may at times feel like you have your own kryptonite set to bring your weaknesses at once when faced to it. The sad truth also lies in the case that most parents, if the choice would be narrowed down to only "this or that" would choose their child to be a bully rather than be bullied, and we all know who among the two has more empathy for how others feel. Evolution through natural selection demands from us to be strong – it's a requirement even, and that doesn't only include physical strength, but mental as well. However, you need to know that in the modern age where our evolution comes down to curing diseases that were once deadly, increasing life span and correcting weaknesses given by nature, sensitivity might not be viewed upon as a weakness – but rather as a crucial skill to connect with people and understand them. With social media booming and communities growing, connecting with people becomes more important, not only for emotional reasons, but also for practical purposes such as working and cooperating together, exchanging thoughts and opinions, as well as making friends and starting relationships. Empathy may be a true gift in these cases for empaths who know how to control the way other people's emotions are affecting them. In case you allow different energies and emotions that don't actually belong to you, to put you in a state of distress and make you feel isolated and over the edge, your empathy may be viewed as a weakness, but once you learn how to control what you feel, your sensitivity in form of empathy becomes your strength that may open many doors for you.

Now that you have learned the basics on what exactly means to be increasingly empathetic and sensitive to emotions and energies around you, we are set to show you some valuable techniques on how to protect yourself and use your empathy as an advantage, while adopting techniques that will help you heal emotionally, spiritually and psychologically.

Chapter 8 Dating Emotional Predators

By this point in our journey to better understand narcissistic individuals, one thing should be crystal-clear: there is no chance for a long-term relationship with a person that has NPD. Any "love story" with such individual will end up with heartbreak, shattered dreams, and maybe even years of your life wasted away.

Even when the victim is held tightly in the narcissist's grasps and is forced to accept the reality that he/she wants, deep down, they are aware of the hopeless situation they are in. No matter how hard you might try to deny the truth and rationalize the actions of a narcissist, in the end, it all boils down to the fact that you fell in love with someone that never existed. A charming, wonderful person that promised you the moon and the stars, and you, a kind-hearted individual with a lot of love in your heart to give, trusted him/her. The reality that your soulmate was "fabricated" by a sick, malicious person is absolutely mind-shattering and heartbreaking, for anyone that has to go through it. The trauma eats you up from the inside, even months after the relationship has ended, and the experience changes you in ways you never knew were possible.

No matter how strong-willed, independent, confident someone was before entering into a relationship with a narcissist, the experience steals all of these good things away from you, reducing you to a shadow of your old self, an empty shell that feels hopeless. Not even celebrities are safe from the grasp of abusive relationships. Reese Witherspoon admitted in an interview with Oprah, to have been involved in an emotionally abusive relationship at a young age, also adding that leaving the said relationship was the hardest decision she ever had to make. Stacey Solomon, the presenter of Loose Women, has as well been outspoken about her abusive experience, going as far as describing on the program how it changed her, "I was in an abusive relationship, and it makes you forget who you are. It made me feel like I'd never be the same person again. No matter what I do, I'll always be this weird version of myself. A part of me does begrudge that person for taking that away from me. If someone says something over and over again, it can embed in you."

Another famous example, that might come as a surprise, is actor Johnny Depp. He was in a physically and emotionally abusive relationship with actress Amber Hart, but, because our society is biased to believe that only men can be abusers, people believed his now ex-wife's lies, and he was blamed for months of being the perpetrator. Hart used his fame and money to propel herself up, and even proudly advocated as a member of the #MeToo movement. It took several hours of video evidence, multiple witnesses, hospital bills, domestic violence reports, and even Hart herself confessing to attacking her partner in two instances, to make the public accept the fact that Depp was the victim all along.

So, to reiterate my point, abuse can happen to anyone, regardless of gender or popularity. Nothing makes us immune in this world filled with wolves in sheep's clothing. It sounds scary and hard to accept, but this is the reality of it. You are not at fault for putting your trust in a mentally deranged person, because you had no way of knowing their real self at the time. And when you did start noticing the truth, you were already strapped in the horror ride of your life, with little to no way out in sight.

Unfortunately, the only way to put an end to narcissistic abuse is for the victim to initiate the break-up, as soon as he/she realizes that their partner is a narcissist. Break-ups take a lot of time, resilience, strength, effort, will-power, and support. It will take every single bit of energy that you may have left, after the constant abuse in your relationship, and, even when the break-up is done, the effective escape is only halfway done. Keep in mind that victims are emotionally and psychologically addicted to their partners and thus, very vulnerable to hoovering attempts. You may have to go through this 'break-up' 20 odd times until you build up the strength necessary to reject any reconciliation attempts. As time goes by, you will become more and more powerful. However, the only way in which you can break-off the control that the narcissist has over you is by adopting a No-Contact stance (or a low/limited contact if that's not possible).

No-Contact is the only solution that prevents relapse into the abusive, intoxicating relationship, and it is the first real step towards getting back control over your life. Think of a relationship with a narcissist as an addiction. You know that it's toxic and harmful. Even if it provides pleasures (in this case small episodes of "love" that makes you feel validated), a long-term relationship could ruin you and destroy you as a person. You realize that it needs to stop, but addiction messes with our brain in such a way that it is very hard to put an end to it. And in order to escape that addiction, you need to stay free of that toxic substance that your brain craves, or in this case, that toxic person. That's why No-Contact should be your first step. Your mind and body need to "detox" in order to truly start healing. Every contact you have with the narcissist, post-breakup, is equivalent to you taking in a small quantity of that "drug" back into your system, which is why the danger to "relapse" is so high in these situations. That little dose will have you wanting more, and after a long, emotionally draining fight to leave them, you will have to fight again, and again to make sure that you stay on the right track.

One of the most challenging types of relationships to end is one with a narcissist, and there are numerous reasons for this. For many individuals, the kindness, loyalty, and desire to keep the promises they have made along the line, make it extremely difficult to do so. The narcissist can also make leaving a problematic process because he wants to be the one to call the shots in the relationship, including when it has to do with ending it. So long as the victim believes keeping the relationship going is a vital element to their lives, the narcissist will have the freedom to control them and the choices they make.

For many individuals in a relationship with a narcissist, the breaking point is when the narcissist performs a specific action that they won't tolerate. However, for many victims, this breaking point differs. However, male victims of a narcissistic relationship are not as likely to leave in comparison to female victims. This may be due to the additional weight of responsibility culturally felt by men to see to the needs of women.

Notwithstanding, when a victim of a narcissistic relationship does take the step to leave, they find it hard to stick to the choice they made. This is mostly a result of pity and guilt they feel for the narcissist. Besides, if the narcissist fails to let the victim leave, they will continuously pressure the victim to have a change of heart, frequently with the typical promise to change and do better, which is often not true. The narcissist can make the life of the victim trying to leave the relationship very stressful so as to keep dominating them alongside the relationship.

Do Narcissists Ever End the Relationship First?

There are situations where a particular circumstance will urge the narcissist to end the relationship. These may include events which change the way life is for either the narcissist or the victim. If the victim falls severely sick, unable to move or not able or willing to go on with the life that has been created by the narcissist any longer, this may urge the narcissist to end the relationship. There are times where good events like having a new kid can change the power dynamics in the relationship. This is common in instances where the narcissist has to show more empathy or become more responsible. Some factors that can make the narcissist end the relationship abruptly with a victim include loss of a job, old age, illness, or a promotion at work.

However, for many victims, the narcissist never leaves and sticks like glue, continuing to dominate the victim as he or she so pleases. How then do you leave the relationship in this instance? Below, we will be looking into a few helpful things that can help make this process a seamless one.

Complete Detachment

The first step, of course, will be to end the relationship, and once you do this, you need to ensure you do not remain in contact. This is extremely crucial because, at this point, you are still in search of closure and want answers to what went wrong. This applies even if you know deep down that no response will arise, and this individual still makes you vulnerable.

You need to remember how you found yourself in the position you are in the first place. Do not put yourself through the process of abuse and incessant pain once again. You need to behave like this individual is not on the same planet as you, which in a way is correct. The individual you are yearning for now is only a smokescreen. Stick to that and make sure you keep them closed out totally.

The narcissist will certainly make efforts to reach out by every means possible. Block their numbers and divert all emails to the junk folder. You need to ensure they do not have access to you at their bidding anymore, as the narcissist will try everything possible to get you back.

If there are kids in the equation, you may need to get the help of a third party who will act as an intermediary if you can. If this is not possible, remember to exercise caution and never meet up by yourself with the narcissist you just barely escaped from. You can get the assistance of a qualified therapist to help you put a parenting plan in place. This is a document which is legally binding and has information about financial responsibilities, time-sharing for the kids, and means of reaching out allowed by both parties involved. This can further help ease the process.

Unfriend Mutual Friends

A friend of your narcissistic partner may not be aware of his lifestyle, and they may tell you that you're making a mistake by leaving him. They'll begin to tell you all he has accomplished and why you should have stayed. To prevent hearing about your partner and how he's doing, cut ties with anyone that keeps discussing him even after you made it clear you don't want to hear anything about them. Unfriend them to keep your sanity and if possible, go somewhere far. Narcissists are very good at persuasion and pretense, and they can send a close friend to make you change your mind, knowing the friend does not know them as much as you do.

Write Down the Things that Made You Leave

Due to the deceitful nature of narcissists, you may find yourself reminiscing on the good times you spent with them. This is why you need always to remember the bad times too. The times that the narcissist made you feel worthless and guilty about what he's supposed to be blamed for.

Remember the times that they made you cut ties with your family and the times you question your sanity because you believed you were going crazy. Most notably, remember when you were manipulated and lied to even when you knew it was all lies, and the narcissist told you it was your mind playing tricks on you. Put all these down in a diary and keep safe. Whenever you start remembering the good times in the relationship, get the journal, and read it.

Remember That Narcissists Heal in a Short Period

Narcissists are very good at getting someone new as soon as you leave. They do not waste time before healing from breakups, and sometimes, they already have a preplanned exit strategy. This is how the narcissists believe they can win the game - since the relationship is a game to them.

Avoid Being Tempted to Stay

Narcissists always try to win back their victim by telling them sweet things. They'll leverage on the fact that they're aware of your weaknesses and use this to sweet talk you into coming back to them. Spend time alone and have a serious reflection about past events. This will enable you to understand yourself better, and you'll recognize any form of deceit when you see it.

Avoid being coerced into changing your mind, as narcissists are very good at coercion. They'll tell you what you want to hear at that moment, but it's all part of their game plan. As soon as you accept and go back to them, be ready for another dose of mistreatment, abuse, and emotional blackmail. It's best not to bother going back when you leave, even if you need to pick an essential item you left behind. If you must visit again, do so with caution and don't be deceived by the kind words you'll hear. Ensure you let them know you've moved on and they should do the same. Wish them the best and block their number. If you can't face them because you're not sure of yourself, do it by calling or texting them.

A narcissist will try everything possible to convince you that you have made a grave mistake by attempting to leave them. You may have developed a kind of disbelief in yourself after many months or years of being with a narcissist. They try to persuade or intimidate you to get back to them by telling you to remember the good times and the good things you've done together. They blackmail you emotionally by telling you that you're overreacting and stressing them. They even tell you that you only see the negativities without looking at the positive side.

Even though they may try to let you see the positive aspects of the relationship and why you should stay, they'll always blame you and tell you you're the one with a problem. They'll manipulate you into believing you're doing the wrong things and not helping the relationship. If you're not strong enough, you'll discover that you're losing your self-esteem and the only option you think of is staying. If they find it difficult to persuade you, they'll start talking about your negative sides to devalue you and make you feel bad. They'd start by telling you how you would have amounted to nothing if you hadn't met them, how poor you were before you met them, how you'll suffer if you leave them and how successful they'll be when you leave. They'll also let you know that finding someone that will really love them and put them first is straightforward. If they still need you, they won't want you to disrupt their plans as leaving them means they can no longer control you as you have more power in the relationship.

Forgive a Narcissistic Partner or Friend

Rather than feelings of hatred and anger towards a narcissist, look beyond the picture and understand that narcissism is a disorder. A narcissist is a weak person who devalues, degrades, and abuses their target to fill a void.

Understanding this will enable you to leave a narcissistic person in peace without further drama. You can then easily forgive them and forgive yourself. Quit blaming yourself, as narcissists are known to be perfect manipulators and it's challenging to differentiate between reality and illusion when you're dealing with them. Yes, they're that good!

Take Time to Heal and Grieve

Yes, you need time to heal completely and grieve about who you thought your partner was. As soon as the narcissist's schemes aren't working again, you're able to really know the person you're dealing with. It may come to you as a big shock because of the kindness and affection shown to you at the early stage of your relationship. By the time you become attached and form an emotional bond with this person, you've already gone far into the relationship. However, always thank yourself and be proud of yourself for taking the bold step by leaving because the emotional abuse would have been worse if you remained with them.

Get Busy

Keeping yourself busy will help you heal faster and move on with your life. If you're not sure of what to do, you can write down a list of exciting things to do and get yourself occupied with this. You can exercise, take a walk, visit the zoo, go on a tour, learn something new or anything that makes you happy. Strive to get better at what you do and learn more. Grow as you learn and concentrate on things that'll make you happy. Ensure you move with people that share the same views and ideas with you. You can join groups on social media platforms to make this easier.

Concentrate on the Future

As soon as you leave a narcissistic person, it is essential that you concentrate on positive thoughts and energy on doing great things for yourself and the people around you. Forget the past and focus more on the present. Thoughts of how to be a better you and heal faster should be your major focus at this point.

Love Yourself

You must have suffered lots of emotional trauma by living with a narcissist for months or years, and you may even have concluded that you don't deserve to be loved. That's what the narcissist has planned, and you shouldn't let it happen. Be kind to yourself and love yourself. Once you do everything to ensure you love yourself, any other person that comes your way will have to reciprocate. Self-love will help you build confidence in yourself and find love again. Don't flog yourself for too long, and ensure you always set proper boundaries.

Believe in Yourself

From time to time, you may find yourself thinking about your experience in the relationship, trying to figure out where you went wrong. This is not right! No one deserves to be mistreated as you were. Don't try to justify their actions. Believe in yourself and know the right thing for you. With time, you'll understand that you deserve a lot better than being stuck in a relationship with a narcissist. You'll regain your self-esteem and have a true understanding of who you are. Soon, you'll be compassionate to yourself and move on to healthy and happy relationships.

It would seem counterintuitive for anyone to want to be with someone who is concerned only with him or herself.

We seek romance and relationships in order to receive validation among other things companionship brings. There are hormones involved that will draw two people together and bind them in a whirlwind of emotions and positive vibes. It is supposed to be reciprocal with lots of give and take.

So it is kind of strange at first blush to see how it would be possible to strike that sort of balance with a narcissist. The incessant need for validating the other person while receiving nothing on the other end would be, to put it mildly, emotionally and physically exhausting. To live in the long shadow of a person who demands attention and will subjugate you to the shadows without a second thought.

Here is how it makes sense. Narcissists have a few things going for them, especially at the beginning of a new relationship.

They are very charming, they enjoy the attention, and they have a lot of charisma. All of this sucks people in to them and causes them to want to be around them. According to Susan Whitbourne at Psychology Today this is very common. She compares it to a chocolate cake, where eating just a little bit is fun and satisfying but eating an entire cake everyday can give you diabetes and heart disease.

Narcissists will make you feel like you are the center of their world. You will be convinced this person wants to marry you and spend their life with you through thick and thin.

This is of course and by nature a very short lived but intense experience. This is not happening because they are so attracted to you, although they may believe it at the time. No, the need is different. This is their way of causing you to need them, to validate them, to admire and adore them.

What is happening is called love bombing. The constant showering of attention and validation leading to the inevitable step of them pulling away and causing you to now need them like a drug. It really is like a drug too. The narcissist was giving freely now the source is gone and the person so used to being showered with attention and in the process getting a little dopamine tick each time is now fiending for more.

Do you want to know if you are in a relationship with a narcissist before it is too late?

Chapter 9 The Narcissistic Translator

Narcissists everywhere have similar taste in targets. Because they almost universally rely on manipulation tactics that follow specific patterns, they also tend to seek out the same kinds of people because those tactics work on those people. Certain traits can make for a particularly attractive target for narcissistic abuse, and if you have all five of the ones that are listed, you may find yourself desired by narcissists around you, seeking you out and wanting to abuse your good nature in order to meet their own narcissistic supply. Recognize that not all of the traits listed here are necessarily negative or bad to have, but when combined, they do leave you vulnerable. Understanding which of these traits you may have will help you better protect from narcissistic traps.

Desirable or Attractive Traits or Possessions

Since narcissists only think about themselves, they are only ever doing things if they want something. It could be money, power, status, or attractive partners, or anything else. Regardless of what the narcissist desires, if she finds someone who has what she wants, she will want to pursue a further relationship with him or her. Attracting a narcissist's attention means you have something that the narcissist values and that are the first criteria to being a narcissist's victim. Even if you do not meet the rest of the criteria on this list, just having something desirable means that the narcissist will be more inclined to try to get close to you just to mirror and emulate you. After all, she might be able to get what you have if she acts just like you.

Caregiver

Some people naturally gravitate toward caring for others. They are frequently very empathetic and loving, and their empathy makes them compassionate towards others and their struggles. Because of that compassion and empathy, these people are more inclined to help others in any way they can, even if that involves plenty of patience and understanding, even if some pain is expected along the way.

That compassion, empathy, and patience that caregiver types exhibit is incredibly attractive to narcissists. Narcissists crave attention and admiration, and someone with a caregiver personality is quite likely to happily provide the kind of attention a narcissist needs in the name of taking care of him or her. Knowing that narcissists actively seek out compassionate individuals who thrive on caring for others because they know that these people will see the narcissist as someone in dire need of caring and compassion. They will regard the narcissist with more grace than could ever be deserved and do everything they can to meet the narcissist's needs.

Grew up with Dysfunction

Dysfunctional upbringings cause people to develop skewed senses for what is and is not normal. People often default to what they grew up with as the norm and often repeat what was seen in childhood. When you grow up in a dysfunctional household, you fail to see the glaring red flags around you in the future. For example, if you grew up seeing people who disrespect each other, you normalize that and when you find yourself being sworn at by a narcissist, it seems normal to you. You do not realize that, in healthy relationships, people do not swear at each other or call each other names when the only relationships that were ever modeled for you involved those behaviors. You do not learn to set up normal, healthy boundaries because the people you grew up around failed to set them.

When you have had that dysfunctional way of life modeled and normalized for you, you are far more likely to accept those abusive tendencies in the future simply because you do not know better. Accepting those behaviors for someone you love is an acceptable compromise when you have never seen any different, and because of that, you are an easy target. Because you lack proper boundaries or a proper idea of what a normal relationship is like when you grow up in a dysfunctional home, you are far more likely to seek out something familiar, even if familiar is unhealthy.

Avoids Confrontation

Narcissists are able to get away with their behaviors because oftentimes, those around them are confrontation avoidant. Since the manipulation tactics a narcissist frequently employs require manipulation, which requires the narcissist to avoid being called out in order to work, narcissists tend to gravitate toward people who are uncomfortable with conflict. These people are far more likely to submit and give the narcissist whatever she may desire in the name of avoiding conflict, which works just fine for the narcissist. She wants to find people who will tolerate her manipulation and abuse, even if that tolerance is hesitant or faked. Since, by nature, no confrontational people avoid arguments, they tend to shy away from calling out manipulation or inconsistencies as they happen, and they are likely to tolerate being mistreated because putting up with the manipulation and abuse is seen as more tolerable than creating a conflict. Unfortunately, though no confrontational individuals attempt to avoid conflict at all costs, their peaceful nature has a tendency to attract the attention of those who would love nothing more than to abuse that peacefulness for their own personal gain.

Lacking Self-Esteem

People with low or virtually nonexistent self-esteem crave love and affection. They want to feel special or as though someone loves them, even though they simultaneously feel as though they are worthless or unworthy for some reason. Their low self-esteem leaves them feeling as though they are unimportant or less deserving of success, happiness, love, and family; though these may be the things they crave more than anything else.

Because people with low self-esteem crave that connection and love more than anything, they will frequently put up with abuse because they think it is the only way they will ever receive it. Even though every person is deserving of love, people with low self-esteem do not believe this. This leaves them vulnerable, as when they do find someone who takes a special interest in them, they are willing to go along with anything. Those with low self-esteem are more susceptible to the love-bombing stage, and will likely cling to any scraps of perceived affection, even if they come with abuse and negativity. Due to feeling as though no one else could love them because of their perceived faults, they are willing to put up with the abuse of the one person they believe will. Because of that willingness to put up with the abuse, narcissists seek those with low self-esteem out, knowing they will be able to be manipulated into believing that the controlling behaviors are an attempt at showing love and are proof that the narcissist loves them. Those with low self-esteem may even believe that the harsh criticisms are true and that the narcissist is actually trying to help correct for those flaws in order to help them grow into the person they ought to be. Unfortunately, that could not be further from the truth, and the narcissist only seeks to keep self-esteem at an all-time low for ease of manipulation.

Chapter 10 Have A Love Affair With Yourself?

You have been in a relationship with a narcissist for years, and that has left you scarred, scared witless, and feeling unlovable. In your mind, you believe you don't deserve to be happy because that is what your narcissist ex had told you all the time.

You are feeling numb, and the pain is eating at you. Let me just ask, "Are you a giver? Do you believe that it is better to give than to receive?" That is all and good for you, but what happens when you have nothing left to give?

When you have given everything, and you are down to nothing, having a love affair with yourself is the way to heal.

Get to Know Yourself

Self-appreciation starts with getting to know yourself. Acknowledge your thoughts, feelings, and emotions, as well as your fears and fantasies. It is great to spend time with friends and family, but don't forget to have some quality time with just you.

Many of us today are addicted to our phones, computers, and TV. Some of us even more addicted to our work. When you are on your alone time, turn these gadgets off to have time off from digital noises. Why don't you spend this time writing in your journal instead?

While doing that, it will be relaxing to listen to your favorite music. Of course, it is okay if you just want to savor the silence. Get to know yourself by clearing your mind of the chatter. Take a deep breath and let your mind wander where it wants to go. Instead of doing, focus on simply being.

Engage in Self-Expression

After losing yourself to narcissistic abuse, we often forget the things we used to like. You can revisit or recover these hobbies by engaging in some self-expressing activities. Doing so helps you connect with inner self and achieve a higher nature of being.

Some self-expression projects you can do include yoga, meditation, dance, or singing. You can also go for a walk, swim, run, or bike ride. Writing a journal is also a form of self-expression. Sometimes, just even laughing out loud or having a good cry is good for your soul.

Treat Yourself with Kindness

The best thing you can do for self-love is to be kind to yourself. Even when you have screwed up so many times in your life, be patient. Criticizing yourself will never change a thing. It only results in you doubting yourself even more and adopting a negative attitude.

Don't shy away from complimenting yourself. Helping others is also a way to treat yourself with kindness. The warm feelings of seeing the smiles of other people you have helped are a fantastic way of countering the self-doubt. This way, you can confidently love yourself.

Pamper Yourself from Time to Time

Part of having a love affair with yourself is pampering and courting yourself. From time to time, it is okay to indulge in aesthetic enjoyment, such as activities for sensory delight. It feels good as well to have all your favorite colors, sounds, smells, and textures surround you as part of self-expression.

Pampering yourself also includes getting dressed up from time to time just for the fun of it. You can take yourself on a dream date and reward yourself with special treats. Get a massage or dance until you drop. Most importantly, tell yourself, "I love you" every day.

Performing these practices are meant to ensure that you don't feel obliged to be with someone for fear of loneliness or desperation. When you know your worth and are never short of showing self-love, no one can make you feel like you are not enough. Because you are and you deserve nothing but the best.

Conclusion

You have by now been able to understand the roles that partners take on in any relationship. You now know yourself as a narcissist or a codependent, or otherwise and interdependent partner. If you are a narcissist, you are now aware of your proneness for power and likely addictions, which are actually in control of you, and not you controlling them. For the codependent you are now aware of your tendencies avoid responsibility of yourself for other people.

Everyone desires for a perfect relationship. But this is not attained in principle alone. It takes effort. The human magnet syndrome has revealed to you how you might have ended up in your relationship without due consideration. But you have also gained helpful insights on how to rectify your behaviors and lead your relationships in a conscious manner in order to bring it to the standards you wish for yourself and your loved one.

Narcissism and codependence do not just erupt in adulthood. These are behaviors that are one adapts to from childhood. Childhood emotional negligence is discussed, and strategies for overcoming its effects explained in adequate detail. These attachment styles occur in different relationship types, but the similarities and differences in each have been explored. Narcissists exhibit self-centeredness in their desires, but so do codependences, though they may seem to have a different disposition on the surface.

A narcissist and a codependent can, however co-exist. This is explained in the healing processes and explaining how you can understand your partner of a different attachment style from your own, and how you can adjust your behaviors to accommodate and probably improve your partner's values and personality. This is explained in the healing process. With commitment from all parties, relationships can become ideal as desired by members. You now know how an ideal relationship works.

Emotional abusers are not going to let go, because there is still the psychic cord between you and the abuser. The invisible rope stops you from getting involved with the narcissist even after the relationship is over.

Because of this relation, you will feel several different and negative emotions. This can lead to a lot of frustration and conflicting emotions such as indignation or disappointment, remorse, rage, and even unfaithfulness. It can be much easier to recover from this form of chronic suffering if you know where to start the healing process.

Emotional abuse is a form of behavioral control, but you can free yourself from this type of suffering. If you have endured any kind of violence, you might not have shown your real feelings because of your lack of emotional maturity. You may still depend on an individual to meet your moving needs.

You must trust that you can meet your emotional needs. You don't have to look endlessly to others to show that you are cherished. Remember that the emotional abusers who won't let go can be solved.

One must bear in mind that narcissism is a mental disorder. We won't change, even if you help them stop abusing themselves and feeling something is wrong. Remove any thoughts you can and will help a narcissist absolutely.

The best thing you can do is to respect yourself and to know how to live unreliably. This will restore your trust and respect for yourself. You're really responsible for your thoughts.

Keep in mind that you will never be able to make a narcissist happy because they lack self-confidence deep inside. You feel good about yourself only if you are hurt in some way.

Remember also that a narcissist wants to control you and will not let you go smoothly. The irony is that they believe, like you, that they are betrayed and abandoned.

You have to wake up and understand what love really means. The good news is that you can get plenty of support for such a destructive relationship that clearly consumes your soul.

BORDERLINE PERSONALITY DISORDER

HOW TO STOP ANXIETY AND DEPRESSION WALKING WITH THE SKILLS OF DIALECTICAL BEHAVIORAL THERAPY. HOW TO PREVENT OUT-OF-CONTROL EMOTIONS FROM DESTROYING YOUR RELATIONSHIPS LIKE EGGSHELLS

Introduction

The thoughts that surround personality disorders has gained a lot of stigma in recent years. Many people are scared by what they will have seen on television or in books and they will often see the person with the disorder not as someone they should associate with, but as someone who is to be feared because they are off or going to do something that is crazy. This guidebook is going to take a look into one of these personality disorders, borderline personality disorder, and help you to discover what it is, if you or a loved one has it, and that it is not the person who is strange and wrong, but the disorder that is preventing that person from living the life that they would like.

tarts out with an excellent summary on what this kind of personality disorder is about. It will take some time to look at a brief description of the signs and symptoms, some of the available treatment options, and even how others will be able to help.

When goes into the meat of the issue a bit more and talks about some of the causes that can start borderline personality disorder. This chapter talks about how it is not entirely understood what causes this kind of disorder and how some facts can be present in those who do not have the disorder. Some of the factors that might be present in those with this disorder, especially if they are mixed together include genetics, brain abnormalities, neurobiological factors, developmental factors, as well as some other things.

One of the best ways that you are going to be able to determine if you or someone else has this kind of disorder is to look for some of the signs and symptoms. There are a lot of different symptoms that can be found with this disorder and this chapter is going to split them up into different categories to make it easier to see where each of them lie. Some of the different signs and symptoms that you will be able to see in a person who has this kind of disorder include emotional symptoms, behavior symptoms, self-harm, interpersonal relationship issues, issues with their own sense of self, and cognition problems.

Talks a bit about how this kind of disorder is going to be diagnosed and some of the ways that you will be able to get a diagnosis from the therapist. Some of the topics that will be discussed in this chapter include the subtypes of the disorder, when the disorder will show up, how to diagnose it when other disorders are present, and so on. One of the best things that a person with this disorder is going to be able to do for themselves is to get a diagnosis so that they can get the kind of treatment that they need. Unfortunately, this kind of help is not always available to patients because they are not diagnosed or they are not willing to get the help that is needed.

Talks about what is going to happen once a diagnosis is made and the client has agreed to get the help that they need. This chapter talks about the management and prognosis that will occur during this phase. For the most part, therapy is the best option and this is what is going to be recommended for most patients. There are some cases where the person is going to need some medications to help out though. These are not going to be used in place of the therapy thought; they are often used to treat a few of the symptoms of the disorder or to help out if there are some other issues that are at play and can make the treatment much more effective.

Next is and it is going to talk a bit about the steps that are going to need to be taken to properly deal with this kind of personality disorder. It is going to start out with some of the steps that the family will be able to do to help out their loved one with their personality disorder to help out with the treatment. It will then go into some more details about what a person who has the disorder is able to do to give themselves the best chance at recovery. Recovery is possible for those who have this disorder, but they need to be willing to work for it and keep working and trusting the therapist to see the best results.

Finally, s going to take a look at some of the controversies that come with this kind of disorder. There are many people who think that those with this disorder are big liars and that they either do not have the disorder or if they do, they are just going to lie about it to the therapist and will never be able to get healed the way that they should. This chapter will go on to talk about some of the stigma that can come with borderline personality disorder, and how society and culture has been portrayed to the mass population.

As you can see, there is a lot of information about this kind of disorder and it can be confusing. It does not help matters that some of the symptoms of this disorder are going to be similar to some of the other disorders that are out there so it is hard to recognize and diagnose the disorder in some people. Use this guidebook to start getting a better understanding of the disorder and to help those who may be going through the issue right now in their lives and simply need the right treatment and support to make things better.

Chapter 1 The World of the Borderline Disorder

Also known as talk therapy, psychotherapy is a treatment approach that involves a variety of types, such as dialectical behavior therapy, cognitive behavioral therapy, mentalization-based therapy, schema-focused therapy, and transference-focused psychotherapy.

Like with any other personality disorder, psychotherapy is commonly used to treat patients to help them overcome their problem. It is important to take note that even though medications can be effective solutions for symptoms, they may have unpleasant side effects.

In addition, medications cannot help patients learn emotion regulation, coping skills, and other important skills that they can use to improve their life. In addition, a major objective of psychotherapy is to prevent a person with a personality disorder from committing suicide.

It is crucial to assess and monitor the tendency to become suicidal all throughout the whole course of treatment. When a person with borderline personality disorder displays severe symptoms, they may need to receive medication or even undergo hospitalization.

The following types of psychotherapy should be tried first, before choosing a more invasive treatment procedure.

Cognitive Behavioral Therapy

Cognitive behavioral therapy involves working with a mental health counselor to become more aware of negative, ineffective, and inaccurate thinking. Patients also work with a therapist so they can see challenging situations more objectively and clearly. In addition, they work with a therapist so they can learn how to practice alternative solution techniques.

What can you expect from it? Well, cognitive behavior therapy focuses mainly on the present moment. This means that you should not dwell on your past experiences. You are still allowed to explain how you came to behave or think the way you do, but you should focus on how you think and act at the present.

Cognitive behavior therapy is also directive. You can expect the therapist to be active during every session. He/she will give you direct advice. In other therapies, the therapists mostly sit back and listen while the patients direct the session.

In addition, in cognitive behavioral therapy, the therapists generally assume that your symptoms are associated with the behavior and thinking patterns that you have adapted throughout the years. Hence, they do not believe that simply spending one to two hours per week in therapy is enough to produce significant results.

They are most likely to give homework and let the patients work on changing their behavior and thinking patterns outside of therapy sessions. Before a session ends, homework sheets and handouts are usually given.

Dialectical Behavior Therapy

Dialectical behavior therapy is especially designed to treat borderline personality disorder. In general, it is done through phone counseling, individual sessions, and group sessions. It makes use of a skills-based approach combined with meditation and physical exercises to help patients learn how to regulate their emotions, improve relationships, and tolerate distress.

During individual therapy, the individual therapist is the main therapist and the patient undergoes individual therapy sessions. The patient goes to the office of the therapist to talk about their thoughts and feelings among other things.

During telephone contact, the patient speaks to the therapist via telephone in between therapy sessions. However, it is important to note that telephone contact is not done for the purpose of psychotherapy. Instead, it provides the patient the support and help that they need to apply the skills that they have learned to real life situations, as well as to help them avoid injuring themselves.

The patient may also call their therapist if they want to mend any issues between them prior to the next therapy session. However, they're not allowed to call within the next twenty-four hours if they injure themselves. This is to avoid the reinforcement of self-injury.

In skills training, a patient speaks with a therapist along with a group of people with the same condition. These patients are taught skills that may be useful to their daily situations. These skills include core mindfulness skills, emotion modulation skills, interpersonal effectiveness skills, and distress tolerance skills.

Core mindfulness skills are based on certain Buddhist meditation techniques, but without any religious allegiance involved. Such techniques are used to enable the patients to be more aware of their experiences, as well as to develop the ability to be mindful of the present moment.

Interpersonal effectiveness skills focus on achieving one's goals with other people. The patients are taught how to ask for what they want, refuse requests or offers, maintain good relationships with other people, and improve their self-esteem.

Emotion modulation skills are about ways to change distressing emotional states. Distress tolerance skills, on the other hand, include techniques for dealing with such emotional states if it is not possible for them to be changed.

In therapist consultation groups, the therapists receive dialectical behavior therapy from one another. The members of the group have to stay focused. They are also required to give a formal undertaking to stay in dialectical behavior therapy mode and avoid making pejorative remarks against the other members.

Schema-Focused Therapy

Schema-focused therapy combines different approaches of therapies, particularly emotion-based techniques and cognitive behavior therapy, to help patients evaluate repetitive life themes and life patterns so they can identify positive patterns and correct negative ones. It focuses on helping them change negative and long-standing self-images through letter writing, role-playing, anger management, assertiveness training, relaxation, guided imagery, and gradual exposure to situations that induce anxiety.

Limited re-parenting is one unique key element of schema-focused therapy. Here, the patients are able to establish a secure attachment to their therapist. This is, of course, within the bounds of a professional relationship. According to Dr. Joan Farrell, director of the Schema Therapy Institute Midwest Indianapolis Center, many people with borderline personality disorder missed emotional learning when they were younger. They were not encouraged to express their needs and emotions.

They also did not receive adequate validation, which is why their core childhood needs are met in schema therapy. Their therapist ensures that such needs are met by expressing compassion, providing nurturance, and setting limitations. After the therapy, patients are expected to become healthy emotionally. They are also expected to be autonomous enough so they will no longer need their therapist to meet their core needs. Instead, they should be able to meet such needs on their own.

Mentalization-Based Therapy

Mentalization-based therapy is a type of psychodynamically-oriented psychotherapy that helps patients identify and isolate their feelings and thoughts from those of other people. It mainly focuses on thinking before reacting.

Patients who undergo this treatment are taught how to separate their feelings and thoughts from the feelings and thoughts of other people.

Individuals with borderline personality disorder usually have intense and unstable relationships that cause them to manipulate or exploit other people unconsciously. They are not able to recognize the effects of their behavior on other people. Through, mentalization, they can learn how to understand feelings and behavior, as well as associate these elements with specific mental states.

According to research, individuals with borderline personality disorder do not have a high capacity for mentalization. You should take note that mentalization is a crucial component in traditional psychotherapy. In mentalization-based therapy, its concept is emphasized, practiced and reinforced within a supportive and safe psychotherapy setting. Mentalization-based therapy is less directive than cognitive behavior therapy.

Transference-Focused Psychotherapy

Transference-focused psychotherapy is also commonly referred to as psychodynamic psychotherapy. It aims to help patients understand their interpersonal and emotional difficulties through the development of relationships between them and their therapists. One of its most distinguishable features is its emphasis on the psychological structure that underlies the symptoms of borderline personality disorder.

Transference-focused psychotherapy also focuses on a deep psychological setup in which the mind is structured around a fundamental split that identifies a way of experiencing oneself and ones surroundings. Such a split determines the perceptions of the patient and results in impulsive self-destructive behaviors and chaotic interpersonal relations. It was actually based on a model of the mind wherein early affectively charged experiences have been established in the psychological structure of the patient.

When you undergo this treatment, you will be taught how to apply your insights into real situations. Your beliefs, attitudes, and internal images will be transferred onto your therapist. By examining this transference, you will be able to work through the distorted images that you automatically impose on external reality. Over time, your capacity for self-reflection will increase and you will be able to adapt to life better. Conversely, your symptoms of borderline personality disorder will decrease.

Every patient needs to be in a structured therapeutic setting, no matter what type of therapy he or she goes through. Individuals with borderline personality disorder usually try to test the limitations of their therapist during treatment. Hence, it is important to establish a well-defined and proper boundary at the beginning of the therapy session.

Clinicians should be aware of their feelings towards their patients, especially when the latter start to show inappropriate behaviors. People with this type of personality disorder tend to be discriminated against unfairly because others see them as troublemakers. A lot of people do not understand the true nature of their condition, which is why they are often shunned.

Dr. Phillip Long notes that these patients may actually need more care than other patients and that their rowdy behavior may only be caused by their personality disorder. He also notes that a therapeutic alliance must develop within the treatment and experiences of the patient with their therapist.

Moreover, the therapists should be tolerant despite repeated episodes of rage, fear, and distrust of their patients. They should also avoid uncovering to boost ego defenses, so the patients can be less anxious about loss and fragmentation. The main goals of therapy must not be in terms of complete personality restructuring, but rather in terms of life gains towards independent functioning.

That is Borderline Personality Disorder?

Have you ever met a person you hated on sight? Someone who appears callous, selfish, and reckless, without a care for consequences? You don't say anything, but you secretly loathe this person who seems to get on everybody's nerves. Or do you have a friend who has a hard time keeping her emotions in check, who doesn't seem to have a lot of friends because of her aggressive and combative tendencies? How about that promiscuous girl who seems to enjoy displaying risqué behavior in public?

Don't be so quick to judge. You may not be aware of it, but this person is probably suffering from something known as Borderline Personality Disorder (BPD). It may sound weird or foreign to the ears, but people with BPD tend to exhibit impulsivity and a tendency to engage in dangerous activities. They can also be aggressive and quarrelsome against people who stand in their way. Often capricious, impulsive, and reckless, these people have few friends and lasting relationships.

Definition

The term BPD caused much confusion for many people who aren't familiar with this personality disorder and its symptoms, which is why the World Health Organization gave it a new name, Emotionally Unstable Personality Disorder. It was first diagnosed in 1980.

People who suffer from BPD tend to be impulsive, capricious and reckless, going after what they want without giving a damn to the consequences. They are also prone to emotional, explosive outbursts, and could turn nasty to people who oppose their actions.

In the long run, people with BPD exhibit a persistent pattern of being unable to maintain close interpersonal relationships. They also tend to have a disturbance in their self-image and the way they feel and express emotions.

BPD usually develops during the early adult years (late teens to early 20s). The impulsivity and instability of relationships may have already been present in recent years, usually driven by the individual's self-image and social experiences. They might even appear shallow and capricious to most other people.

BPD is said to affect two percent of the global population, with female patients more than males. About 7 out of 10 cases of reported and diagnosed BPD are female. BPD may reach its peak during the first few years after its onset, but with proper therapy and treatment, it usually lessens in intensity as the subject grows old. Most patients outgrow its most severe symptoms by the time they reach their 40s or 50s.

Symptoms

As a behavioral disorder, most of the symptoms of BPD have something to do with a person's actions, emotions, and tendencies. The following are just some of the most common symptoms and characteristics of someone who has BPD.

Fear of abandonment

Contrary to being emotionally shallow, BPD individuals are actually full of emotional scars and insecurities. They don't have a lot of self-respect, and they often feel that everyone they care about is going to leave them. In response, they take extra effort to make sure that the people they love won't abandon them.

Unstable relationships

For years, a BPD patient might have difficulty holding on to relationships. He might have a conflicted relationship with his family, or might flit from one romantic relationship to the next. This might be due to an idealized view of relationships, and then disillusionment when reality becomes less than what he expected. They might be clingy to relationships at one time, and bored the next moment.

Disturbed self-image

BPD individuals aren't sure about themselves. They are insecure, and their self-image is constantly changing. They might affiliate themselves with a certain group, and then decide that it doesn't define them. They might follow fads, join cliques, but eventually change their minds about them.

Impulsivity

There's nothing that defines BPD more than reckless impulsivity, which often manifests in risky, potentially dangerous behavior. Individuals with BPD may exercise that impulsivity in different ways, such as reckless driving, overspending, unsafe sex, and even substance abuse.

Suicidal tendencies

BPD individuals often use self-harm and threats as a form of self-defense and manipulation. As such, they might have suicidal tendencies or threats to hurt themselves in order to get what they want. Suicidal behavior is said to be present for 80 percent of reported cases of BPD. Self-harming behavior, on the other hand, is often a result of trying to manage emotions, feelings of guilt or self-blame, or as a means of getting attention from the ones they love.

Mood swings

People who have BPD tend to have extreme varying of moods, which might range from depression, anxiety, irritability, or extreme happiness which only last between a few hours to a few days.

Feeling empty

BPD individuals might feel as if there is something wrong with them, usually feeling like something is missing inside. They feel blank and empty, making them desperate for the love and approval of other people.

Anger management issues

Along with impulsivity, a person who has BPD might have difficulties controlling his anger and temper. They may have anger management issues, along with frequent tantrums or getting into fights. These individuals have excessive hostility and negative emotions, which they cannot control most of the time.

Paranoia

Worse cases of BPD might exhibit fleeting symptoms of paranoia, usually related to stress. They might also have dissociative symptoms ("split personality") because of their varying moods and unstable emotions.

Psychosis

In severe cases, individuals with BPD might experience hallucinations and delusions as part of their symptoms. This is why it was originally called "Borderline Personality" because experts originally thought patients were experiencing a borderline form of another psychotic illness.

Extreme reactions

When a person with BPD feels threatened or fears that she is being abandoned, they tend to lash out with extreme responses and reactions, which may range from extreme depression, panic, or even rage.

These symptoms may manifest as a result of even the pettiest events or occurrences in the person's life. A person with BPD may feel panicked (extreme separation anxiety) even when they become separated from the people they care about for a short time period.

Causes

Like other mental disorders, there is little research to support what are the actual causes of BPD. However, experts generally agree that both environmental and genetic factors are at play when it comes to this disorder.

Genetic factors

There is strong evidence that suggests that BPD is most likely a hereditary illness, especially since a child may inherit certain traits and temperament of his parents, including aggression and impulsivity.

Sociocultural factors

A person's environment and community may have a direct effect to developing BPD. Peer pressure, coupled with poor judgment may lead individuals to make foolish and dangerous choices.

Familial relationships

An individual's relation to his family also plays a major role in the onset of BPD. A person who comes from a dysfunctional family may be more at risk to develop BPD than someone who has a "normal" familial background. Domestic violence and child abuse might also be contributing factors.

Trauma, abuse and neglect are all possible factors, and symptoms might already be present during childhood. However, diagnosis of BPD cannot be officially made unless the patient is already 18 years old. Treatment is difficult but possible, although it tends to take years before full recovery can be made.

Subtypes

The WHO recognizes several major subtypes of BPD individuals, categorized according to the most apparent symptoms that they display:

The discouraged type of BPD individual has avoidant tendencies, coupled with a melancholic mood and a tendency to be overdependent on other people. These individuals are mostly submissive and humble, with feelings of being victimized repeatedly. They have a constant feeling of depression, emptiness and hopelessness because they feel they are powerless to do anything on their own.

The petulant type, on the other hand, features mostly pessimistic and negativistic symptoms of BPD. These people are often restless, defiant, and often impatient. They can get sullen and resentful when they don't get what they want.

BPD individuals who fall under this category tend to be very sensitive—they are easily offended and disillusioned.

The impulsive type of BPD features mostly antisocial or histrionic tendencies. These individuals might appear flighty and capricious, promiscuous even to some. They are easily distracted, and they tend to become clingy in relationships because they have an inner fear of loss. They become anxious, irritable or depressed at times, and might even resort to suicide in order to get attention.

Self-destructive BPD individuals have masochistic and melancholic features. These individuals may be reclusive and introverted, with a tendency to be moody and depressive. They stop conforming or becoming pliant (traits of the discouraged subtype) and their anger becomes directed to themselves, leading to suicidal tendencies.

Coping mechanisms

The behaviors displayed by people with BPD are often a form of self-defense and a means of coping with their symptoms. BPD individuals often react negatively and extremely because they feel like they are a victim, whether of other people or of certain circumstances. They feel misunderstood, and often maltreated by other people.

These people don't see their behavior as dangerous or risky, and when things go wrong, they blame it readily on other people. They turn irrational and forget to see both the positive and negative aspects of a situation. They are also prone to self-pity, and constantly seek assurance and comfort from other people.

Chapter 2 The Borderline Society

There are a lot of different disorders that a person is able to get in their lifetime. Some may have issues with wanting to have everything be in the proper place while others may not get along with others and so much more. But this book is not going to spend time talking and worrying about those kinds of disorders. Instead, it is going to spend a lot of time going on about the disorder that is known as borderline personality disorder.

Borderline personality disorder is actually a cluster B personality disorder and will be marked with impulsivity, instability, and the person is going to have troubles with their own self-image and interpersonal relationships. Basically, it is a mental illness that is going to cause some intense behaviors in the person who is suffering from them. The people who are undergoing this kind of disorder will find that they have severe problems determining what their self-worth is, engage in impulsive behaviors in the hopes of getting an adrenaline rush and without care to how much it could hurt them and others, and very intense mood swings for no reason. If you know someone who has this disorder, you will notice that all of their relationships are troubled, whether it is with parents, siblings, friends, love interests, or coworkers.

In most of the cases, the signs for this kind of disorder are going to appear during their childhood, but the issues are not going to be present until they get a little bit older and enter early adulthood. The treatments for this kind of condition are going to be hard and it is not going to be something that will be done in just a few days or even weeks; this condition is going to take many years to heal and many times it never happens.

So you may be curious as to what is causing this disorder to occur. Unfortunately, experts are not in agreement at the exact causes of borderline personality disorders. Some believe that there are some issues with the chemicals inside the brain, the ones that control your mood and that these are to blame for some people developing the disorder. It also looks like this disorder is carried through families so if you have someone in your family tree that had the disorder, your risk of developing it may go up.

Often, you will find that this kind of personality disorder is going to appear when the person had a childhood trauma of some kind. This could include a death of a close relative or their parent, being neglected, or being severely abused. The risk becomes higher when the child who is going through this trauma also has issues with coping with the stresses and anxieties that are around them. What this means is that just because a child has had a trauma in their life during childhood does not mean that this trauma is going to make them have borderline personality disorder. It does increase the chances of that occurring, but basically if they have a lot of trouble with fears, dealing with things that are happening around them, and do not like change, it is more likely that they are going to develop the disorder if some trauma does occur in their childhood.

For the most part, those with this kind of disorder are not going to get the help that they need. They are not going to recognize that they have any issues at all and so they are not going to get any help. Also, they have pushed away a lot of their own loved ones to the point that they do not have a lot of people who are going to want to have anything to do with them. This makes it very unlikely that they are going to have someone see that there is a problem and will get them the help that they need. This means that the person with the disorder is probably going to go without treatment unless something else comes up and then they are going to be stuck with this condition for the rest of their lives.

For those who are lucky enough to get treatment, they need to be able and willing to take the treatment that they are given. Many of those with this condition are not able to trust their therapists or do not think that they are going to need to stick around for a long time in order to get it done and so they will not get the proper help and will fail. They are going to need to find a therapist who is willing to stick with them and help out and they will need a lot of support to get through this time and seek the help that they need. If they are able to do this, they are more than likely going to succeed since this is what the statistics have pointed out in the past for other patients.

The symptoms are important to look for so that those around the person can get them the help that they need. Most of the time, the sufferer is not going to be able to see that they have a problem and at times they may not admit that anything is wrong at all.

Signs and Symptoms: A Summary

Sometimes, the issues with this disorder are hard to discover because everyone has times when they are struggling with their behaviors and emotions at some point. The difference between those with this personality disorder and those without is that those without this disorder will get over the emotions within a few days or so. On the other hand, those with this disorder will have really severe forms of the problem and they will repeat over and over during a long period of time rather than just showing up and then going away shortly after. These symptoms are also going to be disrupting the lives of those with the disorder because they are so severe and occur so often.

There are a lot of issues that can arise when you are dealing with this kind of personality disorder. The issue that a lot of people have, which will be discussed a bit later in a following chapter, is that a lot of these symptoms will match up with other issues and other personality disorders. This can make it difficult sometimes to diagnose who has this kind of personality disorder and who might have another issue that is unknown. Some of the issues that you should watch out for when you are worried that someone is suffering from this kind of personality disorder include:

- Intense mood swings and emotions. These can show up in several ways. First the person may have something that they can be upset about, but the amount that they react to it is way out of line for what should be called for. They will do this all of the time instead of just once and it really can't be explained away with they are having a bad day.

Other times, there may be absolutely no cause for the intense mood swings and the person will just be extremely happy one minute, angry the next, sad the next, and so on.

- Impulsive and harmful behaviors—the person with this kind of personality disorder is going to enjoy going out and seeking some thrills, no matter how dangerous these tasks may be to them or to someone else. They might go out and perform reckless driving, have risky sex, spend a lot of money that they do not have all of the time, binge eat, and abuse various forms of substance abuse. These people are not thinking about the consequences that might occur with their actions and are only worried about the moment that they are having right then.

- Issues with their relationship—most of the people with personality disorders like this one are going to have issues with their personal relationships. It really does not matter with what part of their lives and they may not have close friends or family either. This is often due to the fact that the person with this kind of personality disorder is only going to see things as good or bad and they will not see things differently or that others have opinions that are valid and different from their own. Also, the opinion that they have of someone else is going to dramatically change over any little thing. At one minute they may think you guys are best friends, but the next you may have to back out of a date or a meeting because of your kids at home, and the person with the personality disorder will start to see you as bad and want nothing to do with you. This makes it almost impossible for them to have relationships with anyone.

- Low self-worth—the reason for this is not fully understood but it could be because they have no one whom they can be close to or because the chemicals in the brain that are responsible for this part of their lives are not working properly. These people are going to feel a lot of the time that they are not worth anyone paying attention to them and they might wonder why anyone would want to be their friend. This can make it difficult to talk to them because they are not going to see the point and may not have a lot to say.

- A fear that is almost frantic of being abandoned or left alone—since this person is dealing with a low self-worth and does not have many relationships that are working well for them, they may fear that the few friends whom they do have are not going to be there when they need them. The person with this disorder may start to do things that are considered frantic to hold onto the ones who may be close to them. On the other end of the spectrum, they may also reject and push away others because they feel it is better to do this before the ones they love can do it to them.

- Aggressive behavior—remember with this that the person with the disorder is going through some intense moments at the time and they are not sure of who they can trust of what they should be doing. These mixed up emotions are going to cause them to act out in ways that are not common for the general populace. Many people with borderline personality disorder are going to exhibit this kind of aggressive behavior.

- Feeling alone and empty inside—this can be two-fold. First, the person is going to feel this way because their emotions are all over and they do not feel like they are worth anything. The few people who are around them may make the person feel like they are not worthy of love so they will push them away. In addition, since the person is not able to hold onto relationships all that well, they may have some issues with feeling alone because they have no one who is there to help them out.

- Problems with violence and anger—in some cases you may think that you are dealing with a little child who has never been told the word no. This is because the person with the personality disorder is prone to getting very angry and since they do not know how to control or express the anger, it is going to erupt in some temper tantrums that can be violent. It is not that they are trying to act like a little child, it is more that they are not sure how to act in society and much like a little child, they just explode with emotions that they do not understand and do not know what to do with.

- Hurting themselves—often those with borderline personality disorder will resort to causing themselves physical harm. This would include things such as burning or cutting themselves. This is going to be a repeat issues, but it may be hard to see because the person is going to be working to hide up the scars so that no one else is able to see what is going on. For example, they may wear long dress shirts, long pants, and refuse to be anywhere that a lot of skin would be showing, such as a swimming pool.

- Suicide attempts as well as suicidal thoughts— this is not uncommon in someone with borderline personality disorder. These thoughts stem from their risky behavior, trouble with emotions, and the fact that they feel all alone in this world.

- Paranoia and losing touch with reality—the human mind is a social creature. It likes to be around others that it can have conversations with, laugh with and have a good time. Doing this is kind of hard for the person with this kind of disorder. They always feel like they are alone and often they are the ones who destroy the relationships that they are in. This leaves them with very few options when it comes to being social with others. As a result, their brains may turn a bit against them, over time, and they may begin to feel like others are after them or that they are not quite in touch with their reality like they should be.

As you can see, a lot of these symptoms are the same ones that you will be able to find in other personality disorders. This is what makes it really difficult to figure out if you have this kind of disorder and which kind you may have if not. It is never a good idea to diagnose yourself or someone else with this kind of personality disorder because you could be wrong and then the wrong treatments are given. It is much better to visit a doctor if there is a possibility of this disorder being present so that the person with it can get the help that they need quickly.

Chapter 3 Communicating with the Borderline

One of the biggest concerns with Borderline Personality Disorders is how you, as a person with BPD, can form healthy relationships with someone and vice versa. We all want someone we can say 'I love you' to, to be happy with the people around us, to have good working relationships with our coworkers, and to perform well in a job we just started working in.

For people who have BPD, life can be challenging. There are intense feelings of anger, desperation, strong emotional pain, feelings of emptiness, and hopelessness and it can also make you feel lonely very often. It's like looking inside a happy home and wishing you were part of it or floating, looking down at people who are happy and wishing you can feel what they feel. Loneliness, desperation, anger, strong and intense emotional pain are all symptoms that can affect every piece of your life. Many people with BPD learn to cope despite these challenges and they work hard to live fulfilling lives.

In this chapter, we will focus on the most crucial segments of life-relationships and the workplace and how it impacts a person with BPD. For children who have yet to be diagnosed or who are already diagnosed with BPD, if left untreated, these could be the struggles that they may go through.

This chapter opens your mind as a parent to the future possibility of what your child may have to go through as they grow older. Hopefully, it will also nudge you towards getting early diagnosis and intervention for your child and emotional support for yourself as a parent. This chapter also endeavors to help adults with and without BPD on how they can manage relationships.

Who are the Ones with Borderline Personality Disorder?

When you read about Borderline Personality Disorder, you may have come across plenty of articles talking about trauma. This is because plenty of people diagnosed with BPD have gone through some form of trauma in their lives. It could also be genetics that plays a role in people developing Borderline Personality Disorder. Research and studies show that if you have a parent, a sibling or a child with BPD, the chances are that you developing it is five times possible. Neurological impairment also seems to be an element that causes BPD, which means in some areas of your brain, there are no proper communication pathways that exist the way a typical brain works.

In many cases, borderline personality disorder begins in adolescence or the latest, young adulthood, and it is estimated that at least 1.6 percent of adolescents deal with BPD. This number could be higher because some cases or people go undiagnosed or untreated. It is also reported that females are generally diagnosed with BPD, but studies have also shown that males tend to be misdiagnosed with either depression or PTSD instead of BPD.

BPD and its Impact on Family

Mental illness, whether it's just you have it, or your child, or your partner or just someone in your family, like your sibling has it it affects the entire family unit. The older the person gets, the more complicated the symptoms can be.

Where personality disorders are concerned, this effect is severe because of the intrinsic impairments that exist in interpersonal relationships. The most affected are partners and family members of the PBD individual as they are the closest and most often in touch. They also have a high impact on the person who has this disorder in return.

There are very limited therapeutic options available for family members of those with BPD. Among the reasons are that there are limited research and studies done on families.

These 5 criteria have been established by the Diagnostic and Statically Manual of Mental Disorders IV. BRD rates range from 0.07 to two percent, which means that there are millions of families out there who are affected as well.

Family members usually play the role of caregiver or case manager. Apart from this, stereotypes and conventional gender roles are the main drivers for women in the household to take up the major responsibility of caring for the individual with BPD. Family members may also field suicidal behavior, a task that crisis prevention and intervention workers are trained and paid to do.

Risks of Depression

Studies that have been done on family members with BPD relatives have shown that they too, suffer the side effects of BPD, primarily depression. A relative with a mental illness also causes family members or primary caregivers to suffer grief, isolation, and burden because of the stress of having to deal with a person with BPD. This also relates to parents who care for children and adolescents with BPD.

Among the biggest aggressors for mental health providers were suicide attempts, patient anger as well as threats of suicide. These three elements are all characteristics of BPD and have a substantial impact on loved ones.

According to observations conducted by researchers Hoffman and Gunderson, families are equally distressed by the exact problems that mental health professionals have, and these problems are, in fact, more demoralizing for families more than the healthcare provider. Families can be severely overwhelmed that they, too, have trouble in managing the symptoms of their loved ones with BPD. What is even more distressing is that family members are not trained for the role of caregiver and usually must learn skills of managing symptoms alongside the PBD adult or child.

Psychological Impact on Families

The impact of BPD psychologically on loved ones cannot be ignored. At times, family members can also feel traumatized, which also confines their emotional responses to be of any help to the BPD individual. Based on reports by the Center for Disease Control and Prevention, the average suicide attempts by a BPD adult are 3.4 times during their lifetime and at least 73 percent of people diagnosed with BPD have attempted suicide at least once in their lives. Unfortunately, an overwhelming 10% of individuals with BPD have committed suicide.

Stress on Families

No doubt that BPD puts an entire family under significant stress, and this level of stress differs differently from parent to a sibling, child to parent and sibling to sibling. The person with BPD has unpredictable behavior and sometimes it just lasts for a few hours but sometimes it can go on for days.

Symptoms are extremely, and triggers are many. The family unit can gain better insight and support from other parental groups, mental health groups, as well as family counseling, family therapy, and advisory groups. Without support, it is practically impossible to deal with a child or adult with BPD.

Families can help ease and calm the loved one with BPD, and the role that families play in the life of the PBD individual is extremely important in helping them manage their condition at home.

Another stress factor for families is the inability to find the right care and therapist it often takes very long to find a good one and even longer to find the one that connects with the patient, makes them feel validated, understood and not judged.

Positive and Negatives of Receiving Diagnosis Family Point of View

The positive aspects of receiving a diagnosis are that when you do, you can seek the right treatment, find the right therapy for both the individual with BPD as well as for caregivers. DBT is one such treatment that we will explore in another chapter it is an extremely helpful therapy that is being practiced more commonly now than before. Other psychological therapies are also available but getting a psychologist that specializes in CBT may not necessarily be the right choice.

It is vital for someone who knows about this condition to treat BPD because it can get very bad, very quickly, and get the correct treatment as soon as possible for the adult, adolescent, or child is imperative. The other good thing about getting a diagnosis is that, through the right treatment, self-harm can be stopped and by extension, suicidal attempts.

The negative aspect of receiving a diagnosis is that BPD is an extremely misunderstood condition, which often comes with its very own stigmatization among people in the community and society at large. However, getting a diagnosis far outweighs this negative aspect. In many ways, it is important not to judge a person no matter how difficult their behavior is because we do not know what they are going through. The family concerned, especially parents, should not be judged as well.

Family Support for a BPD Child or Adult

For parents, one of the best ways to support a child or adolescent with BPD is to make sure they go for their treatments. Parents are encouraged to go for parent-run groups and workshops that help educate family members in convenient and useful ways to help a child cope with BPD. Among the knowledge shared are coping skills as well as strategies to aid someone when they go through any impulsivity or behavioral changes as well as gain a better understanding of the illness. Workshops and support groups also teach parents how to navigate a child with difficult BPD behaviors before they can turn extreme.

The psychologist treating the child or adult will also request that they meet as a family group to explain things, symptoms, and actions. Above all, education is necessary and a vital tool to support the family who, in turn, can better support the individual with BPD.

Support from Mental Health Care Providers

The therapist, psychologist, or doctor is generally the first person who the family contacts if someone is not mentally well. Families have the responsibility of informing the doctor or psychologist about what the individual goes through, what symptoms do they have, any episodes of meltdowns and basically everything that the adult or child experiences. Talking about family history is also vital.

A psychologist that is trained in BPD will be able to talk to the individual in a compassionate way and get them to take their medication and vitamins as well as organize for referrals and evaluations through the period of treatment. The psychologist would also be able to draw up a mental health plan and some sedatives (even if the diagnosis has not been established) to help manage immediate issues concerning the BPD individual, such as anxiety and insomnia.

The right doctor or psychologist will also be able to see the patient as often as possible and talk about ways to get through their episodes and cope with whatever symptoms that kept arising. If symptoms get worse, a psychiatrist or doctor will recommend that the individual admit themselves in the hospital which will also lead to correct diagnosis done. It is extremely important to stay in touch with a doctor that is clear, understanding, direct and above all, non-judgmental.

Doctors, psychologists, and therapists are trained to answer questions from BPD individuals or any individual with a mental disorder.

Impact on Relationships

According to DSM-5, which is the resource material that mental health professionals refer to when making any diagnosis, the intensity of emotions, unstableness as well as conflicted personal relationships are the main manifestations of BPD. At times, there can also be sudden shifts of feelings from feeling smothered to feeling fearful which leads individuals with BPD to withdraw or cling to relationships.

This back and forth innuendo of feelings are stressful for both the partner and the BPD individual. Another impact of BPD is abandonment sensitivity. This sensitivity causes BPD individuals to be constantly watching out for signs that their partners will leave them, and they decipher even minor issues, arguments, or events as signs of their partners leaving them. As a result, the BPD individual acts out in frantic measures to prevent abandonment from causing public scenes, pleading, and even to go so far as to physically prevent them from leaving even if their partners never intended to.

Lying is another complaint partner must deal with in BPD relationships. Deception and lying are not the formal criteria of BPD diagnosis, but there are reports and feedback given from partners saying that lying is a major concern in their relationships because BPD people see things from a different set of lenses.

When it comes to relationships, impulsive sexuality is also another common symptom of BPD. BPD individuals struggle with sexuality as a large percentage of them have experienced some form of sexual abuse as a child, which has sex and sexual relations with their partners complex and complicated.

Self-harm, dissociative symptoms, and impulsivity also make up a large component of BPD symptoms in relationships, which causes major stress among partners. A person with BPD may engage in impulsive tendencies such as binge drinking, fast driving, going on extreme spending sprees, which impact the relationship in both financial and emotional aspects. Suicidal tendencies also present extremely scary episodes for romantic partners who do not want to see the individual get hurt. All these cause extreme stress, depression and anxiety on the partner without BPD.

What does Research tell us about Romantic Relationships and BPD?

A stormy and unpredictable romantic relationship is often the case when it comes to people with BPD. These relationships are distinguished by a great deal of dysfunction and turmoil. It's hard to say that the BDP person has control over things, and it is also to tell their partner without BPD to be extremely understanding. It is like a push and pull game all the time.

When it comes to relationships, it's as complex and complicated. For example, women with BPD symptoms have reported having higher chronic relationship stress and were involved in more frequent fights. Studies have also pointed out that the more serious a person's BPD symptoms are, the less satisfied they are in their relationships. Research has also stated that BPD symptoms relate to a higher number of romantic relationships over a period as well as greater incidences of unplanned pregnancies. Individuals with BPD also have more former partners and shorter romantic relationships than people without any personality disorders. This also suggests that romantic relationships with someone who has BPD has a higher chance of ending up in a breakup or divorce.

Where sex is concerned, research also states that BPD women have more negative perceptions about sex, more uncertain about sex than women without BPD, and are more likely to feel pressured into having sex with their partners. There is very little research done on men with BPD and sexuality. The worst part is watching yourself destroy relationships, knowing that you're doing it as it's happening and not being able to stop it.

Starting a Romantic Relationship with Someone Who Has BPD

Would anyone want to start a relationship with a person who has BPD, given that there are all these complexities and difficulties that exist? A relationship with two typical, non-BPD individuals is complicated, what more one with BPD in the mix?

Firstly, it is vital to keep in mind that despite the disruptive and intense symptoms, people with BPD are like everyone one they are kind, they are good, and they are caring individuals who want the best for their partners. There are plenty of good and positive qualities about them that make them a great partner to be with. Partners who are in relationships with someone who has BPD have said how they are fun, passionate, and exciting. For many people who are in relationships with a BPD partner, they are drawn to the intense emotions and strong desires for intimacy.

Am I able to make a romantic BPD relationship last?

Like most relationships, a BPD relationship also has its honeymoon period where everything is wonderful and blissful. BPD individuals have said that at the beginning of a new romantic relationships, they form an idealization of their partners, often placing their partner in high esteem, as if they have no faults, feeling like they have found the perfect soulmate, a perfect match, the right person who will rescue them from their emotional distress.

The honeymoon period exists with the new partner too, where everything is exciting, the passion is intense, the sex great and the emotions so blissful. The idea is always the same it's nice to finally have someone who feels strongly about you and makes you feel like you are very much needed.

But then this perfect idealization begins to erode, and problems start creeping in when reality kicks in and life unravels. The person with BPD often finds that their new partner does come with flaws, and the perfect image of a soulmate comes starts breaking apart.

The issue here is that people with BPD also struggle with this issue called dichotomous thinking, which makes them see things only in black and white there is no grey area, no middle ground. Because of this, they often have problems identifying or coming to terms that people, average people, make mistakes even with well intentions.

Because of the intensity of their emotions, they are often passion swings both ways they quickly change from idealization to devaluation. To maintain relationships with a BPD partner is to find ways of coping with their turbulent cycles. The key here is also to encourage them to seek professional help to enable them to reduce these cycles. This is often what couples therapy does to help partners in BPD relationships.

How to Manage a Romantic BPD Relationship

Apart from couple's therapy, there are other therapies that need to be undergone in order to have a healthy relationship not just in romantic terms but in life as a general.

- Dialectical Behavior Therapy (DBT)

This is a form of Cognitive Behavioral Therapy which we will explore in greater detail in a separate chapter. But essentially, DBT endeavors to bridge a person's thinking to their behavior. Among the four main skills taught in DBT, managing interpersonal skills is one of them.

- Mentalization Therapy (MBT)

This type of therapy helps to align a person's thoughts and enable them to make sense of what goes on in their mind as well as the minds of the people they communicate with.

- Medications

Medications are often prescribed by doctors to enable the individual to cope with some of their symptoms. Some medications also help improve BPD symptoms, help a person manage their impulsivity, anger as well as depression.

Chapter 4 Taking Back Control of Your Life

Just like any disorder, a mental illness in the family would affect the entire unit as a whole. It has an acute effect on those with personality disorders because it affects interpersonal relationships. The impact of BPD is most felt on the families of those with the illness, an effect that also bounces back on the individual who is suffering.

Families of people with borderline personality disorder are affected in various ways. One or two people are usually designated as the case manager for their family member. It is also common to observe gender stereotyping because the women in the family, by default, are given the responsibility to take care of a family member who is sick; personality disorders included. Studies have also shown that family members of people who suffer from a mental disorder are more prone to becoming depressed. A relative with mental illness such as borderline personality disorder often has feelings of isolation and grief. Naturally, this would also result in feeling emotionally overburdened. In fact, research shows that suicide attempts and patient anger are leading causes of stress for mental health providers. These depressive symptoms are also evident in borderline personality disorder, further proving that the illness remains to have a significant effect on families and loved ones.

Family members also tend to feel overwhelmed in managing the symptoms of a relative with BPD. Additionally, they don't have the training, skills, and experience to manage it effectively while living normal lives of their own. Borderline personality disorder has a strong impact on families, and this fact should not be overlooked. Family members may end up feeling traumatized and this will make them emotionally incapable of taking care of their relative and providing any form of moral support. Statistics show that 10% of individuals with borderline personality disorder commit suicide, placing emphasis on the importance of care a person receives.

However, studies show that when family members are more emotionally engaged with their ill relative, the patient significantly improves their chances of reducing symptoms over the course of a year.

Although limited, there are therapeutic options that family members of those with borderline personality disorder can try. The primary reason behind this is that there the research on family relationships of those with BPD and other mental illnesses remains inadequate today. But given that the statistics estimate around 2 percent of the population are diagnosed with borderline personality disorder, this means that millions of family members are affected. When family members participate in counseling and programs that are designed for their own well-being, this will greatly benefit all parties involved.

Current programs that are aimed at providing support towards family members are derived from Dialectical Behavior Therapy as well as the stress coping and adaptation model. These have proven effective and should be a serious consideration for anyone who has a loved one suffering from borderline personality disorder. The stress coping and adaptation model focuses on healing based on a person's adaptive abilities, resources, and individual strengths. This leads to adaptive coping as it helps strengthen a person's way of dealing with the issue by applying both behavioral and cognitive techniques.

Dialectical behavior therapy is one of the more popular and effective methods of treating borderline personality disorder and its symptoms. This form of therapy is highly recommended for family members of those who have BPD because it focuses on change, coping strategies, and acceptance. The most effective treatment for borderline personality disorder combines teaching communication skills and coping strategies for the patient while also providing support through group networks for the family members.

Dealing with Siblings who have BPD

Sibling relationship can be multifaceted and complex at times. Usually, jealousy and competitiveness are present especially in the desire to seek approval from parents. If a sibling is diagnosed with borderline personality disorder, this may result in intense negative emotional experiences between siblings.

Children and teenagers who have BPD normally are at the receiving end of most of the attention at home. If you have a brother whose emotional behavior demanded that your parents focus more on him, this may cause you to feel resentment, jealousy, and neglect. The burden of witnessing negative behavior and the stress that your sibling's BPD symptoms has on the family also falls on you. However, when your sibling takes action to seek out treatment for BPD, it is crucial that they feel the support of the entire family including you. Working through your own feelings will be an important catalyst in changing the family dynamic, helping you and your sibling move forward for the benefit of the family unit as a whole.

Feeling angry, resentful, and jealous is normal before a sibling is treated for BPD. However, it is recognized that individuals who suffer as a result of a sibling's BPD symptoms have needs that need to be addressed too. While people with BPD need full emotional and moral support from their loved ones, their families are in need of the same things as well. Support groups focused on families of those who have BPD are an excellent place to start and will help you learn more about the disorder. Support groups will also help you work through the complex feelings you are experiencing as a result of being the affected sibling of someone who is borderline.

When facing this challenge, remember that you are not alone because many other brothers and sisters have had to deal with the trauma of growing up with a sibling who suffered from BPD. Support groups provide helpful validation of the experience as a whole and can help you see things in a new perspective. Furthermore, support groups can also teach you about effective communication techniques that you can apply when talking to a sibling who has BPD.

By educating yourself about the disorder, you can identify skills that will prove indispensable in dealing family members with BPD. More importantly you will learn how to best support your sibling at a time when they need you the most, even though they don't act like it. You will also learn to set boundaries as you empower yourself so that you will no longer feel like you are at the receiving end of your sibling's negative emotional outbursts.

Once your sibling begins treatment for borderline personality disorder, they are clearly communicating that they have invested in improving their interpersonal relationships. However, the road to recovery may be full of obstacles and oftentimes won't be easy for them. They may show signs of improvement but with certain stressors may end up taking a step back to destructive behavior. It is up to the family, siblings involved, to help them through the journey as they full recover from BPD. Providing moral support to someone who has BPD also means taking care of yourself emotionally and physically in order to give the best possible support you can.

It is also important to remember that a sibling who has BPD will not have it for life. Borderline personality disorder is a curable disorder, but the earlier it is diagnosed the more effective and successful treatment will be. Since BPD is often characterized by feelings of abandonment, depression, and feeling highly emotional, your sibling will appreciate working through the ordeal with them. Once it's all over you can expect to have a more fulfilling relationship with them.

Mothers With Borderline Personality Disorder and Its Effect on Childhood Development

Childhood is a time where both parents and child learn new things and face challenges. For the child, it is when they are most sensitive to their environment. It is when they are more vulnerable to anything that may affect their development. If a mother has borderline personality disorder, it can create an added battle to the existing trials of growing up.

The National Institute of Health states that mothers with BPD symptoms are considered high-risk caregivers because of the many psychological characteristics that usually lead to negative outcomes in their own children. People with borderline personality disorder commonly have stormy and intense relationships, and mother-child relationships are no different. Mothers may have difficulty controlling their impulses and end up being angry at their child, and may even exhibit suicidal behavior. If a child witnesses BPD symptoms in their mother, who is their primary caregiver, it reduces the opportunity for the mother and child to develop stable environments that are necessary for them to develop healthy attachments to one another. Each child will have their own ups and downs in life, in the same way that there is no such thing as the perfect mother regardless of BPD.

Mothers who suffer from borderline personality disorder should participate in treatment so that they can give their children a better chance to experience stability and security. It is their responsibility to work on getting better so that they can lay out the foundation for developing better relationships with their child. When mothers do this, they also do something that is very important: preventing borderline personality disorder from being passed down to the next generation.

It is also helpful for mothers who have BPD to be educated about child rearing. They can learn additional strategies in child development while coping with the illness.

Mindfulness based strategies are ideal so they can continue to be a source of warmth while monitoring their child.

Dialectical Behavior Therapy provides mothers with the emotional awareness and mindfulness skills that they need to be more effective at child rearing. Mothers who have BPD should seek help in treatment centers who have a strong focus on Dialectical Behavior Therapy so they can recover from their symptoms.

Dealing with Parents Who Have Borderline Personality Disorder

If one of your parents has BPD, you may have had a challenging upbringing. When a parent has BPD it may oftentimes have a negative effect on their children although this is not always the case. Unfortunately, it can have a serious impact on the emotions and psychological health of their child.

Children of parents who have borderline personality disorder don't have a sense of boundaries, suffer from low self-esteem, and have shame and anger issues that go on for a long time unless addressed properly. A parent who has BPD may have neglected their child's emotional, physical, or psychological needs. In extreme cases, all three of these aspects could be completely neglected. Children of those with BPD can benefit greatly from support groups designed primarily for them.

Starting the discussion with someone who has borderline personality disorder because you want them to seek help can have either positive or negative outcomes. Due to their sensitivity this kind of conversation can result in an emotional outburst. Within families, this may result in conflict and distance. People with BPD already feel that they are always being attacked, and confronting them about a mental illness could end up disastrous. The conversation will make a big difference, and should be well-thought about to reduce the chances of it going badly.

However, a parent who has never sought treatment for borderline personality disorder or who denied a diagnosis in the past may pose an added challenge. In fact they may even accuse you as the one who is mentally ill. They may put blame for many problems encountered in your own relationship. If this happens, it is best that you focus on your own healing rather than expecting the other person to change.

How to Cope With A Mother Who Has BPD

If you have a mother who has borderline personality disorder, you are most likely experiencing a difficult relationship with them. Mothers with BPD can behave erratically, ranging from insisting on being over-involved in their children's lives, or neglecting them completely.

Although your mother may not have been diagnosed with BPD, here are some symptoms that you should watch out for:

- Over-control: A common characteristic of parents with borderline personality disorder is the urge to control their children's actions, feelings, and behaviors. At times the desire to control becomes an obstacle to their child's growth and ability to develop.

- Neglect: Mothers with BPD may oftentimes be so absorbed in their seemingly overwhelming emotions that they end up neglecting their children. Sometimes it is so severe that they are completely unable to put their child's needs before theirs.

- Criticism: Mothers with BPD are known to consistently insult or discourage their children, instead of showing them love and nurturing such as a normal mother would do. BPD mothers usually see their children as their extension, which results in the parent projecting negative feelings because it is what they see in themselves.

- Blame: Borderline mothers tend to put the blame for their sadness, anger, and frustration on their children. People with BPD have a difficult time being accountable for their actions and emotions.

Children who are raised by borderline mothers can develop numerous emotional issues as they grow older. They find it more difficult to overcome the hurtful past experienced with the BPD parent and oftentimes need to seek professional help in moving on.

If you are a child of a mother with BPD, you may experience low self-esteem, depression, or anger. The first step towards healing is to recognize that your mother's behavior is not your fault. In order to move forward it is also ideal to talk to family, friends, support groups, and even therapists who can provide moral support. Releasing your feelings in safe places will allow you to validate your own emotions and get rid of pain. There are also many ways you can change the dynamic of your relationship with your mother. It is possible to learn how to create boundaries and help yourself reduce feelings of obligation as well as guilt.

Does BPD Run in the Family?

Many parents with borderline personality disorder worry about passing it on to their children. While it is possible that your children may develop BPD later in life, it is not a guarantee because many BPD parents can learn how to raise their children and allow them to live a healthy life without inheriting the illness.

Some studies show that borderline personality disorder can run in families but there are many factors that contribute to this. Because genetics is a suspected cause of BPD, there is a small chance that your biological children can inherit certain genes from you making them more vulnerable to developing BPD.

More importantly, the kind of environment your child lives in has a greater impact in determining if they will develop borderline personality disorder. For example, if your BPD symptoms cause you to harm your child, this makes them more prone to it because they have been caused harm and possibly trauma. It can be challenging to be an effective parent if you have BPD.

While nothing can be done about genetics, parents with BPD have more control about ensuring that their children have a healthy, happy home to reduce the environmental factors that contribute to the disorder. The kind of environment a child lives in can influence the occurrence of BPD more than any other known factor.

If you are a parent with borderline personality disorder, the most important task you need to do is to ensure you are getting proper treatment. Being under the guidance of a mental health professional or therapist can greatly improve your condition which will benefit your parenting skills as well. In fact, after the first round of treatment many people are no longer considered diagnosed with borderline personality disorder. When you have less symptoms to deal with you will be able to focus on becoming a better parent.

During the course of your treatment, you should be open about asking questions to your therapist. They may be able to assist in evaluating the current home environment, and assess if your parenting skills are affected by BPD. They could also provide you with better resources such as referring you to a program that provides training and coping mechanisms for parents dealing with BPD. Depending on the severity of the illness, some parents with BPD can still turn out to be nurturing and effective although for others it takes some time.

How To Help Your Child Deal With BPD in College

Borderline personality disorder results in highly unstable emotions which can be an obstacle at being successful in school. Managing the symptoms of BPD is crucial so that your child can reach their educational goals. As a parent there are things you can do to help your child cope with BPD and even support them in attaining one or more degrees.

Talk to your child about learning how to cope with stress whenever possible. College and university life can be a high-stress environment where seemingly simple things such as waking up early each day to go to class, making the time to study, and performing exceptionally well can place a strain on children with BPD. Living with BPD also means that one has a more difficult time dealing with stress as compared to their peers. While other schoolmates may perceive stress as a normal part of life in higher education, your child may be overwhelmed simply because they have BPD.

Although the stressors cannot be changed, you can help your child manage them better. Be supportive if they prefer to take on a smaller work load per semester, take online courses, or be a nontraditional student so that they can focus on work with less stress each day. Emphasize the importance of getting adequate sleep and proper nutrition which will be important sources of energy especially with all the studying that they need to do. Your child may also benefit from healthy social connections found in school groups as well as their own family and friends, so you can encourage them to make friends that will aid in alleviating the burden of higher education.

While most children see going away to college as the norm, a child with BPD may feel comfortable studying in a location that is closer to home. Be supportive if they feel this way because their home support system is crucial to them. If your child feels lonely this can worsen the symptoms of BPD by provoking fear of abandonment and other symptoms.

How To Help Your Loved One Start Their Career

Many kids will soon face graduation and along with that comes some daunting questions about major life decisions. If your child is one of them and is suffering from borderline personality disorder, your support will be crucial to their success in the real world.

While these major life decisions can be challenging to anyone, people with BPD may face this with more fear and anxiety than others. This is because they need to be strong in the event of being rejected from a job they have been wanting, be more determined and focused, and make new friends at their new jobs. Remember that individuals with borderline personality disorder already suffer from these symptoms:

- Intense fear of rejection
- Disturbed sense of identity
- Anxiety
- Impulsivity
- Difficulty maintaining stable relationships

Not everyone who has borderline personality disorder will struggle with starting their career. But for others the challenge can be lifelong and oftentimes paralyzing. As parents, you have to be realistic in helping your child succeed. Discuss career goals with children but keep in mind that it takes time, so it is best to avoid putting too much pressure on them because they are dealing with BPD. Since they tend to see everything in black and white they also usually have an all or nothing attitude towards events, people, and situations. If a job interview did not go well they may end up convincing themselves that they made the wrong decision or that they may never find a job at all. Help them realize that there are steps to succeeding and that one rejection doesn't mean they will fail.

Help your child concentrate on making small steps towards reaching their goals. If they focus on only one major goal this can be frustrating and will cause them to give up. Have them focus on small accomplishments that will not only help them move forward but that will also help them to feel good. Encourage them to focus their efforts on sending out at least 5 job applications a day to better improve their chances at landing a job. When they do accomplish these goals, celebrate with them. The moral support lent by parents, family, and friends mean the world to people with borderline personality disorder.

It is also important for parents to keep their cool regardless of the outcome of a job interview. Whether it is positive or negative, be supportive of your child. Recognize their success and also empathize with them if they are dealing with failure or rejection. When talking to your child about the outcome of a job interview or their first day at work, use an even tone of voice that will ensure your support and care for them regardless of their performance at the job. If they find that the learning curve is difficult, provide concrete ways of helping them learn what they need to do in order to work better. For example, they may feel completely in the dark about how to create professional emails and proposals. Sit down with them and teach them how to write emails but encourage them to be independent in seeking resources and information that will help them learn.

Encourage them to keep a routine which will help them stay sane despite what feels like crazy days when one is in the midst of building their career. By having a strong, healthy routine in place it will give them more control. Help them create a routine that works for them, such as certain times of the day that are dedicated to job searches, sending out applications, and making phone calls. It is just as important to ensure that they have a time in the day that they can step away from the job hunt and instead focus on themselves, engaging in activities that make them feel good such as spending time with friends or participating in their favorite hobby.

When young people with borderline personality disorder are just starting out their career, the support of family and friends can make the difference from success and failure. If the symptoms of BPD make it difficult for them to starting or keeping a job, treatment is needed. Once the symptoms are under control they can start their career on the right foot. In fact, many borderline personality disorder treatment centers also offer vocational assistance which can also help your loved one in creating a resume, starting the job hunt, and coaching for interviews. Effective Treatments and Therapies for Borderline Personality Disorder

Borderline Personality disorder can be a scary condition-no one wants to be stuck with someone who is so unstable for the rest of their lives.

But you don't have to because it is not a permanent condition. Many people stick with the condition for longer than usual only because they couldn't identify that there is a problem and get a diagnosis early enough.

Once your loved one has been diagnosed, there are a lot of therapies and treatments that can help them improve and start to get better immediately.

Some of the effective treatments and therapies for Borderline Personality Disorder include:

Psychotherapy

Psychotherapy for Borderline Personality Disorder is also known as Talk Therapy. It involves the use of interpersonal or group interaction to try to change a person's behaviors and teach them better ways to interact with other people and handle the challenges they face with their moods, self-image, and thought process.

There are a lot of psychotherapy methods that are used to treat Borderline Personality Disorder but the most effective ones include:

☐ Dialectal Behavior Therapy

Dialectal Behavior Therapy also known as DBT, is a psychotherapy that helps to teach the patient healthy ways to cope with stress, manage conflicts, regulate their emotions, and improve their relationships.

It can also help to prevent destructive behaviors and eating disorders in people suffering from BPD.

Dialectal Behavior therapy was first introduced in the late 80's by Dr. Mashan Linehan, after discovering that Cognitive Behavioral Therapy(CBT), which commonly worked for people suffering from other personality disorders, was not effective for people suffering from Borderline Personality Disorder.

Dialectal Behavior Therapy is based on the concept of Dialectics, which is a belief that for every force, there is an opposing force that is stronger.

Patients are made to understand that:

- Change is inevitable and constant
- Everything is connected
- Opposing forces can come together to bring out positive results

People who suffer from BPD often have problems dealing with changes and opposing ideas, actions or personalities so this therapy teaches them how to embrace and manage changes, and help them to see that change is inevitable and an inherent quality of life itself.

Patients are also taught how to validate other people's opinions and ideas without necessarily accepting that it is the best approach.

Rather than throw tantrums because you said that Pizza is a better dinner than burger, they would be able to 'respect' your opposing ideas and opinions without necessarily accepting or adopting it.

Dialectal Behavior therapy is one of the most effective treatments for Borderline Personality Disorder and it is often done through group sessions, phone coaching and one on one therapy.

☐ Schema-Focused Therapy (SCT)

Schema-focused therapy helps patients to identify negative behaviors and patterns that they might have developed over time as a coping skill for Borderline Personality Disorder.

For instance, an adult who has suffered from BPD from when they were a child could have developed some negative traits like maybe binge-eating or snapping at people or being too clingy in order to prevent people from abandoning them.

Schema-focused therapy helps to identify these negative coping skills, and helps the patient to learn new, positive coping skills.

☐ Mentalization-based Therapy (MBT)

Another therapy that teaches BPD patients positive coping skills is Mentalization-based Therapy.

Patients are taught how to chart their own thoughts and feelings, and identify what they may be feeling at any point in time so that they can properly ponder on issues before reacting.

BPD patients are prone to impulsive habits and actions-they often react before they think unlike the rest of us who would often think about our actions and reactions carefully before letting them out.

Mentalization-based therapy basically helps patients to think and reflect on the consequences of their actions before acting them out.

☐ Transference-focused Psychotherapy (TFP)

Transference-focused psychotherapy is really great for BPD patients who are married or in romantic relationship, and want to improve their relationship with their partner.

The psychotherapist teaches the patient how to understand their emotions and develop good interpersonal relationship that the patient can duplicate with other people.

All of these therapies are effective and patients can choose one or a combination of therapies depending on what their problem areas are.

However, you would need the help of a mental healthcare professional or a psychologist to recommend the best therapy for the individual.

- Medications: Drugs like antidepressants, mood stabilizers, and antipsychotics are very helpful too especially for reducing symptoms like depression, anxiety, aggressiveness, and impulsiveness.

A doctor can prescribe medications to be used along with therapy because medications alone may only have temporary effects while a combination of both can provide permanent relief from Borderline Personality Disorder.

- Hospitalization: Hospitalization may be necessary where the patient may be suicidal or engaging in self-harm. They would have to be hospitalized and placed on suicide watch where they can start to take medications and therapies that would help to improve their condition.
- Self-help: There are a lot of ways that a person suffering from Borderline Personality Disorder can help themselves outside medications and therapies.

Some helpful self-help strategies include:

- Breathing Exercises: Breathing exercises help you calm down by sending signals to your sympathetic nervous system that is responsible for coordinating your flight or fight response.

Learning how to breathe, especially during distressful situations can help to prevent interpersonal conflicts.

Instead of responding impulsively, the patient can cultivate a habit of taking quick, deep breaths before responding to any situation.

It will not only help them calm down, but also help them ponder on actions before acting them out.

- Journaling and Mood-charting: The brain of a person with Borderline Personality Disorder can be likened to that of a little child. A little child is yet to understand why they are feeling a certain way, and they can't express their feelings so they would cry, throw tantrums and lash out all the time.

But if the child is able to identify what he or she is feeling at that moment, they can easily say "I'm hungry' rather than cry until you ask them if they want food.

Mood-charting can help a patient anticipate and identify their feelings at any point in time, so that they can avoid 'punishing' other people instead of looking inwards and tackling the issue from within them.

Mood-charting can be done with a pocket notebook, where the patient would have to record their moods and feelings at every hour of the day for a period of time, maybe a couple of weeks or months.

After some time, a pattern would emerge and it will be easy to tell how and what the patient may feel at different periods.

The patient would also be able to prepare themselves to handle the people and challenges that they are likely to come across during these periods.

- Family Therapy

The truth is that it is the family and friends that suffer most. If you are living with someone who suffers from BPD, it can take a negative toll on you and since the condition can be passed on to people who grew up or lived with BPD patients for a long time, your children may be at risk of developing Borderline Personality disorder too.

Family therapy is not only helpful for learning how to cope with, and live with patients without conflicts, it can also be a preventive or protective measure for people who have to live with or relate with a person who has the Borderline Personality Disorder.

Family therapy involves all members of the household working together with a therapist. You would all attend sessions as a group, where you would be taught how to communicate and cope with the patient, and how to avoid dangerous BPD family cycles from forming.

You would also be taught how to set boundaries and take care of yourself while caring for your loved one.

Family therapy is often more effective than individual therapy because the patient will still face difficulties at home if family and friends don't know how to communicate and live with them until their condition improves.

There are a lot of family therapy programs for Borderline Personality Disorder but a very common and effective one is Systems Training for Emotional Predictability and Problem-solving (STEPPS). It is a 20-week program that all family members have to attend. The program helps you learn how to predict the patient's reactions to common issues, and help you learn positive ways to respond, communicate and live with them.

Recovery Takes Time

Your loved one will get better as soon as they start receiving treatments but it is important to note that this will not happen overnight.

Some patients will get better almost immediately, while some might take years to respond to recovery so make sure you are patient with your loved one, and you give them as much time as they need to get better.

Chapter 5 BPD and Successful Treatment

All along, we've been talking about how to take care of your partner who has Borderline Personality Disorder but what about you?

Borderline Personality Disorder definitely takes its toll on the partner and family members. In fact, you are the ones who bear the brunt in the relationship because you have to be the bigger one all the time.

You have to ignore a lot of things and be emotionally strong because a lot of what your partner does can hurt you and drive you crazy.

So how do you take care of yourself to ensure that you don't lose it while living with, and loving a person who has Borderline Personality Disorder?

Understand Some of the Ways That Their Illness Can Affect You, and Be Prepared for Them

The first key to caring for yourself is anticipating the difficulties. It's easier to deal with the issues when you already expect or know what would happen.

Living with a person who has Borderline Personality Disorder can affect the partner and the family in a number of ways including:

1. Disruption in Regular Routines

Their mood is hardly stable and so are their desires. You could have planned to attend a family event together during the weekend and when the day comes, your partner decides that they want to stay back at home to watch soccer, or they would rather spend the day with a friend instead.

All of this is bound to get to you, and make you really angry because, how do you tell your mom and dad that he's no longer coming? And for what? Because he wants to hang out with a random stranger instead?

The truth is that, when dealing with someone who has the borderline personality disorder, you have to be flexible, both in your expectations of them, and in what you tell others that they would do.

Even when your partner has promised and swears that they would do something, always have it at the back of your mind that it's possible that they won't be able to do it, not because they don't want to, but because they have a temporary illness that prevents them from taking full control of their actions and decisions.

2. Financial Difficulties

Impulsive behaviors are common with people who suffer from this disorder and impulsive spending is one of the most challenging of their impulsive tendencies.

Your partner can make a mess of the family's finances if they are given total control. You may soon find yourself dealing with a lot of debt repayments due to financial recklessness on your partner's part.

Whilst it may be difficult for you to ask your partner not to do whatever they like with their own money, you can encourage them to use a budget to plan expenditure.

A budget can go a long way in preventing impulsive spending.

3. Changes in Traditional Family Roles

Another problem you may experience in the relationship is the frequent changes in family roles.

Traditionally, the man is like the head or the authority figure in the home-he protects his family, makes decisions and basically, takes charge of the home. The woman on the other hand, is the one who cooks the meals, tends to the household, and takes care of the kids, and so on.

Not trying to be misogynistic here but these are the traditional roles in most households.

But when dealing with a person who has the disorder, you can find yourself switching roles, and standing in for them a lot of times.

She may wake up one morning and decide that she doesn't want to get out of bed that day while she is supposed to be the one who preps the kids for school. So, you would have to step in and fulfill her responsibilities for that day.

A child who has a parent that has Borderline Personality Disorder might find themselves being the caretaker and decision maker a lot of times whereas, it's usually the other way round.

You have to be prepared for these traditional role reversals so as to keep the family functioning; otherwise, the family may become dysfunctional.

Chapter 6 What Is Your BPD Type

Borderline Personality disorder can be a scary condition-no one wants to be stuck with someone who is so unstable for the rest of their lives.

But you don't have to because it is not a permanent condition. Many people stick with the condition for longer than usual only because they couldn't identify that there is a problem and get a diagnosis early enough.

Once your loved one has been diagnosed, there are a lot of therapies and treatments that can help them improve and start to get better immediately.

Some of the effective treatments and therapies for Borderline Personality Disorder include:

Psychotherapy

Psychotherapy for Borderline Personality Disorder is also known as Talk Therapy. It involves the use of interpersonal or group interaction to try to change a person's behaviors and teach them better ways to interact with other people and handle the challenges they face with their moods, self-image, and thought process.

There are a lot of psychotherapy methods that are used to treat Borderline Personality Disorder but the most effective ones include:

☐ Dialectal Behavior Therapy

Dialectal Behavior Therapy also known as DBT, is a psychotherapy that helps to teach the patient healthy ways to cope with stress, manage conflicts, regulate their emotions, and improve their relationships.

It can also help to prevent destructive behaviors and eating disorders in people suffering from BPD.

Dialectal Behavior therapy was first introduced in the late 80's by Dr. Mashan Linehan, after discovering that Cognitive Behavioral Therapy(CBT), which commonly worked for people suffering from other personality disorders, was not effective for people suffering from Borderline Personality Disorder.

Dialectal Behavior Therapy is based on the concept of Dialectics, which is a belief that for every force, there is an opposing force that is stronger.

Patients are made to understand that:

- Change is inevitable and constant
- Everything is connected
- Opposing forces can come together to bring out positive results

People who suffer from BPD often have problems dealing with changes and opposing ideas, actions or personalities so this therapy teaches them how to embrace and manage changes, and help them to see that change is inevitable and an inherent quality of life itself.

Patients are also taught how to validate other people's opinions and ideas without necessarily accepting that it is the best approach.

Rather than throw tantrums because you said that Pizza is a better dinner than burger, they would be able to 'respect' your opposing ideas and opinions without necessarily accepting or adopting it.

Dialectal Behavior therapy is one of the most effective treatments for Borderline Personality Disorder and it is often done through group sessions, phone coaching and one on one therapy.

☐ Schema-Focused Therapy (SCT)

Schema-focused therapy helps patients to identify negative behaviors and patterns that they might have developed over time as a coping skill for Borderline Personality Disorder.

For instance, an adult who has suffered from BPD from when they were a child could have developed some negative traits like maybe binge-eating or snapping at people or being too clingy in order to prevent people from abandoning them.

Schema-focused therapy helps to identify these negative coping skills, and helps the patient to learn new, positive coping skills.

☐ Mentalization-based Therapy (MBT)

Another therapy that teaches BPD patients positive coping skills is Mentalization-based Therapy.

Patients are taught how to chart their own thoughts and feelings, and identify what they may be feeling at any point in time so that they can properly ponder on issues before reacting.

BPD patients are prone to impulsive habits and actions-they often react before they think unlike the rest of us who would often think about our actions and reactions carefully before letting them out.

Mentalization-based therapy basically helps patients to think and reflect on the consequences of their actions before acting them out.

☐ Transference-focused Psychotherapy (TFP)

Transference-focused psychotherapy is really great for BPD patients who are married or in romantic relationship, and want to improve their relationship with their partner.

The psychotherapist teaches the patient how to understand their emotions and develop good interpersonal relationship that the patient can duplicate with other people.

All of these therapies are effective and patients can choose one or a combination of therapies depending on what their problem areas are.

However, you would need the help of a mental healthcare professional or a psychologist to recommend the best therapy for the individual.

- Medications: Drugs like antidepressants, mood stabilizers, and antipsychotics are very helpful too especially for reducing symptoms like depression, anxiety, aggressiveness, and impulsiveness.

A doctor can prescribe medications to be used along with therapy because medications alone may only have temporary effects while a combination of both can provide permanent relief from Borderline Personality Disorder.

- Hospitalization: Hospitalization may be necessary where the patient may be suicidal or engaging in self-harm. They would have to be hospitalized and placed on suicide watch where they can start to take medications and therapies that would help to improve their condition.
- Self-help: There are a lot of ways that a person suffering from Borderline Personality Disorder can help themselves outside medications and therapies.

Some helpful self-help strategies include:

- Breathing Exercises: Breathing exercises help you calm down by sending signals to your sympathetic nervous system that is responsible for coordinating your flight or fight response.

Learning how to breathe, especially during distressful situations can help to prevent interpersonal conflicts.

Instead of responding impulsively, the patient can cultivate a habit of taking quick, deep breaths before responding to any situation.

It will not only help them calm down, but also help them ponder on actions before acting them out.

- Journaling and Mood-charting: The brain of a person with Borderline Personality Disorder can be likened to that of a little child. A little child is yet to understand why they are feeling a certain way, and they can't express their feelings so they would cry, throw tantrums and lash out all the time.

But if the child is able to identify what he or she is feeling at that moment, they can easily say "I'm hungry' rather than cry until you ask them if they want food.

Mood-charting can help a patient anticipate and identify their feelings at any point in time, so that they can avoid 'punishing' other people instead of looking inwards and tackling the issue from within them.

Mood-charting can be done with a pocket notebook, where the patient would have to record their moods and feelings at every hour of the day for a period of time, maybe a couple of weeks or months.

After some time, a pattern would emerge and it will be easy to tell how and what the patient may feel at different periods.

The patient would also be able to prepare themselves to handle the people and challenges that they are likely to come across during these periods.

- Family Therapy

The truth is that it is the family and friends that suffer most. If you are living with someone who suffers from BPD, it can take a negative toll on you and since the condition can be passed on to people who grew up or lived with BPD patients for a long time, your children may be at risk of developing Borderline Personality disorder too.

Family therapy is not only helpful for learning how to cope with, and live with patients without conflicts, it can also be a preventive or protective measure for people who have to live with or relate with a person who has the Borderline Personality Disorder.

Family therapy involves all members of the household working together with a therapist. You would all attend sessions as a group, where you would be taught how to communicate and cope with the patient, and how to avoid dangerous BPD family cycles from forming.

You would also be taught how to set boundaries and take care of yourself while caring for your loved one.

Family therapy is often more effective than individual therapy because the patient will still face difficulties at home if family and friends don't know how to communicate and live with them until their condition improves.

There are a lot of family therapy programs for Borderline Personality Disorder but a very common and effective one is Systems Training for Emotional Predictability and Problem-solving (STEPPS). It is a 20-week program that all family members have to attend. The program helps you learn how to predict the patient's reactions to common issues, and help you learn positive ways to respond, communicate and live with them.

Recovery Takes Time

Your loved one will get better as soon as they start receiving treatments but it is important to note that this will not happen overnight.

Some patients will get better almost immediately, while some might take years to respond to recovery so make sure you are patient with your loved one, and you give them as much time as they need to get better.

Chapter 7 Addressing and Changing Negative Behaviors and Patterns of BPD

The development tasks of the person concerned.

The success of the therapy therefore depends on the competence of the therapist, but also on the motivation of the person concerned and the quality of the relationship between the two.

A therapy can start at different points. It is obvious that the problems are updated in the therapy. Since the borderline disorder mainly affects the interpersonal area, the relationship between patient and therapist is the point at which the problems can be made clear. Updating the problems is certainly not enough, however, if solutions cannot also be found to get the symptoms and problems under control. These solutions usually require that the patient's strengths come to bear. Therapy therefore also serves to activate resources, especially in the search for alternative forms of life. In a certain sense, the therapy serves many affected persons not least to find a new meaning, i.e. to clarify the significance of the symptoms in life history. If the latter is successful, overcoming the disease can also result in maturation.

Specialized therapies differ less in the basic principles of therapy than in their orientation towards a specific disease model of the disorder. The mediation of this model thus represents a central element of specific therapy procedures.

This enables a better concentration on the essential elements of the disease to be achieved, but the general factors of a disease to be given less consideration. Specific therapy methods are thus often embedded in a more general therapy plan.

Types of Therapy

In the history of therapy, a multitude of therapeutic methods have been developed. Essentially, however, biological, humanistic (including conversational psychotherapy, hypnotherapy, Gestalt therapy), psychoanalytic, cognitive-behavioral and systemic therapy methods are differentiated. Apart from a different understanding of illness, these therapeutic approaches differ primarily in their "therapeutic setting". This refers to the conditions under which the therapy takes place. Psychoanalysis works primarily with memory and free narration, cognitive behavior therapy with exercises and systemic therapy with the inclusion of the social environment, especially the family. The experiences with the different approaches and settings can vary greatly from patient to patient, so that it is not really possible to foresee which procedure the patient will benefit most from.

Therapeutic treatment will take place on an outpatient, day-care or inpatient basis. Inpatient treatment can take place in a responsible psychiatric clinic, but also in specialized facilities, such as certain psychosomatic hospitals. The decision as to which form of treatment is appropriate depends on the extent of the symptoms, the degree of risk and the need for help. However, other considerations are also important in deciding whether outpatient or inpatient treatment is more appropriate.

Outpatient therapy usually extends over a longer period of time, with the therapeutic contacts consisting of conversations between which there is usually an interval of at least one week. The advantage of outpatient therapy lies in the fact that contact with the social environment is maintained and the practice field of everyday life enables direct implementation of the therapy progress. In the case of inpatient treatment, the therapeutic programmed is more extensive and thus the therapeutic contact is closer. Instead, there is no opportunity to practice in everyday life. In addition, an inpatient stay involves confrontation with other patients. This can have advantages and disadvantages. However, in the context of an inpatient stay, the distance from the demands of everyday life often makes a beneficial distance and relief possible, so that forces for change can be released.

Some may be admitted to an acute ward of a psychiatric hospital as part of a crisis intervention. Occasionally such an emergency admission represents the beginning of a more intensive therapeutic correction of the disorder. However, psychiatric wards are rarely able to provide specific treatment. However, even treatment wards in psychiatric hospitals are not always geared to the therapy of personality disorders. In such treatment wards one is of course also confronted with patients suffering from other mental illnesses. This can have advantages and disadvantages. In specialised wards, the therapy programmed is usually adapted to the disorder and the group of patients is more homogeneous. However, waiting times and long journeys often have to be accepted.

With all alternatives, it is always advantageous to obtain information beforehand when selecting a suitable setting, so that the special features of the individual options can be carefully weighed against each other.

Expectations of the Therapy

"Even if I am diagnosed with this disorder, I am still the same person and do not intend to see myself as a 'carrier of a disease with certain symptoms', but as a person with personal traits. I will not hide behind a certificate. In general, my fellow human beings either get along very well with me spontaneously or I spontaneously cause allergic reactions, one of them, there is no middle."

In contrast to other mental disorders, it is not to be expected that all aspects of a borderline disorder can be treated and changed during therapy. At the beginning of a therapy there is often the need to do something or the urge of others that something must happen. Expectations therefore often fluctuate between "everything or nothing". But both are unrealistic.

In general, therapy cannot bring about an immediate change in the way we live our lives, but serves to expand the patient's ability to cope with the symptoms caused by the disease. Therapy is therefore a kind of empowerment. The transfer of experiences within the therapy to the handling of symptoms and the general shaping of life is a service that the patient has to provide above all. This transfer will be particularly successful if the expectations and the goals developed from them are as concrete as possible. This is the only way to find a benchmark for the development and success of a therapy. The following questions and answers clearly reflect these expectations and experiences with inpatient therapy.

Changing symptoms and coping with them

What conditions and prerequisites are necessary for therapy to benefit you?

Confidence that you feel well and that you can be helped.

Enlightenment. The therapist should be trained and sometimes rebuke me.

I would have to be halfway balanced, so that I am really receptive. I should be able to develop trust, feel understood and accepted. In the time of the therapy I should be exposed to as little stress as possible from outside (family, friends, colleagues etc.), so that I can stay in the here and now.

Conversations, therapy and that one understands oneself here with the people. That I also see and cooperate.

The important thing is the attitude and the insight to the therapy. To want to give and to get involved in changes. In addition a minimum of confidence belongs to it. Then courage is also needed to let new things in. And the insight that I did not get along with the previous patterns. In addition, learning to accept change.

Confidence to the therapist, best a protected framework.

Structure, clarity, regularity, truth, everything may say, about me speak, sympathy.

Which therapeutic measures do you find helpful?

I like skill trainings, sports and individual conversations.

My experience is that both music therapy and body awareness, social competence training, individual discussions with the therapist and nursing staff, conversations with those affected, the beautiful park for extended walks, all these measures have contributed to strengthening.

Social competence training, skill training, sports, employment, therapy, fitness and the self-help group help me.

At that time I did not want to come here and I went on strike against it because I believed that I did not need therapy and that nobody could help me because nobody understood me. That is why I attempted suicide. Later, training might also be based on the fact that I was here so long and could learn so much.

The most important thing for me is skill training. This is how I learn most about myself, my way of thinking, my mistakes and my behavior. This is the best prerequisite for tackling change.

Both working on current difficulties and getting to know each other better as well as working with dreams.

To be able to talk about everything, a well-reflected therapist who knows when I am lost or when I want to mislead him, i.e. someone who knows his soul and has a map and knows where what lies and how to get there.

How can you help yourself?

By using the skills, I try to calm down or lower myself, otherwise I try to talk to someone. Sometimes I listen to music, try to sleep or talk on the phone.

With the emergency skill training kit. What I learned in the conversations, to use the skills regularly and to try out almost everything that will suggest.

By collaborating and paying close attention to myself, that I can cope later.

I help myself in various ways. Once about the confrontation with myself. I find out what does me good and what the next steps are to implement it. Then I keep a diary in which my feelings get space. I take daily walks. I provide variety. I look at everything from different angles and draw conclusions for today. I create positive ideas about the future and ask myself what I need for it.

Which topics bring you closer to your goal of becoming healthy?

How best to cope with the disease, for example what you can do in case of a crisis.

Topics that concern everyday life and the various areas of life, such as partnership, social environment, workplace, leisure activities, family and friendships.

The most important thing for me is the past, which I would have to deal with.

What information will help you better understand your condition?

How to calm down better. How to get rid of anger without hurting anyone and breaking objects.

Anything that helps to analyze the disease.

Experiences of others in similar situations to mine.

Information that I would otherwise not be able to access, which is very much in the medical field. Information, which refers to empirical values.

What significance does your family have in participating in the therapy?

It has the meaning that everyone can see what the experience is like for me. The acceptance of being able to leave something behind, to find new possibilities for an independent life of one's own.

I am dependent on the support of the family, the understanding and their patience, if not everything is to break.

How do you know you're feeling better?

I can tell by how I manage to fulfill my life's desires and cope better with S. and also have a lot of understanding for her.

I am calm, feel well, no tension, positive thoughts, feelings, future plans, can be more patient.

I scratch much less, have a normal weight and only very rarely suicidal thoughts and tensions.

On my sleeping behavior, when I live in the here and now, when I feel the joy of life, when I can make plans again, when I get out of bed well in the morning.

Therapy is always a process in which goals and expectations change continuously. In the best case, the developments within the framework of therapy open up new avenues. The solution through therapy is often the fact that the spectrum of possibilities expands.

Reasons for a Therapy

As a rule, the thought of a therapy comes when the pressure of suffering has become so great that one can no longer progress with one's own means. The advice of friends, perhaps also occasionally coincidences, then consolidate the intention. Of course, the therapy should relieve the strain of suffering and reduce the symptoms. It should be remembered that no real success is conceivable without an inner change. Therapy does not only mean that something changes, but also that the affected person is ready for a change and can also carry out this change. Some people literally flee into therapy because they can no longer bear the pressure of the disease.

This motive is initially legitimate, after all therapy is also a shelter. But the shelter must be left strengthened, because the demands of life still have to be met. Therapy is also not an end in itself. It can only be a component of the personal life organization and life accomplishment. This spectrum becomes clear in the following report:

I decided to save my life after I "made myself go away" every day with brutally a lot of alcohol. My best and only friend was alcohol and my biggest enemy was myself. The first thing I did was to detoxify myself and I received a lot of positive support. To protect myself I stayed there for two months (the rule is two weeks). I then decided to go to a day clinic because I still thought I was strong enough to cope with life and therapy at the same time. The day clinic was not worth the name. So I started to organize a long-term therapy for myself. I didn't get any support from the clinic side, so I did everything on my own (pride). Then I had different clinics send me therapy concepts (not these cute house brochures) and decided afterwards.

Therapy concept: deep psychological orientation. Forms of therapy: Art, sport, Gestalt, group and individual therapy. The concept points out that borderlines are increasingly to be found among the patients and that the clinic is not necessarily able to do justice to them. I found that honest.

Conclusion: I went into therapy with a sense of self-esteem that I was under the turf and went out with my shoulders over the grass. I pulled the best out of every single form of therapy for myself (I can't believe it, but you can learn to even get rid of your anger in the artistic field - I didn't even count the brushes afterwards). Otherwise, I have learned to perceive feelings and to endure them, to better differentiate myself. In short, I got to know myself better.

Afterwards I did a follow-up therapy, which consisted of individual and group therapy and was excellent. My individual therapist has never been obsessed with the subject of addiction, but has dealt with the subject of borderline.

In conclusion, I can only say that there is no "wrong" or "right" therapy. A therapy can only bring as much benefit as one is willing to contribute. The prerequisite for this is, on the one hand, surrendering to oneself and, on the other hand, the willingness to endure the consequences of a therapy.

I cannot say that my life today has become simpler, but at least more understandable, and I know today how and where I can find help when life is no longer bearable.

Experiences with Therapists

The experiences with therapists are quite different. Thus, bad experiences do not mean that a therapy cannot be used. It is not easy to define the suitability of a therapist. Experience certainly plays a major role, but the therapist's attitude towards the affected person and his attitude towards the disorder also have an influence on the quality of the therapeutic contact. The therapy of the borderline disorder was also burdened for a long time by the fact that violent conflicts were expected from the therapist in advance. Nevertheless, the patient also bears responsibility for the success of the therapeutic relationship.

All those who have dealt with the treatment of borderline disorders emphasize the importance of the "container" function in therapy. This refers to the therapist's ability to absorb and endure the patient's emotions - the "supporting" function of the therapy. An important prerequisite for this is that a therapist is able to cope with crises of the

and patients can deal with. It is also necessary to strike a balance between closeness and distance. If a therapist behaves distantly and prefers critical comments, it is very difficult to achieve sufficient openness in the therapeutic relationship. On the other hand, being too close to the problems makes sober reflection more difficult and increases the risk of uncontrolled reactions. In this sense, it is always an advantage if the therapist can also question himself and consider his own limitations.

It has already been mentioned above that the person concerned can also contribute to a good therapeutic relationship. For example, a certain reliability in keeping agreements is important. Refusal to cooperate, for example due to a lack of openness, can also put a lasting strain on the therapeutic relationship. This includes concealing additional alcohol and drug consumption.

Many of the symptoms associated with the disorder may overburden therapists. Considering the limitations of a therapist is a protection against the failure of the therapy. It is important that the private area remains protected. Even enduring threats has its limits. For example, frequent announcements of suicidal actions are a permanent threat to therapy. Due to the relationship disorder within the framework of the borderline disorder, those affected tend to adopt a "hostile" attitude towards the therapist. It is not to be expected that a therapist can directly offer a solution to all situations. Impatience will therefore negatively affect the therapist's motivation to comment on the person's stories. A therapeutic relationship in which mutual reproaches and devaluations occur in the first place cannot succeed in the long run.

There are many behaviors on the part of the therapist that play a role in therapeutic relationships. The necessary distance has already been mentioned above. It cannot be helpful for a therapist to be anxious to make the patient dependent on himself. Such a danger is particularly present when a therapist overestimates his own possibilities. But also a strong uncertainty as well as the disregard of one's own emotions can have a negative influence on the course of the therapy. It is actually necessary for a therapist to establish a balance between acceptance and willingness to change. Such a balance becomes particularly clear in the above example.

It is important for a therapist to insist on adherence to rules while maintaining flexibility. The therapist's openness is also important, because it is usually of great interest to the person concerned what a therapist thinks. If mutual openness is achieved, critical remarks can also be better accepted.

Finding the right Therapist

"My first therapy was after a suicide attempt. My therapist at that time asked me (I was abused by my own father) as nice questions as I did: What did you do to irritate your father? Or: Could you imagine sleeping with me? Nevertheless, I risked trusting a therapist again and didn't regret it."

It is always difficult to find the right therapy and the right therapist for the diversity of the offer. As a rule, the possibilities of information are also limited. It is advantageous if the experiences of other patients can be used. However, this is only possible in exceptional cases. Perhaps the situation will improve with the introduction of the Internet. At first, however, one is usually dependent on the principle of trial and error. At the beginning of this search there should be a consultation. The consultation can take place from a professional, in addition, from friends and possibly from co-affected ones. Occasionally it is no mistake to consult a doctor with this question. It is also possible to seek advice from a psychiatrist or information from outpatient psychotherapists. In many places there are also counselling centers that can help in the search for a suitable therapist. Sometimes health insurance companies have information at their disposal.

Psychotherapy is the primary treatment for borderline disorders. It can therefore be carried out by an appropriately trained doctor or psychological psychotherapist. It has already been mentioned above that the inpatient services are also specialized in different ways. As a rule, the individual clinics have information material from which the degree of specialization can be seen.

The addresses of outpatient therapists can be obtained from the telephone directory, better still from the health insurance company or within the framework of the above-mentioned consultations. Since in many cases an outpatient treatment is carried out first, it is possible to ask for the addresses of the clinics in question. If possible, an initial consultation should be arranged before starting the therapy. The treatment conditions can be clarified and a first impression can be gained about the way of dealing with the disorder. For example, in the case of additional alcohol and drug abuse, an upstream detoxification treatment is sometimes required.

It is not only important to find the right therapist, but also to correct wrong decisions. In this sense, it is a good idea to reflect together with the therapist on the course of treatment at certain intervals and to evaluate it with regard to expectations. If there is no noticeable progress, a break in treatment or a change in therapy can possibly be agreed.

Chapter 8 Reconstructing Your World and Building a New You

Talking treatment, psychological therapy and talking therapy all mean the same thing. These terms have the same meaning and all cover treatments that you may know as: • Psychotherapy • Counseling • Therapy Some will use one of the terms while others will use another term. This can be confusing, but they are all talking about the same thing. Specially trained mental health professionals practice therapy. A therapist can also be referred to as a psychiatrist, psychologist, psychotherapist and counselor What Talking Treatments Can Help You With

You open your mouth to talk to your counselor and words just tumble out of your mouth. That's okay, because your therapist will still likely make sense of it all, and translate it back so it even makes sense to you.

Talking treatments can help you deal with difficult feelings or experiences you are going through like: • Bereavement • Anger • Fear • Guilt • Low self-esteem • Redundancy • Sadness • A relationship breakup • Anxiety • Depression Talking treatments can help you to cope and to come to terms with the symptoms you experience, along with your mental distress, illness, disability or physical problems.

Cognitive Behavior Therapy or CBT

Cognitive Behavioral Therapy helps you tackle day-to-day difficulties using problem-solving techniques. You will learn how you can replace negative thinking patterns with positive ones.

Cognitive Behavioral Therapy generally focuses on the present, but when used for BPD, it also takes into account your past experiences, which have had an influence on your current fundamental beliefs and how you think.

Problem-Solving Therapy (PST)

Problem Solving Therapy is a talking therapy that is based on the use of cognitive-behavioral techniques. It is helpful if you are depressed or if you are in a crisis after an attempt to commit suicide. The focus of Problem Solving Therapy is the present and there are five stages: • Adopt a problem-solving strategy • Define the problem and select your goals • Think of potential solutions • Predict possible results and choose the solution that is best • Try it and look at the effects Generally, there are four to eight sessions for PST. During these sessions your therapist and will work with you to identify the problems you are facing, and then you will focus on one or more of the problems while your therapist teaches you a structured approach to help you solve your problems. Your therapist will also teach you a general approach to your problems.

Your therapist will decide whether to use PST as a complete structure for your therapy sessions or to use PST with other therapies.

Problem Solving Therapy is a series of seven steps, which we will look at.

1. Problem Orientation

This is your attitude to solve issues and problems. This is not your actual problem solving skills, but rather it relates to your thoughts and feelings about the problem(s) and your ability to solve the problem(s). These two components determine how you are going to respond when you face a stressful problem. That's why it is such a key part of your PST.

Positive problem orientation is associated with an effective, rational style of solving problems while negative problem solving is associated with a problem solving style that is one of avoidance. You are likely to make careless, impulsive decisions. One of the main goals of PST is to help you develop positive orientation through education and helping you to recognize when your attitude is negative.

2. Recognize and Identify Problems

Step 2 aims to teach you how you can recognize a problem, identify the problem correctly and begin to solve it. While it sounds pretty obvious written down, it is not always that straightforward, because you are accustomed to avoiding your problems or impulsively responding.

There are three parts to Step 2:

- Invite you to impulsively report current problems
- Learn how to track problem indicators
- Using a problem checklist

3. Select and Define a Clear Problem

The third step in problem solving therapy helps you to choose one clear problem to work on and define. Learning how to define a problem clearly is important because the more clearly you can define a problem the easier solutions will be to find. Fuzzy problems get fuzzy solutions. You can achieve clear definition by gathering all the facts and then clearly and objectively writing them down.

4. Generate Solutions

Once you have selected and defined the problem you are going to work on, you will need to begin problem solving to identify possible solutions. You will learn how to brainstorm. The more ideas you have, the more you are likely to find a solution that will work.

5. Decision Making

Once you identify some possible solutions, you need to make a decision by weighing the advantages and disadvantages of each potential solution. You might find this stage difficult because there are so many possible solutions going around in your mind. Your therapist will teach you a systematic way to make these decisions.

The Hidden Signs of Borderline Personality Disorder

While many of the symptoms of borderline personality disorder are difficult to miss, there are also traits of the illness that are much more subtle. A person exhibiting these more subtle signs is said to be experiencing "quiet" borderline personality disorder.

Whereas people with BPD often experience violent mood swings which are easy to recognise, those with quiet BPD are more likely to internalize their feelings. While they still experience the same fluctuation of emotions, the disorder can be much more difficult to spot.

To recognize "quiet" BPD in either yourself or a loved one, look out for the following traits and symptoms:

- Struggling to maintain relationships: People with quiet BPD may speak about how they find it hard to keep relationships, whether romantic or otherwise. These relationships will often have been ended by the other person, unable to cope with the BPD sufferer's wild mood swings and aggression.

- Low self-esteem: While quiet sufferers of BPD may be less prone to self-damaging behavior such as reckless driving or violence, they are still likely to suffer from a severely diminished sense of self-worth. Often, this will only be noticeable to others by paying attention to the way they speak about themselves. They may say things like "I can't do anything right," or "Why would you want to spend time with me?"

- Self-harming tendencies and talk of suicide: As with the above example, to recognize these traits in quiet sufferers of BPD, it is important to pay attention to the way they speak. Their comments relating to self-harm or suicide might seem on the surface to be flippant, throw-away lines such as

"It makes me want to bash my head against a brick wall," or but this seemingly innocuous comments can be a mask for much deeper issues.

- Having Unhealthy Boundaries: In the same way that BPD sufferers are prone to black and white thinking, people with quiet BPD will often obsess about a person, seeming to care greatly what this person thinks of them. On the flip side, they may also have times of needing to completely detach from others, pulling away to the point of isolating themselves in order to create what they perceive as a safe space between them and the world.

- Heightened Emotions: People suffering from BPD generally experience emotions much more easily and deeply than the general population. This can have both negative and positive effects. People with BPD often exhibit great levels of excitement, enthusiasm, joy and love but, conversely, can often feel overwhelmed by negative emotions such as anxiety, depression, guilt, anger. Everyday emotions are often highlighted, with sadness being transmuted to grief, for example, mild embarrassment being replaced by intense humiliation and panic taking the place of nervousness.

- Lack of concentration: Another more subtle trait of BPD is the inability to concentrate. This is often due to the intense emotions building up inside one's head, leaving them with little room to think about anything else. Inability to concentrate is a form of disassociation and can appear as though a person is simply zoning out. A BPD sufferer who has zoned out can be identified by an expressionless face and/or flat vocal delivery. They may also appear distracted.

Familiarizing yourself with these more subtle symptoms of borderline personality disorder can help you identify whether you or a loved one may be suffering from the illness. If you suspect yourself or someone you love is experience borderline personality disorder, it is important to seek professional help.

The Different Faces of Borderline Personality Disorder - Types of BPD

J Borderline personality disorder can also be broken down into four different types, as proposed by American psychologist Theodore Million, in his 1995 book Disorders of Personality DSM-IV and Beyond.

Million's four categories of BPD are as follows:

- Discouraged Borderline: People suffering from discouraged borderline personalities often exhibit avoidant, depressive, dependent tendencies. People with this form of BPD are often submissive and humble, and prone to pliant behavior. They often feel hopeless, powerless and vulnerable. Someone with a discouraged borderline personality can be clingy and tends to go along with the crowd for fear of upsetting the people around them. They can behave in a somber and dejected manner. Below the surface, however, is an anger waiting to erupt. When it does so, it can lead sufferers to self-injury and even suicide.

- Petulant Borderline: A petulant borderline personality is characterized by a heightened sense of negativity. Sufferers of this form of BPD are often highly impatient, stubborn and resentful. They are sullen and defiant and feel easily slighted. They are easily disillusion and disappointed in life. People with a petulant borderline personality disorder fluctuate between desperately relying on people and keeping their distance out of fear of being disappointed or let down. Their emotions are prone to swing between feelings of unworthiness and rage.

- Impulsive borderline: Sufferers of impulsive borderline personalities are prone to histrionic or antisocial behavior. This form of BPD is characterized by frenetic, flighty behavior. They can often be flirty and charismatic, able to draw people to them. They are highly energetic and are constantly seeking the next thrill. However, when things do not go their way, sufferers are quick to become agitated, gloomy and irritable. They fear any form of loss, leading them to frequent suicidal tendencies.

- Self-destructive borderline: Self-destructive borderline personalities are often highly depressive and masochistic. They carry around a constant sense of bitterness, which they regularly turn inwards. People with this form of BPD are often prone to self-harming and self-punishing. They are often angry, highly strung and moody and are prone to suicidal thoughts and behaviors. Their self-hatred is prone to reach extreme levels, leading them to many types of destructive behavior, ranging from reckless driving, to poor healthcare, to performing derogatory sexual acts.

In addition to these four borderline types proposed by Million, psychologist Dr. Christine Lawson also identified four types of borderline personalities in her book Understanding the Borderline Mother.

- Borderline Queen: Someone with a borderline queen personality is prone to perfectionism. They are prone to take mild criticism very personally and will become aggressive and indignant if anyone suggests they have made a mistake. Thanks to their perfectionism, borderline queens often disassociate from their own negative traits and emotions, believing them a flaw, so is often unable to accept his or her own mistakes. People with this borderline personality regularly feel the need to one-up people around them, particularly their therapists and loved ones.

- Borderline Waif: Unlike many other borderline types, the borderline waif does not exhibit a great deal of aggression or outward hostility. Instead, they appear to be fragile and victimized by all life has thrown at them. Waifs are generally depressed and discontented and worry easily. Borderline waifs believe themselves to be helpless victims and often refuse to accept help in order to keep their 'victim' mentality alive.

- Borderline Witch: Someone exhibiting a borderline witch personality can be extremely aggressive and controlling. They seek to punish people for the smallest of indiscretions and are prone to "borderline rage" -- the destruction of objects that are of value to those they believe have wronged them. Borderline witches are adept at black and white thinking, particularly when it comes to their loved ones. Parents with this personality will often idealize one of their children over the rest or seek to play one family member off against another. People with a borderline witch personality can be extremely domineering and intrusive, often violating the boundaries of those around them. They are prone to using the thoughts and feelings of those around them a weapon, leading their loved ones to become withdrawn and restrained in their presence. Borderline witches can be extremely paranoid and suspicious, with their hostile behavior masking their own fear of loss of control.

- Borderline Hermit: People with a borderline hermit personality view the world as an inherently dangerous place. They have large amounts of paranoia and suspicion and have trouble trusting those around them. Thanks to their belief that everyone is out to get them, borderline hermits will withdraw from the world and isolate themselves. For many sufferers of a borderline hermit personality, the disorder stems from sexual abuse or other equally damaging childhood trauma.

Diagnosing Borderline Personality Disorder

A BPD can lead to violence, damaged relationships, any number of dangerous behaviors, and even suicide. It is not something that you should attempt to handle without the help of a trained psychologist, or other mental health professional.

Self Diagnoses:

- Do your emotions change very quickly?
- Do you often experience extreme anger, sadness or distress?
- Do you often feel empty or unfulfilled?
- Are you constantly afraid the people I care about with leave me?
- Are most of your romantic relationships intense and unstable?
- Does the way you feel about the people in your life tend to fluctuate from one extreme to the other?
- Are you ever tempted to engage in self-injury or attempt suicide?

- When you feel insecure in a relationship, do you ever lash out or behave impulsively in a desperate attempt to keep your lover close?
- Do you ever engage in dangerous behavior such as binge drinking, drug use, unsafe sex or reckless driving?

If you or your loved one answered yes to several or all of these statements, it may indicate borderline personality disorder.

Professional Diagnoses:

BPD will be officially diagnosed following a clinical assessment by a mental health professional. The generally accepted method of diagnosis involves presenting the patient with a list of characteristics and asking them whether they feel such characteristics accurately represents them. By actively involving patients in their own diagnosis this way, sufferers are likely to come to terms with the disorder more quickly.

Mental health experts have produced a list of nine symptoms associated with borderline personality disorder. For a person to be diagnosed with BPD, they must exhibit at least five of the following traits:

- Fear of abandonment
- Unclear or changing self-image
- Unstable relationships
- Impulsive and/or self-destructive behaviors

- Tendency towards self-hard or suicide attempts
- Extreme mood swings
- Difficulty controlling rage
- Paranoia or suspicion of others' motives.
- Persistent feelings of emptiness

Such an evaluation will also discuss the severity of these symptoms and when they began, along with determining when they may have begun. Of particular relevance are any suicidal thoughts a patient may have experienced, along with thoughts of self-harm, or doing harm to others.

An assessment may also include physical tests to rule out other triggers of these symptoms, such as thyroid conditions or drug and alcohol abuse.

As a result, mental health professionals might experiment with a range of treatments and therapies in order to identify the most suitable path towards recovery.

So what if you or a loved one has been diagnosed with borderline personality disorder? What does this mean for your relationships, and your life in general? There is no doubt that BPD presents an enormous array of challenges to both the sufferer and those around them. But all is not lost.

What to Expect if You Have Been Diagnosed with Borderline Personality Disorder

So you have been diagnosed with borderline personality disorder. Perhaps this has come as a cruel shock. Or perhaps you may even welcome the diagnosis as an explanation to your previously unexplainable emotional outbursts and mood swings. It feel like a relief to know that this behavior is the cause of an illness, rather than another part of yourself.

Regardless of how you feel about your diagnosis, there is no doubt that living with borderline personality disorder can be a hellish experience, both for you and your loved ones. BPD can affect every part of your life, from your relationship to yourself and others, to your education, career and recreational life. Your tendencies to act out and behave in violent and aggressive mean that both you and your loved ones are prone to being hurt, both physically and mentally.

Learning to manage the disorder begins with understand. By knowing exactly what to expect, you can prepare and develop coping skills to help you weather the emotional storm. Having a deep understanding of your illness and its traits will also help you communicate better with your loved ones about BPD, making it easier for them to assist you with the struggles you will face.

Chapter 9 Maintain success on a personal level

The most important part of an abusive relationship might be the first moment within it—the first contact you make with your abuser. This first contact you make may be the most important part of that relationship. The way that we make first contact with a person and the way that an abuser makes first contact with a person are massively different, and this shows most of all when we first meet them. That first stage of that relationship is led by that first touch, the first impressions of both parties.

As a victim, when we meet someone, we think about what they're thinking and what that might lead to. As people who have a tendency to live in fear and anxiety for most of our lives after being in the cycle of abuse, we look for a way to escape from almost everywhere we find ourselves. When we're trained as people to be afraid of our partners, we don't have the positive experiences with other people, which would assure us to act more calmly.

However, we look at new people we meet as just that—as normal people, more or less. Normal people grow up meeting new people by spending time around them and checking for themselves if they get a good feeling from that person. This is how we're used to interacting with people, and we treat most other people we meet like non-threatening presences. We understand the world around us as relatively safe and we connect with people out of a desire for security and companionship. We check if their "vibe" is one that we connect with.

Most normal people have a sense of character and are able to read people for their true characters easily. Some people are a better judge of character than others, but most normal people have in common that they spend their time understanding someone better simply through practice. Spending time with someone you know better is the fastest way to get to know them on a more personal level. It's through this repeated interaction that we become closer to other people. That interaction forges a new relationship with them over time, and we get to know them even better. This is the cycle for most normal people, socially.

Abusers, on the other hand, very rarely act this way when they first meet someone. When an abuser first meets someone, they try to sniff out the weaknesses of other people. They look at a person as someone who could act as a steppingstone or another pawn for them to get where they think they need to go. They use everyone they meet is they think there's something in it for them, and that mainly includes potential victims for a relationship. When you first meet them, they'll analyze you to try to find out how you function. Abusers usually have a lack of understanding of how people function, so they're mainly focused on understanding people they meet on the most literal level.

This is where abusers locate empaths, in particular—highly sensitive people are usually able to be picked out of a crowd, especially by manipulative people and abusers. Empaths are usually very reactive to meeting new people and will show their emotions on their faces very plainly. They react expressively to the feelings of other people, and the abuser understands this and uses it to their advantage by trying to draw emotional responses out of them. When they do so, the confirm to themselves that they're meeting someone very empathetic, likely to try to sympathize with them whenever they can. In addition, the abuser will try to see if they can gauge how submissive you are when the two of you first meet.

As you spend more time with them, they will offer you more opportunities to defer to them and let them do what they want instead of offering you that opportunity. The more you allow them to exert their will over you at these opportunities, the more the abuser is assured that they can do so farther into the relationship. This entire set of first meetings between the abuser and their victim is the set-up for abuse. They groom their victims, trying to scope out what part of their personality they can take advantage of and to what degree.

When they come into contact with a new person, they immediately begin to look at that person as either someone expendable to their grand plan or someone who they need to keep around for at least the time being. Those who he does keep around are the victims who are often the most empathetic, the most kind to them, the most willing and able to see the good in people and the good in bad people, in particular. Seeing this potential for good things in all people, no matter their past actions, is good and kind.

However, not being able to balance this kind lens with a sense of realism and what the person is likely to do of their own volition, can end with you getting hurt by that person.

The same person who you may have thought you could save at one point, could end up being your undoing, your new abuser. They can turn out to be someone who manipulates and uses you for a large portion of your life in the future, a portion of your life that's incredibly hard to fight your way out of. Being able to just look at everyone you meet more sensibly can be your answer. Dodging the potential for meeting a terrible and manipulative person by developing your ability to be cautious around new people, instead of either blindly latching onto them or blindly avoiding them. Picking and choosing who you associate, instead, can be a much more positive solution.

After you make that first important contact with your abuser, and they decide you're someone they want to keep around for their own sake, they'll initiate the second phase of their plan. This phase is often referred to as "love-bombing," the infamous phase in which the abuser showers their victims with affection and praise and essentially induces a high in the victim.

When we first enter a relationship, we enter the honeymooning phase of that relationship, in which we experience elation pretty much every time we're around that person. Our new partner is put on a pedestal in our eyes, and we can't stop thinking about them. We romanticize just about everything they do, right down to the way they move and breathe. This first infatuation phase happens because the new partner and a new relationship introduce a lot of dopamine into our system.

This dopamine, a neurotransmitter often associated with rewards and risk-taking, floods our brains when we think about or interact with that new partner. This is what infatuation is, chemically speaking. The dopamine floods the brain over and over again and this heightened level of the chemical leads to extended and heightened feelings of giddiness, joy, elation, and excitement. This is the feeling of falling in love when we first meet our partner and enter a serious relationship with them. That feeling can last a long time, and the abusive partner knows how to take advantage of it. When we're right in the middle of this honeymooning phase, the abuser will love-bomb us by showing us lots of tender affection.

In a way, this softer version of their normal beginning praise and attention offsets the dopamine flooding our brain, but the abuser is also keen on how most abuse victims think and react. Large, over the top shows of love can be frightening at first, especially to someone who's afraid of attachment or being left behind, so the abuser pulls back.

Instead of these massive shows of love or infatuation on their end, they introduce the victim to flowers, handholding, gentle and soft ways, they show affection and love. In addition to this softer side of the new partner, they know how to make the abuse victim feel special as well. They'll introduce parts of themselves that are vulnerable, even secret, assuring the partner that they've never told anyone else these things about themselves. They pretend to bare their heart and soul to their partner, in an attempt to get their trust almost immediately—and it usually works.

While this act of vulnerability usually earns the trust of their newest victim, it also ensnares them into thinking that their new partner can be saved, helped, turned around down the road when the relationship begins to turn sour. When the abuser starts to act out, the victim is under the impression that they do these things and act sourly because of the damage they might have endured when they were younger. The abuser sets the precedent when the relationship is still good and pleasant, revealing some damaging truth to you beforehand. It helps them to garner sympathy from you. You want to help them and try to heal them as best you can, especially if you're someone who considers yourself an empath. This is the other reason most abusers will try to pick out an empath as their newest partner and victim—an empath is most likely to connect to them and their story, whichever story that is. When the abuser presents themselves as something like a victim of abuse in their younger years, they develop a kinship with their victim. The victim will usually reciprocate the feeling, as they're usually trying to forge some kind of bond with the people they meet anyway.

Someone who has probably been abused before is going to try their hardest to connect to people who have also endured abuse before. Therefore, the abuser has the means and the ability to forcibly connect themselves and their feelings to those of their partner, who is likely an empath—someone who feels a heightened connection to the emotions of others. After that connection is made, it's hard for the victim to separate from the other side of the connection on their own. The abuser has made room for themselves to act out and begin abusing and more brashly manipulating their victims. They feel more able to now, as they've established themselves as someone who can connect with their partner on a deeper level than most other people.

After that precedent is established along with their connection through trauma, the victim is compelled to give them more chances, to offer them more help. They're convinced that their abuser is simply misguided, just misdirected and in need of help. They're more than willing to outstretch their hand, feeling the pain of their partner, and try to give their partner help. The victim, like I've said before, can develop a bit of a hero complex—they believe that because they weren't able to receive the help they wanted when they needed it, they can be the saving grace of other people who are being abused or going through a hard time.

Ultimately, the abuser will use this optimism against the partner, which will keep the victim of their abuse closer to them as time goes on. The more strongly the victim believes they can save their partner, the less likely it is that the victim will be able to leave of their own volition. To them, if they leave their abuser behind, they'll be giving up on them and the cause they had been dedicating themselves to. In reality, this is exactly what the abuser wants out of their victim—any reason for them to want to stick around and be helpful to the abuser. The more the victim is willing to help, the more subservient they tend to be when the victim plays them right.

The next phase might come as a surprise to most victims who are coming right out of the honeymooning phase of their new relationship. The part of the abusive relationship that follows this phase full of praise and love-bombing is the exact opposite—the devaluation phase. This is the sadder part of the relationship where the partner starts to draw back all of that praise and excitement, they had given you for so long. They start to replace the praise and the intimacy you had with them with strict rules and backhanded compliments to break you down and make you feel worthless.

In normal, healthy relationships, what comes after the honeymooning phase is the opposite of that rush of dopamine. The feel-good chemical which had been flooding the brain for months, even years, dries up back to a relatively normal level.

Because dopamine, along with most other neurotransmitters, can be chemically addictive, we get used to that rush of dopamine that we had when we began the relationship. We want to ride that high forever, and so the crash afterward is just that much harder. The emotional low after the honeymooning period is where most relatively short-term relationships will come to an end because the two people will start to want to be around one another less and less as time goes on.

As they have this falling out, they get into fights more often and generally feel less and less in tune with each other. The high of infatuation and the elation of wanting your happy ending fades and you're faced with a flawed human in front of you. This revelation is jarring to people, and they usually can't help but feel more than a little disappointed. Hence, the two separate and see other people, for the cycle of elation and disappointment to perhaps repeat. The emotional low in a normal relationship is healthy—it's just the hormones in the human brain going back to a normal level.

Although it can feel as though you're drained, waiting out the emotional low will allow your brain to adjust to the new level of dopamine and other neurotransmitters. Your emotional responses to the person will also become calmer and more moderate. Your connection with that person becomes less infatuation and more actual intimate human connection—this is where "true" love actually begins.

In an abusive relationship, however, that infatuation was manipulated by the abuser to make the victim think that their elation was how the relationship should always be. That level of elevated happiness and elevated reaction, in general, is set as the standard for the two people by the manipulative partner. Then, after that connection is built and the victim is made to feel responsible for the abuser, the abuser takes back the kind things they had done for them. The intimacy and the vulnerability that the two had shared is erased, and a lot of changes happen between the two people. Where there was once kind, gentle gestures of love, the abuser now shows their "caring" nature by setting rules and restricting the victim. They withdraw their affection from you, make you feel like less of a person. The frequent texts and charming surprises slow or halt entirely, and their interactions with you might become colder, more isolated. They give you the cold shoulder, ignore you and your efforts, and treat you more like an inconvenience than a partner.

That connection you might have felt you shared through trauma or through the issues the two of you shared may feel like it's vanishing. In the place of that vulnerability, the abuser suddenly has this massive cold wall between you and them. They seem distant and like they don't want to do much with you, like go out or have dinner. The cute moments you had with them where you really clicked stop. They might even make it seem as though they feel sad, alone, frustrated, angry about something. They close themselves off from you and from other people, and you feel pressured to do the same for their sake. This is where the victim falls for the abuser's ultimate trap, one that's been laid out since the beginning of the relationship.

Because the victim already feels as though they and their abuser are connected through trauma, hardship, or something else intimate that the abuser revealed to their victim, they also feel like they have to suffer with the abuser. They think that they should sacrifice their social life or their happiness because it seems that their partner is being forced to do the same.

Because they feel like the intimate connection from before has been lost, they also feel that they have a responsibility to rekindle that relationship now with some other form of camaraderie. Alternately, the victim might feel like this colder version of their partner has been created by something the victim did. They might feel like they've been doing something wrong, not listening well enough to their partner or not doing something expected of them. They want to right that wrong, and so the victim doubles their efforts to help their partner, further investing themselves in that relationship, even though it's tearing them apart from the inside.

This hero complex that the victim has, and which has been developing with their partner for some time really comes into effect now as they do everything they can to please their abusers. When their partner seems upset or is ignoring them, the victim feels responsible for that. They feel like everything bad that happens to the both of them is somehow their fault—and the abuser knows this. They're aware of the effect they're having on their victim because they've had it intentionally set up that way since they first began interacting with each other.

From the moment the two people met, the abuser knew exactly how to ruin the positive feelings of their victim and how to get rid of them with little to no mess for them to clean up afterward.

That mess is also known as the discard phase. This is the part that hurts the most for the victim, as they may finally realize that the relationship and the connection, they had been building up inside their head doesn't actually exist. The love and responsibility they felt over caring for, protecting their partner, wasn't reciprocated. This is where the damage is done in the long term to the victim of the abuser, as they reel and have to take in that they weren't cared about at all during their relationship after all. Coming to terms with the fact that your relationship was actually hollow and wasn't filled with the love and compassion that you have thought was inside it, is incredibly hurtful for the victim in question.

After that realization on the part of the victim, they'll often get caught in the cycle of abuse where they want to leave and know that they should. But they keep getting drawn back in over and over again until they either find the courage to leave for good, or the abuser simply discards them for their next victim. As a victim, you come to the crushing conclusion that you were never seen as a human being with feelings and thoughts—you were just a vehicle to get closer to what they wanted.

The minute you didn't obey them or do as they asked, you become worth less and less in their eyes. Someone who you thought was vulnerable with you, and who you felt very personal and vulnerable with, turns out to be someone just trying to hurt you for their personal gain.

However, the abuser will very rarely discard their victim of their own volition. They usually want to keep their victim around for as long as possible, squeeze every last bit of "use" out of them as much as they can. When the victim understands that they're being abused, they might try to leave the relationship almost immediately. Unfortunately, the victim—an empathic one, in particular—will still likely have some kind of attachment to their partner. They still feel the need to help them, even if they also want to leave and distance themselves from that emotion. This need to help others, even if they don't really deserve that treatment, is usually what drives the victim back to their partner. If this isn't the case, most abusers also know just how to get their victims back where they want them.

A staple of abusive personalities is that the "best" and most manipulative abusers are incredibly charismatic. They understand precisely how to get to their victims and make them feel loved again. They might suddenly turn up in behavior, begin rewarding them with presents and genuine sentiment again. Most importantly, they'll credit this change to them. Assuring their victim that they've helped them be a better person reverses the feelings that the victim might have had prior. They go back to the abuser, thinking that things will be different now that the partner has started being better and more in control of their actions.

In reality, however, this is usually just a part of the abuser's plan. They know that they don't have to change, and they never plan to. They just know that they have to do this over and over for as long as they need until they have everything they wanted out of that victim. They'll keep acting out and trapping the victim in the cycle of abuse, then pulling them back in with a feigned change of heart just as they're about to quit on the relationship and leave.

It seems hard to believe that someone would fall for this same trick more than once—it's difficult for most people to give out chances beyond the second mistake. However, victims of abuse are connected to other victims of abuse. They feel compelled to stay with them and to make good on the love and attention that they never got to receive themselves.

In a way, the victim trying to care for their partner is the victim attempting to live vicariously through the people they try to help. The abuser of that victim, who has probably long given up on healing properly from their own experiences and trauma, understands this desire and is sure to take advantage of this at every turn. As time progresses, the victim feels more and more lost. They keep going back and forth between the hope that they can improve their own relationship and the crushing defeat when they go back only to visit that same conclusion—that they're going to be trapped in that relationship with someone who mistreats them.

This is the entire over-arching dilemma of an abusive relationship. When the abuser grows tired of the false kindness, they make all bad things feel as though they're the fault of the victim. The victim is used to having these feelings pushed on them, and they rarely learn how to really deal with that blame coming from other people, in addition to coming from their own internal narrative. They don't want to feel as though they're the root of all their relationship problems, but they also can't help but instill this own fear inside them.

Once you can get rid of this crushing fear inside you and shed the responsibility you feel over the wellbeing of other people, especially other people in your life who might not even care about you, you can learn to actively defend yourself against your abuser's emotional manipulation tactics. You can unlock the part of your life that you were meant to live—the part which is full of love and care, the part that was always waiting for you. This part of your life may have been held back from you by other people trying to pull you down, but you're the only one who can truly unlock it for yourself.

Chapter 10 Using mindfulness to manage emotions

Overcoming narcissistic abuse is one of the most difficult things you might ever experience. It takes a lot of effort to find the momentum to jump from the pain that has engulfed your life to a better future. The most natural reaction to abuse is pain. Your life is shattered, your heart is broken, you lose everything. But all is not lost. There are solutions for you, effective solutions that will help you get your life back.

Meditation

Narcissistic abuse leaves victims in emotional trauma. The kind of trauma you experience in such a relationship has long-lasting effects on your life. One of the most effective ways of healing, managing and overcoming the negativity you experience from a narcissist is meditation.

Meditation is useful for virtually any condition that is either caused or exacerbated by stress. Meditation helps your body relax, in the process reducing your metabolism rate, improving your heart rate, and reducing your blood pressure (Huntington, 2015). It also helps your brain waves function properly, and helps you breathe better. As you learn how to relax through meditation, the tension in your muscles oozes out of your body from your muscles where tension resides.

The best thing about meditation is that you can perform it even when you have a very busy schedule. You only need a few minutes daily, and you will be on your way to recovery. During meditation, try and focus on your breathing. Listen to the air flowing in and out of your body. This action helps you focus by following the path the air takes in and out of your body. It is one of the easiest ways to calm down.

As the air moves in and out of your body, try and scan your body to identify the areas where tension is high. Observe your thoughts so you are aware of what you are trying to overcome through meditation. It is okay to feel the overwhelming sensations, but do not judge yourself. Recovery is not a sprint. It might take you a few sessions, but your commitment will see you through.

Do not reject your emotions. Your emotions are a part of who you are. It is normal to react in a certain way to someone's actions or behavior towards you. Embrace the feelings and overcome the negativity. Meditation will help you make the neural pathways to and from your brain healthier and stronger by increasing density of grey matter. You learn to be mindful of your feelings and emotions again, and with time, you break the toxic connection you had with your narcissistic abuser.

Trauma and distress affects your brain by disrupting parts of the brain that regulate planning, memory, learning, focus, and emotional regulation. Over the years, meditation has proven a useful technique in overcoming these challenges by improving the function of the hippocampus, amygdala and prefrontal cortex.

As a victim of narcissistic abuse, once your abuser gets control over your life, you have nothing else but to follow their command. However, meditation gets you back in control of your life. You can reclaim your realities, heal and become empowered to overcome all challenges you experienced under their control.

Group therapy

Group therapy is one of the options you can consider when healing from narcissistic abuse. One of the first things you will learn in group therapy is that you cannot fix your narcissistic abuser. However, what you will learn is how to deal with narcissism.

Most of the time victims are encouraged to walk out of such abusive relationships, because there can only be hurt and trauma from them. Narcissists are ruthless in their pursuit of adulation, attention and gratification. They are aware that what they seek is impossible to achieve, so they delude themselves in the idea that they can make you achieve it for them.

Group therapy for narcissistic abuse is helpful because you get one thing you haven't had in a very long time, support. Each time you hear about the experiences of other group members, you realize you are not alone. The overwhelming feelings you have been going through become lighter, because you learn that there are people out there who can relate to what has been eating you inside.

While group therapy has its benefits, you will have to play your part to enjoy these benefits. Your willingness to heal is signified by the fact that you are taking the first step to seek help. Commit to the therapy sessions by taking a pledge of what you want out of it. Once you are in, participate. It might not be easy at first because you have to open up to strangers, but you will get the hang of it. It is okay to sit and listen to others tell their story at first. Once you feel comfortable, you can open up. Remember that it gets easier over time as you keep sharing. Never hold back. Therapy is a safe place. By sharing your experience, you are not just letting the group in on your pain, you might also be helping someone else in the group open up about theirs.

Cognitive behavioral therapy

Cognitive behavioral therapy (CBT) is a therapeutic process that combines cognitive therapy and behavioral therapy to help patients overcome traumatic events that have wielded control away from them. Cognitive therapy focuses on the influence your thoughts and beliefs have in your life, while behavioral therapy is about identifying and changing unhealthy behavioral patterns (Triscari et al, 2015).

CBT is effective because your therapist doesn't just sit down and listen, they also act as your coach. It is a healthy exchange where you learn useful strategies that can help you manage your life better. You learn to recognize your emotional responses, behavior and perceptions.

CBT is ideal for victims of narcissistic abuse because it helps them understand their emotional experiences, identify behavioral patterns, especially problematic tendencies, and learn how to stay in control over some of the most difficult situations in their lives.

Cognitive processing therapy

CPT is a subset of CBT. It is one of the most recommended methods of treating trauma patients. Victims of narcissistic abuse usually go through a lot of trauma, and they can develop PTSD. When you develop PTSD, you might have a different concept of the environment around you, your life and people you interact with. PTSD affects your perception of life in the following areas:

- Safety

After experiencing abuse, you are conditioned to feel unsafe about yourself and everyone else around you. PTSD can exacerbate these fears about safety. You are afraid you cannot take care of yourself, or anyone else.

- Trust

Narcissists break you down to the ground. They make sure you can no longer trust anyone, or yourself. In the aftermath, PTSD can cause you to not trust yourself to make the right call.

- Control

You don't just lose control over your life, you depend on your abuser to guide you through your life. Narcissism does this to you. Narcissists are happy when they have control over your life because it shows them they have your attention and can do anything they please with you. After leaving a narcissist, PTSD can reinforce a feeling of a loss of control, which makes getting back on your feet a very slow process.

- Esteem

One of the painful things about surviving a narcissist is the way they erode your confidence. Even some of the most confident people who have ever lived ended up unable to recognize who they are or what their lives are about anymore. You shy away from situations that require confidence and astute decision making, which you would have embraced willingly earlier on. Your perception of yourself is a broken, unworthy person.

- Intimacy

Among other manipulative tricks narcissists use, triangulation makes you feel so insecure about yourself and intimacy. You feel insecure because no one understands you, and at the same time, you cannot understand why they behave towards you the way they do. Following narcissistic abuse, PTSD may give you moments of flashbacks to the points when your intimacy was insecure. It can make it difficult to start new relationships.

All these thoughts end up in negative emotions clouding your life, like anger, guilt, anxiety, depression, and fear. Through CPT, you learn useful skills that help in challenging these emotions. The negative emotions create a false sense of being that embeds in your subconscious, making you feel like a lesser being. CPT helps by repairing your perception of yourself and the world around you. You learn how to challenge the abuse and gain a better, positive and healthy perspective of your life.

Yoga

For a trauma survivor, yoga can offer an avenue to healing. The restorative benefits of yoga have long been practiced in Eastern traditional societies for wellness. Yoga helps you establish a connection between the mind and your body. It helps you stay grounded. This is one of the things that you need when you survive a narcissistic relationship.

Yoga has been demonstrated in the past to be effective in treating different physical and mental conditions, trauma-related problems, and stress (Criswell, Wheeler, & Partlow Lauttamus, 2014). By combining breathing exercises, physical movement and relaxation, yoga helps you cultivate mindfulness and become more aware of your environment, internal and external.

Breaking up and walking out of a relationship with a narcissist is just the first step. Healing takes more steps. You need to find your bearings. You need to end the confusion that has engulfed your life to the point where you lack an identity.

During yoga, you will focus on breathing exercises. Breathing is one of the most effective and free ways of getting relief. Whether you are going through a difficult period, emotional upheaval or a moment of anxiety, all you have to do is breathe.

Each time you feel the urge to bring the narcissist back into your life, find a comfortable place where you can sit quietly and relax. Close your eyes and breathe. Focus on your breathing, counting your breaths to take your mind away from the problem. Gentle yoga classes can help with this.

Art therapy

Art therapy is founded in the idea that mental well-being and healing can be fostered through creativity. Art is not just a skill, it is also a technique that can be used to help in mental health. Art therapy has been used in psychotherapy for years. Art allows patients to express themselves without necessarily talking to someone about what they feel.

It is ideal for people who struggle to express themselves verbally. Art can help you learn how to communicate better with people, manage stress and even learn more about your personality. Through art therapy, experts believe that their patients can learn how to solve problems, resolve conflicts, ease stress, learn good behavior, develop or sharpen interpersonal skills, and increase their esteem and awareness (Lusebrink, n.d.)

Art therapists have a lot of tools at their disposal that can be used to help you overcome the trauma of a narcissistic relationship. From collages, to sculpture and painting, there is so much to work with. Art therapy is recommended for people who have survived emotional trauma, depression, anxiety, domestic abuse, physical violence and other psychological problems from an abusive relationship with a narcissist.

The difference between an art therapy session and an art class is that in therapy, the emphasis is on your experiences. Your imagination, feelings, and ideas matter. These are things that your narcissist partner might have conditioned you to give up. You will learn some amazing art skills and techniques, but before you do that, your therapist will encourage you to express yourself from deep within. Instead of focusing on what you can see physically, you learn to create things that you imagine or feel.

EMDR

Eye Movement Desensitization and Reprocessing (EMDR) is another technique that you can consider to heal from narcissistic abuse. It is a technique that helps to reprogram your brain away from trauma, so it can learn how to reprocess memories. Exposure to persistent trauma might see your brain form a pattern which perpetuates the negativity you have experienced for a long time (Mosquera & Knipe, 2015)

Traumatic memories cause victims a lot of psychological distress. EMDR is a unique method of treatment because you don't have to talk through your feelings and problems. The brain is instead stimulated to change the emotions you feel, months or even years after you walk away from a narcissist.

EMDR works because the eye movement enables the brain to open up, making it easier to access your memories in a manner that the brain can reprocess in a safe environment other than the environment in which your trauma was perpetuated. After accessing your memories, it is possible to replace them with more empowering feelings and thoughts, so that over time you dissociate from the pain and embrace more fulfilling responses to the triggers in your environment. Flashbacks, nightmares, and anxiety soon become distant memories as you embrace a new life and free yourself from their hold.

For victims of narcissistic abuse, your brain remembers the painful memories of verbal, sexual, psychological, emotional and even physical abuse. In an EMDR session, you are encouraged to focus on the details of any such traumatic events, while at the same time viewing something else for a short time.

What happens is that while you focus on both the negative memories and a new positive affirmation, your memory feels different. You will also learn self-soothing techniques to help you continue dissociating from the pain. EMDR helps to unchain the shackles in your life and allow your brain to think about experiences differently.

Self-hypnosis

Hypnotherapy has been used successfully to help victims of narcissistic abuse heal for so many years. There are specific conditions that must be met however, for this to work. You must ensure you are in the presence of specific stimuli that can encourage hypnosis. You will also learn how to narrow down your focus and awareness, and finally, allow yourself to freely experience your feelings without making a conscious choice to do so.

Narcissists are not capable of genuine connection, but instead they project their feelings and insecurities about loneliness and abandonment to their victim. How do you get into a trance state for hypnosis? Emotional abuse has a significant impact on your life. Hypnosis allows you to relax effortlessly. Effortless relaxation is one of the last things you might have experienced throughout your ordeal with a narcissist. The moment you are capable of allowing yourself to relax without struggling, you open doors to healing your mind and your body.

Self-hypnosis is a transformative process that restores your belief in yourself, encourages you to learn important emotional tools that can help you recover from abuse, and also help to protect yourself in the future. With each session, you become stronger, and calm. The waves of emotional upheaval you used to experience reduce and you become at peace with yourself and your environment.

Self-hypnosis also gives you a clearer picture of what your life is about. You let go of the negative vibes and embrace peace. You are set on a path to rediscovery. You find more value in yourself than you ever had throughout your narcissistic relationship. As you go on with these sessions, you learn how to take the necessary steps towards healing, and moving in the right direction in life. The most important thing behind self-hypnosis is that you start looking forward to a new life, and you actually believe in your ability to succeed while at it.

Aromatherapy

Even though it might feel like you are at the edge of a cliff and there is no way back for you, it is possible to recover from narcissistic abuse. Many people have done it before and you can do it too. Recovery from this kind of trauma is very sweet. Each time you make progress, you can look back at how far gone you were, and the changes you have made. It helps you appreciate your life, and realize how toxic it was earlier on.

Aromatherapy is one of the conscious efforts you take towards healing and recovering from narcissistic abuse. Think about aromatherapy in the same way you think about exercise. If you feel you are unfit, you exercise regularly. You can schedule three or four training sessions weekly to help you stay in shape.

The same applies to aromatherapy. Narcissists leave you so unfit emotionally. You need to get your emotions in shape so that you can live a happy and fulfilling life. To free yourself of emotional distress, you need to stimulate your amygdala. Smell is one of the best ways to stimulate the amygdala. There is a strong connection between your emotions and sense of smell, a connection that has been there since you were a child.

The sense of smell is closely associated with emotional connections, whether positive or negative. This explains why each time you smell your favorite food being prepared, it reminds you of an event during which you enjoyed it. Smell, therefore, helps to induce comfort, and nostalgia. If smells can take you way back, it can also help to remind you of the traumatic events that you suffered through narcissistic abuse.

Essential oils used in aromatherapy can help you access emotions buried so deep you never realize they are present (Kirksmith, 2004). They can also bring back memories so that you can embrace them and release those that are no longer useful. The difference between emotions and words is that while they both charge through your body, emotions are faster. It might take you a while to listen, speak and read something during therapy and allow your body enough time to process it. On the other hand, your body will respond to emotions faster. This is why most people are prone to making emotional reactions.

- Basil
- Cedarwood
- Lavender
- Bergamot
- Lemon balm
- Hyssop
- Frankincense

During aromatherapy, you must remember that it is very possible you might not derive the same level of comfort from the essential oils as someone else did. If you don't like the scent of some oil, you might not get positive results from using it.

Chapter 11 The Narcissist's Target

Once you have been able to get away from the narcissist, some of the hard work is going to begin. It is time to figure out the steps that are needed to heal and feel better once the narcissist is out of your life. Healing from the abuse that a narcissist put on you, whether it was mental, physical, or emotional abuse is going to be hard. And sometimes, since you were in that relationship for a long time without realizing what was happening to you in the first place, it may seem impossible even to know where to get started. Some of the different things that you can do to help yourself heal from the narcissistic abuse that you endured includes:

Don't blame yourself that the relationship didn't really work out. If you spent a good deal of your time in a relationship with a narcissist, it is important to not beat yourself up for the challenges that were faced in that relationship. You must remember in this that your partner, no matter how much you loved them, was dealing with a mental disorder, one that you really had no control over. In fact, there is a lot with that relationship that you had no control over at all.

What you can control through all of this mess is who you are in a relationship with, whether you want to maintain this kind of relationship or not, and even your expectations for how the other person in the relationship is supposed to be treating you. While the narcissist may have tried to take some of that away from you, these are still some of the decisions that you can control.

During this time, there are a few steps that you are able to take in order to help you get through the blame game. First, don't dwell so much on how things have changed, or ever think about how these changes have happened only because of some actions that you took. And, any of the abuse that you received was not your fault, it was because of the narcissistic personality of your partner, and in no way, shape, or form because you actually deserved the abuse.

The net thing that we need to explore is understanding that it is just fine to leave your narcissistic partner. While it is true that most targets are going to fall in love with their partner over the years, it is important to remind yourself that the narcissist does not love you in this process and that this person you thought you loved as changed. Do not feel guilty or allow any blame or shame to come upon you when you are considering whether it is time to leave the relationship and heal from it or not.

Remind yourself during this time that you really do deserve to be with someone who isn't going just to use and abuse you; you deserve to be with someone who loves you and respects you and will show these through actions rather than meaningless words. If you find that you are not getting that out of the relationship that you are in right now, it is time to consider leaving your own partner.

Despite what some may lead you to believe, and despite what the narcissist may have been telling you all this time, it is not selfish to walk out from the relationship and heal yourself. Instead, it is going to be an act of self-preservation that should be done in order to ensure that you get the amount of respect that you deserve.

Once you are out of that relationship, it is time to do your best in order to move on and start a new life. Extracting yourself out of a relationship that is not that healthy can be hard and even emotionally draining at times. Even though this can happen, removing yourself from the relationship that is abusive can end up causing you less pain in the long run.

Getting over someone who you have loved for some time is hard, even if the relationship is bad for you. Remind yourself that the relationship has ended, and it is perfectly fine to feel mad, sad, or a whole bunch of other emotions in the process. This is nothing to feel mad or guilty about at all. Never let this pain and sadness just sit there inside of you. Bottling up the emotions and ignoring them because you don't want to feel bad or you don't want to let the relationship bring you down, is just going to make it worse. If you need to, consider talking about this relationship with another person to help you out.

During this time, you are going to feel pretty sad. You have gone through a relationship that was hurting you for a long time, but it still ended, and this can be hard to deal with. Plus, all of the feelings of insecurity the narcissist sent your way are still going through your head. During this time, remind yourself that you are a wonderful and beautiful person, and you deserve to find someone who truly loves you.

Another thing that you need to focus on here is that you must remember that the narcissist is not really capable of having feelings. It is hard to get over a person who is trying so hard to get you back, which is exactly what the narcissist is going to try to do when they are not abusing you. But to help you not get dragged back into this cycle and stuck with the narcissist again, you have to remember that all of these declarations of love, no matter how much you desire to hear them, are going just to be another form of manipulation from the narcissist to get you back to them.

The narcissist doesn't want you to go. And they will continue to reach back into your life and try to get your healing off track. When you leave, they lose their source of love, their attention, and admiration that they have been getting off you. They will use every technique that they can find in order to convince you back. They will manipulate, yell, scream, talk to you, profess their love and more in order to try and get you back. But they don't mean this. They have not changed, and if you do jump back into the relationship, without actually working on the healing that you need, you are just going to get harmed again.

One thing that you may notice when it comes to healing from a narcissist and realizing that they are incapable of real feelings is that they like to keep their target on the hook. The way that this works is that the narcissist is going to treat the target poorly, but they flip the switch and pretend to be back in love their target just enough times that they can keep the relationship on track and together. In moments where you are reflecting on the relationship, remind yourself of the declarations of love from your partner and see if you can recognize how often these were just another form of manipulation from that person.

During the healing time, it is likely that the narcissist is going to try and get ahold of you. They will call to say that they miss you, that they will change, and that they want to continue the relationship or get back together with you. Try to remember during this time that these words are empty promises and that they are just a way for the narcissist to try and get back in with you. Stay strong, and if you can, cut out all of the communication that you have with this narcissistic person.

You can also work on finding a good support group to help you out. Healing from the narcissist is not something that you are going to be able to do all on your own. It would be nice to escape all of the red tape and emotional drain that the narcissist put you through on your own, but since the narcissist already had you used to the isolation and more, it is time to get away from that and try something new.

Without a good support group behind you to help you succeed and feel better, it is likely that you are not going to see success. This allows the narcissist to have more time to get into your life, to have more chances to tell you that they are the only one who is right for you. They can get into your head so much easier if you let them and without a good support group. Having people around you to keep your spirits up, to remind you why the narcissist was so bad, and to help you figure out the right steps to take now that the narcissist is gone can be so important.

The first person you need to consider getting on your side when you are healing from a narcissist is a therapist. You should work with one who has experience with narcissists and helping targets heal from this abuse. This therapist will be perfect for talking your feelings out with, for understanding what you are going through, for answering your questions, and for being there to give you guidance and the right steps so that you can learn how to let go and live the rest of your life free of the narcissist.

In addition to having a therapist on your side, you may also want to consider having a support group of friends and family members who are happy to be there to support you. If you can contact the people you were close to before the narcissist entered your life, and these people are willing to come back in and be that support that you need, then you are off to a good start.

The trouble here though is that a lot of narcissists made sure that tier targets were isolated. When a target is isolated, they are not able to get the support or any outsideideas that are not supported by the narcissist. Basically, when no one is around to tell the target that they are doing things that don't make sense and no one is there to check the actions of the narcissist, the narcissist is then able to get free reign and has more control.

This may mean that you will come out of this relationship without anyone who will be there to support and love you as you need. This can be a hard realization, but it doesn't mean that you are stuck with no solutions to help you out. You can still find some great people who will be there to support you and love you along the way; you just need to get creative.

Getting out there and making new friends can be a great way to heal from a narcissistic relationship as well. This means that you can't just sit around at home and hope that things get better. You have to get out there, try something new, rediscover your old favorite hobbies or some that are brand new to you if you can't think of any. You have to be willing to jump out of your comfort zone, and perhaps even have some fun. When you are able to do this, then it is easier to have friends and a good support group who will always be there to help you out.

There is nothing better than a good support group when you are dealing with the effects of a narcissist on your life. Many people worry that the narcissist is going to come back and cause problems again. But with a support group who can be there to talk through your emotions with, who may go and meet up with the narcissist with you if you still have to see them, and someone who can help you understand what is normal behavior and what is not when it comes to the narcissist, and it won't be long before you are getting yourself out of that situation, and moving on thanks to your healing.

As you go through this healing process, it is always best if you can try to move on. Extracting yourself out of a relationship that is really unhealthy is going to be hard, and it is often going to drain a lot of energy out of you. Many times, the potential pain is enough to keep people away from even trying to get away in the first place. They have been trained well enough to assume that nothing could be better, and the relationship with the narcissist is the best that they can get, so they never leave.

However, you will find that the pain that you feel inside the relationship, especially over the long term, is going to be so much more than what you are going to experience when you end the relationship. Sure, ending the relationship with someone you truly love, someone who seems like the best person in the world for you, and someone you imagined spending your life with is going to be tough, the emotional, mental, and physical abuse that you went through with the narcissist is going to be so much worse.

It is going to be hard. And there is going to be a time frame when you first leave the relationship where you will question your decisions and wonder if you made a big mistake with what you did. But if you are able to focus on taking care of yourself, and building up a support group, slowly but surely you will start to think about the narcissist less and less. And before on, you will be able to move on to bigger and better things.

Through this part, try to remind yourself often that you are a wonderful person, someone who deserved to be loved by someone, rather than the one who does all of the loving and giving. Love yourself as much as possible by setting aside a part of each day to do "me time" and just focus on something that is good for you something that makes you happy, and something that you love to do. Soon, you will start to see the wonders of this new life without the narcissist, and you will feel so much better.

Take some time to work on yourself during this time. When you were with the narcissist, it is likely that your own self-care was put to the side. You didn't take proper care of yourself at all, because you put the needs of the narcissist ahead of your own needs. Now that the narcissist is out of your life and you are trying to find the most effective ways to heal after all of this, it is time to pay attention to yourself.

Self-care is so important, and it has to be a part of the healing process here. You don't have to go crazy and spend hours a day trying to do this stuff. But even a few minutes a day can make a difference and can help you get back to your old self. The methods you use for self-care are going to depend on your own personal likes and wants, so consider this when making a decision.

Some people decide to just take better care of their health and eat better while working out more. Even half an hour of exercise that you can control can be enough to help with this. Some people go out and purchase the new clothes they have wanted in a long time so they can feel better being dressed up for once. Taking time to enjoy a soaking bath, reading a book, doing meditation, seeing a therapist, and spending time with friends can all be examples of the different options you have available when using self-care for your life.

Eventually, move on and find someone else who makes your heart flutter and who treats you right. In the beginning, it is going to feel like no one else can take the place of the narcissist. Even though they really had no love for you at all, you were in love with them, and perhaps thought that you were going to be with them for the rest of your life. Now that this is over, you are likely going to feel abandoned, and as nothing will ever get better.

The good news is that things will get better. The narcissist is not going to maintain their hold on you forever. In fact, if you are able to remain strong long enough, they will realize that you are not worth their time, and they may go away on their own. And while you should not jump right into the first relationship that presents itself at this time, eventually, you will find someone. You will find someone who loves you and cares about you and who wants to be in the relationship because of who you are, not because of what prestige or other things that you can offer. It may take time, and it is likely to come at a time when you are not expecting it, but no one deserves to be in a relationship with a narcissist, and everyone deserves to find true love. You will find yours when the time is right.

Healing from the narcissist is not always the easiest thing for anyone to do. The narcissist made sure that they were able to have as much control over you as possible. They enjoy being able to get that love and attention, even though they are not sharing any of it back with you. And they understand that if they didn't do the work the right way, then their target would walk away and never come back again.

This is why the narcissist delves in so deeply with their target. They want to make sure that the target stays put and that they are not tempted to run away and not come back again. The healing process, and getting over all of the mind games and more that the narcissist did to you is not always going to be easy. In fact, sometimes it can be very difficult and often the narcissist is going to be able to get back in your head, even with very little communication in the first place.

Taking your time with the healing, and really focusing on yourself can help with this. It allows you to break away from the narcissist, to start to value yourself and to start to understand what is most important to you. Of course, the narcissist is going to be unhappy with the way that things are. They are starting to lose control and are no longer getting their own way. But stick with it, because your mental well-being, as well as your physical health and emotional health, are worth it.

Conclusion

BPD is classified "the Good Prognosis Diagnosis" because, despite the fact that it is one of the more difficult mental health analyzes to contend with, numerous individuals have a high possibility of getting better or recovering altogether. If you have faith in your beloved one and stick by him during treatment, you may see genuine prizes. Many, numerous individuals who once experienced pervasive trouble in interpersonal relationships because of BPD are now healthy and completely functioning after treatment and a ton of self-work. Keeping a receptive outlook, working on your very own portion responses and reactions, and being honest with yourself about the substances of BPD may bring you to a fuller feeling of self and happiness in time.

Living with a borderline personality disorder is hard for the patient and friends and family. If you care about this person, support his or her treatment, figure out how to communicate viably, set limits, and make sure to think about yourself as well. Be patient and understand that BPD treatment sets aside some effort to work. Continue to give appropriate support, and your adored one will show signs of improvement.

The emotional sequence that a person with BPD experiences can be contrasted with a line of dominos. One elicit, one push of the first domino, and the whole range fall in fast succession. Your responsibility is to attempt to expel your own "domino" from the column. You can likewise realize what makes the dominos fall. Focus on your encounters, and anticipate approaches to keep things quiet. If you can quiet yourself, the adrenaline doesn't course through your structure, and you can begin to attempt to guide the volatile relationship.

Made in the USA
Middletown, DE
06 June 2020